# Child Slavery before and after Emancipation

If we are to fully understand how slavery survived legal abolition, we must grapple with the work that abolition has left undone, and dismantle the structures that abolition has left in place. *Child Slavery before and after Emancipation* seeks to enable a vital conversation between historical and modern slavery studies – two fields that have traditionally run along parallel tracks rather than in relation to one another. In this collection, Anna Mae Duane and her interdisciplinary group of contributors seek to build historical and contemporary bridges between race-based chattel slavery and other forms of forced child labor, offering a series of case studies that illuminate the varied roles of enslaved children. Duane provides a provocative, historically grounded set of inquiries that suggest how attending to child slaves can help to better define both slavery and freedom.

Anna Mae Duane is Associate Professor of English at the University of Connecticut. She is the author of *Suffering Childhood in Early America: Violence, Race and the Making of the Child Victim* (2010), the editor of *The Children's Table: Childhood Studies and the Humanities* (2013), and the coeditor of *Who Writes for Black Children?: African American Children's Literature before 1900* (forthcoming, 2017). She is also the coeditor of Common-place.org.

Slaveries since Emancipation

*General Editors*
Randall Miller, *St. Joseph's University*
Zoe Trodd, *University of Nottingham*

*Founding Editor*
Robert E. Wright, *Augustana College*

Slaveries since Emancipation publishes scholarship that links slavery's past to its present, consciously scanning history for lessons of relevance to contemporary abolitionism and that directly engages current issues of interest to activists by contextualizing them historically.

# Child Slavery before and after Emancipation

*An Argument for Child-Centered Slavery Studies*

Edited by

## ANNA MAE DUANE

*University of Connecticut*

**CAMBRIDGE**
UNIVERSITY PRESS

# CAMBRIDGE
## UNIVERSITY PRESS

One Liberty Plaza, 20th Floor, New York, NY 10006, USA

Cambridge University Press is part of the University of Cambridge.

It furthers the University's mission by disseminating knowledge in the pursuit of
education, learning, and research at the highest international levels of excellence.

www.cambridge.org
Information on this title: www.cambridge.org/9781107566705
10.1017/9781316412312

© Cambridge University Press 2017

First published 2017

Printed in the United States of America by Sheridan Books, Inc.

*A catalogue record for this publication is available from the British Library.*

*Library of Congress Cataloging-in-Publication Data*
Names: Duane, Anna Mae, 1968– editor.
Title: Child slavery before and after emancipation: an argument for child-centered
slavery studies / [edited by] Anna Mae Duane, University of Connecticut.
Description: New York, NY: Cambridge University Press, 2017. |
Includes bibliographical references and index.
Identifiers: LCCN 2016041125| ISBN 9781107127562 (hardback) |
ISBN 9781107566705 (paperback)
Subjects: LCSH: Child slaves – United States – History. | Slavery – United States – History.
Classification: LCC E441.C486 2017 | DDC 306.3/620973–dc23
LC record available at https://lccn.loc.gov/2016041125

ISBN 978-1-107-12756-2 Hardback
ISBN 978-1-107-56670-5 Paperback

# Contents

# Figures

# Notes on Contributors

**Jonathan Blagbrough** has been conducting research and managing programs on child labor and slavery issues with nongovernmental organizations, multilateral bodies, and local groups for the past twenty-five years. He is currently an independent consultant on child exploitation and is the head of technical advice for Children Unite, an organization dedicated to protecting child domestic workers from exploitation and abuse and promoting their rights worldwide.

**Gary Craig** is Emeritus Professor of social justice at the Wilberforce Institute for the Study of Slavery and Emancipation, University of Hull, England, and Visiting Professor at several other universities. He has written widely about forced labor, child slavery, human trafficking, and modern slavery more generally, including issues of race, racism, and ethnicity.

**Audra A. Diptee** is an associate professor in the department of history at Carleton University. Her research explores various themes relevant to humanitarianism, historical memory, and critical applied history. She has held a visiting fellowship at Yale University, and her research has been supported by various institutions and granting agencies, including the Atlantic History Seminar at Harvard University and the Social Science and Humanities Research Council of Canada.

**Anna Mae Duane** is an associate professor of English at the University of Connecticut. She is the author of *Suffering Childhood in Early America: Violence, Race and the Making of the Child Victim* (2010), and the editor of *The Children's Table: Childhood Studies and the Humanities* (2013) and coeditor of *Who Writes for Black Children?: African American*

*Children's Literature before 1900* (forthcoming). Her work has been supported by awards from the National Endowment for the Humanities (NEH) and the Fulbright Commission. She currently coedits *Common-place, the Interactive Journal of Early American Life.*

**Sarah L. H. Gronningsater** is an assistant professor of history at the California Institute of Technology. She is writing a book titled *The Arc of Abolition: The Children of Gradual Emancipation and the Origins of National Freedom* (forthcoming).

**Kelli Lyon Johnson** is an associate professor of English and an affiliate in justice and community studies at Miami University Hamilton, where she teaches courses on human trafficking, nonprofit studies, writing, and literature. The author most recently of an article on contemporary slave narratives and a book chapter on children in contemporary slavery, she is currently completing a book manuscript on the child as an object of international relations in transnational trafficking discourses.

**Micki McElya** is an associate professor of history at the University of Connecticut. She specializes in the histories of women, gender, sexuality, and racial formation in the United States from the Civil War to the present, with an emphasis on political culture and memory. She is the author of *The Politics of Mourning: Death and Honor in Arlington National Cemetery* (2016) and *Clinging to Mammy: The Faithful Slave in Twentieth-Century America* (2007). She is currently at work on a book titled *Liberating Beauty: Feminism, the Civil Rights Movement, and Miss America* (forthcoming).

**Erica Meiners** is a professor of gender and women's studies and education at Northeastern Illinois University. She's the author of several books, including *Flaunt It! Queers Organizing for Public Education and Justice* (2009), *Right to Be Hostile: Schools, Prisons and the Making of Public Enemies* (2009), and articles in a wide range of venues. She has been a visiting scholar at the Institute for Research on Race and Public Policy and a Lillian Robinson Scholar at the Simone de Beauvoir Institute in Montreal. Currently writing a book titled *Intimate Labor* (forthcoming), Meiners is supported by funds and awards from organizations such as the Illinois Humanities Council, the Woodrow Wilson Foundation for Public Scholarship, and the U.S. Department of Education. In 1998, she cofounded an alternative high school for men and women exiting prisons and jails.

**Jessica R. Pliley** is an associate professor of women's, gender, and sexuality history at Texas State University. She is the author of *Policing*

*Sexuality: The Mann Act and the Making of the FBI* (2014) and coeditor of *Global Anti-Vice Activism, 1890–1950: Fighting Drink, Drugs, and "Immorality"* (Cambridge University Press 2016).

**David M. Rosen** is a professor of anthropology at Fairleigh Dickinson University in Madison, New Jersey. He is the author of *Armies of the Young: Child Soldiers in War and Terrorism* (2005) and *Child Soldiers* (2012). His recent articles include "Child Soldiers: Tropes of Innocence and Terror," "Who Is a Child? The Legal Conundrum of Child Soldiers," and "Child Soldiers, International Humanitarian Law, and the Globalization of Childhood." He is finishing a manuscript titled *From Patriots to Victims: Child Soldiers in the Western Imagination*.

**Karen Sánchez-Eppler** is a professor of American studies and English at Amherst College. The author of *Touching Liberty: Abolition, Feminism and the Politics of the Body* (1993) and *Dependent States: The Child's Part in Nineteenth-Century American Culture* (2005), she is currently working on two book projects, *The Unpublished Republic: Manuscript Cultures of the Mid-Nineteenth Century US*, and *In the Archives of Childhood: Personal and Historical Pasts*. She is one of the founding coeditors of *The Journal of the History of Childhood and Youth* and past president of C19: The Society of Nineteenth-Century Americanists.

**John Wall** is a professor of religion, with a joint appointment in childhood studies, at Rutgers University, Camden. He is a theoretical ethicist whose research and teaching focus on moral life's relation to language, poetics, narrative, culture, religion, time, age, and children's rights. He is the author of *Children's Rights: Today's Global Challenge* (2016), *Ethics in Light of Childhood* (2010) and *Moral Creativity* (2005), as well as the coeditor of *Children and Armed Conflict* (2011), *Marriage, Health, and the Professions* (2002), and *Paul Ricoeur and Contemporary Moral Thought* (2002).

**Sarah Winter** is a professor of English and comparative literary and cultural studies at the University of Connecticut. She is the author of two books, *Freud and the Institution of Psychoanalytic Knowledge* (1999) and *The Pleasures of Memory: Learning to Read with Charles Dickens* (2011). Her current research, supported by an NEH Faculty Fellowship for 2016–2017, focuses on the history of habeas corpus, abolitionism, and human rights.

# Acknowledgments

This book began as an email, written to the organizers of a conference that first introduced me to possibilities and challenges of thinking of slavery as a transhistorical phenomenon. In my email, I asked why, when so many scholars readily acknowledged the prevalence of children in both past and present iterations of slavery and trafficking, so few placed children at the center of analysis? James Brewer Stewart's generous response to that email – and his continued encouragement to pursue the questions I was asking – led to this volume being published. The Yale Gilder Lehrman Center for the Study of Slavery, Resistance and Abolition (GLC) hosted that conference – just one instance of the intellectual leadership and nourishment the Center provides for students and scholars. The GLC has been shaping my thinking and writing since my graduate school days, and I'm profoundly grateful to David Blight, Thomas Thurston, Dana Lanier Schaffer, David Spatz, and Melissa McGrath for the incredible work they do, and for their kindness and generosity throughout the years. Many thanks to Robert Wright, who helped me shape my initial questions into a book project and to Historians Against Slavery and Deborah Gershenowitz at Cambridge University Press for moving forward with a series that asks us to imagine slavery before and after emancipation. It has been a pleasure working with Deborah, Kristina Deutsch, and Ami Naramor as we moved from manuscript to finished volume.

This book has benefited from many conversations since that initial email. David Blight, Cathy Schlund-Vials, James Brewer Stewart, and Samuel Martinez provided valuable commentary in an early workshop on this topic. Mary Kelley kindly read and responded to a draft of the introduction. UConn's English Department and the UConn American

Studies program provided funding for a one-day colloquium that allowed contributors to present their work and receive feedback from UConn faculty and students, as well as from members of Connecticut's larger anti-trafficking community. I'm grateful to UConn's Humanities Institute for funding the Unfree Labor working group, and to group members Jane Gordon, Thomas Meagher, Vanessa Lovelace Christopher Clark, and others, whose own work on slavery and trafficking taught me a good deal. The Unfree Labor group also brought Joel Quirk to campus, whose scholarship has greatly inspired the work of this volume, and whose kind words have encouraged me to bring it into being.

From its inception, this book has been a collective effort, and it has been an honor to have such brilliant and generous interlocutors. The contributors to this volume have added immeasurably to the conversation that we hoped to bring forward, and I'm grateful for their hard work, their intellectual courage, and their friendship as we worked through the complicated relationships between children and slavery. At the University of Connecticut, I am fortunate to have brilliant colleagues such as Alexis Boylan, Kate Capshaw, Martha Cutter, Victoria Ford Smith, Kathy Knapp, Micki McElya, Cathy Schlund-Vials, and Chris Vials, whose scholarship and friendship have been sustaining. Everything I have written or edited has benefited from the careful attention and generous feedback of my writing group, and this project is no exception. Many thanks to Jeff Allred, Sophie Bell, Sarah Chinn, Joseph Entin, Hildegard Hoeller, Meg Toth and Jennifer Travis. At colloquiums and conferences, I learned about race, childhood, and slavery through the work and conversations of Karen Sánchez-Eppler, Lucia Hodgson, Brigitte Fielder, Jonathan Senchyne, Britt Rusert, Sari Edelstein, Sari Altschuler, Paul Erickson, Pat Crain, Martin Brückner, Hester Blum, Corinne Field, Catherine Jones, Sarah Adelman, Natalia Cecire, Elizabeth Marshall, Pier Gabrielle Foreman, Courtney Weikle-Mills, Tyler Bickford, Caleb Smith, Nazera Wright, Philip Nel, Rebekah Sheldon, Kathryn Bond Stockton, Cliff Rosky, Mallory Cohn, Julian Gil-Peterson, and Mary Zaborskis. While this book has benefited enormously from all these encounters, any oversights or missteps that remain in these pages are entirely my responsibility.

The biggest thanks are due, as always, to Matthew and Connor, who make everything possible.

# Introduction: When Is a Child a Slave?

## Anna Mae Duane

In the 2011 memoir *My Stone of Hope: From Haitian Slave Child to Abolitionist*, the narrator witnesses a woman brutally abusing a little girl. The girl is enslaved within the woman's house as a *restavec*, or domestic servant. As the "mistress" beats the child mercilessly, the woman screams, "I am not of your race!"[1] This wrenching moment illustrates the challenges of bringing knowledge of past slavery to present-day abuses. Reading this passage as a scholar of antebellum slavery in the United States, my first thought was that a scene in which an "owner" abuses a slave is, unfortunately, nothing new. The abuser's assertion of racial distinction echoes earlier justifications for dominating and abusing another. Cadet, the scene's narrator, points out that the French had invoked racial superiority to justify their cruelty in the days before slavery was rendered illegal. So in many ways, this twentieth-century scene of physical brutality, justified by racism, appears to be a seamless continuation of older models. But once we look closer, this model's explanatory power slips. To begin with, both aggressor and victim are black, and both are desperately poor. The narrator of this scene, Bobby, a self-identified slave, was significantly lighter in complexion than his owner, who nonetheless insulted him for his blackness. It is this very disjunction – modern slavery both is and is not a reiteration of models of pre-emancipation enslavement – that provides insights that could not be gleaned if we viewed this scene in isolation. Grappling with this Haitian mistress's seemingly nonsensical allusion to racial difference in the twentieth century reminds us anew of how arbitrary the lines of racial distinction were when they were first developed. Certainly these lines strained the limits of credibility in the eighteenth and nineteenth centuries as blood relatives were placed in different racial categories, often when the difference in skin tone was barely perceptible.

This scene of a child being beaten – in some ways alien, and in others deeply familiar – opens up the questions at the heart of this book. As a transhistorical endeavor, *Child Slavery before and after Emancipation* brings together scholars of pre-emancipation U.S. and Atlantic slavery with scholars working on twenty-first century slavery and trafficking. Ideally, knowledge of the past can help us to better understand the present. But as Jean-Robert Cadet's narrative illustrates, the present also has the capacity to shift our perspective on the past, illuminating what we may well have overlooked, or even changing what we thought we knew in the first place. In particular, this volume suggests that a focus on the child – a subject of contention and continuity in pre- and post-emancipation versions of slavery – opens opportunities both to rethink how we teach and write about historical slavery and to reconsider the assumptions we bring to scholarly and activist engagements with twenty-first-century abuses.

In short, we believe that asking the question "When is a child a slave?" is necessary if we hope to answer when *anyone* in the modern world is a slave. As the contributors to this volume know well, risks accompany invoking the word *slavery* in a modern context. Even as the terminology of modern slavery has been gaining purchase on many fronts, vociferous arguments oppose its proliferation. Anyone who has attended a conference on this question has likely witnessed more than one stormy dispute over terminology. This volume will not settle the debate. Readers will almost certainly disagree with some arguments included here – indeed, some of our essayists disagree with each other, as in any good conversation. We don't propose definitive answers: rather, this volume seeks to tug on vital conceptual threads undergirding the complicated tapestries supporting modern-day slavery. We hope that this conversation invites others to work on further unraveling the knots we identify.

Undoubtedly, the term *slavery* itself is a particularly knotty problem. On one side of the debate, critics, including some of this volume's contributors, argue against sloppily deploying the term *slavery* as shorthand for "bad." As David Rosen argues in his discussion of child soldiers and Jessica Pliley discusses in her analysis of the white slavery debate, reformers have been – and continue to be – quick to apply the word *slavery* to describe modern practices they find morally repugnant, particularly when those practices disrupt largely unexamined ideas about childhood innocence and passivity.[2] Put simply, the term *slavery* can be historically imprecise.[3] Particularly for scholars who have spent years studying the Atlantic slave trade, using the term *slavery* to account for a host of present-day practices, all with different levels of consent, coercion, and harm, diminishes the horror of chattel slavery, and distracts us from the experiences of the millions of people enslaved under that system. As Micki McElya points out in her contribution to this book, the white slavery scare traded on a comparison that diminished the sufferings of enslaved African Americans, by suggesting that the trials of antebellum slaves were trivial compared to the indignities young white girls suffered. Further, it can be argued that to focus on child slavery specifically only reiterates the same infantilizing apparatus long deployed to enslave and disenfranchise women and people of color.

In response to such concerns, many human rights activists and policy makers prefer the term *trafficking*.[4] This alternative is also not without problems. The term is rooted in twentieth-century laws like the 1910 Mann Act that forbade transporting women across state lines.[5] As such, *trafficking* implies the movement of people for nefarious purposes. And certainly, there is validity within this definition – much coerced and exploitative labor involves removing people from their home countries with the intent of exploiting them. Yet movement itself doesn't invariably involve the coercion or exploitation associated with the slave-like practices that now come under the term *trafficking*.[6] Further, people can find themselves reduced to slave-like conditions without leaving the borders of their home countries. Particularly in the case of children, exploitative practices often take place in private homes, in natal villages.

Even as we are aware of the problems and risks of deploying the term *slavery*, this volume – and the series in which it appears – argues that insisting on different nomenclature for slavery before and after legal emancipation(s) risks obscuring powerful historical continuities that underlie many modern atrocities.[7] There are dangers inherent in broad comparisons, but there are also compelling reasons for engaging them. Ronald Weitzer and others argue persuasively about the need to invest in micro-level research about modern slavery to gather better data about divergent circumstances in widely different parts of the globe. We agree, but we also contend that it is precisely the overwhelming complexities of modern slavery that render the task of creating global definitions vital. As Joel Quirk has argued in his remarkable work *The Antislavery Project*, any approach to the question of modern slavery has to invoke big questions: "How many 'slaves' are there? How do we know?"[8] This volume seeks to provide one part of the intellectual scaffolding needed to enhance our "capacity to move beyond particular cases, and thereby situate [diverse examples] within a shared frame of reference."[9] To ask such questions offers a necessary counterpart to the vital work of gathering data in the field. Just as surely as we need new data to inform our analyses, we need to interrogate the rubrics we bring to that information. Our aim in this volume is to trace how undertheorized assumptions about childhood dependence and adult power have allowed structures of enslavement to persist, even as laws across the globe strictly forbid chattel slavery. As feminist approaches can provide a framework for illuminating an interlocking set of assumptions undergirding a wide range of particular oppressions women face throughout the world, we argue that a child-centered approach to slavery studies will allow us to see underlying beliefs that facilitate enslavement, in conjunction with a need to increase our attention to the particularities of individual instances of enslaved children.

Evidence continues to accrue that children have often provided both the conceptual underpinning for justifying slavery and much of the labor within slavery's machinations. This volume seeks to excavate the embedded concepts at work in these machinations, many of them rooted in an engagement with an imagined child who functions as the counterpoint to the autonomous citizen. More precisely, the very concepts that undergird slavery – infantilization, paternalism, and guardianship – all invoke such an imagined child to make their arguments. In each case, power is given to those who can "prove" that they are not childlike, and are thus deserving of rights. Both sources engaging the past, such as David Eltis' Transatlantic Slavery Database (which estimates that in the latter years of the slave trade, perhaps up to 50 percent of those subjected to the middle passage were children), and modern-day statistics compiled by UNICEF, the ILO, and others demonstrate that children constitute a sizable proportion of slavery's victims. Yet children are often bracketed from discussions and analyses of slavery, both past and present.[10] For example, the most recent estimate provided by the Global Slavery Index suggests that roughly 29.8 million people suffer slave-like conditions throughout the world. However, recent figures from UNICEF indicate that 171 million children in the developing world are engaged in the worst forms of coerced and exploitative labor, including sex work and warfare.[11] Certainly these statistics leave room for error: it is notoriously hard to get solid data on illegal practices that are hidden from view. That said, these are the sorts of metrics that currently guide public and scholarly discourse on the issue and that are cited in policy decisions: we need to attend to the story they collectively tell. In particular, we need to consider how the startling disconnect in the statistics (enslaved *children* somehow constitute more than five times the number of enslaved *people*) testifies to how historians, analysts, and activists often either don't "see" child slaves, or don't include them in their analyses because children's needs and vulnerabilities complicate the already difficult work of creating viable definitions.[12] Children don't count, or at least they are not counted in the same way. In many ways, it's not surprising that scholars often avoid the problem of integrating child slavery into larger slavery studies: thinking about children as a fundamental element within slavery forces us to confront questions about power and dependence, about authority and force that structure how we think about rights, about citizenship, and about human development. Because slavery and childhood have been defined in relation to one another since antiquity, enslaved children are a paradox for analysts who wish to engage the complex relationship between slavery and freedom. A focus on children is not a way out of the contradictions and inconsistencies facing scholars, activists, and policy makers. Rather, children reside at the heart of these contradictions, and that is precisely why we must turn our attention to them.

### "The Child Is the Natural Slave": Childhood and Slavery as Mutually Defining Terms

Although children are often excluded from the calculus of who counts as a slave, they have long been central to defining slavery itself. Aristotle's definition of a child as a subject whose personhood is derived from their relationship to an adult – still reflected in modern children's lack of independent legal standing – offers an early but influential example of how the vulnerability and dependence that is a natural part of the human life cycle justify a lack of rights, or indeed, a lack of full personhood. In his description of the "natural slave," Aristotle views a child as the embodiment of the incomplete subjectivity that is central to enslavement: "The Child is imperfect and therefore obviously his virtue is not relative to himself alone, but to the perfect man and to his teacher, and in like manner the virtue of the slave is relative to the master."[13] The child by definition here is incomplete, and thus imperfect. His incompleteness renders him an appendage of an adult – a perfect man, arguably in full possession of the rights and "virtues" of adulthood. In turn, the child's humanity emerges only in response to the demands and the tutelage of such a virtuous, and thus self-reliant man. The child's "natural" state of dependence and incompleteness provides the terminology for explaining how slavery itself functions. In ancient Rome, the terms for *youth* were literally the words for *slave*. As Sandra Joshel points out, Roman "slave owners (re)named a male slave by combining the Latin word for boy (*puer*) regardless of the slave's age and the genitive of his owner's name." Thus "*Marcipor*, for example was *Marci puer* (Marcus's boy)."[14] Those scholars familiar with conventions in the antebellum United States readily recognize the staying power of that particular infantilizing tradition, as enslaved African Americans were often called "boy" or "gal" no matter what their age.

The conceptual entanglements between childhood and slavery are so profound that these relationships formed much of the rhetorical scaffolding for the racial justifications of slavery that would emerge in the West during the eighteenth and nineteenth centuries. During the Atlantic slave trade, the figure of the child created a conceptual bridge that attached race to slavery, as blackness was increasingly equated with childishness. Thomas Jefferson famously quipped that freeing a slave would be akin to abandoning a child.[15] Stanley Elkins' often-critiqued description of the stereotypes surrounding plantation slaves suggested that slaveholders felt that the African American slave's "childlike quality" was "the very key to his being." Uncle Tom, perhaps the most famous fictional slave in global history, is portrayed as "simple and *childlike*" and spends much of his time in the novel as the playmate of a six- or seven-year-old child.[16] The relationship, once forged, between childhood, slavery, and blackness was so powerful that both slavery apologists and abolitionists often could not see African Americans outside a paternalistic framework.

As childhood was often deployed to justify and explain enslavement of masses of people, the definition of childhood itself has been recalibrated in response to slavery's encroachments. The contributors to this volume work with the United Nations' rubric that defines people under the age of eighteen as legal children. But of course, the definition of a child has varied widely over historical and geographical space. Often those variations shifted in response to evolving definitions of slavery itself. For example, one way that colonial Americans began to differentiate between white apprentices and black slaves was in their attention to the age of children. As a law passed in colonial Virginia testifies, ascertaining the precise age of youth destined to be apprenticed was very important, as the terms of their service often came to an end at the age of twenty-one.[17] The law required that white and Indian apprentices provide their age so that the terms of servitude could be assessed, but no such requirement was made for African youth. For black servants, childhood was both illegible (no one knew or cared when it began) and interminable, along with their servitude. In the post-emancipation-era United States, as contributor Jessica Pliley reminds us, the age of consent (an increasingly vital marker between childhood and adulthood) was increased in the United States and the United Kingdom in response to the perceived encroachments of "white slavery." As the age was pushed up, a girl's childhood lengthened, and her role as a sex worker became an easily recognizable form of "slavery." In colonial Africa, as contributor Audra Diptee details in her essay, French authorities sought to shift traditional ideas that had aligned people in generations, rather than according to individual ages. Colonization rendered childhood an individual rather than a communal life stage. As they sought to impose Western concepts of childhood dependence and protection on African children, French colonial authorities also found ways of keeping such children under the control of stakeholders in the colonial enterprise.

Because concepts of childhood and slavery have long been used to define one another, those who sought to claim freedom have long cast themselves as empowered adults who could break with the "childlike quality" of slavery. For instance, *The Narrative of the Life of Frederick Douglass* (1845), a text that occupies a central role in U.S. antebellum slavery studies, is often read as a coming-of-age narrative that aligns freedom with adulthood. At a key point in the narrative, Douglass comforts himself by acknowledging that "all boys are bound to someone." In doing so, he creates parallel journeys aligning moving from childhood to adulthood with moving from slavery to freedom.

Douglass's rhetorical journey was so powerful because it tapped into Enlightenment formulations of who can and should wield the right to self-government. When John Locke wrote that children are "not born in [a] full state of equality, though they are born to it," he simultaneously both changed the definition of what government meant, and removed children from its workings.[18] Locke and other Enlightenment thinkers made children's exclusion from political power not only necessary, but natural as they sought to imagine power that would reside in reason, rather than heredity. As Holly Brewer has argued, Locke's emphasis on consent rendered children incapable of participating in the contractual obligations that would come to occupy center stage in liberal democratic thought and would emerge as key rubric for distinguishing between slavery and freedom.[19] The social contract, and the insistence that participants in the

transaction come to it as fully consenting, independent subjects, effectively excludes those who do not fit the bill.[20] If one is not a self-reliant
adult, the Enlightenment version of Aristotle's "perfect man," then one
is relegated to the children's table. Women, African Americans, the disabled, and others have all been aligned with childhood and childishness
to explain why they were exempt from the contract.[21] As Lucia Hodgson
points out, "the child subject's exclusion is the *foundation of* the adult
subject's inclusion."[22] Adults deserve rights precisely because they are not
children.

## Children as Property

The 2012 Bellagio-Harvard guidelines for defining slavery, building on
the foundational 1926 UN protocol, argue that slavery "is the status
or condition of a person over whom any or all of the powers attaching
to the right of ownership are exercised." The guidelines further explain
that "the exercise of 'the powers attaching to the right of ownership'
should be understood as constituting control over a person in such
a way as to significantly deprive that person of his or her individual
liberty, with the intent of exploitation through the use, management,
profit, transfer or disposal of that person."[23] Children, who are largely
considered the property of their parents, offer particular challenges to
this definition.[24] As Karl Marx and Fredreich Engels famously noted,
capitalism's investment in individual assets was created in tandem with
a model that rendered slaves, women, and children all different forms
of property.[25] The Western world has largely rejected the morality
of the first two arrangements, but for the most part, children are the
exception.

In many places across the globe, including the United States, the notion
that children have a right to liberty (and thus are oppressed if that liberty
is denied) is a highly contentious assumption.[26] Behaviors and activities
that would be viewed as exploitive if imposed upon adults, such as working on a family farm for no pay, having to hand over all of one's pay to
an older relative, or having minimal to no control over one's emotional
and sexual relationships, are often considered completely appropriate for
children. Like no other class of people, children are largely considered
the domain of others, particularly their parents. The United States is the
only nation that still refuses to ratify the 1990 UN Convention on the
Rights of the Child, in part because of objections raised by American
parents who feared they would be barred from exercising their "natural"

rights to physically coerce their children into obedience.[27] Throughout the world, traditions of bride price, apprenticeship fees, and other forms of commodification work on the assumption that the child is an asset that belongs to their parents. Rather than children existing as a special case within slavery's larger schema, enslaved children actually demonstrate how people come to function as property. As Karen Sánchez-Eppler writes in her contribution to this volume, the "slave child epitomizes, after all, the dual demands of productive labor and being oneself a possession, commodity, and investment."

## Children as Naturally Protected by Kin and Family Structure

Because many children are often treated *de facto*, if not de jure, as the property of their parents, distinguishing between the slave child and the free child can be a very difficult process. Leonie J. Archer, who argues that we should define slavery as a state of social alienation, rather than a lack of self-ownership, acknowledges that many women and children are incorporated in slave-like structures, but suggests that their inclusion in kin networks exempts them from the "social death" that is the lot of the slave alone.

> In certain respects, the status if not condition of the slave has often paralleled that of wives, concubines, children and other minors, all of whom have been forbidden to hold property in their own name, participate in political decision making, give legal testimony and so forth. Such significant parallels can make it seem that slavery has grown out of primitive patriarchy. There may be an element of truth in this but it should not obscure the discontinuity and distinction between the status of dependent kin and that of the slave. Women and children, if not enslaved, helped to constitute the family and the lineage – even more essentially they brought together different kin groups and lineages, a function and role with its own moment of autonomy.[28]

In response to such arguments, this volume contends that a reliance on the protective role of family ties to make the distinction between a free child and a slave child reiterates the very beliefs that ensure the oppression and, yes, the enslavement of both children and women. For women and children, the kinship lineage they inhabit often increases the property and status of the male householder, but offers very little in the way of empowering their own lives. We cannot reserve the term *slave* only for those few individuals who upon securing "freedom" could fully inhabit established structures of property, labor, and rights assigned to adult male citizens.

Indeed, the alleged benefits of marital or filial ties to a benevolent patriarch are often the very structures that trap modern children in enslavement. As Audra Diptee argues in her contribution to this volume, colonial forces in Africa often relied on parental and kinship structures – parents, guardians, and husbands – to provide cover for their appropriation of children's labor within systems formerly considered slavery. Looking at more recent events, we might ask where one might find the "moment of autonomy" the schoolgirls sold into forced "marriages" with the Nigerian terrorist group Boko Haram have found.[29] In one of the more recent first-person accounts of forced child marriage, Nujood Ali describes how her father sold her into a forced marriage in rural Yemen as she approached ten years of age. Although technically Nujood was afforded the benefits of kinship status (ostensibly being "married" protected her from rape by men other than her "husband" – a man three times her age), her trauma from her "husband's" frequent rapes surely meets the criteria of degradation and utter control that constitutes the Bellagio-Harvard definition of ownership and exploitation.[30] She managed to apply for a divorce and received one in court. Even after the international attention her case garnered, Nujood Ali's subjection to her father kept her from benefiting from her story or her actions. Both law and custom demanded that the proceeds from her book be paid to her father, not her. As a child, and particularly as a girl, she can only *be* property. She cannot be the owner of it. Her father declined to spend the money on Nujood's schooling, as was intended, choosing instead to add two wives to his own retinue. According to a recent report, the father has sold Nujood's younger sister into a forced marriage.[31]

Undeniably, parents, husbands, and other kin in the twenty-first century can be as impervious to the logic of sentimental protection as the nineteenth-century slaveholders who fancied themselves benevolent patriarchs. While girls are particularly vulnerable to oppression within and because of familial rights, boys are far from immune. Historians of antebellum slavery in the United States have long chronicled how often and how easily white fathers disowned and sold their mixed-race children. In the twentieth century, Jean-Robert Cadet's narratives describe how his own father orchestrated his life as a *restavec*. In the past, the extramarital birth of certain children has rendered them more vulnerable to slavery by their own kin. This continues to be true, as it was for Cadet, but modern slavery also involves the abuse and sale of children by their legally recognized parents. In many cases, poverty reduces the options for parents, who must sell or indenture their children as a means of survival. In India, for instance, debt bondage places millions of children in factories or in domestic servitude, working at wages so small that buying their way out is all but impossible. In the words of one activist, it is precisely the child's double subjection to parents and to employers that renders them ideal slaves. "Children are very compliant.... On the one hand they are afraid of the employer, on the other of their parents, so they just do as they are told."[32] In short, to argue, as Archer does, that familial structures provide protection as "a more or less well-defined pact between the social and natural order, and between one human group and another," is to perpetuate a deadly fallacy that suggests that kinship inoculates members against the worst sorts of cruelties.[33]

When it comes to children, a dizzying array of laws and customs represent variations on a persistent belief that absolute power over children is permissible because that power will be checked by the paternal love all children will inevitably elicit. As scholars of U.S. antebellum slavery have demonstrated, slave laws sought to both justify and erase the violence of slave systems by suggesting that those in power would be naturally restrained by the vulnerability of those under their dominion. Under this logic, the tears and smiles of the powerless – particularly children – will naturally stay the hand of otherwise unchecked power. In 1857, slavery apologist George Fitzhugh argued that "the dependent exercise, because of their dependence, as much control over their superiors in most things as those superiors exercise over them." For Fitzhugh it was "an invariable law of nature, that weakness and dependence are elements of strength, and generally sufficiently limit that universal despotism, observable throughout human and animal nature."[34] This concept is particularly powerful when children are concerned – it seems only natural that their weakness will translate into a certain power over adults who feel compelled to care for them. Saidiya Hartman explains the tautology this way: "the dominated exert influence over the dominant by virtue of their weakness and therefore more formal protections are unnecessary."[35]

In this model, the rights of the powerless – as the child is rendered by contract theory and the legal structures built on it – come into existence solely through the feelings they evoke in the powerful. The child, legally considered incapable of consent, is naturally expected to submit to adults who are moved by feeling and duty to act in the child's best interest. In return, adults, particularly those charged with a child's care, cannot help but be guided by benevolent feeling. Then as now, the fantasy of benevolent paternalism – based on the assertion that charming children can win power through tears and smiles – enables slavery. Of course, parents do often love and protect their children. No one denies that fundamental reality. However, it is an equally fundamental truth that depending on the best elements of human nature to always prevail is a dangerously naive approach to policy.

The belief that children bind their parents by love manifests in different forms to be sure, but nonetheless remains prevalent in both law and custom throughout the world, and thus underlies the philosophy informing human rights statutes and funding. Even the most well-meaning advocates for children often present their cases within a framework that reasserts adult control and emphasizes childlike subjection and vulnerability. In the nineteenth century, antislavery material often focused on heart-wrenching scenes of children torn from parents in the hopes of arousing protective instincts. Harriet Beecher Stowe pulled no punches when she painted slavery's ills through the desperate struggles of a mother faced with losing her child in her 1852 novel *Uncle Tom's Cabin.*

For the child slept. At first, the novelty and alarm kept him waking; but his mother so hurriedly repressed every breath or sound, and so assured him that if he were only still she would certainly save him, that he clung quietly round her neck, only asking, as he found himself sinking to sleep,

"Mother, I don't need to keep awake, do I?"

"No, my darling; sleep, if you want to."

"But, mother, if I do get asleep, you won't let him get me?"

"No! So may God help me!" said his mother, with a paler cheek, and a brighter light in her large dark eyes.

"You're *sure*, an't you, mother?"

"Yes, *sure*!" said the mother, in a voice that startled herself; for it seemed to her to come from a spirit within, that was no part of her; and the boy dropped his little weary head on her shoulder, and was soon asleep. How the touch of those warm arms, the gentle breathings that came in her neck, seemed to add fire and spirit to her movements! (106)

In this iconic scene, the vulnerability of her sleeping, helpless child gives Eliza nearly superhuman powers. She carries her child through the night, and, like an action hero, she jumps across crashing ice floes, traversing the Ohio River to safety. It's worth pausing on the representation of Harry himself here. In an earlier scene in the novel, he's old enough and clever enough to engage in a series of canny impersonations and performances, but here he is infant vulnerability incarnate. In fact, he's unconscious for most of the trip, unable to speak, and when he does, his mother soothes him back to passivity. This pattern reasserts itself later in the text, when both parents dress Harry as a little girl to better disguise/infantilize him, and he is admonished not to talk at all. As a child, Harry becomes a precious object to be rescued by adults who speak on his behalf rather than an agent who can lay claim to rights and protest their infringement. Stowe's strategy was a successful one. The image of Eliza saving her endangered child appeared everywhere in the mid-nineteenth century – on stage, on tableware, on engravings, in paintings, and beyond.

In our own era, when humanitarian organizations, activists, and scholars have sought to raise awareness about human trafficking, forced labor, and modern slavery, they often introduce a suffering child as the ambassador for international empathy. The sentimental logic of paternal power animates this circulation of images of vulnerable children as an antislavery tool – as we look at children's helpless faces, we are supposed to be compelled by our feelings, if not by law, to act on their behalf. Such a model can do much to raise awareness, but it also can perpetuate the idea that children need to be helped solely because of their emotional appeal, not because they can claim self-possession. Ad campaigns, book covers, and even television shows feature images of an endangered child, looking out in a silent plea for our care, our rescue, and our dollars. Because of the visceral, parental response children are expected to evoke, children render the story of modern slavery a compelling morality tale, in which we – as free, autonomous adults – are fully empowered to play the hero. As contributor Erica Meiners discusses in her analysis of anti-incarceration campaigns, an investment in children's suffering can often reify the disempowering fantasy that children's rights depend on the emotions they evoke.

This investment in the innocent, passive child as a perpetually appealing victim continues to skew analyses, both official and informal, of what constitutes child slavery, and of how to address it. Assessment of a situation's severity can hinge on ideas of what childhood is *supposed* to represent, rather than the lived experience of actual children. Thus when children suffer within the realm of what scholars and policy makers imagine the child *should* do – such as domestic work in private homes – it is often met with far less outrage than other practices elicit.[36] As Gary Craig and Jonathan Blagbrough discuss in this volume, because domestic servitude so closely correlates with the sort of power relations we believe children *should* experience – living in private homes, among families, doing chores – it seems more difficult to identify these situations as slavery. On the other hand, when the public sees people under eighteen engaging in the sort of actions we like to tell ourselves that children never do on their own – like have sex or be violent – we often can see *only* slavery.

In some of the more controversial arguments found in this volume, Jessica Pliley, Micki McElya, and David Rosen argue that our attachment to viewing children as the innocent reflections of parental desires not only renders actual slavery invisible, but can also invoke a definition of slavery when it does not apply. Micki McElya's chapter, for instance, focuses on how a single statue depicting a young girl endangered by "white slavery" was considered far more scandalous than any other form of exploitation imposed on children, including the chattel slavery imposed upon generations of African Americans. In our own day, the heated debate over child sex trafficking – one area in which children take center stage in discussions of modern enslavement – often relies on the idea that both parents and law enforcement are best suited to protect an innocent child from an outside world of strange predators. Thus the remedy for child sex trafficking adheres to a model in which children are safe at home, where they belong, free from outside dangers. Yet as work by Heather Montgomery, Laura María Agustín, and Elizabeth Bernstein amply demonstrates, women and girls often find themselves coerced into prostitution because of, rather than in spite of, their families.[37]

Undoubtedly, many children are coerced into sex work, as they are coerced into other forms of work, including domestic servitude (as Gary Craig, Jonathan Blagbrough, and Kelli Johnson detail in their chapters), military work (as David Rosen discusses), and agricultural and factory work. It is sex trafficking – and to some extent, child soldiering – however, that garners the lion's share of attention, largely because these forms of work blatantly contradict the idea that children are beings largely defined by their parents' wishes. This insistence that children somehow occupy a wholly different realm of consent and coercion imposes a false binary that presumes that someone under eighteen engaging in these acts is a wholly defenseless victim, while a nineteen- or twenty-year-old doing the same thing is a criminal or at the very least, a fully consenting agent.

In addition to critiquing infantilizing narratives, the authors of this volume also engage in the risky but necessary work of confronting the very truths that infantilization manipulates and exploits. All human beings need support and nurturance, though the extent of that need varies according to age, gender, ability, and circumstance. Children, of course, often require more care than adults do, but they are not alone in needing support. To return to that exemplar of self-won freedom, Frederick Douglass, we too often forget that he arrived in New York vulnerable and afraid. He did not strike out boldly on his own, but rather needed the help of antislavery networks in order to find lodging and work.

The binary of child and citizen, victim and agent, prevents us from fully engaging the plight of people on either side of the divide. "This is a false dichotomy," Sara Vida Coumans reminds us. Not "only can we exercise our agency at every point in life, but also we might rely on protection at every point in life. Furthermore, agency and protection are not mutually exclusive concepts; they contribute to and rely on each other as well."[38] By foregrounding children as part of a continuum of human need, rather than as a wholly different class of person, essays by John Wall, Gary Craig and Jonathan Blagbrough, and Sarah L. H. Gronningsater posit how we might come to a more capacious understanding of positive rights and collective freedoms. Together, our essays work though the powerful narrative we've inherited from the abolitionists of the past. In response to the oft-told story of a transformative movement from infantilizing slavery to adult freedom that still structures much of Western thinking, these essays provide resources for thinking through how these very assumptions can lend themselves to coercion, abuse, and slavery.

Because this volume seeks to trace how conceptual entanglements between slavery and childhood impact material conditions and political responses to them, the essays are organized around attributes that entangle definitions of children with definitions of slaves. We begin by considering children in their most natural of habitats – the home – to consider how assumptions about power and property in the family allow coercion to go unquestioned. Our second section focuses on how our assumption of "natural" innocence – itself a highly racialized characteristic – harms children by demanding they inhabit the very sort of passivity and ignorance that renders them especially vulnerable. Our third section argues that liberal theory's emphasis on consent – and the insistence that children are always incapable of it – skews our definitions of slavery for both children and adults. The fourth and final section foregrounds children's voices to ask how we might better listen to enslaved children, past and present.

The first section begins with Karen Sánchez-Eppler's argument that we read the American WPA Slave Narratives as testimonies of childhood experiences of enslavement, in which they were uniquely vulnerable to "paternalism's double-binds of exploitation and devotion." She suggests that once we acknowledge that the majority of people enslaved in the antebellum United States were actually children, we can begin to recalibrate our historical methodology. For instance, if we recognize childhood as a crucial characteristic of the antebellum U.S. slave regime, those very traits and conditions that have seemed to undermine the reliability of the WPA narratives become a source of insight. Sarah Winter's essay offers a different take on how the workings of slavery and of family can be indistinguishable. Her essay focuses on an eighteenth-century

British legal case to explore how the child's legal inability to own property became complicated during the practice of "gifting" slave children to other children. Not quite siblings, but not fully master and slave, these childhood relationships were a means of training white and black children for their future roles. Such gifts were also an act of theater. No child, free or enslaved, was legally able to own property. Winter then turns to a remarkable eighteenth-century British probate case in which it was determined an enslaved child gifted to his mistress could accept the property his mistress bequeathed to him in death. Tellingly, this outcome was only possible because he had reached the age of majority.

If our first section examines how the dependence we naturally attribute to childhood facilitates the often ruthless power structures children find themselves "protected" within, the next two sections explore the flip side of that coin. The authors in the second section explore how the potent image of an innocent child can reduce the complexities of coerced labor to a simple moral equation, in which lawmakers and reformers overlook large economic, social, and legal issues in favor of rescuing individual, appealing children. In their chapters, authors Micki McElya and Erica Meiners think about how visual images of childhood innocence evoke and sometimes erase memories of abolitionist tactics against chattel slavery. For McElya, the sensationalizing statue *The White Slave* provides an object for meditating on how fetishizing the sexual innocence of young white girls worked to diminish attention to memories of sexual abuse in U.S. chattel slavery. Erica Meiners highlights another reform movement that draws on associations with U.S. chattel slavery – the prison abolition movement. Meiners pays particular attention to how some prison abolitionists invoke a well-known image from nineteenth-century abolitionism: the figure of an innocent and endangered child. She argues that now, as then, this image carries a powerful emotional punch. But relying on discrete emotional responses threatens to reduce the wide-scale structural issues that need to be addressed in favor of the fantasy of individual rescue. Certainly incarceration is a terrible fate for juveniles. It is also often a grave injustice for adults, who are denied the claims to the sort of naturalized innocence that are deployed on behalf of children.

The first two essays in this section focus on how an idealized innocence is used to keep children separated from both adult choices and adult consequences. In the third essay in this section, Sarah L. H. Gronningsater asks why eighteenth-century reformers in New York found children the most suitable candidates for a freedom from which their parents were still disqualified. Specifically Gronningsater focuses on Northern gradual emancipation statutes that first emancipated children born on a certain date, rather than adults currently enslaved. Strikingly, Gronningsater argues that it was the children's dependence that rendered them particularly attractive as the recipients of gradual emancipation. Ironically, it was because they could not fully access freedom right away that masters felt less threatened by freeing them in the first place. Under these legal compromises, older children had to work for years to "repay" masters for the trouble of feeding them before they could produce valuable labor. As in so many of the instances we explore in this volume, a child's need for care, her inability to work, and thus her "innocence" of market forces justifies the caretaker's claim to ownership.

The third section works through how formulations of consent – what it means, who can wield it – represent particularly fraught ground for scholars who wish to parse the relationship between childhood and enslavement. Jessica Pliley's chapter focuses on how the legal response to the white slavery scare pivoted on changing the age of consent in the United States, thus extending the definition of childhood itself. Pliley further complicates the now commonsense denial of consent to children by excavating archival material in which young girls refused to be "rescued," insisting that their sex work was consensual. David Rosen offers a startling perspective on another highly visible form of child slavery when he questions current human rights policy defining all military service by people under eighteen as *de facto* slavery. While Rosen acknowledges that children are indeed enslaved into military service, he also draws from historical and contemporary examples that defy the notion that people under eighteen are incapable of consenting to fight. If we face this reality, Rosen argues, then we must question whether the term *slavery*, as applied to child soldiers, provides a comforting buffer from the reality that children can and do make hard choices in morally ambivalent circumstances. Audra Diptee's essay turns to colonial Africa, where, she argues, Europeans saw the future of the continent embodied in a battle for the future of African children. Yet even as children occupied the heart of antislavery colonial rhetoric, colonial policies intensified the demand for coerced child labor. By exploring several incidents in which former slaves are transformed into wards, and former masters into guardians and husbands, Diptee charts how French colonial authorities mapped Western ideas of childhood onto existing structures of slavery, exploiting notions of familial protection to provide cover for the same relationships of coercion and exploitation that they were allegedly there to reform.

Our final section challenges us to listen to children themselves as speakers, to recognize them as activists and abolitionists, and to recalibrate human rights discourse and law in ways that empower, rather than simply rescue, children. Kelli Lyon Johnson's essay engages the testimonies of formerly enslaved children to explore the rhetorical and political work they do. Here too, we see the theme of innocence invoked, this time by children themselves to assert their lack of culpability in what happened to them. The next essay, by Gary Craig and Jonathan Blagbrough, both of whom have worked extensively with children enslaved as domestic servants, draws on their own considerable expertise. Perhaps even more important, they draw on the expertise of the child survivors they've worked with to offer concrete suggestions about how to improve conditions. Children, like adults, want dignity, social connection, and legal protection. Finally, John Wall argues for creating a child-centered version of human rights discourse and law that will position children as agents entitled to participate in the public sphere as well as to expect protection from it. As he contends, the roots of child slavery itself gain sustenance from adult-centered, neoliberal conceptions of freedom. He, like all our contributors, claims we need to radically rethink who deserves rights and why if we want to craft a meaningful path to dignity, empowerment, and, yes, freedom across the vast spectrum of human difference, need, and ability.

Collectively, the contributors to this volume seek not just to make the argument that invoking the child requires different questions, different methodologies, and different ways of thinking in slavery studies. We also seek to provide concrete examples of how those different approaches and perspectives might function across a range of chronology, geography, and methodology. There is much work to be done. We argue that in order to do it, we must challenge our own scholarly and intellectual attachments that weld freedom to adulthood, and thus skew our understanding of slavery's workings in both the past and the present. Our purpose is to demonstrate how childhood and adulthood are continually reconstructed in a host of contexts – cultural, political, and economic – and to interrogate how those constructions serve those in power. We offer a variety of perspectives, but we contend that attending to the rights of children can push us to find a model of freedom that can accommodate vulnerability as well as autonomy, and that doesn't find dependence a disqualifier for, but rather a vital aspect of, a fully realized life.[39]

## Notes

1  Jean-Robert Cadet, *My Stone of Hope: From Haitian Slave Child to Abolitionist* (Austin: University of Texas Press, 2011), 52–3.

2  For a nuanced and instructive reading of how childhood innocence has been distributed along the racial lines of slavery in the United States, see Robin Bernstein, *Racial Innocence: Performing American Childhood from Slavery to Civil Rights* (New York: New York University Press, 2011).

3  See Orlando Patterson, "Trafficking, Gender & Slavery: Past and Present," in Jean Allain, ed. *The Legal Understanding of Slavery: From the Historical to the Contemporary* (Oxford: Oxford University Press, 2012).

4  One of the main documents on this issue produced by the United States is the *Trafficking in Persons Report*, for instance. Yet even within this document *slavery* and *trafficking* are sometimes used interchangeably as in Secretary of State Hillary Clinton's introduction to the State Department's 2009 *Trafficking in Persons Report*: "We have seen unprecedented forward movement around the world in the fight to end human trafficking, a form of modern-day slavery." The United Nations notably uses the word *slavery* in much of its literature. Still other analysts split the difference, using both terms, as in Siddharth Kara's important work *Sex Trafficking: Inside the Business of Modern Slavery* or Joel Quirk's powerful *The Antislavery Project, from the Atlantic Slave Trade to Human Trafficking* (Philadelphia: University of Pennsylvania Press, 2011).

5  See essays by Jessica Pliley and Micki McElya in this volume for a discussion of this issue with particular attention to white slavery's worries about the innocence of young girls and the infantilization of female sexuality. See also Jo Doezema, *Sex Slaves and Discourse Masters: The Construction of Trafficking* (London: Zed, 2010).

6  An addendum to the 2010 *Trafficking in Persons Report* states that an individual "need not be physically transported from one location to another" to be a victim of the oppressive practices that *trafficking* has come to connote. U.S. State Department, *Trafficking in Persons Report* (June 2010), 8–9. Another line of critique argues that the emphasis on trafficking allows for the intensifying of border policing and the criminalization of migrant workers. See Ratna Kupur, "Migrant Women and the Legal Politics of Anti-trafficking Interventions," in Sally Cameron and Edward Newman, eds. *Trafficking in Human Beings: Social, Cultural and Political Dimensions* (Tokyo: United Nations University Press, 2008) 113; Catherine Dauvergne, *Making People Illegal: What Globalization Means for Migration and Law* (Cambridge: Cambridge University Press, 2008); Craig McGill, *Human Traffic: Sex, Slaves & Immigration* (London: Vision, 2003) I am grateful to Joel Quirk for pointing me to these resources.

7  In this we take inspiration from Joel Quirk's *The Antislavery Project*; Gary Craig's *Child Slavery Now: A Contemporary Reader*; Benjamin Lawrence and Richard Roberts, eds. *Trafficking in Slavery's Wake: Law and the Experience of Women and Children in Africa*; Gwyn Campbell, Suzanne Miers, Joseph C. Miller, eds. *Children in Slavery through the Ages* (Athens,

Ohio University Press, 2009) and *Child Slaves in the Modern World* (Athens, Ohio University Press, 2011).

8   Quirk, *The Antislavery Project*, 3.

9   Ibid., 4.

10  Certainly the plight of enslaved children has received attention from international organizations and initiatives, with the UN Special Rapporteur on Trafficking in Persons, Especially Women and Children (2004), or the Asian Regional Initiative Against Trafficking in Women and Children (2000). My larger point is that children are often treated as a particular, separate aspect of slavery, apart from the larger scope of modern slavery studies. Notable studies that do foreground enslaved children include Wilma King, *Stolen Childhood: Slave Youth in Nineteenth Century America* (Bloomington: Indiana University Press, 1997); Mary Niall Mitchell, *Raising Freedom's Child: Black Children and Visions of the Future after Slavery* (New York: New York University Press, 2010); and the aforementioned works of Gwyn Campbell et al., Gary Craig Benjamin Lawrence, and Robin Bernstein.

11  www.globalslaveryindex.org/report/; www.unicef.org/protection/ files/child_labour.pdf

12  As Kevin Bales has noted, a primary indicator of a nation's likelihood to export enslaved and trafficked people is a high proportion of the population being under fourteen years old. Kevin Bales in Jean Allain, *Legal Understanding of Slavery from the Historical to the Contemporary* (Oxford: Oxford University Press, 2012), 506.

13  Aristotle, *Politics*. trans. Benjamin Jowett (Kitchner: Batoche Books, 1999), 21.

14  Sandra R. Joshel, *Slavery in the Roman World* (Cambridge: Cambridge University Press, 2010), 95. Also William Linn Westermann, *The Slave Systems of Greek and Roman Antiquity* (Philadelphia, PA: American Philosophical Society, 1955), 58.

15  *The Writings of Thomas Jefferson*. Memorial Edition. Andrew A. Lipscomb and Albert Ellery Bergh, eds., 20 vols. (Washington, DC, 1903–4), vol. 19, 41.

16  Harriet Beecher Stowe, *Uncle Tom's Cabin* (Cleveland, OH: John P. Jewett & Co., 1852), 79.

17  *Laws Pertaining to Slaves and Servants, Virginia 1629–1672*, William Waller Hening, editor. *The statutes at large; being a collection of all the laws of Virginia, from the first session of the Legislature in the year 1619*, vol. 1. New York: Printed for the editor, 1819–23. vol. 1. October 1670-ACT XII. For a canny discussion of this phenomenon, see Lucia Hodgson, "Nature, Nurture, Nation: Race and Childhood in Transatlantic American Discourses of Slavery" (*DAIA*) February 2010, 70 (8): 3005–6, University of Southern California.

18  John Locke, *Second Treatise of Civil Government*, Sixth Edition (London: A. Millar et al.) VI. Par. 55.

19  Holly Brewer, *By Birth or By Consent: Children, Law and the Anglo-American Revolution in Authority* (Chapel Hill, NC: Omohundro Institute, 2007).

20 For two different perspectives on how to realign our vision of rights and the social contract from which they are derived, see Martha Nussbaum, *Frontiers of Justice: Disability, Nationality, Species Membership* (Cambridge, MA: Harvard University Press, 2006) and Martha Fineman, "The Vulnerable Subject: Anchoring Equality in the Human Condition," 20 *Yale Journal of Law and Feminism* 1 (2008–2009) 1–23.

21 See Anna Mae Duane, *Suffering Childhood in Early America: Violence, Race and the Making of the Child Victim* (Athens: University of Georgia Press, 2010).

22 Lucia Hodgson, "Infant Muse: Phillis Wheatley and the Revolutionary Rhetoric of Childhood." *Early American Literature* 49.3 (2014): 663–682.

23 "Harvard Bellagio 2012 GLOBAL DIALOGUE" in *Slavery Today* 14.2 (2012): Guideline 2.

24 Anna Mae Duane, "Does Dependence Create Ownership? The Problem of Defining a Child Slave." opendemocracy.net November 17, 2015. www .opendemocracy.net/beyondslavery/anna-mae-duane/does-dependence-create-ownership-problem-of-defining-child-slave.

25 Marx and Engels both noted the relationship between slavery and familial modes of ownership. Freidrich Engels, *The Origin of the Family Private Property and the State 1884* (New York: Penguin, 2010) and Karl Marx and Friedrich Engels, *Marx and The German Ideology: Including Theses on Feuerbach 1845* (New York: Prometheus, 2011). Robin Blackburn's engages these works in his essay in *Unfree Labor* in Jean Allain's *The Legal Understanding of Slavery.*

26 Amar, Akhil Reed, and Daniel Widawsky. "Child Abuse as Slavery: A Thirteenth Amendment Response to DeShaney." *Harvard Law Review* 105, no. 1359 (1992).

27 For an official rendition of these objections, see Comments of Senator Jesse Helms (R-SC) on Senate Resolution 133–Relative to the United Nations Convention on the Rights of the Child, *Congressional Record*, June 14, 1995. http://pangaea.org/street_children/world/helms.htm

28 Leonie J. Archer, *Slavery and Other Forms of Unfree Labor* (New York: Routledge, 1988), 264.

29 www.washingtonpost.com/news/morning-mix/wp/2014/04/30/hundreds-of-kidnapped-nigerian-school-girls-reportedly-sold-as-brides-to-militants-for-12-relatives-say/

30 Nujood Ali with Delphine Minoui, *I am Nujood, Age 10 and Divorced* trans. Linda Coverdale (New York: Broadway Paperbacks, 2010).

31 Joe Sheffer, "Yemen's youngest divorcee says father has squandered cash from her book," *The Guardian*, March 12, 2013. www.theguardian .com/world/2013/mar/12/child-bride-father-cash-spend

32 Director of a nongovernmental organization running schools for former child laborers, Varanasi, Uttar Pradesh, March 12, 2002. Cited in "Small Change: Bonded Labor In India." Human Rights Watch, 2002, 4. www .hrw.org/sites/default/files/reports/india0103.pdf Also see: Natasa Kovasevic, "Child Slavery," *Harvard International Review*, Summer 2007, 29, 2.

33 Archer, *Slavery and Other Forms of Unfree Labor*, 264–5.

34   George Fitzhugh, *Cannibals All! Or Slaves without Masters* 1857 (Cambridge: Belknap, 1971) 204–5.

35   Saidiya Hartman, "Seduction and the Ruses of Power," *Callalloo* 19.2 (1988): 547.

36   For more on the disparate attention to particular practices, see Gary Craig and Jonathan Blagbrough's essay on domestic labor, and David Rosen's essay on child soldiering, both found in this volume.

37   For just a few examples, see: Heather Montgomery, *Modern Babylon? Prostituting Children in Thailand* (New York: Berghahn, 2001); Laura María Agustín, *Sex at the Margins: Migration, Labour Markets and the Rescue Industry* (London: Zed, 2007); Elizabeth Bernstein, *Temporarily Yours: Intimacy, Authenticity, and the Commerce of Sex* (Chicago: University of Chicago Press, 2007).

38   Sara Vida Coumans, "How Age Matters: Exploring Contemporary Dutch Debates on Age and Sex Work." Masters' Thesis. http://repub.eur.nl/pub/ 51411 Page 26.

39   For more on vulnerability as a precondition we all share, see Martha Fineman, *The Vulnerable Subject: Anchoring Equality in the Human Condition* (Princeton, NJ: Princeton University Press, 2013); Karen Sánchez-Eppler, *Dependent States: The Child's Part in Nineteenth Century American Culture* (Chicago: University of Chicago Press, 2005); and Lennard Davis, *Enforcing Normalcy: Disability, Deafness, and the Body* (New York: Verso, 1995).

# THE CHILD AS GIFT: THE LOGIC OF THE *PECULIUM* IN PERPETUATING LOGICS OF ENSLAVEMENT

## Anna Mae Duane

In 2015, when asked about the ongoing debate over vaccinations, Senator Rand Paul drew on a centuries-long tradition entangling proprietorship with parenthood. "The state doesn't own your children," he insisted. "Parents own the children, and it is an issue of freedom and of public health."[1] For Paul, an American politician who identifies with libertarian ideals of radical independence, the ownership of children is inextricable from personal freedom. The first two chapters in this book explore the logic behind such a claim by focusing on how property relations within the family provide a point of continuity between the most privileged of positions (the indulged, cosseted child) and the most abject (the commodified, dehumanized slave). They do so by looking at moments of gift giving, an act that at first glance seems to represent the antithesis of slavery. Yet, as Karen Sánchez-Eppler and Sarah Winter's chapters argue, giving gifts to those who cannot own property – both free and enslaved children – triangulate the forces of affection, proprietorship, and control.

In one example that emerges in both chapters, a white child is given an enslaved child: an act that infuses power with generosity, love with domination. In their analyses of this scene, Sánchez-Eppler and Winter demonstrate how, even as the white child gains status from the exploitation of the black child "given" to her, the very logic that enshrines white childhood innocence denies *all* children the ability to claim themselves – or anything else – as property. As such, the very "innocence" of privileged childhood – an innocence propped on being excluded from the right to consent, to own property, or to enter the public sphere – makes it all the easier to exploit more vulnerable children.

As Sarah Winter argues, such moments of performative gift giving conflate parental love and paternalistic power. The act of giving one child to another illustrates how children – both those treasured for love, and those valued for money – are denied the possibility of laying claim to any form of property, including themselves. Such acts of manipulative generosity provide a particularly powerful view into how often children are caught between what Karen Sánchez-Eppler calls "paternalism's double-binds of exploitation and devotion" in the pre-emancipation world. As Sánchez-Eppler argues, we need to radically revisit "the concept of paternalism … once we acknowledge that the majority of enslaved people in the antebellum United States [and a great proportion of people subject to coerced labor throughout the globe today] actually were children." Both of these authors linger on paternalism's ability to create moments of claustrophic domesticity in which slavery, particularly child slavery, seemingly exceeds the stark logic of "social death," in which power rules by alienating the slave from social bonds. These children, rather than being victimized by being cast outside familial and kinship structures, are bound all the more tightly by their (provisional) inclusion in domestic structures.

Together, these chapters illuminate an aspect of enslavement understood in Roman law as a *peculium* – a sort of token, an aspect of property allotted by the slaveowner to the enslaved to encourage loyalty and obedience.[2] This token could range from a plot of land to a garden, Christmas candy, clothes, money, or other forms of status. An account featured in Karen Sánchez-Eppler's chapter, in which an enslaved girl is "given" property to hold while Yankee soldiers search the house, provides an ample demonstration of the work of the *peculium* – property is given with the explicit understanding that the child may hold on to it only as long as the giver allows it. Orlando Patterson, who articulated the notion of social death, noted how the *peculium* – rather than weakening slavery's power, actually strengthens it by providing the gloss of consent and reward between master and slave. "The universality of the *peculium* is not difficult to explain," Patterson insists. "It was the best means of motivating the slave to perform efficiently on his master's behalf."[3]

Scholars have noted that manumission itself can be considered the *peculium* taken to its farthest extent: the master who promises eventual manumission makes clear that freedom remains the master's property, to be bestowed when and if the slave qualifies as worthy of receiving it. This analysis takes on particular weight when applied toward children, for whom even the possibility of freedom was always postponed until some future date. As Sarah L. H. Gronningsater describes in Section II of this volume, manumission laws in the United States and elsewhere were often structured to mimic the progress from childhood to adulthood. In both the cases of the temporary gifts bestowed by masters in the case studies described by Sánchez-Eppler and Winter, and in the gradual manumission laws that dominated early abolitionism, the dependence of the child and the slave were cast as mutually reinforcing, to be alleviated only by the passage of time and the indulgence of adults.

The *peculium*'s tendency to conflate alleged acts of love with expressions of control not only trouble certain definitions of slavery, they also trouble many coveted ideas about childhood. As Karen Sánchez-Eppler writes, the debate over whether enslaved children in the antebellum United States "had a childhood" starts with a common premise: "a definition of childhood as a protected time of nurture and free-spirited play." In other words, the child is the very opposite of the slave, because in an idealized childhood the logic of the *peculium* is never made explicit: the care accorded to youth, the gifts given to ensure love and loyalty, are never acknowledged as a down payment on a future monetary payoff. But as Sarah Winter's chapter makes clear, even the most privileged of children do not possess the right to own property. Mary Prince's slave narrative, Winter reminds us, details how her child-mistress was distracted with grief over "her" slaves being sold away from her. Neither the child's genuine affection for her enslaved companions, nor her father's affection toward his own child, provides the "young mistress" with any power over "her" enslaved companions.

Attending to how familial bonds of affection were overlaid on the bonds of slavery illuminates how children – as they are imagined in many legal, humanitarian, and cultural forums– have provided and continue to provide an appealing cover for the belief that financial and physical dependence renders one closer to property than to person. "The notion of the child as property not only survived abolition," argues Barbara Bennett Woodhouse, "but also hitched a ride on the freedom train as an essential element of the liberties of 'free men.'" Even though children in families were rarely explicitly claimed as property, paternalistic family structures rendered childhood a particularly apt location to smuggle through concepts that cast ownership as benevolence. "Although only children held as slaves were ever actually designated by law as 'chattels personal,'" Woodhouse writes, "in many ways, the laws applying to children as a group had much in common with the laws of property."[4]

Take for example, U.S. Senator Jacob Howard's argument for civil rights in 1866, which resonates with the same proprietary logic Senator

Paul invoked in 2015: "Is a free man to be deprived of the right of having a family, a wife, children, home?"⁵ In both these nineteenth- and twenty-first-century sound bites, adults' freedom is figured as inextricable from their freedom to "own" (Paul's word) or to "have" (Howard's word) children whose rights – are, at best – a *peculium* allowed by parents: "What definition will you attach to the word 'freeman,' Senator Howard demanded, "that does not include those ideas!" This section – and this volume – seeks to pose a different question than Howard's: What definition could we attach to freedom that doesn't have the word "man" at its center?

## Notes

1   http://thehill.com/policy/healthcare/231501-rand-paul-the-state-doesnt-own-your-children
2   I am grateful to Thomas Meagher, whose work introduced me to the concept of the *peculium*.
3   Orlando Patterson, *Slavery and Social Death: A Comparative Study* (Cambridge, MA: Harvard University Press, 1982), 186. See also: M. L. Bush, *Servitude in Modern Times* (Cambridge, UK: Polity, 2000), particularly 6–8.
4   Barbara Bennett Woodhouse, *Hidden in Plain Sight: The Tragedy of Children's Rights from Ben Franklin to Lionel Tate* (Princeton, NJ: Princeton University Press, 2010), 61.
5   Congressional Globe, 39th Congress 1st Sess. 504 (1866).

# "Remember, Dear, when the Yankees came through here, I was only ten years old": Valuing the Enslaved Child of the WPA Slave Narratives

## Karen Sánchez-Eppler

No Ma'm, there was never any money given to me in slavery time. Remember, Dear, when the Yankees came through here, I was only ten years old. Misses Fannie and Ann Crawford were Major Crawford's daughters, and they kept house for Marse John. That morning in May I was wearing a sleeveless apron, and they (Miss Fannie and Miss Ann) put a bag of gold and silver, and some old greenback Confederate money in my apron and told me to hold on to it. Miss Fannie and Miss Ann, both of them, patted me on the head and said: "Now be a good little girl and don't move." On came the Blue Coats: they went all over the house searching everything with their guns and swords shining and flashing. I was so scared the sweat was running down my face in streams. Bless your life! When they came to the bedroom where I was standing by a bed, holding that money inside my apron, they didn't even glance at me the second time. Little did they think that little slave girl had the money they were hunting for. After the Yankees were gone, I gave it all back to Miss Fannie, and she didn't give me the first penny. If any of the money was given to my mother she didn't tell me about it.[1]

On a hot July day in the late 1930s, seated in her parlor at 168 Pearl Street in Athens, Georgia, Mary Colbert recalled an incident that probably occurred in May 1864 when Union troops occupied Athens and raided nearby plantations. Colbert told this memory to Sadie Hornsby, a white woman the Federal Writers' Project (FWP) had sent to interview men and women "born in slavery." These New Deal Work Progress Administration (WPA) efforts to collect and preserve memories of slavery recorded well over 2,000 interviews with elderly African Americans in seventeen states. This enormous oral history repository has gradually become one of the most widely used evidentiary streams for the study of antebellum U.S. slavery, but also among the more contested. As a source of information on the experience of slavery, these interviews have been viewed with persistent, and in many ways appropriate, skepticism, on a wide range of grounds. No scholar employs them without a discussion of their limitations. One strand of historiographic critique of this material reflects the misunderstanding of the relationship between slavery and childhood that this volume seeks to rectify: the false belief that slavery and childhood are antithetical categories, a failure to "see," as Anna Mae Duane put it in her initial proposal for this project, "the children who often represent the majority of enslaved people." As the essays in the final section of this volume make clear, failures to listen to the voices or to see the actions and conditions of enslaved children continue to hobble contemporary antislavery policies and activism. Thus the historiographic blind spots probed in this chapter carry important implications for contemporary antislavery efforts. Conversely, it is my hope that the kind of attention this chapter affords to the childhood facets of the WPA Slave Narratives may prove a useful model for the ongoing efforts to end child slavery.

The story Mary Colbert tells here is a story about the invisibility of slave children: "the good little girl" who "don't move," "the little slave girl" the Union soldiers "didn't even glance at ... the second time." She had been rendered invisible by race, by gender, by status, by docility, by stillness, and by age, but of course the desired treasure was in her apron pocket all along. The tale of invisibility and value Mary Colbert tells in this FWP interview serves as a provocative emblem for the difficulties present-day antislavery activists have in responding to child slavery and historians have in making use of the FWP interviews and in recognizing their worth. Interviews conducted more than seventy years after emancipation necessarily rest on distant memories and raise all the interpretive issues associated with the workings of memory. They also, and just as necessarily, recall childhood experiences of and perspectives on slavery. Thus one significant strand of the historiographic resistance to the WPA Slave Narratives results from a failure to recognize recollections of enslaved childhoods as valid accounts of slavery. As John Blassingame early explained: "Since only 16 percent of the informants had been fifteen years or older when the Civil War began, an overwhelming majority of them could only describe how slavery appeared to a black child." Blassingame's phrasing suggests an implicit presumption that "how slavery appeared to a black child" is a perspective on slavery of only marginal historical interest.[2] The slave experience of the vast majority of those interviewed, Van Woodward wrote in an influential and largely celebratory review of the 1972 publication of the WPA Slave Narratives, "was, in fact, mainly that of childhood, a period before the full rigors and worst aspects of the slave discipline were typically felt and a period more likely than others to be favorably colored in the memory of the aged."[3]

The many historians who now draw on the FWP interviews have developed two very different strategies for navigating the childhood bias of this material. Since the WPA Slave Narratives appear most reliable for understanding childhood experiences of enslavement, some scholars have restricted their use to this and related subjects. The two recent book-length histories fully devoted to describing enslaved childhoods draw heavily on these interviews, as do studies of childhood that include the experiences of slave children and most studies of the slave family.[4] This focused approach has produced fine histories of this restricted field, but in doing so it has served to discount the utility of the FWP interviews for broader assessments of the slave system. Conversely, those historians who have used the interviews to discuss general and adult experiences of enslavement have mostly done so in a way that disregards the childhood context and content of these accounts, often simply not mentioning that bias at all, or failing to evoke it in the evaluation of any specific piece of evidence. Rather than acknowledging issues of age and discussing how and why the testimony of such young and long-ago observers is relevant, such work – and generally this is very important, insightful work – has tended to ignore the childhood circumstances of these accounts.[5] Both sorts of responses rest on the same misconception: the felt irreconcilability of ideas of slavery and ideas of childhood.

We know, however, that in 1860 at least 56 percent of the enslaved population in the United States was under twenty years of age, even though the infant mortality rate for black children in the Southern states was twice that of whites.[6] Indeed, analysis of the U.S. Census from 1830 (when census questions on age first permit such analysis) through 1860 demonstrates that consistently over these decades more than 30 percent of all US slaves were less than ten years old (Table 1.1).

These slave demographics are strikingly different than those of other American slaveholding nations where a continual international slave trade produced large percentages of prime hands: men in their twenties and thirties. In the United States, after the outlawing of the international slave trade, most of the growth in slavery – as this table shows, there was prodigious growth – depended on natural increase, that is on the birth and rearing of slave children.[7] How might recognition of the prominence

TABLE 1.1. *Percentage of US Slaves Who Were Young Children: 1830–1860*

| Decade | Slaves under 10 | Total slave population | Percentage under 10 |
|--------|-----------------|------------------------|---------------------|
| 1830 | 43,223 | 117,549 | 36.77% |
| 1840 | 87,330 | 253,532 | 34.44% |
| 1850 | 110,663 | 342,844 | 32.28% |
| 1860 | 135,537 | 435,080 | 31.15% |

*Note*: These figures were derived using tools available through the University of Virginia, Geospatial and Statistical Data Center, "Historical Census Browser," n.d., http://mapserver .lib.virginia.edu/. I also consulted "Historical Statistics of the United States, Earliest Times to the Present: Millennial Edition," New York: Cambridge University Press, 2006, http:// hsus.cambridge.org/HSUSWeb/HSUSEntryServlet. Interestingly, while the latter includes ten tables on slavery, including one that details "slave population by state and sex," its standard tables do not account for age; Schwartz, *Born in Bondage*, 5, finds similar overall percentages to those I produce here.

of enslaved children in the demographics and economics of U.S. slavery change our attitudes toward the WPA's repository of recollections of enslaved childhoods? I postulate that once we recognize childhood as a crucial and devastating characteristic of the antebellum U.S. slave regime, those very traits and conditions that have seemed to undermine the reliability and relevance of the WPA Slave Narratives become instead a source of insight. This chapter draws on close readings of individual FWP interviews to braid three strands of analysis. It offers a historiography of the uses of these interviews that demonstrates the lacuna produced by historians' resistance to recognizing children as slaves and slaves as children. It meditates on the roles of memory, nostalgia, and cultural idealizations of childhood in these narratives. Most comprehensively, it demonstrates the kinds of insight about slavery, childhood, and the relations between them that become possible once we approach these testimonies as the recollections of people enslaved as children.

Read with such attention, Mary Colbert's story of girlhood invisibility raises a host of issues about money, mistresses, mothers, Union soldiers, loyalties, fears, the interview situation, and how all these express attitudes toward and expectations of "the little slave girl." The white FWP interviewer, Sadie Hornsby, clearly asked a question about money or wages, and Colbert's response registers her sense of the interviewer's dual miscomprehensions: her failure to grasp Colbert's experience of the economic structures of slavery and her failure to remember that Colbert was "just ten years old" when slavery ended. Colbert, like many other elderly African Americans the FWP interviewed, repeatedly stresses that she is describing events from her childhood. To her, the relationship between childhood and slavery is not paradoxical but salient, yet she is well aware that these are connections that her interviewer and the WPA project as a whole are prone to forget.

Nevertheless, in telling of this one anomalous experience in which her "owners" did give her money – lots of it, Colbert gleefully detailing gold, silver, and old greenback Confederate notes – Colbert reassesses the uncompensated nature of her labor and loyalty, seeming to imply that she now recognizes herself as deserving a payment she did not receive. Such a recognition strikes at both the exploitative economy of a slave system in which labor received no monetary reward, and the exploitative expectations of childhood where monetary compensation is also generally deemed unnecessary. As the "good little girl" Fannie and Ann Crawford asked her to be, Colbert returned "all" the money stored in her apron. Her mistresses did not consider this service worth paying her "the first penny," but Colbert also wonders about her mother's role in this transaction. Might the slave woman have received some reward for her daughter's performance? Colbert's speculations here demonstrate her own sense of childhood powerlessness and ignorance, raising the possibility that her capacity for risks and for obedience might be equally exploited and unrecognized by mistress and mother alike, by the normative economic patterns of slavery and of childhood. As Marie Jenkins Schwartz notes, in slavery, "children occupied an unusual position in that two sets of adults valued them, laying claim to their economic worth and attaching emotional significance to their presence."[8] The conflictive, difficult nature of such double allegiances and exploitations is just one of the many conditions of slavery that become evident through heeding the experiences of slave children.

Of course it is precisely the ease of overlooking children that makes Colbert's apron such a good hiding place. Both her youth and her slave status render Colbert insignificant. I suspect the Crawford mistresses may have chosen to hide their gold in the pockets of the little girl, rather than in her mother's apron, less out of a fear that the Blue Coats would search the slave woman than out of the worry that the woman herself might make off with the family's money. The Crawfords successfully bank on the invisibility and docility of childhood. But what of young Mary Colbert's choices and actions? Her invisibility enabled her to serve as a witness, a role that at least at this moment of narration, decades later, she can recognize and claim as a role of historical agency. Back then, if she had shown the contents of her apron to the Union soldiers with their

flashing guns and swords, they might have taken her with them as more
contraband. That she didn't may point to her anxieties about the risks
of separation from family and friends in such a move, as well as to the
ties of loyalty to her mistresses, and to her fear of angering them. It is
also worth noting that Fannie and Ann Crawford are themselves dependents, the unmarried sisters of "Marse John," and that this money may
well have belonged to him. Beyond all this lies, of course, the Civil War
contest itself. In short, this scene is riven with questions of dependency
and agency, union and autonomy, in which age plays an important part,
but in which childhood is not the only site and source of these issues, but
entangles with them all.

The injunction for Mary Colbert to be a "good girl," the pats on
her head, demonstrate what Eugene Genovese – one of the first historians to derive a significant portion of his evidence from the WPA Slave
Narratives – characterizes as the "paternalism" of the peculiar institution,
where affiliation, even affection, serves as a powerful tool of control.[9]
The apron marks Colbert's more intimate status as a house servant; if
she worked in the fields, she would probably not have worn one, and
the structures of paternalism in her servitude would likely have been less
direct. As a pattern for institutional labor and domination, the concept of
paternalism obviously rests on the metaphor of the family – drawing an
analogy to the relation between child and father. Whether or not U.S. slavery was a paternalistic institution, or one in which the paternalism of
plantation rhetoric merely served to mask the system's brute violence,
remains a question of historical debate. But I think it is important to ask
what happens to the concept of paternalism (and perhaps of "maternalism") once we acknowledge that the majority of enslaved people in the
antebellum United States actually were children. Surely paternalism is one
of those arenas where the history of slavery and the history of childhood
should prove mutually illuminating.[10] In the case of Colbert, her compelling account of her fear during the search does not specify its source (fear
of the soldiers, of her mistresses, of the situation and her own conflicted
position and desires?), but it sweats with paternalism's double-binds of
exploitation and devotion. Green Willbanks, another Georgia slave even
younger than Mary Colbert at the time of the surrender, explains his fear
in a similar scene:

Old Boss and Old Miss hid their valuables. They told us children, "Now, if they
ask you questions, don't you tell them where we hid a thing." We knowed enough
to keep our mouths shut. We never had knowed nothing but to mind Old Boss,
and we were scared 'cause our white folks seemed to fear the Yankees.[11]

Fear of "Old Boss" and of what the old boss fears would surely have been difficult for Colbert to parse as well. She too, at ten, may have known nothing but the pressures of obedience. For a child caught in such a confusing web of power and allegiance, knowledge and ignorance, invisibility might truly be one of the assets of childhood.

The discounting of childhood voices repeats patterns of reception – the rampant questioning of truthfulness, authenticity, and bias – that have characterized the reception of slave narratives since the beginning of the genre, and that continue to undermine contemporary antislavery activism. It was only in the late 1960s and early 1970s that U.S. ante- and postbellum published slave narratives began to be recognized as serious historical sources. If before the civil rights era the accuracy of early slave narratives was regularly undermined by charges of abolitionist propaganda, since then the WPA Slave Narratives have garnered suspicion on opposite grounds as interviews constrained by the white supremacist conditions of their collection. The reasons for this distrust of the WPA Slave Narratives are well known and legion: collected between 1936 and 1938 through decentralized state efforts, largely restricted to the Southern states, they suffer from a lack of sampling methodology and interview protocols that account for much of the haphazard and uneven quality of the interviews. Most importantly, the FWP relied almost exclusively on white Southerners as interviewers, some of whom were themselves the descendants of slaveholders. The WPA preference that the interviews be recorded in dialect graphically marks the racial distance between interviewers and the "ex-slaves" whose stories they collected. Moreover, FWP interviewers were government employees in a Depression-era South where at least some of the elderly African Americans interviewed seem to believe that their cooperation might earn them pension checks. "Yes, ma'am. Come on in. Is you taking lists of folks for old age pensions?" Anna Woods greeted her FWP interviewer in 1938. "Can you tell us what we going to get and when its's going to come? … Cause we sure does need the pension."[12] Woods wonders if she could at least receive groceries, and discussions of food prove one of the most detailed and frequent topics of the FWP interviews, surely an index of Depression-era scarcity and hunger.[13] In short, there was a great deal about the structure of this project besides the age of the people being interviewed and the childhood content of their memories of slavery to skew these recollections toward the polite and halcyon: narrations of what elderly African Americans who had remained in the Depression-era South might imagine that white Southern government workers would want to hear about slavery days.[14]

The now easily ridiculed racist insistence that slaves cannot offer reliable testimony resonates against the still prevalent presumption that children cannot. The historiography of slave women is informative for the new field of childhood studies since early feminist work on slavery confronted similar dynamics of intersectionality and invisibility to those I have been discussing here: "All the women are white, all the blacks are men ... but some of us are brave."[15] In an influential 1982 essay that drew importantly on the WPA Slave Narratives, Jacqueline Jones explained:

[M]ost historians continue to rely on the gender neutral term "slave": – which invariably connotes "male." ... Slave women were something of a historical aberration, a "special case" that has little relevance to current theoretical and methodological perspectives on women's work.... The purpose of this article is to suggest that the burdens shouldered by slave women actually represented in extreme form the dual nature of all women's labor within a patriarchal, capitalist society: the production of goods and services and the reproduction and care of members of a future work force.[16]

A conception of slavery that excludes women, and a conception of womanhood that ignores the experiences of slaves, precisely mirrors the continuing treatment of slave childhoods. Expanding Jones's analysis to the situation of enslaved children, I propose that their experiences can similarly and productively be understood as representing the institution of slavery and the institution of the family "in extreme form." My earlier discussion of paternalism begins to suggest one of the ways that paying attention to enslaved childhoods might let us see slavery itself differently, and thus to suggest more generally how childhood studies insights might serve to reconfigure the field of slavery studies, much as feminist historical work did in this earlier period. Childhood certainly proves resonant for the mesh of patriarchy and capitalism that Jones describes. The slave child epitomizes, after all, the dual demands of productive labor and of being oneself a possession, commodity, and investment. Indeed, at least for the more eastern and northern exporting states of the domestic slave trade, an enslaved child was invariably worth far more than any goods he or she could produce at the time.[17] In this chapter, I do not attempt to draw a comprehensive historical portrait of antebellum slave childhoods, and I am delighted that others have begun to do that work. I do raise questions, however, about how little pressure even historians of childhood slavery have put on the rhetorical imbrications of those terms.

"Despite a quota of abuse and danger, the slave children had a childhood," Eugene Genovese concludes from his readings of the WPA narratives.[18] In titling her book *Stolen Childhoods*, Wilma King presents her work as a contestation of that claim, holding that "enslaved children had virtually no childhood because they entered the workplace early and were subject to arbitrary authority, punishment and separation, just as enslaved adults were."[19] Even as they debate over whether enslaved people *had* childhoods, Genovese and King fully agree as to what it would mean to possess this life stage. They share a definition of childhood as a protected time of nurture and free-spirited play; that is, they concur in understanding childhood to be the very opposite of slavery. Marie Jenkins Schwartz's conclusions about her use of the WPA Slave Narratives similarly appears to derive from Van Woodward's critique of these narratives as centered on a period of life exempt from "the full rigors and worst aspects of the slave discipline."[20] Although she does not supply statistical evidence for this claim, she avers that the narrators' "recollections reflected their age of understanding when slavery collapsed," noting that "some people spoke of early childhood, when owners sought to instill in them a sense of love and loyalty towards masters and mistresses; others recalled a harsher version of slavery associated with the age at which children began to work and to pay dearly for the mistakes of youthful inexperience."[21] As my discussion of Mary Colbert's experiences as "a good little girl" already demonstrates, such dichotomies between affection and punishment oversimplify the complex dynamics of enslaved childhoods expressed in these narratives. Schwartz's hypothesis, like the work of Genovese and King, rests on the assumption that the more of a child one is, the less of a slave. This definition of childhood as a time of innocent and imaginative delight buffered from the crueler realities and requirements of adulthood, and therefore certainly of slavery, is a very specific historical phenomenon. In the United States, this conception of childhood had its greatest cultural force between the mid-nineteenth and the mid-twentieth centuries, that is, precisely during the period spanned by the FWP interviews. While such a notion of childhood appears irreconcilable with the facts of child slavery, there is much evidence that slave labor and the figure of the "pickaninny" were instrumental in constructing this idealization of childhood for white families and as a general cultural ideal.[22]

Federal Writers' Project interviewers certainly shared this celebratory sense of what childhood should be like. Concluding one report, Miriam Logan acknowledged the mismatch between her expectations and the experiences she had recorded for the Ohio collection of narratives, noting that the men and women she interviewed for the FWP did not have

the kind of a story to tell that I was expecting to hear from what little I know of colored people. I may have tried to get them on the songs and amusements of their youth too often, but it seems that most that they knew was work; did not

sing or have a very good time. Of course I thought they would say that slavery
was terrible, but was surprised there too.[23]

Logan's expectations both of the "terrible" and of the "good time" are
jarred by the stories she hears. Her assumption that she would find songs
and amusements in these narratives conflates what she believes she knows
about "colored people" with what she believes she knows about "youth."
The racist tendency to view African Americans as children poses opposite and undoubtedly even more pernicious problems from those issues
raised by the misperception of childhood and slavery as irreconcilable.
Focusing on enslaved childhoods certainly carries this potential for viewing slaves as "childlike" and treating slaves like children, and so proves
one of the many ways in which the power imbalances of the FWP interviews can serve to infantilize. "The blacks were carefully editing what
they told whites," Blassingame concludes. "Generally, they told them only
children's tales and songs."[24] Indeed, the project's initial director, John
Lomax, was curator of the Archive of American Folk Song at the Library
of Congress, and questions about songs, stories, games, and other forms
of play feature significantly in the model questionnaires he developed for
FWP interviewers.[25] "What games did we play? Let me see ... " Mary
Colbert muses.

Anderson Bates does describe the "good time" Logan and interviewers
like her wanted to hear about:

a big plantation, one hundred slaves, and a whole lot of little slave chillum, dat
him wouldn't let work. They run 'round in de plum thickets, blackberry bushes,
hunt wild strawberries, blow cane whistles, and have a good time.[26]

"How we played and played!" Fannie Yarborough exclaims. "I was
little and stayed wid Mammy up at de big 'ouse and jus' played all over it
and all de folkses up der petted me," Neal Upson recalls.[27] These nostalgic
celebratory strands of the WPA Slave Narratives – the places where they
describe protected, happy, indeed petted childhoods – can seem difficult
to reconcile with a sense of slavery's horror. "The very things that supposedly shield children from enslavement (youth, leisure, affection)," Anna
Mae Duane observes, "are often the tropes deployed against children's
voices when they seek to tell a different story."[28] Much of the challenge of
working with the WPA Slave Narratives is learning to recognize slavery
when it comes framed in the rhetoric of childhood – when youth, leisure,
and affection prove part of the story of slavery. Jim Allen's account of
his childhood as a "pet" "stray nigger" can at first glance appear a sanguine and nostalgic celebration of benign paternalism. Yet if we give these

narrations a second glance, the images accrue, and the dehumanizing, and perhaps sexually exploitative aspects of this pet status become clear.

As I done tol' you, I was Marse Allen's pet nigger boy. I was called a stray. I slep' on de flo' by old Miss an' Marse Bob. I could'a slep' on de trun'le bed, but it was so easy jes to roll over an' blow dem ashes an' mek dat fire burn.
[…]
I car'ied water to Marse Bob's sto' close by an' he would allus give me candy by de double han'full, an' as many juice harps as I wanted. De bes' thing I ever did eat was dat candy. Marster was good to his only stray nigger.
[…]
Marse Bob lived in a big white house wid six rooms. He had a cou't house an' a block whar he hired out niggers, jes like mules an' cows.[29]

Recognizing the extent to which FWP interviewers like Miriam Logan desired and asked for cheerful narratives is helpful. But it is also import-ant to think about the stakes for the African American men and women interviewed in this project in claiming for themselves, in their acts of telling, the very sorts of playful childhoods their labor and status helped produce for others. Clearly it matters to Allen to note that he "could'a slep' on de trun'le bed," and thus to characterize sleeping on the floor as his own choice, even if chosen so as to ease his nightly labor of blow-ing the fire and warming his masters' room. Jonathan Blagbrough and Gary Craig's accounts in Chapter 10 of this volume of the exploitation of contemporary child domestic workers stress the psychic costs of such demeaning conditions as sleeping on the floor, as well as the high level of sexual abuse for children engaged in such intimate service. Marse Bob's gifts of candy by the handful may smack of seduction if we read these narratives listening to what P. Gabrielle Foreman calls the "undertell" of slavery's sexual abuse.[30] The acknowledgment of such possibilities of abuse should not prevent recognizing and honoring how – savoring a memory of that "bes' thing" candy – Allen's manner of telling his experi-ence of slavery asserts childhood choice and pleasures even in the midst of slavery's horrors. These are the juice harps (or jews harps) he "wanted," not music to entertain masters. Kelli Johnson's chapter on contempo-rary enslaved children details how "narrators enslaved as children … recognize the ways that their status and identity can thin their agency" and this sense of the vulnerability of childhood is certainly expressed by the WPA narrators and evident in Allen's status as a "stray," but it is striking how often WPA narrators, as Allen does here, use sentimental figurations of childhood playfulness and innocence instead to "thicken" their agency, to grasp choice and delight. As Johnson recognizes in the

writing contemporary enslaved children produced, narration itself can
be a means of claiming agency and empowerment.[31] Surely Allen knows
what he is doing when he follows his praises for the ways that "Marster
was good to his only stray nigger" with an account of the block where the
same master "hired out niggers, jes like mules an' cows."

Between the late eighteenth and the early twentieth centuries historians have charted a shift in the primary valuation of children from sources
of labor to objects of love.[32] This redefinition unfurled in jagged, uneven
ways in the United States, with slavery accounting for much of that jag-
gedness, as it both increased the leisured preciousness of white children
and exploited the labor and ruptured the families of black children. The
fractures within the WPA narratives, I am suggesting, point not only to
what is conflated and contradictory about the figure of a "slave child,"
but also to felt instabilities within the concept of childhood itself. From
the time she was eight years old, Lou Williams was charged with taking
care of white children, yet in describing her experiences of slavery, she
focuses on the ways in which her own childhood was cherished and
playful:

I's have de bes' white folks in Maryland. I's born in a three-room frame house and
I had one of them statements (birth certificates). When I five years old, my old
missy she say, 'Dat gal, she sho' am gwine be dependable and I makes nursemaid
out of her.' When I eight years old she trusts me with dem white chillen. I loves
to fish so well I'd take de li'l chillen to de creek and take off my underskirt and
spread it out on de bank and put de chillen on it while I sho' cotch de fish. Massa,
he start lookin' fer me and when he gits to de creek he say, "Dar's de li'l devil."
He know dem chillen safe, so he jus' laugh.[33]

Lou Williams notes with pride the privileges her owners granted her: a
frame house, a birth certificate, the luxury of a petticoat, and trust.
Williams appears pleased with her mistress's assessment that she was
"gwine be dependable" – a good nursemaid – her capacity for work
already assessed when she is a mere five years old. Childhood is a marker
of class status; it is an identity, a pleasure, and a way of being in the
world that only some kinds of people have the affluence, leisure, and
security to possess. Despite the rarity of a slave birth certificate, or of
a young slave dressed not in a shift but in a skirt with a petticoat, the
mistress's evaluation of "dat gal" casts Williams as a worker, not a child.
In telling her story, Williams counters her mistress's demands for dependability and docility. A chasm of discontinuity separates "she trusts me
with dem white chillen" from the gleeful assertion "I loves to fish so
well" – on the period between these phrases, identity pivots from slave to

child. Instead of her nursemaid dependability, Williams emphasizes her childhood naughtiness, her love of and skill at fishing, and her master's amusement at her prank. An edge of tension and threat runs through this vignette: it could so easily have ended terribly differently. But wonderfully, the master "jus' laugh," and does not punish her or stroke her bare legs, and the sobriquet of "li'l devil" functions as an endearment, rather than a curse or a threat of rape. Williams's skill at catching fish no doubt helped feed her. She resourcefully uses her underskirts to create a safe nest for her charges on the shore. Thus there is much in Williams's narration, and its possible "undertell," to demonstrate the shrewdness and acumen with which she negotiates the burdens and threats of the slave system. But the transformative power of this story lies not in these glints of slavery's oppressions, but in how, as Williams tells it, the naughty slave girl, not the "white chillen," gets to be the playful child bathed in affectionate laughter.

Samuel Sutton – one of the four "ex-slaves," as her reports call them, who Miriam Logan interviewed in Ohio – provides a similarly provocative account of the very different meanings childhood carried within the slave system, and the symbiotic relationship between his enslaved childhood and the childhood of his "baby master":

Ol' Mars. tuk us boys out to learn to wuk when we was both right little me and Baby Mars. Ah wuz to he'p him, and do what he tol' me to – an first thing ah members is a learnin to hoe de clods. Corn and wheat Ol' Mars. raised, an he sets us boys out fo to learn to wuk. Soon as he lef' us Baby Mars, he'd want to eat; send me ovah to de grocery fo sardines an' oysters. Nevah see no body lak oyster lak he do! Ah don' lak dem. Ol Mars. scold him – say he not only lazy hese'f, but he make me lazy too.[34]

Mastery and servitude are learned roles. Sutton's master, "Mars. Ballinger," set out to teach these roles to his son and to his slave, two boys he raised along with his corn and wheat. The narrative patterns in Sutton's story thus reveal two lines of affiliation that entwine and tug at each other: the potency of an age cohort that links "us boys" and of a plantation system that insists on distinguishing masters – "Ol' Mars" and "Baby Mars" – from their slaves.[35] Sutton's repeated phrase "tuk/set us boys out to learn to wuk" likely repeats something Master Ballinger said as it calls attention to the joint nature of the boys' learning and of their equality in age: "we was both right little." Despite the commonalities implicit in his frequent use of "us" and "we" to join these boys, Sutton's narrative is very clear about the differences in their situations, experiences, and even desires.

While the enslaved boy learned to hoe clods and follow orders, "Baby Mars" learned self-indulgence. In joking about and distancing himself from his young master's oyster feast, Sutton, through his story, allows himself to participate in Baby Mar's boyish gluttony and yet to remain blameless. He insists that he does not like oysters and was not himself the one scolded. There may be an element of revenge on his baby master in Sutton so gleefully revealing the other boy's wrongdoings and punishment. Certainly in telling this story Sutton exposes the inequities and contradictions inherent in the idealization of children's play. The threat that slave-owning children would grow up tyrannical and indolent offers an exaggerated perversion of the ideal of childhood as a time of play. Abolitionists frequently leveled this charge, and slaveowners did worry, as Mars Ballinger clearly does, over slavery's corrupting effects on their children.[36] Conversely, Ol' Mars's concerns about raising a lazy slave boy are grounded in the same sorts of "Sambo" stereotypes that prompted Miriam Logan to expect African American "ex-slaves" to entertain her with songs and stories of good times. Thus the notion of childhood as a time of play does not fit easily with the lessons and experiences of either the baby master or his young slave.

Conventional icons of childhood delight and protection can indeed serve in these narratives to instigate the most violent and cruel aspects of slavery. In one of the more brutal of the WPA narratives, Henrietta King tells a story in which a peppermint stick and a rocking chair become instruments of torture.

Well, here's how it happened. She put a piece of candy on her washstan' one day, I was 'bout eight or nine years ole, an' it was my task to empty de slop ev'y mornin'. I seed dat candy layin' dere, an' I was hungry. Ain't has a father workin' in de fiel' like some of de chillum to bring me eats – had jes' little pieces of scrap-back each mornin' throwed at me from de kitchen. I seed dat peppermint stick layin' dere, an' I ain't dared go near it 'cause I knew ole Missus jus' waitin' for me to take it. Den one mornin' I so hungry dat I cain't resist. I went straight in dere an' grab dat stick of candy an' stuffed it in my mouf an' chew it down quick so ole Missus never fin' me wid it.

Nex' mornin' ole Missus say:

"Henrietta, you take dat piece o' candy out my room?" ... Well, she got her rawhide down from de nail by de fire place, an' she grabbed me by de arm an' she try to turn me 'cross her knees while she set in de rocker so's she could hol' me.... I twisted 'way so dere warn't no chance o' her gittin' in no solid lick. Den ole Missus lif' me up by de legs, an' she stuck my haid under the bottom of her rocker, an' she rock forward so's to hol' my haid an' whup me some mo'. I guess dey must of whupped me near a hour wid dat rocker leg a-pressin' down on my haid. ...

Seem like dat rocker pressin' on my young bones had crushed 'em all into soft pulp. ...

Here, put yo' han on my face – right here on dis lef' cheek – dat's what slave days was like.[37]

Children crave candy. Rockers lull babies to sleep. King's mistress, perversely and deliberately, uses these items of childhood pleasure and safety to tempt, punish, and disfigure this young girl. In her narrative, King calls attention to these childhood props and the evil of their misuse. She repeatedly emphasizes the childhood context of her experience. She estimates her age at the time of this beating. She presents the lack of a father, who might have provided her with "eats" or protection, as one of the sources of her tragedy. Her "young bones," she explains, were not yet tough enough to withstand such abuse. Telling the story of her disfigurement in searing and childhood-saturated detail, King thus crafts a narrative in which her vulnerability as a slave and her vulnerability as a child collapse into each other. The idealization of childhood as a sweet time of pleasure and safety haunts this narrative and demonstrates what is unnatural about "slavery days." The mistress wielded conventional emblems of childhood happiness as physical weapons that snare and beat this child. King in her narration turns the peppermint stick and rocking chair into rhetorical weapons; she uses their childhood associations to reveal the perverse cruelty of this mistress and of the slave system as a whole. Eighty-six years after this wounding, Henrietta King demands a confirmatory and tender gesture from her listener: "here, put yo' han on my face."

As Stephanie Camp has argued, the historiography of slavery needs to get beyond "accommodation versus resistance" polemics to "explore the contradictory and paradoxical qualities of bondpeople's lives," what Ariela Gross refers to as the "double character" of slavery.[38] My efforts to chart the multiple ways in which WPA narrators employed the rhetoric and emblems of an idealized childhood seek to reflect this "double character." Paying attention to the special situation of enslaved children serves to accentuate both the logic of childhood and the logic of slavery. This is true not only for vulnerability, docility, and amusement, but also for labor and commodification. "Children were taught to experience their bodies twice at once, to move through the world as both child and slave, person and property," Walter Johnson explains in his study of the New Orleans slave market. Johnson explicitly decided against using the WPA narratives for his study, but these narratives confirm his observation that even as young children the enslaved understood their commodity

status.³⁹ "Children were not allowed to do much work," Green Willbanks
explains to his interviewer, "because their masters desired them to have
the chance to grow big and strong."⁴⁰ Such desires may have produced
somewhat easier slave childhoods, the "whole lot of little slave chillum,
dat him wouldn't let work" that Anderson Bates describes. But as Bates
and Willbanks intimate, this space of play, so dependent on what the
master would or wouldn't allow, probably derived less from benevolence
than from economic self-interest.

Richard Sutch's index of slave values in 1850, calibrated by age, sex,
and region, demonstrates what a good investment children could be,
slave children's value increasing far more rapidly in the years between
five and fifteen, and in any move between the Old and the New South,
than could be accrued for any other age cohort.⁴¹ Sutch's data suggest
that a male child under five valued at $100 in the Old South, for exam-
ple, could be sold in the cotton belt for $400 by the time he was seven
years old and for more than $600 by the time he was eleven or twelve;
and even if kept in his native region the boy would still likely triple or
quadruple in value over five or six years. According to Sutch's data, the
price increases for girls over similar temporal and geographical spans is
only slightly less. In contrast, even if kept for a longer ten-year period so
as to reach the most highly valued "prime hand" category of the mid-
twenties, a fifteen-year-old East Coast slave sold to the cotton plantations
of the New South would at best double in value. This does not suggest
that enslaved children were more profitable than older slaves from whom
far more labor could be extracted: "Me an' a girl worked in de fiel', car-
ryin' one row; <u>you</u> know, it tuk two chullun to mek one han," Jim Allen
explained, his phrasing stressing his sense that anyone in Mississippi,
even this FWP interviewer, should know the economic calculus of slave
ages in the field.⁴² What it does suggest is that in the hybrid valuations
of the slave system where all enslaved people both produced goods and
were themselves commodities, enslaved children were more valuable as
goods themselves than as workers.

Jim Allen recounts his master's claim of preferring to "raise little
niggers; den I won't have to buy 'em." Raised as plantation products,
enslaved children not only understood their commodity status, but had a
clear sense of their financial price. "A Mr. Covington offered Old Master
$700 for me when I was about ten years old, but he wouldn't sell me. He
didn't need to for he was rich as cream and my, how good he was to us,"
Lou Smith boasts, equally pleased, it seems, both of his own high price
and of his master's wealth and the security it afforded his slaves. Less

confident, Julia King muses, "When I was born, mother's master said he was worth three hundred dollars more. I don't know if he ever would have sold me."[43] These monetary valuations, remembered for decades and told to FWP interviewers, suggest how deeply these "ex-slaves" had learned as children to feel price as an aspect of their identities. They all know that this value put on their bodies and their labor does not belong to them. This value is the master's wealth, and their accounts make clear that even if high price feels in some real way like a source of validation – a recognition of vigor, strength, and skill that they want to include in their autobiographies and tell these government workers – it also proves a source of vulnerability. To know one's price is also to know that one is an object of trade, and that the stability of any and all human relationships rests precariously on the whims of the market. "For slaves born in the exporting states, one in five marriages would have been destroyed by the trade and one in three children aged under fourteen years would have been separated from one or both parents," Michael Tadman concludes in his study of the interregional slave trade.[44]

Does I lak to talk 'bout when I wuz a chile? I sho does. I warn't but 4 years old when de war wuz over, but I knows all 'bout it.

I wuz born in Floyd County sometime in October. My pa wuz Erwin and my ma wuz Liza Lorie. I don't know what dey come from, but I knows dey wuz from way down de country somewhars. Deere wuz six of us chilluns. All of us wuz sold. Yessum, I wuz sold too. My oldest brother wuz named Jim. I don't riccolec' de others, dey wuz all sold off to diffunt parts of de country, and never heared from 'em no more. My brother, my pa and me wuz sold on de block in Rome, Georgia. Marster Frank Glenn buyed me, I wuz so little dat when dey bid me off, dey had to hold me up so folkses could see me. I don't 'member my real ma and pa, and I called Marster 'pa' an' Mist'ess 'ma', 'til I wuz 'bout 'leven years old.[45]

Easter Brown's account of the devastation the trade wrought on her family, seems to take comfort in the cute littleness of her childhood self. Because she was born after the start of the Civil War, what Brown "knows" about slavery must come as much from things told her as from her own recollections, as well as from the way in which, remaining post-emancipation as a servant in her master's household, her experiences of slavery and of domestic service blended into one another. Perhaps other members of the slave community helped her to keep in memory at least the names of her parents, if not those of all her sold siblings or where they came from. But it seems possible that it may have been the master and mistress she called "pa" and "ma" who identified the site of her sale and who described how the trader had held her up when she was too small to be seen on the auction block. Similarly, in reporting what "her mother's master said" when she was born, Julia King must be passing on not her own memory of this speech, but a valuation her mother had told to her. In both these reported memories, the affective bonds of family and the economic bonds of property are layered on each other. Such layering proves a generalized characteristic of childhood, as Barbara Woodhouse notes, "Although only children held as slaves were ever actually designated by law as 'chattels personal,' in many ways, the laws applying to children as a group ... as well as the actual treatment of children, remained deeply analogous to assumptions made in the prevalent thinking about property."[46] Under slavery such concepts are not simply analogous: birth and sale quite literally amount to the same thing.

Gracie Gibson describes how her master gave Gibson as a birthday present to his daughter: a potent symbol of how birth means differently for these two young girls, and the scene with which Sarah Winter begins her chapter in this volume. A few lines earlier in Gibson's FWP interview, she lists all the members of her family – parents, siblings, grandparents – owned by the Kinzlers and moved together by them from Florida to South Carolina: "Captain John wouldn't sell his niggers and part de members of de family." Her status as a birthday present does indeed evade sale and keep her within the family, but it only heightens her status as a proprietary object.[47] How does a master tell and how does a child hear the story of the day they were acquired? What might it mean for a mother to repeat her master's smug claim of ownership and profit to her daughter? Or for one girl to recall being gifted to another as a birthday present? How is it possible to untangle the value, love, possession, pathos, and threat in these practices of exchange and these details of price? Such questions permeate the WPA narratives, where "to talk 'bout when I wuz a chile" is to talk about slavery. It is easy to discount Easter Brown's claim that she "knows all 'bout" a system of slavery that officially ended before she turned five, but my aim in this chapter has been to try taking her claim seriously, and to see what new things can be learned about slavery and about childhood by paying attention to those times and places – such as the WPA Slave Narratives – "when a child is a slave."

## Notes

1  The Federal Writers' Project Slave Narratives of the Work Progress Administration were first widely disseminated in Federal Writers' Project,

*The American Slave: A Composite Autobiography*, ed. George P. Rawick, 19 vols. (Westport, CT: Greenwood Publishing Company, 1972). Scans of the interview typescripts are now available online, searchable by narrator or state, and provide page numbers that refer to the pagination in the original nineteen-volume set. Federal Writers' Project, WPA and Library of Congress Manuscript Division, "Born in Slavery: Slave Narratives from the Federal Writers' Project, 1936–1938," 2001, http://memory.loc.gov/ammem/snhtml/. Mary Colbert, Georgia, 216.

2   John W. Blassingame, "Using the Testimony of Ex-slaves: Approaches and Problems," *Journal of Southern History* 41 (1975): 486. Blassingame draws these age percentages from Norman R. Yetman, "The Background of the Slave Narrative Collection," *American Quarterly*, no. 3 (1967): 534–5. Yetman found the percentage age composition of interviewees in 1865 to be 1–5 years – 16%; 6–10 years – 27%; 11–15 years – 24%; 16–20 years – 16%; 21–30 years – 13%; older than 30 years – 3%. By counting from the beginning of the Civil War in 1860, Blassingame presents each cohort as five years younger.

3   C. Vann Woodward, "History from Slave Sources," *The American Historical Review* 79.2 (April 1, 1974): 473.

4   The two full-length studies of children in slavery are Marie Jenkins Schwartz, *Born in Bondage: Growing Up Enslaved in the Antebellum South* (Cambridge, MA: Harvard University Press, 2009); and Wilma King, *Stolen Childhood: Slave Youth in Nineteenth-Century America*, Second Edition (Bloomington: Indiana University Press, 2011). Steven Mintz, *Huck's Raft: A History of American Childhood* (Cambridge, MA: Belknap, 2004) devotes significant attention to the experiences of slave children; for accounts of specific aspects of childhood such as play or education, see Thomas L. Webber, *Deep Like the Rivers: Education in the Slave Quarter Community, 1831–1865* (New York: W. W. Norton, 1978); David K. Wiggins, "The Play of Slave Children in the Plantation Communities of the Old South, 1820–1860," *Journal of Sport History* 7.2 (Summer 1980): 21–39; Heather Andrea Williams, *Self-Taught: African American Education in Slavery and Freedom* (Chapel Hill: University of North Carolina Press, 2005); on the slave family, see Herbert G. Gutman, *The Black Family in Slavery and Freedom, 1750–1925* (New York: Vintage, 1977); Herman R. Lantz, "Family and Kin as Revealed in the Narratives of Ex-Slaves," *Social Science Quarterly (University of Texas Press)* 60.4 (March 1980): 667–75; Elizabeth Fox-Genovese, *Within the Plantation Household: Black and White Women of the Old South* (Chapel Hill: University of North Carolina Press, 1988); Brenda E. Stevenson, *Life in Black and White: Family and Community in the Slave South* (New York: Oxford University Press, 1997). All these works rely in significant ways on FWP interviews.

5   Since the 1970s, most broad, general accounts of antebellum slavery rely on these interviews to at least some extent. Let me demonstrate my point with two works I particularly admire that make strong use of the WPA narratives and write in nuanced ways about their use. Saidiya V. Hartman, *Scenes of Subjection: Terror, Slavery, and Self-Making in Nineteenth-Century America*

(New York: Oxford University Press, 1997) provides an insightful discussion of the kinds of attention needed in interpreting such "an overdetermined representation of slavery," but does not discuss age; see especially p. 12. Stephanie M. H. Camp, *Closer to Freedom: Enslaved Women and Everyday Resistance in the Plantation South* (Chapel Hill: University of North Carolina Press, 2004) describes the differences between what various kinds of sources can tell about the experience of slavery in a way that I find particularly helpful in thinking about the FWP interviews, but while she provides a sensitive account of the difficulties posed by memory and by race in these interviews, she does not mention childhood; see especially loc. 171–3.

6    King, *Stolen Childhood*, loc. 69–72.

7    Robert William Fogel, *Without Consent or Contract: The Rise and Fall of American Slavery* (New York: W. W. Norton, 1994), see his chapter "The Population Question," 114–53; Walter Johnson, ed., *The Chattel Principle: Internal Slave Trades in the Americas* (New Haven, CT: Yale University Press, 2005).

8    Schwartz, *Born in Bondage*, 8.

9    Eugene D. Genovese, *Roll, Jordan, Roll: The World the Slaves Made* (New York: Vintage, 1976).

10   For the debates on paternalism that reference the WPA Slave Narratives, besides Genovese, *Roll, Jordan, Roll* see Norman R. Yetman, "Ex-slave Interviews and the Historiography of Slavery," *American Quarterly* 36 (1984): 181–210; and especially for comparisons with "maternalism" Katherine van Wormer, David Walter Jackson, and Charletta Sudduth, *The Maid Narratives: Black Domestics and White Families in the Jim Crow South* (Baton Rouge: Louisiana State University Press, 2012).

11   "WPA Slave Narrative Project: Born in Slavery," Green Willbanks, Georgia, 145.

12   "WPA Slave Narrative Project: Born in Slavery," Anna Woods, Arkansas, 224.

13   Stephanie J. Shaw, "Using the WPA Ex-slave Narratives to Study the Impact of the Great Depression," *Journal of Southern History* 69.3 (August 2003): 623–58, demonstrates the utility of the WPA narratives for studying the African American experience of the Great Depression, that is, as a history not of the nineteenth century, but of the period when the interviews took place. One of the most successful recent uses of the WPA narratives has been as a compendium of African American foodways. See Herbert C. Covey and Dwight Eisnach, *What the Slaves Ate: Recollections of African American Foods and Foodways from the Slave Narratives*, American Mosaic (Santa Barbara, CA: Greenwood Press, 2009).

14   For provocative and detailed accounts of this historiography, see: Yetman, "The Background of the Slave Narrative Collection"; Woodward, "History from Slave Sources"; Blassingame, "Using the Testimony of Ex-Slaves"; Jerrold Hirsch and Tom E. Terrill, "Conceptualization and Implementation: Some Thoughts on Reading the Federal Writers' Project Southern Life Histories," *Southern Studies: An Interdisciplinary Journal of the South* 18.3 (July 1979): 351–62; Ira Berlin, Marc Favreau, and Steven F. Miller, eds., *Remembering Slavery: African Americans Talk about Their*

*Personal Experiences of Slavery and Emancipation* (New York: The New Press, 1998), xiii–lii; Sharon Ann Musher, "Contesting 'the Way the Almighty Wants It': Crafting Memories of Ex-slaves in the Slave Narrative Collection," *American Quarterly* 53.1 (2001): 1–31.

15  Gloria T. Hull, Patricia Bell Scott, and Barbara Smith, eds., *But Some of Us Are Brave: Black Women's Studies* (New York: Feminist Press at City University of New York, 1982).

16  Jacqueline Jones, "'My Mother Was Much of a Woman': Black Women, Work, and the Family under Slavery," *Feminist Studies* 8.2 (1982): 236.

17  Gregory D. Smithers, *Slave Breeding: Sex, Violence, and Memory in African American History* (Gainesville: University Press of Florida, 2012); King, *Stolen Childhood*, loc. 580–90.

18  Genovese, *Roll, Jordan, Roll*, 503.

19  King, *Stolen Childhood*, loc. 128.

20  Woodward, "History from Slave Sources," 473.

21  Schwartz, *Born in Bondage*, 210.

22  For a general overview of shifting ideas of childhood, see my entry for "Childhood" in Philip Nel and Lissa Paul, eds., *Keywords for Children's Literature* (New York: New York University Press, 2011), 35–41. For accounts of the ways in which race and slavery enabled an ideal (white) childhood, see Robin Bernstein, *Racial Innocence: Performing American Childhood and Race from Slavery to Civil Rights* (New York: New York University Press, 2011); and Caroline Field Levander, *Cradle of Liberty: Race, the Child, and National Belonging from Thomas Jefferson to W. E. B. Du Bois* (Durham, NC: Duke University Press, 2006).

23  "WPA Slave Narrative Project: Born in Slavery," Celia Henderson, Ohio, 44.

24  Blassingame, "Using the Testimony of Ex-Slaves," 484.

25  Lynda M. Hill, "Ex-slave Narratives: The WPA Federal Writers' Project Reappraised," *Oral History* 26.1 (April 1, 1998): 64–72 provides rich insight into Lomax's goals for this work, and on the role of WPA interview guidelines and assessments of the oral histories collected.

26  "WPA Slave Narrative Project: Born in Slavery," Anderson Bates, South Carolina, 42.

27  "WPA Slave Narrative Project: Born in Slavery," Fannie Yarborough, Texas, 226 and Neal Upson, Georgia, 51.

28  E-mail correspondence, Anna Mae Duane, August 9, 2014.

29  "WPA Slave Narrative Project: Born in Slavery," Jim Allen, Mississippi, 2–4.

30  P. Gabrielle Foreman, "Manifest in Signs: Reading the Undertell in Incidents in the Life of a Slave Girl," in *New Essays on Harriet Jacobs*, ed. Deborah M Garfield and Rafia Zafar (New York: Cambridge University Press, 1996), 76–99.

31  Johnson discusses how these contemporary narratives of enslaved childhoods offer empowerment through the act of narration. She draws the concept of thick and thin agency from Natascha Klocker, "An Example of 'Thin' Agency: Child Domestic Workers in Tanzania," in *Global Perspectives on Rural Childhood and Youth: Young Rural Lives* (New York: Taylor and Francis, 2007), 83–94.

32   For a cogent summary of this shift and its implications, see Peter N. Stearns, *Childhood in World History*, second edition (London, New York: Routledge, 2010), chapter 6: "Forces of Change and the Modern Model of Childhood: Developments in the West Eighteenth Century to 1914."

33   "WPA Slave Narrative Project: Born in Slavery," Lou Williams, Texas, 166.

34   "WPA Slave Narrative Project: Born in Slavery," Samuel Sutton, Ohio, 92.

35   Sarah Winter's chapter in this volume (Chapter 2) further probes the inherent contradictions in the legal status of children and in notions of proprietorship at stake in one child's so-called possession of another child.

36   See Winter's and Blagbrough and Craig's chapters in this volume (Chapters 2 and 10, respectively) for historical and contemporary instances of the negative effects on slave-owning children of growing up "with a sense of innate superiority over others."

37   Henrietta King's narrative, collected by the FWP in Virginia, was not forwarded to Washington, DC, and therefore is not included in the "Born in Slavery" collection. It has, however, been published in Charles L. Perdue Jr. and Thomas E. Barden, *Weevils in the Wheat: Interviews with Virginia Ex-Slaves* (Charlottesville: University of Virginia Press, 1991), 190–2; and in Berlin, Favreau, and Miller, *Remembering Slavery*, 19–21.

38   Camp, *Closer to Freedom*, loc. 64–8; Ariela J. Gross, *Double Character: Slavery and Mastery in the Antebellum Southern Courtroom*, new edition (Athens: University of Georgia Press, 2006).

39   Walter Johnson, *Soul by Soul: Life Inside the Antebellum Slave Market* (Cambridge, MA: Harvard University Press, 2001), loc. 288. Johnson says of his decision not to use WPA testimony: "I have not used the WPA narratives for two reasons (1) because those whose testimony was recorded in the 1930s would generally have been too young to recollect the level of detail about the slave trade that the nineteenth-century narrators provided. (2) because I believe the rhetorical situation of the interview by a white recorder in the 1930s South to have been a great deal more inhibiting than that which characterized the production of the abolitionist narratives," loc. 3149–50.

40   "WPA Slave Narrative Project: Born in Slavery," Green Willbanks, Georgia, 139.

41   Richard Sutch, "Index of Slave Values, by Age, Sex, and Region: 1850. Table Bb215-218," *Historical Statistics of the United States, Earliest Times to the Present: Millennial Edition*, New York: Cambridge University Press 2006, http://dx.doi.org/10.1017/ISBN-9780511132971.Bb209-218. Sarah L.H. Gronningsater's discussion in Chapter 5 of this volume of the process of gradual emancipation in New York demonstrates the inverse of these equations – the expense of raising slave children.

42   "WPA Slave Narrative Project: Born in Slavery," Jim Allen, Mississippi, 2.

43   "WPA Slave Narrative Project: Born in Slavery," Jim Allen, Mississippi, 4; Lou Smith, Oklahoma, 300; Julia King, Ohio, 58.

44   Michael Tadman, "The Interregional Slave Trade in the History and Myth-Making of the U.S. South," in Walter Johnson, ed., *The Chattel*

*Principle: Internal Slave Trades in the Americas* (New Haven, CT: Yale University Press, 2005), 131.

45 "WPA Slave Narrative Project: Born in Slavery," Easter Brown, Georgia, 136.

46 *Hidden in Plain Sight: The Tragedy of Children's Rights from Ben Franklin to Lionel Tate* (Princeton, NJ: Princeton University Press, 2010), 61.

47 "WPA Slave Narrative Project: Born in Slavery," Gracie Gibson, South Carolina, 113. See Winters' chapter in this volume and the discussion of Gibson's narrative in Orlando Patterson, *Slavery and Social Death* (Cambridge, MA: Harvard University Press, 1982), 12.

## 2

# The Slave Child as "Gift": Involutions of Proprietary and Familial Relations in the Slaveholding Household before Emancipation

## Sarah Winter

In the opening pages of his seminal study, *Slavery and Social Death*, Orlando Patterson draws attention to the recounting of a childhood memory by Gracie Gibson, a former slave from South Carolina. She recalled a singular transaction between her master and his daughter, Adelaide, called Ada:

I was called up on one of [Miss Ada's] birthdays, and Marster Bob sorta looked out of de corner of his eyes, first at me and then at Miss Ada, then he make a little speech. He took my hand, put it in Miss Ada's hand, and say: "Dis your birthday present, darlin'." I make a curtsy and Miss Ada's eyes twinkle like a star and she take me in her room and took on powerful over me.[1]

Gibson was eighty-six years old when she told this story in 1937 to an interviewer from the Federal Writers' Project (FWP) of the Works Progress Administration (WPA). (On these WPA narratives, see also Sánchez-Eppler, Chapter 1, this volume.) While he does not comment on its details, Patterson positions the quotation in his discussion of the complete lack of "authentic human relationship where violence was the ultimate sanction" (12). As Patterson explains, in the relation between master and slave, "[t]here could have been no trust, no genuine sympathy; and while a kind of love may sometimes have triumphed over this most perverse form of interaction, intimacy was usually calculating and sadomasochistic" (12). This scene of a child being given as a "birthday present" to another child seems to enact for Patterson a particularly disturbing demonstration of "what slavery really meant: the direct and insidious violence, the namelessness and invisibility, the endless personal violation, and the chronic inalienable dishonor" (12).

The act of giving or receiving another human being as a "gift" and personal possession also seems to indicate the way enslavement treats human beings as things, or forms of property.[2] Yet Patterson finds fault with definitions of slavery that construe ownership, following Roman and European continental law, as consisting in "a set of absolute rights in rem – things, usually tangibles, sometimes intangibles." Such a notion of absolute property rights fails to describe modern practices of slavery for several reasons: "[F]irst, in sociological and economic terms (as in the view of [Anglo-American] common law) there can be no relation between a person and a thing. Relations only exist between persons. Second, relations between persons with respect to some object are always relative, never absolute" (20). In addition, the concept of property in persons lacks specificity in relation to slavery because "Proprietary claims are made in respect to many persons who are clearly not slaves," such as husbands, wives, or children (21–2). Patterson contends that the condition of enslavement should instead be viewed as an extreme example of the circumstance prevailing in various legal systems and across history "that all human beings can be the object of property and that, strictly speaking, property refers to a set of relationships between human beings" (31). Slavery's distinctiveness for Patterson therefore lies not solely in the status of the slave as alienable human property, but in the "total" power of the master "over all aspects of the slave's life" (26).

The abundance of the master's power, then, and the ways it overlapped with his paternal role are both manifested in the young Gracie Gibson's master's "gift" of the child slave to his own child, whose freedom is correspondingly demonstrated by ostensibly taking ownership of another child within a slaveholding family.[3] Perhaps it is the exchange of glances between father and daughter and the "sparkle" in Miss Ada's eyes as she receives her human "present" that makes this incident exemplary of Patterson's theory that "the slave was not a slave because he was the *object* of property, but because he could not be the *subject* of property" (28). When we compare it to Mary Colbert's WPA testimony, as discussed by Karen Sánchez-Eppler, about being "given" valuable property (later reclaimed) by her mistress during a search by Union soldiers so that she could become a sort of receptacle or hiding place, we perceive that Gracie Gibson's story is important to Patterson's study because the experience seems to have made explicit to the child the difference of her slave status and the utter disregard shown for her personhood, and thus both stories give the outsider a glimpse into the "calculating intimacy" of enslavement (12).

Historian Wilma King explains that because "the enslavement of Africans in the New World was … based on color and was transferred from mothers to children in perpetuity, … [s]uch a system demanded that mothers and fathers and others teach girls and boys how to be slaves and children simultaneously."[4] By uncovering the psychological, social, and legal implications of the enslaved child given as a gift, we can begin to investigate the ways the child slave's peculiar status as subjected both to adult authority and to enslavement brings to light "the nature and inner dynamics of slavery and the institutional patterns that supported it" (ix), particularly because childhood involves the inculcation and reproduction of such dynamics in both the children of slaveholders and the slave children themselves. The situation of a slave child given as a gift, however, also points to the complexity of the legal status of slaves and of childhood generally, as well as the psychological and social dimensions of the proprietary relations entailed in slavery.

In his comparative study of the major forms of human bondage in modern societies – slavery, serfdom, indentured service, debt bondage, and penal servitude – M. L. Bush highlights the differences between the status of slaves in law and in customary practice. He argues that although by law "the slave was formally the disposable possession of his master," without "autonomous rights to family and property," some slave systems in practice did allow slaves a *peculium*: "that is, the wealth a slave was allowed to acquire and possess; partly the family relationships slaves were able to sustain; partly the right slaves were awarded to share their master's religion; partly the slaves' ability to create an independent culture; partly the traditional practices and liberties established as customs that masters were obliged to respect."[5] These restricted and partial property rights of slaves provided masters with a further means, in addition to force, to overcome slaves' resistance to enslavement. In surveying many slave systems across history and worldwide, Bush makes the case that some slaves could manage to create "a social identity" through the "possession of an independent culture that masters resented but could not deny."[6] King similarly points out that American slaves in the rice-producing coastal areas of Georgia and South Carolina were able to accumulate property because they worked on a task-based system requiring a certain amount of labor every week, leaving them free to work for themselves during their remaining time to provide food and clothing for their families, and even eventually to save money to buy their freedom. By insisting on these "customary rights" to keep their own property, King argues, slaves in these regions also promoted their children's self-esteem: "With encouragement

from their parents or by their own initiative, some children had possessions of their own."[7] Such children under the care of enslaved parents
would have learned how it was possible for them to be both subjects and
objects of property.

In his history of American childhood, Steven Mintz emphasizes that
although "slavery instilled in some children a profound sense of degradation and shame," many slave children still succeeded in "'stealing' a
childhood":

They devised games that prepared them psychologically for the traumas of whip-
pings and family separation. A surprisingly large number learned how to read and
write. Above all, they contributed to their family's well-being by supplementing
their families' meager diets and assisting in their parents' work. For all its depri-
vations, childhood in bondage promoted an early sense of personal responsibility
and strong communal loyalties.[8]

Mintz nevertheless stresses the psychological damage that enslavement
inflicted on children: "Much more than a system of labor exploitation,
slavery was a complex set of social relationships in which masters strove
to make their property obedient, tractable, and dependent" (103). Mintz
reports that "A slave had to call even a young [white] child 'Young Massa'
or 'Young Missis'" (106).

Patterson and Bush's comparative accounts of slavery, alongside King
and Mintz's historical understanding of American slaves' and slave children's resourcefulness under conditions of severe deprivation and psychological and physical coercion, provide a launching point for this
chapter's investigation of the status of child slave owners and child slaves
as both objects and subjects of proprietary relations. The following analysis encompasses multiple geographic locations included in the Atlantic
slave trade. I focus on two well-known nineteenth-century slave narratives involving the West Indies and the United States, and a little-stud-
ied eighteenth-century English Chancery case concerning a former child
slave's ability to receive a bequest – all of which describe incidents of a
slave child being given as a gift or willed by an adult to a younger family
member – in order to provide insight into the involuted, redoubled nature
of the slave child's condition of inferiority as the property of another
child, and to highlight the complications of emotional attachment and
exploitation between children and adults in such relations. Like Sánchez-
Eppler, I am interested in investigating circumstances "when youth, leisure, affection prove part of the story" of child enslavement (Chapter 1,
this volume), with particular attention to family dynamics and legal

definitions. If the enslaved child Gracie could be given as a "birthday present" to another child, then her subordination and vulnerability are reinforced by becoming the "property" of a person who was not capable legally of ownership independent from her parents' legal guardianship. This scenario produces a set of interlocking legal and moral conundrums: not just, in what respect can a child "own" another child, but also how can a child enslave another child, and finally, how can a human child, born with natural rights according to common-law legal systems, also be born a slave? While not being able to own herself or anything else, the slave child living as the so-called possession of another child presents an acute case of the more general legal disability of childhood, thus also exposing the illegitimacy of the gift of one child to another and revealing its status as a ritual for inducting the children of slaveholders into the privileges and powers of mastery. By studying such instances and taking note of their exemplarity in the history of slavery, we can perceive that childhood represents a crux where the deep connections between familial relationships and the proprietary relations of slavery become visible in ways that could lead some observers of slavery to call into question its apparent legality. Considering slavery and childhood together, we can also gain insight into the central role of paternalism in defining both the male head of household's familial authority as power over wife, children, and dependents and the authority of the master over the slave, a reinforcement that indicates the proprietary nature of the bonds that render the family into a legal entity.

## Birthday: The Gift of Life

Gracie Gibson's description of being given away at a birthday party calls attention to this familial transaction as an enactment of the enslaved child's deprivation of birthrights, or her inherent and inalienable rights as a human being. In the first volume of his enormously influential *Commentaries on the Laws of England* (4 vols. 1765–9), Sir William Blackstone defines "natural liberty" as one of the "absolute rights of man, considered as a free agent" and as "a right inherent in us at birth, and one of the gifts of God to man at his creation, when he endued him with the faculty of free-will."[9] Related to this absolute natural right of personal liberty, that becomes a legal right guarded by the English constitution, are the fundamental rights to personal security and private property (129). In the context of this transition from natural rights to legal rights, then, the child slave immediately becomes an anomaly, thus foregrounding that she is the target from birth of what Blackstone refers to as an "artificial" that is, social and legal, arrangement (123), in this case, a system of enslavement. In Blackstone's specific discussion of the status of children, the duties of parents to provide maintenance, protection, and education for their children seem to correspond to and form the basis of children's entitlement to these fundamental rights (449–50). Here Blackstone focuses on parents as the givers of life to their children: "By begetting them therefore, [parents] have entered into a voluntary obligation, to endeavour, as far as in them lies, that the life which they have bestowed shall be supported and preserved. And thus the children will have a perfect *right* of receiving maintenance from their parents" (447; emphasis in original). The "empire" (453) and guardianship of a father over his children holds sway until their full majority at the age of twenty-one, when a son or daughter legally may sell or otherwise dispose of his or her property, whether "lands, goods, or chattels" (463). This right to dispose of property holds true in the female's case provided she is not married, since a woman's property, with very few exceptions, was transferred to her husband upon marriage, although he could not sell real property, such as land, without his wife's consent.[10] Blackstone explains, however, that before the age of majority, "a father has no power over his son's *estate* than as a trustee, or guardian; for, though he may receive the profits during a child's minority, yet he must account for them when he comes of age" (452–3; emphasis in original). Teresa Michals observes that in volume three of the *Commentaries*, Blackstone "defends the property that husbands, fathers, and masters have in their wives, children, and servants," so that "[a]lthough these relations involve reciprocal duties, their element of ownership goes only one way." Michals concludes that "the slave differs from such persons [other members of the household] not in being property, but rather in being nothing but property."[11]

Given slavery's codification in the criminal and civil laws of South Carolina and other Southern states, the "birthday present" of one child to another can be understood as a familial performance of legal impunity for the violation of the slave child's natural rights, becoming the inversion that Patterson refers to as "the chronic inalienable dishonor" of enslavement (12). This familial ritual, in fact, enacted legalized slavery's very tightly engineered contortion of the fundamental inherency of rights and duties between parents and children initiated by the gift of life, as Blackstone and the Anglo-American common-law legal tradition conceived it, while reinforcing the common-law property rights of the male head of household. Former slaves and other abolitionist writers would draw attention to the unjust and destructive effects of this system: that slave parents and their children were deprived of both duties and rights, while the children of slaveholders became, in an insidiously domesticated manner, the usurpers of the natural rights of other children.

## Child Proprietorship, Paternal Right

Despite variations in the laws governing majority and inheritance among the slaveholding states of the United States and in the British West Indies before abolition, Blackstone's formulations also provide a useful framework for discerning the lived contradictions in children's proprietorship of slave children. For example, what might have been the effects on a child of believing herself to be the owner of another child? In a narrative of her life as a slave in Bermuda, Turks Island, and Antigua, published in 1831 by the British Anti-Slavery Society, Mary Prince recounts that she was purchased as a young child along with her mother as part of a division of family property and given by her new owner to his grandchild, "little Miss Betsey Williams … who was about my own age":

> I was made quite a pet of by Miss Betsey, and loved her very much. She used to lead me about by the hand, and call me her little nigger. This was the happiest period of my life, for I was too young to understand rightly my condition as a slave, and too thoughtless and full of spirits to look forward to the days of toil and sorrow.… The tasks given out to us children were light, and we [Mary and her two brothers and three sisters] used to play together with Miss Betsey, with as much freedom almost as if she had been our sister.[12]

Like Gracie Gibson's narrative, Prince's account focuses on the gesture of the child owner leading the slave child by the hand as a daily ritual of childish pretend proprietorship and the familial practice of initiating children into slave ownership, with the racial stigmatization that Miss Betsey verbalized as a sort of lesson learned and repeated in order to justify the separation in status of playmates of the same age. Betsey's and the slave children's "freedom" to play together "almost" as if they were sisters and brothers, however, suggests that childish proprietorship lends a heightened visibility to the quasi-kinship or even friendship that could emerge in relations between enslaved and free children, even as true freedom remained inaccessible for child slaves.

Prince further reports that at the age of twelve, after her kind mistress, Mrs. Williams, died, her master, a captain of a merchant vessel, decided to sell her and two of her sisters to pay for his wedding to a woman with whom he had been involved in a liaison during his marriage. This sale meant that Prince and her siblings would be separated from their mother. Prince does not believe this is possible at first, since she and her mother belonged to Miss Betsey by the gift of her grandfather: "We were by right *her* property, and I never thought we should be separated or sold away from her" (10). Miss Betsey too was "in great distress" over the impending sale, but had no power to prevent it; she tells Mary, "'You are *my* slaves, and he has no right to sell you; but it is all to please her [the new wife]'" (10; emphases in original). Miss Betsey's ownership is repeatedly asserted by the children and emphasized in Prince's narrative, which presents the scene in dramatic colors. But the children are all mistaken, and instead this incident introduces the break-up of Prince's family and unleashes her anguish at her impending sale the next day. Prince recounts her mother's intense sorrow, and her own feelings of sadness in recollecting her pain over their separation, together with Miss Betsey's distress:

Oh dear! I cannot bear to think of that day, – it is too much. – It recalls the great grief that filled my heart, and the woeful thoughts that passed to and fro through my mind, whist listening to the pitiful words of my poor mother, weeping for the loss of her children. I wish I could find words to tell you all I then felt and suffered. The great God above alone knows the thoughts of the poor slave's heart, and the bitter pains which follow such separations as these. All that we love taken away from us – Oh, it is sad, sad! and sore to be borne! – I got no sleep that night for thinking of the morrow; and dear Miss Betsey was scarcely less distressed. She could not bear to part with her old playmates, and she cried sore and would not be pacified. (10)

Miss Betsey's lack of control over her slave "property," even though her family members had recognized her ostensible ownership, provokes her realization of her own disempowerment in relation to her father's decisions, perhaps also heightening her grief at the death of her own mother. Revealing once again the pivotal role of paternalism, this collapse of the household after Mrs. Williams's death also shows how, as Amy Dru Stanley describes, "slavery and marriage amounted to symmetrical bonds, categorized together as relations of domestic dependency, entitling the master of a household to the persons and labor of both his wife and his slaves although one bond originated in coercion and the other in consent."[13] Betsey's plight is indicative of this symmetry, also revealing how childhood shares with slavery a lack of legal capacity to consent.

Prince describes how the following morning, before departing for the slave market to render her children up for sale, her mother brought them to Miss Betsey, saying, "'Take your last look of them; may be you will

see them no more.'" Miss Betsey responded with embraces and proprietary sentiments: "'Oh, my poor slaves! my own slaves!' said dear Miss
Betsey, 'you belong to me; and it grieves my heart to part with you'"
(10). To the extent that this incident reflects common events, we can read
the scene that Mary Prince recounted as indicating the emotional attachment bound up with everyday assertions of disparaging attitudes and
privileges that children of slave-owning households learned to exercise
toward enslaved playmates.[14] Such attachment reportedly motivated the
sons of Dred Scott's original owner, Peter Blow, to purchase and emancipate Scott, their childhood friend, and his wife and children after they
lost their suit for freedom before the U.S. Supreme Court in the infamous
*Dred Scott v. Sandford* decision of 1857.[15] This act of loyalty presents a
brighter possibility on the spectrum of "perverted intimacy," as Patterson
describes it (12), which often involved situations where slave children
actually were siblings to their master's children.

The common disempowerment of Miss Betsey and Mary Prince in
relation to the legal authority of the male head of household also brings
into sharp relief the drastic difference in the two girls' status, since Miss
Betsey was not subject to enslavement and sale. Harriet Jacobs's *Incidents
in the Life of a Slave Girl, Written by Herself*, first published in Boston in
1861 under the pseudonym Linda Brent, provides another variation on
the relation between a child slave and her so-called child owner. Jacobs
recounts her comparatively sheltered early childhood in North Carolina,
where she lived with her parents and brother, not knowing that they
were all slaves until her mother died when she was six years old. She
subsequently was sent to serve as a personal attendant to her mistress,
who was the "foster-sister" of her own mother, since they had both been
nursed as infants by Jacobs's grandmother. Jacobs reports that "My mistress was so kind to me that I was always glad to do her bidding, and
proud to labor for her as long as my young years would admit." When
her mistress died almost six years later, Harriet hoped that she and her
brother would be set free, both because her mistress "had promised my
dying mother that her children should never suffer for any thing" and
"on account of my mother's love and faithful service." But instead, her
mistress's will "bequeathed me to her sister's daughter, a child of five
years old. So vanished our hopes."[16] As in Prince's narrative, repeated references to "love" convey the writer's assumption during childhood that
such feelings across status lines had been genuine, thus emphasizing the
experience of rupture when domestic ties of loyalty and affection are dis-
regarded and terminated by slavery's economic transactions.

After two years serving in the household of the father of her new child mistress, physician James Norcom (called Dr. Flint in the narrative), Jacobs was besieged by the sexual insinuations of "my master, whose restless, craving, vicious nature roved about day and night, seeking whom to devour." He tells her "that I was made for his use, made to obey his command in *every* thing; that I was nothing but a slave whose will must and should surrender to his" (20; emphasis in original). Despite these claims that Harriet's body and will are his own property, Dr. Flint publicly insists on his daughter's ownership of Harriet:

Dr. Flint occasionally had high prices offered for me; but he always said, "She don't belong to me. She is my daughter's property, and I have no right to sell her." Good, honest man! My young mistress was still a child, and I could look for no protection from her. I loved her, and she returned my affection. I once heard her father allude to her attachment to me; and his wife promptly replied that it proceeded from fear. This put unpleasant doubts into my mind. Did the child feign what she did not feel? or was her mother jealous of the mite of love she bestowed on me? I concluded it must be the latter. I said to myself, "Surely, little children are true." (22)

Acting in a legally proper manner as "trustee" of his daughter's inheritance, in Blackstone's sense, Dr. Flint nevertheless hopes to exploit his daughter's property sexually. For her part, Harriet is the caregiver rather than the playmate of the much younger girl, but their relationship is still confused by the bonds of proprietorship, which, as we have seen, did not give the child any rights of ownership that could be executed until she came of legal age. In acknowledging that her young mistress cannot protect her from the predations of Dr. Flint, Harriet also exposes the weakness and ambiguity of the child's proprietary claims, despite the legal validity of her former mistress's bequest in transferring Harriet's ownership to the Flint household. Instead, Harriet resorts to the hope that the child's affection for her is genuine, despite the compromised relationships perpetuated by slavery. She imagines herself as the preserver of the childhood innocence of her master's daughter.

This particular "incident" in Jacobs's narrative, then, also works like other antislavery arguments discussed in this volume to expose the way the innocence associated with childhood is corrupted within the slave owner's household. Dr. Flint's simultaneous claims in public that Harriet is his daughter's property, when combined with his private claims to Harriet that he may master her body and will completely, exemplify Patterson's account of slavery as a system of absolute control, but also show how fully Flint's paternal role is complicit with and reinforces his ability to express his mastery through sexual aggression. Exposing "the underlying beliefs that facilitate enslavement" (Anna Mae Duane, "Introduction," this volume), Jacobs's text interrogates the logic of Dr. Flint's combined public and private assertions to make apparent that Flint's daughter's ownership of Harriet functions in her father's mind as support for his assertion of a paternalistic right to rape a female slave residing in his own household. This claim was not extreme, but rather typical of chattel slavery in the United States, since North Carolina law did not recognize sexual assault against a slave as rape. As Saidiya V. Hartman states, "[t]he rape of black women existed as an unspoken but normative condition fully within the purview of everyday sexual practices, whether within the implied arrangements of the slave enclave or within the plantation household."[17]

James Norcom's "trusteeship" of his daughter's human property during her childhood, then, functioned similarly to the way that, according to Audra Diptee's account in this volume (see Chapter 8), under a system of guardianship devised for emancipated child slaves by French colonial authorities in Africa, "the majority of children were entrusted to traders and merchants ... who had a vested interest in keeping child slavery as a thriving institution." In other words, a legal arrangement, whether trusteeship or guardianship, meant to protect the rights of child dependents is employed to facilitate a practice of child enslavement and to cloak children's domestic exploitation. Jacobs's narrative also points to the paternalistic logic often supporting the exploitation of child domestic workers today, as Jonathan Blagbrough and Gary Craig discuss (Chapter 10, this volume). This contemporary context underscores Jacobs's narrative's indictment of the U.S. slaveholding family for the insidious practice of what would be termed today in multiple jurisdictions as the unlawful sexual abuse of enslaved domestic workers.

### The "Gift" Returned (or a Child Slave's Wages Paid): *Shanley v. Harvey,* 1762

Up to this point, we have been exploring the legal implications and social and psychological dynamics of the giving of child slaves to other children as gifts or bequests, finding an impetus in Patterson's approach. I want to focus now on the role that the giving of gifts played in a legal case in mid-eighteenth-century England involving the bequest of a dying woman to a slave who had been a child when he was given to her by a relative. Although the woman in question was not a child owner of another child, her reception of the "gift" of a child slave brings to light once again not only the complex and involuted forms of proprietorship, attachment, and exploitation that we have been examining so far, but also the possibility of a limited reciprocity or reparation.

This case also brings us to the debate over the legal status of slaves and the legality of slavery in England, a question that remained inconclusive and that therefore formed the focus of legal and political activism by British abolitionists, including those of African descent, in the late eighteenth and early nineteenth centuries until the British Parliament abolished the Atlantic slave trade in 1807, and slavery in British dominions between 1833, the date of legislation, and July 31, 1838, when final emancipation took place.[18] A number of signal legal decisions permitted public debate in the British press of significant antislavery arguments prior to the political breakthrough that abolished slavery in the British dominions. In the *Somerset v. Stewart* decision of 1772 on a writ of habeas corpus, perhaps the most famous of the eighteenth-century cases testing the legality of slavery in England, Chief Justice of King's Bench, William Murray, Lord Mansfield confirmed the freedom of a former slave, James Somerset, who had been brought to England from Virginia (by way of Massachusetts) by his master, Charles Stewart. After Somerset absconded, he was recaptured by Stewart and placed aboard a ship bound for Jamaica, where he was to be resold. Before the ship's departure, however, several of Somerset's abolitionist friends were able to obtain a writ of habeas corpus from Lord Mansfield, resulting in Somerset's rescue by an officer of the court from his shipboard confinement. Following a series of hearings that took place from December 1771 to June 1772 before the High Court of King's Bench, Chief Justice Mansfield ruled on the reasons stated for Somerset's capture and detention in the return to the writ that "So high an act of dominion was never in use here; no master ever was allowed here to take a slave by force to be sold abroad, because he had deserted from his service, or for any other reason whatever. We cannot say the cause set forth by this return is allowed or approved of by the laws of this kingdom; therefore, the man [Somerset] must be discharged."[19] The ruling was seemingly a narrow one, based on the illegality of sending Somerset out of the country under the 1679 Habeas Corpus Act, specifically, section 11 titled "No subject to be sent Prisoner into Scotland, &c. or any Parts beyond the Seas."[20] However, the great public interest in the case as it unfolded, the abolitionists' promotion of Lord Mansfield's ruling as a decision against the legality of slavery in England, as well as the incorporation of the *Somerset* decision into later legal decisions in various jurisdictions in the independent United States, gave it a wide-ranging legal and cultural influence.[21] According to Douglas A. Lorimer, *Somerset* had a greater impact on "the slave's life chances" in England than most scholarship focusing on its strictly legal effects has allowed, because "by declaring that blacks could not be compelled to leave the country ... the law had confirmed their right to resist this most threatening and arbitrary aspect of their masters' authority."[22]

In his publication of the statement he delivered before the court, Francis Hargrave, one of James Somerset's lawyers, cites several earlier cases where slavery had been declared unlawful in England, one of which hinged on the status of a slave given as a gift when he was a child. This case before the Court of Chancery, *Shanley v. Harvey*, involved a dispute over the legacy of a dying woman, Margaret Hamilton, to her servant, Joseph Harvey, a former slave who had been given to her by one of her uncles, Francis Shanley. The other uncle, Edmund Shanley, sought either to nullify or reclaim this bequest by declaring that the slave's ownership reverted to his brother, Francis Shanley, and therefore the legacy should remain part of his niece's estate. In his ruling dated 15 March 1762, Lord Chancellor Robert Henley (later Baron Northington) upheld the validity of the deathbed bequest as a *donatio causá mortis*, ruling further that "As soon as a man sets foot on English ground he is free: a negro may maintain an action against his master for ill usage, and may have a *Habeas Corpus* if restrained of his liberty."[23] In quoting this decision as a precedent for James Somerset's claim to freedom in England, Hargrave notes the "strong expression of the late Lord Chancellor," reporting that "Lord *Northington*, as I am informed by a friend who was present at the hearing of the cause, disallowed the master's claim with great warmth, and gave costs to the negro."[24]

The published report on *Shanley v. Harvey* is quite brief:

This was a bill brought by *Edward Shanley*, esquire, as administrator of *Margaret Hamilton*, deceased, against *Joseph Harvey*, a negro, and two persons of the name of *Gossop* and *Thorpe*, his trustees, and *Francis Shanley*, one of the next of kin, for an account of part of her personal estate under the following circumstances.

The plaintiff had twelve years before brought over the defendant, *Harvey*, as his slave, then only eight or nine years old, and presented him to his niece, *Margaret Hamilton*, who had him baptized, and changed his name.

On the 9th of *July*, 1752, being then very ill, she, about an hour before her death, directed *Harvey* to take out a purse, which was in her dressing-case drawer, and delivered it to him, saying, "Here take this, there is £700 or £800 in bank notes, and some more in money, but I cannot directly tell what, but it is all for you, to make you happy; make haste, put it in your pocket, tell nobody, and pay the butcher's bill." He then knelt down and thanked her. She said, "God bless you, make a good use of it."[25]

This report, followed by the Lord Chancellor's ruling quoted earlier, suggests that the vehemence Lord Chancellor Henley [Lord Northington] exhibited went beyond the dismissal of the bill of complaint, and was also expressed in his further statement of the rights available to blacks in England, making the case appropriate for Hargrave's later purposes in arguing for James Somerset's freedom. The original Bill of Complaint brought by Edmund (not Edward, as in the report) Shanley, and Joseph Harvey's Answer to the Complaint, both held at the UK National Archives, are much more detailed and afford additional insight on the circumstances of Margaret Hamilton's bequest and the Lord Chancellor's ruling, which evidently did not settle the issue of slavery's legality in England. The English High Court of Chancery oversaw cases where the dispositions of property in wills or the terms of contracts were uncertain or contested and therefore required remedies not available in the common-law courts. The more detailed case records suggest that the Lord Chancellor's ruling extended into the question of slavery's legality because the case directly implied the capacity of a former slave to receive a bequest, and therefore to be a subject and not simply an object of property. The case thus turned on whether Joseph Harvey was still a slave at the time of Margaret Hamilton's death, but his status also depended on the court's understanding of his relation with his mistress as a child servant grown up in her household, and of Margaret Hamilton's intentions in giving Joseph such a large sum on her deathbed.

Both the Bill of Complaint and Joseph Harvey's Answer reveal that Joseph Harvey's ability lawfully to receive the deathbed gift directly depended on the psychological dynamics of the slaveholding household, specifically the ties of affection and duties of maintenance that could be proven to have existed between Margaret Hamilton and her servant, in contrast to the assertion of mastery over the child slave highlighted in Gibson's, Prince's, and Jacobs's narratives. In his Bill of Complaint, the lawful administrator of Margaret Hamilton's estate, Edmund Shanley (also spelled Shanly), an Irish merchant residing in Dublin, refers to Joseph Harvey as "a Negro Slave" and as "the property of the said Francis Shanly," his brother. He further asserts that Harvey, in combination with two associates, Gossett (not Gossop) and Thorp, have "taken possession of money and bank notes belonging to the deceased, Margaret Hamilton, amounting to over £1000, as well as £300 in New South Sea Annuities," which she had allegedly directed Harvey to take "at or shortly before her death … out of Friendship and Regard for him." Edmund Shanley further complains that his brother, Francis Shanley, "also insists that the said Harvey being his Slave and property he was and is Incapable by Law of Acquiring or taking any Estate or Effects whatsoever for his own Benefit but that he the said Francis Shanly is intitled [*sic*] to such Money Bank Notes and South Sea Annuities."[26] Edmund Shanley insists that even if such a bequest took place, which he does not admit, then it should be invalidated by the court due to the dying woman's mental instability caused by her approaching death, with the likelihood of her insanity demonstrated by the bequest itself, "it being highly Improbable that she should be willing to give so Large an amount … to a Slave or even a free menial Servant to the Prejudice of your Orator [himself] and his said Brother who were her next of Kin." As proof of his assertion that Joseph Harvey was still a slave and thus the property of Francis Shanley, Edmund Shanley also asks for verification "whether the said Margaretta Hamilton did not often or at some time or times in her life when the said Joseph Harvey misbehaved threaten she would send him to his said master the said Francis Shanley." He also demands to know who else might have been present at the time of Margaret Hamilton's death "and the whole of the Conversation which then passed," and whether the gift was "Solicited or desired by any," and "whether she did not express herself or seem unwilling that the said Harvey should take or have" the bank notes and money.

The Answer to the Bill of Complaint, sworn March 7, 1760, is signed "Jo Harvey," and is presented as Joseph Harvey's personal statement, as framed by his lawyers. The "Defendant" Harvey begins by stating that "he is a Negro and that he was a Slave and that he was such several years since and when he was only a child brought from Algiers into England by Francis Shanley … to be given as or by the way of present to Margaretta Hamilton … in return for some favours conferred on the said Francis Shanley."[27] However, he immediately begins to undermine that slave status and to question the proprietary behavior allegedly exhibited by his mistress. Harvey explains that "at the time he was so brought into England a Lad only of tender years the said Margaretta Hamilton took a particular fancy to this Defendant and although she sometimes spoke sharply to this Defendant yet in general she treated him with great civility and kindness." Margaret Hamilton also arranged for his baptism on December 4, 1752, at the Parish of Saint George Hanover Square in the county of Middlesex (London) "by the name Joseph Harvey," standing as his godmother herself and arranging for two of her gentlemen friends to stand as his godfathers, one of whom, "Edward Harvey Esquire," "at her request had agreed ... to permit this Defendant to take the name of Harvey." It appears from Joseph Harvey's testimony that Margaret Hamilton, a wealthy woman with her own house at Paddington, frequently entertained a group of friends who gave Joseph gifts of money amounting over the years to more than £100, which Margaret put aside for him. Harvey further states that to his knowledge Margaret Hamilton did not correspond with her uncles, Edmund and Francis Shanley, after the time that "this Defendant was so given to her," "nor did the said Margaretta Hamilton ever profess any regard or kindness either for the said Edmund or Francis Shanley but on the contrary ... whenever their names were mentioned she always spoke of them both in a disregardful manner and used frequently to declare that neither of them should ever have any part of her fortune declaring that they had both used her very ill." Harvey reinforces the idea that the bequest had been long planned as a quasi-parental provision for his future well-being, explaining that "Margaretta Hamilton being greatly pleased and satisfied with this Defendants [sic] honesty and good behaviour hath frequently declared as well to this Defendant as to her Friends and Acquaintance in general ... that she intended to reward this Defendant for his faithful service and that she would provide for him at her death in such a manner as to enable him to live without going again into Service."[28]

Harvey further testifies that despite frequent ill health due to "a decay occasioned by Indiscretions in her Youth," Margaret Hamilton put off making her will. On the day of her death, July 6, 1759 (not the mistaken day and year of 1752 noted in the report), after undergoing a "violent purging" at approximately "half of an hour past two of the clock in the afternoon," she sent the maidservant for the minister and apothecary to attend her bedside. Joseph Harvey, however, remained with her, along with another witness not mentioned in the record of the case, Mrs Mary Stapylton, a widow and an "intimate acquaintance" of Margaret Hamilton. Harvey reports that, after praying together as they "frequently used to do and in which the said Margaretta Hamilton then very fervently joined ... the said Mrs Mary Stapylton said to the said Margaretta Hamilton [you] always promised to do something for this Defendant She the said Mary Stapylton hoped she the said Margaretta Hamilton would not leave him destitute but would provide for him to which the said Margaretta Hamilton immediately answered yes I will." Harvey then recounts Margaret Hamilton's direction that he retrieve her purse from her dressing table, and her bequest and blessing, in words similar to those contained in the report. When the minister and apothecary arrived forty-five minutes later, Mrs Mary Stapylton and Joseph explained to them what had occurred and asked them to serve as witnesses to the bequest, but Margaret could no longer speak, and she died shortly afterward. This lack of multiple corroborating witnesses may have contributed to Edmund Shanley's decision to pursue a Chancery suit.

In responding specifically to Edmund Shanley's questions about the money, Harvey admits that Margaret Hamilton died intestate, and he renounces any claim to her estate other than to the "Money and Bank Notes to the amount in the Complainants Bill set forth" contained in the purse or bag given to him by Margaret Hamilton as a *donatio causá mortis*. Although the receipts for the New South Sea Annuities were also part of these contents, Harvey also gives up any claim to them. But he defends his own legal capacity to receive the bequest, and confirms Margaret Hamilton's sanity and clear understanding of her intentions and actions just prior to her death. Harvey denies Francis Shanley's claim that ownership of Joseph should revert to him, but instead "humbly insists that he was not at the time of the Decease of the said Margaretta Hamilton the property of the said Francis Shanly nor did this Defendant live with the said Margaretta Hamilton only by the permission of the said Francis Shanly on the contrary this Defendant saith that he was so given to the said Margaretta Hamilton by the said Francis Shanley as aforesaid and that from thenceforth he was always looked upon and Deemed the Servant of the said Margaretta Hamilton only." Being given as a "gift" in his childhood, as Joseph Harvey carefully construes it for the court, becomes the commencement of his separation from his slave status, an informal process that could be contrasted with the legislated, gradual emancipation of slave children in eighteenth-century New York State analyzed by Sarah Gronningsater (Chapter 5, this volume). Supplying further evidence that he was no longer a slave, Joseph stipulates that he was not subjected to resale or being repossessed, since Francis Shanley never sought to "reclaim" him, but "the said Francis Shanley was himself so well satisfied that this Defendant was none of his the said Francis Shanleys [*sic*] property that when the said Francis Shanley returned to Ireland he never offered required or desired this Defendant to go with him … but permitted this Defendant to go freely away without the least molestation." In addition, Mrs Mary Stapylton's intervention in bringing about the bequest should not be distrusted, Harvey claims, because after the two had prayed together, Margaret "was quite composed and in her perfect senses and understanding," and he "verily believes the said Margaretta Hamilton was well pleased with the said Mrs Mary Stapylton" for reminding her of her plan to make Joseph independent through a bequest. Far from considering Joseph mere chattel, all the friends of the deceased were solicitous for his welfare as a valued member of her household, knowing Margaret's regard for him from childhood. Furthermore, immediately after Margaret Hamilton's death, Harvey sought the help and advice of her friends, including Gossett and Thorp, in securing her possessions with bankers until her heirs could claim them, and he insists that there had been no dishonest confederacy among them to take possession of her estate as Edmund Shanley had "most wrongfully sustained."

As one mid-nineteenth-century American legal commentator on *Shanley v. Harvey* observed, "The claim does not appear to have been for the negro, but for the money; and the question to have been whether he was capable of receiving the money as a gift."[29] Lord Chancellor Henley was not required to rule on the legality of slavery in England in *Shanley v. Harvey*, but he did so anyway, also confirming both the validity of Margaret Hamilton's gift, since it took place prior to her decease rendering her intestate, and Joseph Harvey's legal right to receive and keep it.[30] If the Lord Chancellor had found for the complainant, Joseph Harvey might also have been re-enslaved according to Francis Shanley's claims or as part of Margaret Hamilton's estate.[31] According to Harvey's approximate age as noted in the report on the case, he would have been twenty or twenty-one years old at the time of his statement before the court in 1760, and therefore of legal age to own property. Lord Chancellor Henley's vehemence in declaring, "As soon as a man sets foot on English ground he is free," makes sense as a direct response to the Shanley brothers' insistence on Joseph Harvey's continuing enslavement, their ownership of him, and their attempts to profit by it in Chancery, a remedial court of equity which was charged with discerning and carrying out as far as the law would allow the intentions of testators such as Margaret Hamilton.[32]

It would seem in retrospect that Margaret Hamilton's deathbed gift also had the status of a legally valid manumission, if such were needed, as implicitly confirmed by the Lord Chancellor. Harvey also reports in his statement that the group of Margaret Hamilton's close friends who acted as his trustees after her death helped him to "Invest the sum of Nine hundred and forty four pounds nine shillings part thereof in the purchase of one thousand one hundred and fifty pounds Bank [of England] three percent annuitys [*sic*]," thus contributing toward fulfilling Margaret

Hamilton's intention that Joseph Harvey should be able to live comfortably without going into service again.[33] Included in her gift, presumably, was Joseph Harvey's own savings of monetary gifts amounting to £100 that Margaret had put aside for him over the years.[34]

A crucial element of the case that emerges from the legal documents but becomes more apparent in the context created for it here lies in Margaret Hamilton's ability to dispose of her personal property and estate as she saw fit because she was an unmarried woman, or in law, a *feme sole*. The combined proprietary, familial, and legal powers of the dominant paternal head of household and slave master, so evident in Gibson's, Prince's, and Jacobs's narratives, seem to have been completely absent in Margaret Hamilton's household, where she was in charge. Although Margaret Hamilton and Joseph Harvey were still mistress and servant at the time of her death, Margaret could have felt a parental (maternal) regard for Joseph in carrying out her duty to a dependent, as Blackstone would define it, to secure Joseph's future "happiness" and financial independence.[35] These quasi-familial bonds would still be implicated in slavery, since Margaret Hamilton inevitably participated in Joseph Harvey's enslavement as a child by accepting him as a gift from her uncle, and by employing him as he grew up, presumably as an unpaid servant. In this respect, her gift could be viewed as the rendering of wages she owed to him. Her concern for Joseph's welfare after her death and her gift of financial independence in her bequest nevertheless seem to make a partial return or reparation for the tainted gift she had received stemming from the slave child's likely kidnapping and sale away from his natal home and family and purchase by her uncle in Algiers. In the most resonant aspect of the case for the history of a child slave's gradual self-emancipation – an uncommon case for its time and for many years to come in British and U.S. slaveholding dominions – Joseph Harvey also gained official recognition of his own casting aside of his enslavement over the course of his youth and years of domestic service.[36] This process of self-possession that Harvey accomplished, it would seem, in concert with Margaret Hamilton led to the ratification of both his truthfulness and his property rights in the English High Court of Chancery.

## Conclusion

The foregoing analysis of historical slave children given as "gifts" or bequests leads to greater understanding of the ways that child slavery creates fissures in legalized slavery's seemingly naturalized relationships

by existing in intimate connection with other familial relations of proprietorship.[37] Underscoring the challenges of locating and interpreting the
voices and testimony of children and the importance of paying attention
to them, as discussed in multiple contributions to this volume, this chapter's study of the *Shanley v. Harvey* case allows one voice of a former
child slave to emerge from the legal archives. This is a significant case in
the history of slavery and abolition because, unlike James Somerset in
the *Somerset* case, who could not speak in court but instead was represented by his lawyers before the King's Bench, the rules of the Court of
Chancery allowed Joseph Harvey to refute his accusers directly through
his formal response to their complaint, to have his testimony granted
legal standing, and to have his rights upheld on the basis of the convincing story about his free status in the Hamilton household which the legal
process enabled him to tell.[38] The powerful antislavery arguments embedded in the depictions of slave children and their child owners in Prince's
and Jacobs's slave narratives further indicate that such sources do not
simply reflect the historical experience of child slaves, but also that they
contributed to shaping public understanding of the deleterious effects
of institutionalized slavery on childhood and family relationships, thus
contributing to political debates over accountability for the institution
of slavery and its abolition. These depictions of child enslavement do not
simply demonstrate violations, but also convey through their expression
of protest against injustice, what a child's freedom, agency, and social
participation would look like (see Johnson, Blagbrough and Craig, Wall,
Chapters 9, 10, and 11, this volume, respectively). Such entanglements of
family life and slavery persist today, contributing to the complex causes
of contemporary children's forced labor investigated by multiple contributors to this volume. Viewing enslaved children not just as objects
but also as subjects of property and its accompanying socially recognized forms of selfhood may aid in understanding how exploited children
today are capable of exercising, and not just receiving, economic, social,
and human rights (see Wall).

## Notes

1  "Gracie Gibson, Ex-Slave 86 Years Old," in *The American Slave: A Composite
   Biography*, Vol. 2, South Carolina Narratives Parts 1 and 2, edited by George
   P. Rawick (Westport, CT: Greenwood Publishing Company, 1972), Part 2,
   113; qtd. in Orlando Patterson, *Slavery and Social Death: A Comparative
   Study* (Cambridge, MA: Harvard University Press, 1982), 12. Further refer-
   ences to Patterson's study are included parenthetically in the text.

2  I place the word "gift" in quotation marks in the title and opening para-
   graphs of this chapter to call attention to the morally unacceptable nature of
   the transfer of one enslaved human being to another, who becomes his or her
   master, implied in this transaction. These objections remain in place throughout the subsequent analysis, but the quotation marks around the word gift
   are omitted.

3  While a detailed study is beyond the scope of this chapter, certain case
   reports suggest that the validity of gifts of slaves to children could be doubt-
   ful. For example, the report of a Virginia case, *Shirley v. Long*, 6 Randolph
   764, August 1827, states: "Held: if a father gives a slave to a child, and the
   donor retains possession of the slave, and exercises control over it, the gift
   is not the less fraudulent because the child always lived with the father, and
   the slave was always called the child's in the family and neighborhood." A
   similar case, *Durham v. Dunkly*, 6 Randolph 135, February 1828, reads:
   "Dunkly in 1804 delivered a slave, Jenny, 'to the female Plaintiff [Nancy] ...
   being both at that time under one year old,' and on the same day executed a
   deed of gift conveying Jenny to Nancy, stipulating that Dunkly was 'to keep
   the said negro, and raise it for' Nancy 'until the said Nancy is thirteen years
   old.' Immediately after the deed was executed, Jenny was taken back into
   the possession of Dunkly who has held the slave ever since. The donee never
   lived with him, nor was the deed ever recorded. Held: the gift is void under
   the act of assembly [I Rev. C., 432, sect. 51]." *Judicial Cases Concerning
   American Slavery and the Negro, Vol. I Cases from the Courts of England,
   Virginia, West Virginia, and Kentucky*, edited by Helen Tunnicliff Catterall
   (Washington, DC: Carnegie Institution of Washington, 1926), 150–1.

4  Wilma King, *Stolen Childhood: Slave Youth in Nineteenth-Century America*,
   2nd ed. (Bloomington: Indiana University Press, 2011), 33.

5  M. L. Bush, *Servitude in Modern Times* (Cambridge, UK: Polity, 2000), 6–8.

6  Ibid., 9.

7  King, *Stolen Childhood*, 67.

8  Steven Mintz, *Huck's Raft: A History of American Childhood* (Cambridge,
   MA: Harvard University Press, 2004), 95. Further references are included
   parenthetically in the text.

9  Sir William Blackstone, *Commentaries on the Laws of England*, 9th ed., Vol.
   I (London: Strahan, 1783), 125. Further references are included parenthetically in the text.

10 On the history of married women's property rights, see Susan Staves, *Married
   Women's Property in England, 1660–1833* (Cambridge, MA: Harvard
   University Press, 1990).

11 Teresa Michals, "'That Sole and Despotic Dominion': Slaves, Wives, and Game
   in Blackstone's *Commentaries*," *Eighteenth-Century Studies* 27.2 (Winter
   1993–4), 202.

12 *The History of Mary Prince, a West Indian Slave*, ed. Sarah Salih (London:
   Penguin, 2000), 7. Further references are included parenthetically in
   the text.

13 Amy Dru Stanley, "Instead of Waiting for the Thirteenth Amendment: The
   War Power, Slave Marriage, and Inviolate Human Rights," *American*

*Historical Review* 115.3 (June 2010), 734. See also Amy Dru Stanley, *From Bondage to Contract: Wage Labor, Marriage, and the Market in the Age of Slave Emancipation* (Cambridge: Cambridge University Press, 1998).

14 *The History of Mary Prince* is a joint work with Prince's abolitionist collaborators, Susanna Strickland (later Moody), to whom Prince told her story, and the editor, Thomas Pringle, who was also secretary of the Anti-Slavery Society. For an analysis of the authentication debates and libel suits resulting from this publication, see Kathryn Temple, *Scandal Nation: Law and Authorship in Britain, 1750–1832* (Ithaca, NY, and London: Cornell University Press, 2003), chapter 4.

15 See Paul Finkelman, *Dred Scott v. Sandford: A Brief History with Documents* (Boston, MA: Bedford/St. Martin's: 1997), 3.

16 Harriet Jacobs, *Incidents in the Life of a Slave Girl Written by Herself*, ed. Nell Irvin Painter (London: Penguin, 2000), 7–10. Further references are included parenthetically in the text.

17 Saidiya V. Hartman, *Scenes of Subjection: Terror, Slavery, and Self-Making in Nineteenth-Century America* (New York and Oxford: Oxford University Press, 1997), 85. Hartman also analyzes the rationales and precedents in slave law for not recognizing the rape of a slave as a crime (82–6). For a discussion of North Carolina cases where the master was deemed to have "uncontrolled authority of the body of his slave," see also Andrew Fede, *People Without Rights: An Interpretation of the Fundamentals of the Law of Slavery in the U.S. South* (New York and London: Garland Publishing, 1992), 106–11.

18 Coerced labor nevertheless persisted after emancipation in British colonies, and slavery remained an object of active political and moral concern among abolitionists, missionaries, and colonial administrators in subsequent decades as the slave trade continued in various territories impinging on the areas coming under British colonial governance during the nineteenth century, particularly in Africa. Ending slavery became a rationale for further colonial expansion into Africa. Joan Anim-Adoo provides an account of the king of Dahomey's "present" in 1850 of a captured eight-year-old West African girl to a British naval captain engaged in suppressing the slave trade, as part of trade negotiations involving the exchange of gifts between the African slave-trading ruler and the British queen's representative. The girl would be named Sally Bonetta Forbes, after Captain Forbes of the HMS *Bonetta*, who decided to keep and rescue her as "property of the crown" and to transfer her to the custody of Queen Victoria, whose protégé she became. Anim-Adoo, "Queen Victoria's Black 'Daughter,'" in *Black Victorians/Black Victoriana*, edited by Gretchen Holbrook Gerzina (New Brunswick, NJ: Rutgers University Press, 2003), 11–19. Anim-Adoo explains that for King Gezo, "presents of slave children to ship's captains were part of a traditional pattern of interaction with slavers" (13).

19 "Historical Chronicle, *Monday* 22 [June]," *The Gentleman's Magazine* XLII (June 1772), 293–4. This quotation is excerpted from an abbreviated text of Mansfield's ruling. For discussions of the various extant transcriptions of the ruling and their implications, see David Brion Davis, *The Problem of*

*Slavery in the Age of Revolution, 1770–1823* (New York: Oxford University Press, 1999), 469–522; James Oldham, "New Light on Mansfield and Slavery," *Journal of British Studies* 27.1 (1988): 45–68; and George van Cleve, "Somerset's Case and Its Antecedents in Imperial Perspective," *Law and History Review* 24.3 (2006): 601–45.

20  *The Habeas Corpus Act of 1679, legislation.gov.uk*, National Archives, United Kingdom, www.legislation.gov.uk/aep/Cha2/31/2 (Accessed April 2012).

21  On the reception of the *Somerset* case in the British press, see Folarin O. Shyllon, *Black Slaves in Britain* (London: Oxford University Press, 1974), 141–64. For discussions of the *Somerset* decision as precedent for later decisions involving freedom suits of American slaves and in constitutional and political deliberations involving the legality of slavery in the United States, see William M. Wiecek in "*Somerset*: Lord Mansfield and the Legitimacy of Slavery in the Anglo-American World," *The University of Chicago Law Review* 42 (1974–5): 86–176, and Alfred W. Blumrosen, "The Profound Influence in America of Lord Mansfield's Decision in *Somerset v. Stewart*," *Texas Wesleyan Law Review* 13 (2006–7): 645–58.

22  Douglas A. Lorimer, "Black Slaves and English Liberty: A Re-examination of Racial Slavery in England," *Immigrants and Minorities* 3.2 (1984), 131. Lorimer argues that black slaves provided the initiative for the ending of slavery in England between the 1760s and the 1790s through their "common practice [of] fleeing from their masters to make their way as free, wage-earning servants or labourers" (135).

23  This brief report of the *Shanley v. Harvey* case appears in Robert Henry Eden, *Reports of Cases in the High Court of Chancery, from 1757 to 1766*, Vol. 2 (London: Charles Hunter, 1818), 126–7; and is also included in Catterall, *Judicial Cases Concerning American Slavery and the Negro, Vol. 1*, 13.

24  Francis Hargrave, *An Argument in the case of James Sommersett, A Negro, Lately Determined by the Court of King's Bench, Wherein it is attempted to demonstrate the Present Unlawfulness of Slavery in England* (Boston, MA: E. Russell, 1774), 41–2; emphasis in original. The first edition was published in London by W. Otridge in 1772.

25  *Shanley v. Harvey*, 126–7; emphases in original.

26  UK National Archives C12/1853/23/001, *Shanley v. Harvey*.

27  UK National Archives C12/1853/23/002, *Shanley v. Harvey*.

28  For a recent study of the relations between domestic servants and their employers in eighteenth-century England, including the roles of black slaves and servants in English households, see Carolyn Steedman, *Labours Lost: Domestic Service and the Making of Modern England* (Cambridge: Cambridge University Press, 2009).

29  John Codman Hurd, *The Law of Freedom and Bondage in the United States*, Vol. 1 (Boston, MA: Little, Brown, and Company, 1858), 186.

30  James Walvin observes on *Shanley v. Harvey* that, "Henley's statement was a complete denial of the legal view which had held sway since 1729, and went back for its inspiration to 1569." *Black and White: The Negro and English Society* (London: Alan Lane The Penguin Press, 1973), 113. Walvin

refers here to the January 1729 opinion of Sir Philip Yorke, the Attorney-General (later Lord Hardwicke), and the Solicitor-General, Charles Talbot. They responded in writing to a request made by a group of West Indian merchants at a dinner held at Lincoln's Inn that they comment on the legality of slavery in England: "We are of the Opinion, that a Slave by coming from the West-Indies to Great Britain, doth not become free, and that his Master's Property or Right in him is not thereby determined or varied: And that Baptism doth not bestow freedom on him, nor make any Alteration in his Temporal Condition in these Kingdoms. We are also of the Opinion, that his Master may legally compel him to return again to the Plantations." Qtd. in Shyllon, *Black Slaves in Britain*, 25–6. The 1569 opinion was "Cartwright's Case," which pertained to a slave brought from Russia, the ruling being that "England was too Pure an Air for Slaves to breath in." Qtd. in Walvin, *Black and White*, 109.

31 Lawrence Brown, *The Slavery Connections of Northington Grange*, published online by the University of Manchester (June 2010), 21. www.englishheritage.org.uk/publications/slavery-connections-northington-grange/slavery-connections-northington-grange.pdf. In this history of the Northington Grange property commissioned by the English Heritage project "Researching Slavery Connections," Brown traces the ties of the Henley family, who owned the property between 1662 and 1787, with the Atlantic slave trade (15–28). He comments on Lord Chancellor Henley's ruling in *Shanley v. Harvey* that it "was far more expansive" than Mansfield's later ruling in *Somerset* because it meant that "the law could directly intervene in the economic relationship of master-slave" (23).

32 In controverting the Shanleys' proprietary claims in relation to Joseph Harvey, the Lord Chancellor's judgment also seems to outline at least three areas of law within which "Negroes" and former slaves in England could have the same rights as other English subjects: the fundamental right to possess property; access to the common-law writ of habeas corpus, as well as protection under the 1679 Habeas Corpus Act; the law of equity concerning wills and bequests, adjudicated by the Court of Chancery; and a fourth area involving the right to bring a complaint against a master for ill treatment, which seems to pertain to contracts of servitude and apprenticeship under the 1747 and 1757 Master and Servant legislation, discussed in Steedman, *Labours Lost*, 180–98. British abolitionists would soon realize that the writ of habeas corpus could become an instrument to extract legal decisions on the question of slavery from English courts, as in the *Somerset* case.

33 I have found two documents in the Sessions Papers, Justices Working Documents from the Middlesex Sessions, dated January 1771 and July 1771, which mention a Joseph Harvey, Victualler, residing at Portland Row in the Parish of St Mary Le Bone. If this is the same Joseph Harvey, he may have used Margaret Hamilton's bequest to establish a business. These documents are accessible at *London Lives 1690–1820, Crime, Poverty, and Social Policy in the Metropolis*, www.londonlives.org/index.jsp (accessed March 12, 2014).

34   Walvin remarks of Henley's ruling in *Shanley v. Harvey* that "Once again one
     searches in vain for evidence that the new legal position in any way altered
     daily practice, with the pleasant exception of Joseph Harvey of course,
     who was allowed to keep the change from the butcher's bill" (*Black and
     White*, 113). In his testimony, Harvey states that Margaret Hamilton always
     promptly paid her bills to "her Tradespeople at Paddington," that the butch-
     er's bill amounted only to seven shillings, and that her remembering to dis-
     charge this debt just before she died "is rather a Strong indication of her then
     being in her Senses and of her then having her Memory and Understanding."
     The "change" on the butcher's bill was essentially the entirety of the bequest.
     In his complaint, Edmund Shanley calculated that Margaret Hamilton's
     estate was worth more than £3,000, so that her gift to Joseph Harvey rep-
     resented approximately a third of that amount. But Harvey stated that he
     estimated the value of Hamilton's estate to be much higher than Shanley
     had claimed. The value of £1,000 in 1762, according to the historic stan-
     dard of living value in 2012 would be approximately £126,400. Lawrence
     H. Officer and Samuel H. Williamson, "Five Ways to Compute the Relative
     Value of a UK Pound Amount, 1270 to Present," *Measuring Worth*, 2014,
     www.measuringworth.com/ukcompare/ (accessed March 18, 2014).

35   Folarin Shyllon writes favorably of the familial attachments displayed in the
     *Shanley v. Harvey* case: "Margaret Hamilton did not consider or treat Joseph
     Harvey as a chattel or plaything. On the contrary, she stood *in loco parentis*
     to the African boy." *Black People in Britain 1555–1833* (London: Oxford
     University Press, 1977), 39. I have not been able to ascertain Margaret
     Hamilton's birth date or her age at the time of her death, so I cannot say
     what the relative ages of Margaret and Joseph were, though she must have
     been a younger woman than her two uncles at the time Joseph became a
     member of her household.

36   In a discussion of the lawsuits and public contestations of the picture of
     colonial slavery presented in Mary Prince's narrative after its publication,
     Kathryn Temple points out that "Despite the myths that circulated about
     English liberty in English law, only property owners experienced freedom in
     the sense that the abolitionists imagined it. Slaves, apprentices, most women,
     and all others without property experienced only a restricted version of free-
     dom." *Scandal Nation*, 188.

37   I am grateful to Anna Mae Duane for supplying this formulation of the chap-
     ter's aims in response to my initial draft.

38   James Somerset's inability to testify in his own behalf was not due to dis-
     crimination against him, but rather was a general restriction of the habeas
     corpus judicial process. In 1816, a new statute would permit the prisoner
     to give testimony in a habeas corpus proceeding. Paul D. Halliday, *Habeas
     Corpus: From England to Empire* (Cambridge, MA: Harvard University
     Press, 2010), 246.

## SECTION II

# THE PUBLIC'S CLAIM TO THE PRIVATE CHILD: SLAVERIES DEFINED BY A CHILD'S VALUE

## Anna Mae Duane

In this section, our contributors move from nineteenth-century New York homes to twenty-first-century Chicago schoolyards to analyze how reform movements aimed at children often demand innocence as the price of protection. Innocence, far from an inherent quality of childhood, is constructed and distributed across racial and class lines.[1] Sarah L. H. Gronningsater's chapter charts how antislavery legislation sought to dismantle slavery as an institution by focusing first on children whose vulnerability and need for support rendered them among the least valuable commodities in the New York slave market. Erica Meiners and Micki McElya's chapters both concentrate on moments in which the term *slavery* is evoked by very different constituencies to denote harm done, particularly to children. In all three cases, children's economic standing – intimately tied to their racial and class status – determines their participation in various marketplaces and public institutions is deemed worthy of the term *slavery*. Together, these three chapters demonstrate how often slavery itself is defined and combatted in relation to how particular children are perceived and valued.

Viviana Zelizer has argued that, in the West, children's emotional value increased just as social conditions in the nineteenth century conspired to diminish the commercial value of white middle-class children's labor. As an idealized home became increasingly cordoned off from the marketplace, both women and children were deemed too innocent for the sordid business of capital accumulation. Indeed, they required protection from it.[2] This investment in the home as a wholly private sphere provides the basis for political identity and the grounds for political recognition, particularly in the United States.[3] The ability to maintain private property – and a recognizable family within it – is considered a prerequisite for entering the public sphere in the first place. On the other hand, those who do qualify as part of the "normal" privatized family imagine themselves the product of personal responsibility, acting as if they had little dependence on state resources, but on whose behalf state power will be exerted at any perceived threat. As Mark Rifkin has discussed, "various kinds of populations are denied access to social resources based on their supposed failure to embody an idealized vision of conjugal domesticity."[4]

Children, as the three essayists in this section note, are a vital part of maintaining this ideological balance between private and public – indeed, their ability to be fed, clothed, and cared for solely within the private home is central to the concept of an ideal childhood. Those children whose racial and/or economic status renders them reliant on state resources find themselves in a precarious condition – often turned away from education or other social support, yet rigorously policed and regulated in an attempt to either corral them back into an idealized private setting (as in the white slavery scare) or to remove them from the realm of childhood and privacy altogether by incarcerating them (as Meiners describes in her chapter on the School-to-Prison Pipeline).

Micki McElya's chapter – one of two chapters in this volume focusing on the white slavery scare of the twentieth century – deftly analyzes how a particular investment in white female childhood created a new definition for slavery. In this new formulation, the suffering of enslaved African American men, women, and children was relegated to a lesser form of violation because, the argument ran, no one in that population had access to the sort of innocence embodied in Sarah Eberle's famously controversial statue *The White Slave*. The statue, depicting a prepubescent white girl sold on an auction block, was a scandalously effective work of reform propaganda. Through that statue, childhood became a marker of a harm coded as slavery. Since white girls were allegedly innocent of sexual desire and could only survive in the privatized, sheltered home, far from the sordid male realm of the market, any sexual commerce related to them would qualify as *a priori* slavery.

Remarkably, the very work designed to help allegedly victimized children was considered too dangerous for actual children to engage, and scandalized middle-class parents cancelled subscriptions to a magazine featuring *The White Slave* on its cover. It's a scenario that we've found echoed in our own time as the handwringing over foul language in the 2011 documentary *Bully* kept the film from getting a rating that would allow children – the people most vulnerable to the very abuse being depicted – to be exposed to curse words.[5] Similarly, the continued resistance to sexual education in U.S. schools speaks of a logic that aligns knowledge with a fall from grace.[6] These acts of supposedly protecting imagined childhood innocence deny actual children the agency to make choices in difficult circumstances. Further, such acts of protection demand that, to qualify as the sort of child that deserves our help, the child-victim must be innocent–unaware of what its own victimization would look like.

Erica Meiners' chapter deals with another post-emancipation practice equated with slavery – the mass incarceration of black and brown people in the late twentieth and early twenty-first centuries.[7] She explores how activists in this field also point to a harmed child to highlight the abuses of a system they wish to abolish. Many youth-led protests against what has been deemed the School-to-Prison Pipeline foreground an argument that casts the inmates as children, who would thus be entitled to the sort of protection and care that Americans believe children need and deserve. Here as in McElya's chapter, we find that this sort of child – the innocent child who should be sheltered from the public realm – is defined along racial and class lines. Robin Bernstein's magisterial *Racial Innocence* demonstrated how innocence was denied to American black children by, among other practices, depicting them as impervious to pain. Thus, by depicting young people harmed by the School-to-Prison Pipeline as particularly vulnerable to pain and suffering, twenty-first-century activists seek to enroll black children in the exclusive realm of protected innocence assigned to white children. Yet, as McElya and Meiners demonstrate in this section and David Rosen, Jessica Pliley, Audra Diptee, and others note elsewhere in this volume, access to the privileges of innocent childhood almost invariably requires losing access to rights both real and imagined. In the United States, Meiners points out, "[T]hose identified as 'childlike' do not merit rights or due process and can be subject to a host of violations from the state." Formulated as unable to think or act on his or her own behalf, the innocent child, to survive, must be controlled and "protected" in a private realm that public institutions monitor and regulate.

The first two chapters in this section focus on how post-emancipation antislavery advocates fear that an idealized child would be endangered by free access to adult choices and pressures. In this section's third chapter, Sarah L. H. Gronningsater asks why eighteenth-century reformers in New York found children the most suitable candidates for a freedom from which their parents were still disqualified. As becomes clear in her discussion of the relative ease with which children could occupy the role of slave or pauper on the poor rolls, late eighteenth-century abolition laws defined the imagined privacy of the domestic sphere against the needs of those who were not enclosed by a home with self-sufficient parents. The overlap between the patriarchal home and the slave master's dwelling was openly acknowledged as the emancipation law urged masters to "act the part of the father."[8] As Gronningsater points out, the difference between a father and a master, in the eyes of emancipators, "revolved around the question of profit." To turn a slave into a child, it seems, it was necessary to imagine that child ensconced in a familial relationship. And indeed, once black children were no longer a guarantee of future profit, administrators had additional incentive to move them from the public rolls to the care of their parents.

As Gronningsater notes, the move to free children first is not unique to the northeastern United States. Cuba and Brazil would implement "free womb laws" in the late nineteenth century that were similar in many ways to the laws she describes in New York. As she writes, and as all three authors in this section demonstrate, studying how children functioned as pivot points, alternately defining and combating slavery, "compels us to examine normative definitions of freedom with great subtlety." For children, and for the people who love them, freedom does not involve the move into the public sphere that Habermas, Locke, and other thinkers have marked as the prerequisite for citizenship and its attendant rights. Rather freedom involves the ability to move safely between the public and private, and to claim both protection and agency.

## Notes

1   See Robin Bernstein, *Racial Innocence: Performing American Childhood from Slavery to Civil Rights* (Cambridge, MA: Harvard University Press, 2011).
2   Viviana A. Zelizer, *Pricing the Priceless Child: The Changing Social Value of Children* (Princeton, NJ: Princeton University Press, 1985).
3   Elizabeth Maddock Dillon, *The Gender of Freedom: Fictions of Liberalism and the Literary Public Sphere* (Stanford, CA: Stanford University Press, 2004); Carole Pateman, *The Sexual Contract* (Stanford, CA: Stanford University Press, 1988); Lauren Gail Berlant, *The Queen of America Goes to Washington City: Essays on Sex and Citizenship* (Durham, NC: Duke University Press, 1997).
4   Mark Rifkin, *When Did Indians Become Straight?: Kinship, the History of Sexuality, and Native Sovereignty* (New York: Oxford University Press, 2010), 25.

5   For an argument about protecting children from knowing about threats to childhood evocative of the handwringing over *The White Slave*'s influence on children in the home, see the following commentary from Focus on the Family: http://pluggedin.focusonthefamily.com/harsh-truth-is-weinstein-39-s-bully-movie-too-profane-for-kids/.

6   For one of the many studies disproving this logic, see Pamela K. Kohler, Lisa E. Manhart, and William E. Lafferty. "Abstinence-Only and Comprehensive Sex Education and the Initiation of Sexual Activity and Teen Pregnancy." *Journal of Adolescent Health* 42.4 (2008): 344–51.

7   The scholarship on this subject is voluminous. See, for example, Ruth Wilson Gilmore, *Golden Gulag: Prisons, Surplus, Crisis, and Opposition in Globalizing California*. Vol. 21 (Oakland: University of California Press, 2006); Michelle Alexander, *The New Jim Crow: Mass Incarceration in the Age of Colorblindness* (New York: The New Press, 2012); Dennis Childs, *Slaves of the State: Black Incarceration from the Chain Gang to the Penitentiary* (Minneapolis: University of Minnesota Press, 2015).

8   David Cooper, *A Mite Cast into the Treasury: Or, Observations on Slave-Keeping* (Philadelphia, 1772), 16.

# 3

# The White Slave: American Girlhood, Race, and Memory at the Turn of the Century

## Micki McElya

When American sculptor Abastenia St. Leger Eberle introduced *White Slave* (Figure 3.1) at the 1913 Armory Show in New York City, she sought to ignite a sense of social responsibility in her audiences and to shock them into action in the Progressive-era fight to eradicate prostitution. It would have been one of the first pieces exhibition goers saw as they entered through the gallery dedicated to American Sculpture and Decorative Arts. The *New York Evening Sun* explained that as one entered "the first big room" of the show, "there stood a small piece of sculpture which arrested the attention even of those who rush through exhibits with unseeing eyes. It was called 'The White Slave' and represented a young girl whose hands were in the tight grip of the man who was – obviously – selling her." Remarking again on the statuette's small size – it is not quite twenty inches high – the paper noted that it nonetheless had a big impact. One critic called it "monumental."[1] A scene of auction, the sculpture aimed to make even the most distracted viewer see slavery and child exploitation, rather than inevitability or a "necessary evil," in commercial sex, and to feel the implications of their inaction as complicity. At the same time, Eberle worked to distance her piece and its intent from other representations in a popular culture awash with white slavery narratives, imagery, and titillation. Regardless, the sculptor was accused of having a perverse mind, condemned for allowing "her imagination to go deep in the haunts of vice."[2] Eberle's concerns about reception and the criticism her work received highlight the slippage between arousing outrage and desire, and the place of *seeing* in both.

In the early twentieth century, Americans were gripped – and simultaneously tantalized – by fears of a national and international traffic

FIGURE 3.1. *The White Slave*, Abastenia St. Leger Eberle, 1913. Plaster cast. Courtesy of Wikimedia Commons.

in young, native-born, white girls coerced into prostitution by Eastern European and Asian immigrants. This so-called white slavery scare, which peaked from 1908 to 1915, motivated the creation of extensive activist networks and state and local governmental agencies aimed at protecting white girls and women, abolishing prostitution, and limiting

immigration; it fueled the passage of significant state and federal legislation (most notably the White Slave Traffic Act, or Mann Act of 1910),
and generated an enormous and varied popular culture of white sexual
enslavement that included novels, films, magazines, art, and popularized
social science.[3]

The iconography of the white slavery panic was spectacular, pervasive,
and often the key selling point for these varied texts. One reform study published in 1908 proclaimed on its title page to be an analysis of "Beautiful
white girls sold into ruin ... illustrated with a large number of startling
pictures."[4] Texts such as these and films like *The White Slave* (1907), *To
Save Her Soul* (1909), *Traffic in Souls* (1913), and *Inside of the White
Slave Traffic* (1914) promised titillating imagery of young, white girls and
women forced into prostitution in ways reminiscent of nineteenth-century
abolitionist political culture that had focused increasingly on the sexual
coercion rampant in American slavery, lurid accounts of the "fancy trade,"
and images of light-skinned and brutalized bodies of enslaved African
Americans. Donning the mantle of New Abolitionists, early twentieth-
century opponents of prostitution, capitalist exploitation, and immigration all traded in the iconography of sexual slavery to bolster their claims,
as others capitalized on the panic to sell entertainment in papers, novels,
and movie tickets. As a historical legacy and contemporary threat, slavery
became a primary vehicle for grappling with the eroticism, inequalities,
aspirations, and degradations of modern consumer capitalism.

It was in this complicated nexus of allure, the marketplace, and social
activism that Eberle sculpted *White Slave* for the Armory Show. This
chapter considers Eberle's statuette within the contexts not only of the
wider white slavery panic that surrounded and informed it, but also as a
critical example of the ways in which popular memories of the enslavement of Africans and African Americans in the United States propelled
American modernity and set the contours of subsequent understandings of slavery and abolition to the present day. One of the organizing
questions of this collection – "When and how can we see enslaved children?" – is at play in two important and interconnected ways here. Eberle
hoped that *White Slave* would allow viewers to see prostitution as sexual
slavery and as a particular threat to innocent girlhood in 1913 in order to
inspire activism and generate change. At the same time, considering her
most notorious work anew and the racialized narratives and silences it
embodies allows us to see the centrality of antebellum slavery not only to
the culture and politics of the early twentieth-century United States, but
to our own twenty-first-century historical moment.

This past case of one artist's desire to make people see the sexual enslavement of children as part of wider efforts to abolish prostitution presents an opportunity to examine critically the historical claims and associations between old and new slavery in today's activism and policy making to end human trafficking in which many have termed themselves "The New Abolitionists." Not unlike the turn of the past century, contemporary American political and entertainment cultures dwell on sexual slavery, particularly that of white girls and women, when talking about trafficked people. Popular entertainments are ripe with trafficking narratives and images from television procedurals high and low like *The Wire* and *Law and Order: Special Victims Unit* to the Liam Neeson white slavery film franchise *Taken* (2008), *Taken II* (2012), and *Taken III* (2015). This persistent attention to sexual slavery, including the personification of innocence in the child, blocks from view other forms of coerced labor and trafficked people. At the same time, policy, activism, and advocacy coalescing around the New Abolitionist moniker equates all prostitution and many other forms of commercialized sex with slavery and trafficking. Today's advocacy, activism, and policy initiatives concerning trafficked people and traffickers are caught – and often complicit – in webs of memory, representation, and titillation that have their historical roots not only or even mostly in nineteenth-century slavery and abolition, but in the Progressive-era white slavery panic.[5]

Although *White Slave* was her most overtly political work, Eberle was a successful sculptor who had long been committed to Progressive reform, the settlement house movement, and feminist politics, and usually looked to the working-class girls and women of her Lower East Side and West Village neighborhoods in New York for subject matter and inspiration. Celebrating the quotidian joys and beauty found in often hard lives and sometimes ugly places, Eberle was most well known for her work with playful girl subjects, such as *Girl Skating* (1906), *Bubbles* (1908), and *On Avenue A (Dance of the Ghetto Children)* (1914). These were not the streets of her childhood or her own young experience. Eberle was born in Webster City, Iowa, in 1878, and raised in Ohio. When the United States claimed possession of Puerto Rico among other insular holdings in the Caribbean and Pacific after the Spanish American War in 1898, Eberle's army doctor father was transferred and her family moved to the island. She moved to New York and began taking classes at the Art Students League, making periodic visits to Puerto Rico, which provided some of the subject matter for her early work.[6]

Unlike her exuberant depictions of poor, urban girlhood, *White Slave* turns with great directness to the depravations and potential horrors of poverty in the city.[7] The piece depicts a scene of auction. A young, white, nude girl, head bowed, is clutched, her hands bound behind her back, by a bearded man in a shabby, rumpled suit who gestures with his free hand toward an unseen audience. The drape and drab of his clothing stand in stark contrast to the girl's smooth nakedness. While highlighting Eberle's formal sculptural abilities, the surface distinction between the two figures marks their difference, read as both racial or ethnic and moral as it pits brutality against endangered purity. The girl's pigtails, small breasts, hairless form, and hint of a child's pudge mark her as being on the verge of puberty, cementing the narrative of the piece as a depiction of virginity for sale. While the panderer offers this girl to an imagined audience of potential buyers, it is ultimately the viewer of the sculpture to whom he beckons.[8] With a strategy echoed in later pleading child appeals described by Anna Mae Duane in the introduction to this volume, Eberle sought to appall viewers into action, as she simultaneously suggested their voyeuristic complicity. Arguably, she wanted viewers to recognize their own roles in this problem through inaction as well as in their titillated gazes and voracious consumption of salacious white slavery narratives.

Both the indictment and the call to action are embodied in depicting the act of sale, which makes visible the commodification and sexual enslavement of the girl. Eberle first conceived of *White Slave* in 1909. That same year, one of America's most famous "white slave crusaders," Chicago Assistant State's Attorney Clifford G. Roe, opened his contribution to *War on the White Slave Trade: A Book Designed to Awaken the Sleeping and Protect the Innocent* (1909) with a scene of auction:

"Hear ye! Hear ye! How much will you give for a human being – body and soul?"
  "What is a soul worth?"
  "Nothing," cried the auctioner, "I throw that in with the sale of the body."
  This is the value the White slave traders place upon the soul of a girl when she is auctioned off to the highest bidder for a house of ill repute.[9]

This kind of melodramatic narrative fueled anxieties and national obsessions with white slavery, moving well beyond the local political and reform circles of any one city or community. Congress would soon be debating the White Slave Traffic, or Mann Act, known for its sponsor James R. Mann, Republican congressman from Illinois and chairman of the House Committee on Interstate and Foreign Commerce. Audiences devoured newspaper articles, magazine exposés, reform tracts like Roe's, and films depicting white slavery. Eberle later explained to a journalist that she did not actually model the statue earlier because she worried it would be taken as crass "sensationalism" by critics and audiences.[10] It seems she feared her work being folded into the actual market in white slavery iconography that emerged from and in turn fueled the sex panic.

Representations of early twentieth-century white slavery in popular culture, politics, and policy appealed to popular outrage and drew moral energy from comparisons to the historical enslavement of Africans and African Americans. As his bill was coming to a vote, James R. Mann made a summary argument that Congress had the constitutional authority and human obligation to act "because all of the horrors which have ever been urged, either truthfully or fancifully, against the black slave traffic pale into insignificance as compared with the horrors of the so-called 'white slave traffic.' "[11] Popular reform and entertainment cultures were similarly infused with the association, invariably naming "white slavery" far worse and more pervasive than past American slavery. In his sensational tract of 1910, *Chicago and its Cess-Pools of Infamy*, Samuel Paynter Wilson claimed "the Congo slave traders of the old days appear like Good Samaritans" compared to the white slavers of his city. A year later in its published findings on prostitution there, the Chicago Vice Commission argued that white slavery was "more terrible than any black slavery that ever existed in this or any other country."[12]

Like the white slavery panic itself, these moral and historical associations reached back to earlier feminist and social purity campaigns to raise state age of consent laws from the common standard of ten or twelve years of age. When an activist with the Florence Crittendon Missions argued in 1893 that an "organized traffic in girls is constantly going on, and worse than any race-slavery is the slavery of the brothel into which thousands of our loveliest girls are mercilessly thrust," the central emphasis was on imperiled children and teenage girls likened to children.[13] By criminalizing those seeking sex with girls in and out of the contexts of prostitution, activists not only sought to eradicate sex work – or at least pull the rug from beneath those arguing for legal, regulated prostitution – but to uproot the gendered double standard and enshrine bourgeois notions of a long and protected girlhood across class lines. This was illustrated in leading feminist and suffrage activist Elizabeth Cady Stanton's 1892 argument that low age of consent laws were an "invasion of the personal rights of woman, and the wholesale desecration of childhood."[14] In the contexts of the animating comparison with ante-bellum chattel slavery, however, imperiled childhood and innocence were equated with whiteness, forging associations and a racialized hierarchy of victimization over time that would underpin the white slavery scare of the new century, and, as Karen Sánchez-Eppler and Erica Meiners both argue in this volume, persist.

Slavery and the constraints to human agency and consent it delimited became a key framework for marking the horrors of unfettered indus-trial capitalism and the particular exploitation of children as workers and consumers, as desiring subjects and desired objects. Similar to Progressive anti-prostitution work, campaigns to end child labor in American facto-ries, mills, and mines and to set minimum age and hour regulations drew on analogies to chattel slavery and took on the mantle of abolitionists in popular reform texts such as *Children in Bondage* (1914).[15] In the contexts of prostitution and "white slavery," as Jessica Pliley details in her chapter for this volume (see Chapter 6), the casting of all white sex workers as girls infantilized adult women, rendering them only as victims incapable of agency. The white slavery panic was part of an expansive reimagining of modern American childhood that swelled the ranks of who should be considered a child while keeping the identification clearly demarcated by race.

A passage from a 1912 exposé and fundraising pamphlet for the Chicago Rescue Mission's Women's Shelter, tellingly titled *Chicago's Black Traffic in White Girls*, makes evident the ranging contours of the panic from the presumed youth of its victims to its defining lines of race and nation. Its author, Jean Turner Zimmerman, argued that the white slave trade to which she equated all prostitution was "carried on and exploited by a foaming pack of foreign hellhounds ... the moral and civic degenerates of the French, Italian, Syrian, Russian, Jewish, or Chinese races." Bluntly, she asserted, "Open prostitution – White Slavery, as it exists to-day in Chicago is almost entirely under **foreign** control."[16] On the cusp of the massive immigration restrictions of 1917, 1921, and 1924, this literature consistently repeated the same narrative – immigrant, barely white, or non-white men preyed on native-born, white girls from rural places who were either lured to cities like Chicago, New York, and San Francisco or were newly arrived in them seek-ing employment. Zimmerman's reference to white slavery as a "black traffic" necessarily conjures as it displaces its historical antecedent, the traffic in and enslavement of Africans and African Americans. The scene of auction, for Zimmerman and others, was the crucial location for

highlighting the depravity of contemporary prostitution, its special victimization of children, and for likening it to historical forms of slavery:

the saddest story America has ever known since the black mothers of our
Southland were torn from their black and white babies and with shrieks of agony
and heart strings bleeding and soul rent with blackened horror were sold to death
on the plantations of Louisiana and Mississippi, and I want to tell you who read
this and who think there is little truth in the now much agitated question of White
Slavery in America, that in the dives and dens of our City's underworld I have
heard shrieks and heart cries and groans of agony and remorse that have never
been surpassed at any public slave auction America has ever witnessed.[17]

In centering the exploitation of children and equating commercial sex
to slavery, reformers sought to fire moral outrage and obligations, while
persistently arguing that modern white slavery was more pervasive and
far more horrifying.

These comparisons urged consumers and readers to see the possible
contemporary enslavement and sexual degradation of white girls, and
by association white women, as necessarily and fundamentally worse
than the known history of the enslavement, rape, and sexual coercion
of black children, men, and women. This simultaneously produced two
other racialized elisions in the frameworks of prostitution reform in the
early twentieth century. First, this hierarchy of victimization erased all
non-white people from the category of the endangered or those in need of
protection and rescue, suggesting that their presence among the ranks of
sex workers was to be expected and their supposed fall or sexual depravity their own racial destiny. On the other side of this coin, to call white
prostitutes the victims of "slavers" suggested that no white person would
ever willingly become a prostitute or turn to periodic sex work, and that
those who did were acting against their will and their natures.[18] This was
compounded by likening all white prostitutes, "white slaves," to young
dependents in need of protection and incapable of consent.

Pinned between the controlling images of black women's sexual devi-
ance and lasciviousness and white female purity and danger, African
American Progressives, clubwomen, and church leaders had to negotiate the dominant effects of the white slavery narrative as they sought to
address prostitution within black communities. They struggled to make
visible black female endangerment, on one hand, while confronting the
disproportionate policing of black women's sex work, on the other. This
ran headlong into the overriding sense within a politics of respectability
and racial uplift that black women's visible prostitution was itself det-
rimental to racial progress and social justice, meaning the women often

slipped from the status of victim to themselves being a community threat. As historian Cynthia M. Blair argues in her study of black women's sex work in early twentieth-century Chicago, this led black reformers to their own narrow focus on imperiled girl children as figures of unquestioned innocence and deserving of protection. The move to characterize all white sex workers as unable to consent to their labors due to mutually constituted enslavement and childlikeness was similarly employed within black reform politics, but to very different aims. At the same time, black activists flipped the source of danger within the dominant white slavery narrative to focus on white men as predators and purchasers of sex, rather than on traffickers.[19]

Self-styled white slavery abolitionists of the early twentieth century were not the first to focus disproportionately on the relative horror of the enslavement – and its implied sexual abuse – of white or white-looking girls and women. By the 1850s, the trope of the sexually endangered "white slave" girl was prevalent in abolitionist activism and iconographies.[20] Most famous, perhaps, and critical to historicizing Eberle's *White Slave*, was Hiram Powers' sculpture *The Greek Slave* (1844) (Figure 3.2), which toured the United States, including several Southern cities, in the 1840s and 1850s. Although the stated context of the piece was the Turkish–Greek wars of the 1820s, viewers in the United States and Europe often took *The Greek Slave* as a tragic and compellingly stoic representation of the brutality of American slavery – horrors crystallized in the auction and impending sexual violation of a woman who, in Henry James' words, was of "sugar-white alabaster."[21] The British magazine *Punch* published an engraving depicting a black woman in the same pose titled "The Virginia Slave, Intended as a Companion to Powers' *Greek Slave*" to draw the connection explicitly in 1851.[22] One American reviewer noted the distinct possibility that *The Greek Slave* could depict the sale of a light-skinned woman for concubinage in the slave markets of New Orleans, commenting in 1847, "Everyday does our own sister city of New Orleans witness similar exposures, with a similar purpose. Let no one keep down the natural promptings of his indignation by the notion of wooly heads and black skins."[23]

Just as Eberle's *White Slave* implicates viewers in the act of purchase and as witness-participants in a slave auction, Powers' work enacted a similar effect. This is illustrated in an 1857 engraving depicting the exhibit of *The Greek Slave* at the Dusseldorf Gallery in New York City (Figure 3.3). Highlighting the power of looking or inspection in the auction of people as well as art, the engraving shows compositional similarity

FIGURE 3.2. *The Greek Slave*, Hiram Powers, 1844.
Courtesy of the Library of Congress.

with British illustrator George Cruikshank's popular scene from Harriet
Beecher Stowe's abolitionist novel *Uncle Tom's Cabin* (1852) titled
"Emmeline About to Be Sold to the Highest Bidder." Notably, the Stowe
scene details the New Orleans sale of a very light-skinned girl – not the
young adult woman of Powers' sculpture – for the express purpose of

FIGURE 3.3. Hiram Powers' *The Greek Slave* at Dusseldorf Gallery in New York City, *Cosmopolitan Art Journal*, 1858.
Courtesy of the Library of Congress.

sex as her mother is forced to watch, devastated for her daughter. Before the auction, Stowe describes the mother's pain: "She knows that to-morrow any man, however vile and brutal, however godless and merciless, if he only has money to pay for her, may become owner of her daughter, body and soul ... she holds her daughter in her arms and wishes that she were not handsome and attractive."[24] The 1857 engraving suggests a circle of associations completed, as Cruikshank likely modeled his Emmeline, standing on a block before three large statues of female figures, after Powers' *The Greek Slave*.[25] Exhibited in galleries and detailed in the press, the statue was simultaneously folded into New York's urban nightlife of commercial sex. Performances of *The Greek Slave* as a pornographic tableau – a precursor to the striptease or burlesque – were popular in the 1840s and 1850s.[26]

The Progressive-era white slavery panic and Eberle's *White Slave* drew on this visual culture, history, and abolitionist rhetoric to make claims about imperiled girls and their childhoods while participating in larger discourses of rewriting and re-remembering slavery in the early twentieth century. Dominant representations downplayed slavery's horrors or ejected it altogether from political narratives and popular memories for the sake of white supremacist nationalism, regional reconciliation, and the continued maintenance of Southern apartheid and segregation around the country. American modernity was suffused with warped histories of slavery and the antebellum South, which were largely white supremacist fantasies of old plantation grandeur and contented, faithful slaves. New forms of consumer advertising, prepared foods, and product branding consistently pulled from this iconography of faithful slavery to sell ease, taste, and status. Store shelves, periodicals, and public broadsides were full of enslaved figures like Aunt Jemima selling everything from pancake mix, flour, rice, cereal, and cleaning supplies to tobacco.[27]

As images of faithful slavery became more prominent in the consumer marketplace, the realities of enslavement and the emancipationist function of the Civil War were pushed out of the dominant culture, replaced by images of Union and Confederate troops coming together in common valor to reunite the nation, whether that be in the context of imperial wars overseas or remembrances of battles past.[28] Fitz W. Guerin, himself a decorated Union Civil War veteran, produced the photo tableau *Cuba Libre* (1898) (Figure 3.4) promoting the entwined notions of America's obligation and national gains from war with Spain, including the unified military endeavor of former Union and Confederate foe. Critically, both are illustrated through the act of protecting and liberating a small, enslaved white girl. The image depicts a Union and Confederate officer clasping hands, as if they are in the act of shaking hands. Between them rises a diminutive, white, blond girl wearing a white, classically draped garment and a crown labeled "Cuba." Her left hand rests atop the men's

FIGURE 3.4. *Cuba Libre*, F. W. Guerin, ca. 1898.
Courtesy of the Library of Congress.

while the other is held aloft in a loose fist displaying the broken chain
of "her" colonial "enslavement" to Spain that hangs from both wrists.
The tableau is framed by thick bunting of stars and stripes, curtain-like
against a studio background of ocean waves, suggestive of the overseas
action of the war and subsequent empire building. The staged scene not
only makes stark the argument for patriotic white men's reconciliation

and national reunification, but relocates the national and embodied scene of slavery in the white child representing Cuba, marking this a clear iteration of the modern white slave narrative. Union and Confederate veterans would famously clasp hands several times over in the early 1910s as Civil War fiftieth anniversary events and reunions celebrated white nationalism and regional reconciliation by minimizing black freedom struggles and slavery as the cause for war and self-proclaimed new abolitionists pushed non-white girls and women from the ranks of the potentially endangered and crafted new versions of slavery in which white people were the primary victims. The Gettysburg 50th Anniversary Blue-Gray Reunion of 1913 occurred just a few months after Eberle exhibited *White Slave* in New York and was depicted in newsreels shown in movie houses around the country, many of which would be playing one of the most popular feature films of the year, *Traffic in Souls*, in December.

Eberle had returned to the idea of the *White Slave* in early 1913 when she was invited to submit work to the Armory Show, completing the piece in the four weeks between her invitation and the opening. America now had its first Southern president since the Civil War, who, elected on a platform of "New Freedom," would set quickly about formalizing segregation in federal workplaces as well as housing, public accommodations, and entertainments in DC. The white slavery scare continued but was on the wane, the Mann Act was now law, and some activists were outlining more radical positions citing economic exploitation and gender oppression as the underlying causes of prostitution.

One such activist was Jane Addams, a leader of the settlement house movement and a prominent activist for child welfare, woman suffrage, and economic justice. Eberle often cited Addams as a major influence on her politics and her work. Just months after the Armory Show's opening, *The Survey*, a popular reform journal, used *White Slave* as its cover illustration for an issue devoted to the problem – an editorial choice that would spark great controversy and accusations of the very sensationalism that Eberle had feared. The accompanying article on *White Slave* and Eberle's body of work generally noted that "Jane Addams' books have, more than anything else, [the artist] says, helped to clarify and mould her vision of the constructive part the sculptor may play in social readjustment."[29] This was most likely a reference to Addams' book on abolishing white slavery and prostitution generally, *A New Conscience and an Ancient Evil*, published in 1912. The book opens with a discussion of popular analogies between white slavery and the enslavement of African Americans, both to caution against hyperbole and to focus on the abolitionist movement of the nineteenth century, arguing a link between contemporary prostitution abolitionists and their antislavery predecessors. Crucial to understanding Eberle's decision to complete *White Slave* for the Armory Show, Addams also made a call for artists to work to generate a "new conscience" among the American people – to make them *see*.[30] Addams explained, there are:

great artists [of] every age [who] enter into a long struggle with existing social conditions, until after many years they change the outlook upon life for at least a handful of their contemporaries. Their readers find themselves no longer mere bewildered spectators of a given social wrong, but have become conscious of their own hypocrisy in regard to it, and they realize that a veritable horror, simply because it was hidden, had come to seem to them inevitable and almost normal.[31]

It is likely that Addams' call combined with the opportunity for publicity presented by the Armory Show invitation led Eberle back to her project of sculpting the *White Slave*. Arguably she sought to shake her audience from its torpor, from the notion that prostitution was "normal" and "inevitable" or that white slavery was political farce or mere sensation. Given the number of positive and positively moved responses to the work, in some ways she succeeded. One Armory Show attendee reported, "I was passing through that room of the exhibit when suddenly I faced it – I could not go on. I had vaguely realized that this horrible thing was in the world, but it had never touched *me*. I sat there for perhaps an hour, thinking – and thinking."[32]

Eberle's statuette gained wider notice, celebration, and notoriety when it was featured on the May 3, 1913, cover of *The Survey* and circulated nationally. The cover image prompted controversy, cancelled subscriptions, and congratulations that played out over three months of letters from readers and editorial responses. All grappled with the problems, pleasures, and social power of showing and seeing sexual slavery and the exploitation of children. Some lauded the cover's visual power to make real the threat and need for social action in ways mere words could not. Ray F. Carter, educational director of the First Congregational Church of Oakland, California, echoed the unnamed visitor to the Armory Show. "That picture was like a blow from a clenched fist at the end of a strong arm. I sat looking at it for quite half an hour, and never before did the horror of the traffic it represents so sink in my soul." He concluded, "Most of our sermons, talks to boys and girls, lectures to women's clubs, etc., lack 'punch' – no one's feelings are hurt. That picture has more punch in it than anything ever written."[33] Rabbi Rudolph I. Coffee, who identified himself as also a member of the Pittsburgh (PA) Morals Commission, concurred, thanking the magazine and calling Eberle's cover a "finished sermon on the subject" of white slavery, while Howard A. Kelly of Baltimore, Maryland, wrote, "This picture of a low human brute hawking into slavery a poor little immature girl will, I believe, be yet more effective in rousing the sluggish consciences of our American people." He closed his letter asking if he could borrow the original image "to make a lantern slide to use in my public talks on vice."[34] Many asked for photographs or plaster reproductions of the work to employ in their own activism and conscience-firing exhibits. Noting the paucity of "sociological art" available in the West, Albert E. Selcer, vicar of Omaha, Nebraska's St. Stephen's Church, requested copies of the statuette. "I cannot, with the spoken word – do the work as effectively as might be done were it possible to illustrate," he explained, as Eberle's composition does, "the awfulness of the white slave traffic." He noted that the cover image and Eberle's work made him see the terrible depths of the problem in a way his own work with endangered urban youth had not. "The reproduction on the cover page brought it home to me very forcibly – in such a way as it has never been brought home to me – and I have a record of four year's work in the juvenile court and slums of Chicago."[35] While so many noted their religious, medical, or institutional credentials, Julia G. Babcock of Bakersfield, California, wrote, "Permit me, as a mother of a son and daughter and as one who is interested in the welfare of other people's sons and daughters, to thank you" for the cover.[36] These and other men and women were moved by the image, or the controversy it subsequently generated, to commend the magazine for facilitating the *White Slave's* wider circulation, which they in turn hoped to expand.

Yet many charged that the cover image itself represented not only sensationalism and poor judgment, even if in the aim of a worthy cause, but posed a danger to the girls and boys who might come in contact with it, particularly within the privacy of their homes. One married couple from New York, identifying themselves as "friends of *The Survey*" nonetheless said the cover was "sensational" and "ill-advised" and was especially problematic for a periodical "which finds its way into private houses where decency and modesty are inculcated." Given the importance of the issue, particularly to the social work professionals who read *The Survey*, they concluded that placing the image "*inside* of its covers is excusable, but its *outside*, open to the observation of all, young and old, should to our minds be severely censured."[37] The twinned concerns that refined domesticity, or bourgeois private spheres removed from urban worlds of poverty, diversity, and vice exhibited in white slavery narratives and reform literatures, would be invaded by that world via reform work, and would imperil the morals and sensibilities of the youth within those spaces was a common chord across outraged letters and public subscription cancellations. "With several boys in my family, the only way I could lay the issue on my library table was *after* tearing off the cover, which is certainly glaringly offensive," complained William Hager of Lancaster, Pennsylvania. A Morristown, New Jersey, man similarly feared for the moral health of his sons should they confront such an image, cancelling his subscription because he was "altogether unwilling to expose myself to the risk of having any such picture ... [again] sent into my home at the risk of its being seen by my four sons," three of whom "are under age."[38] It is striking how often the imperiled child in this situation was understood to be a boy, his immature sexual health at risk and his desire potentially warped. But not all letter writers feared only for their sons. In similarly declaring her subscription cancellation, Estelle R. McVeckar of Mount Vernon, New York, was "grieved," but said she could not "run the risk of having another cover similar to that by Miss Eberle come into our home circle." She declared her "hearty sympathy" with the cause Eberle "so eloquently depicts," but said she could not "permit the sanctity of my home to be invaded by another of that sort." McVeckar described her "young daughters" staring at the cover and Eberle's work "with wonder and amazement on their faces," and expressed her disgust at the image's wide circulation. "I felt badly enough when it came into my home," McVeckar lamented, "but when I saw it lying on the newsstand I felt worse."[39]

After the first round of letters and cancellations at the end of May, *The Survey*'s editors published a long response and justification for their cover decision that relied on various levels of comparison to antebellum slavery and nineteenth-century abolitionism. The situation was dire, they explained, and the magazine had "this spring added fire and conviction to the abolition movement against prostitution – that 'twin of slavery, as old and outrageous as slavery itself and even more persistent,' to use Miss Addams' phrase." Jane Addams had been a bit more careful in her comparisons, although as a member of the magazine's editorial board she likely approved this use of her study in arguments that the cover was, above all, "a challenge to public conscience searching." Finally, the editors made a direct comparison to the controversies of abolition movements past, citing the antebellum work and abolitionist strategies of Henry Ward Beecher who had staged mock slave auctions in his Brooklyn

FIGURE 3.5. *The Haymarket, Sixth Avenue*, John Sloan, 1907. Oil on canvas, 26 1/8 x 34 13/16 in. Brooklyn Museum, Gift of Mrs. Harry Payne Whitney. Courtesy of the Brooklyn Museum.

church.[40] "New times bring new needs," the response concluded. "Miss Eberle has modeled the auction block of a new slavery."[41]

Ultimately, however, the "New Conscience" Addams, Eberle, *The Survey*, and other Progressives sought concerning prostitution did not emerge in the ways that they hoped. Reformers succeeded in closing most red-light districts in the early twentieth century and criminalizing prostitution, but they did not abolish sex work, organized or otherwise. By the time Eberle showed *White Slave*, a pronounced backlash against the moralizing of anti-prostitution activists was evident, some of which came from other prominent New York artists. Although distinct in a number of ways, Eberle's work is most often compared to that of the Ashcan circle, a group of left-leaning painters and illustrators, who also depicted everyday life and the working communities of the city's Lower East Side in the early twentieth century. Scenes of urban prostitution and female sex workers appear in several Ashcan works and illustrations for *The Masses*, but with a very different political valence from Eberle's *White Slave*.[42] John Sloan's *The Haymarket* (1907) (Figure 3.5) depicts three women entering a popular New York concert hall that was a well-known venue for prostitution. Their lavish clothes, plumed hats, and very presence at the club encode the women as prostitutes or potential prostitutes, yet nothing about them suggests coercion or degradation. This is not a damning portrayal of urban vice, an attempt to encourage prostitution's prohibition, or a comparison to slavery. The only suggestion of approbation comes with the pairing of a mother and daughter in the lower left-hand corner of the painting. As the daughter's eyes follow the women into the well-lit door of the Haymarket, apparently enthralled, the comparably drab and dark mother figure hauling laundry looks on with concern. The white dress and hat of the young girl mimics the color of the prostitutes' attire, suggesting not only a potentially linked fate, but also a shared desire.

This is not the first time we have seen a young girl encountering overtly eroticized female bodies and scenes of sexual commerce. Recall the outraged former *Survey* subscriber's "young daughters" staring at Eberle's *White Slave* "with wonder and amazement on their faces," or the young female figure in the opposite bottom corner of the engraving of Powers' *The Greek Slave* on display in New York from 1857. The similarity in composition of these two, watchful girls is striking. They speak to wider concerns about commerce, sexuality, scopic knowledge, and endangered girlhood and young women's potential resistance to protection.

We write for this collection at the turn of another century – in the midst of the Civil War sesquicentennial and a popular culture similarly brimming with narratives and images of white sexual slavery and trafficking – to consider the crisis of modern slavery, the place of children within it, and the conditions of neoliberal global capitalism and coerced labor and exploitation. The similarities do not end here, but include activists' assumption of the New Abolitionist moniker and appeals to the moral authority of historical comparisons to the nineteenth century. This is evidenced by another example from the intersection of activist and arts communities in a December 2008 panel discussion, titled "Sex Trafficking and the New Abolitionists," hosted by the Brooklyn Museum of Art's Elizabeth A. Sackler Center for Feminist Art. In seeking to impress the audience with the gravity of the situation, Gloria Steinem argued, "At this stage in history, there are more enslaved people than there were in the 1800s." Later in the discussion, Steinem got to the heart of her argument and call to activism through more historical analogy, arguing that sex trafficking – her label for all prostitution in all locations – "is, indeed, a new form of slavery," and a "reality of life that is hidden in plain sight."⁴³ Like Eberle, Addams, and so many before them, today's New Abolitionists make comparisons to chattel slavery to mark horrifying exploitation and injustice, and to ignite moral urgency, to compel others to see the problem as they do. But historical comparison to the early twentieth-century white slavery panic is far more apt, and points to the potential dangers and elisions inherent to these uses of the past to frame the problems and abuses of the present.

### Notes

1   "A Woman Sculptor Who Is 'Different,'" *New York Evening Sun* (May 28, 1913): 14. On the layout of the Armory Show, see *The Armory Show at 100: Modernism and Revolution*, Marilyn Kushner and Kimberly Orcutt, eds. (New York: New York Historical Society, 2013), 35.

2   RI Newport letter to *The Survey* vol. 30, May 31, 1913, quoted in Gretchen Soderlund, *Sex Trafficking, Scandal, and the Transformation of Journalism, 1885–1917* (Chicago: University of Chicago Press, 2013): 167.

3   For general studies on the white slavery panic and prostitution in the early twentieth century, see: Elizabeth Alice Clement, *Love for Sale: Courting, Treating, and Prostitution in New York City, 1900–1945* (Chapel Hill: University of North Carolina Press, 2006); Christopher Diffee, "Sex and the City: The White Slavery Scare and Social Governance in the Progressive Era," *American Quarterly* 57.2 (June 2005): 411–37; Brian Donovan, *White Slave Crusades: Race, Gender, and Anti-vice Activism, 1887–1917* (Chicago: University of Illinois Press, 2006); Timothy Gilfoyle, *City of Eros: New York City, Prostitution, and the Commercialization of Sex, 1790–1920* (New York: Norton, 1992); Frederick K. Grittner, *White Slavery: Myth, Ideology, and American Law* (New York: Garland Publishing, Inc., 1990); Laura Hapke, *Girls Who Went Wrong: Prostitutes in American Fiction, 1885–1917* (Bowling Green, OH: Bowling Green University Press, 1989); Ruth Rosen, *The Lost Sisterhood: Prostitution in America, 1900–1918* (Baltimore, MD: Johns Hopkins University Press, 1982); Margit Stange, *Personal Property: Wives, White Slaves, and the Market in Women* (Baltimore, MD: Johns Hopkins University Press, 1998).

4   John D'Emilio and Estelle Freedman, *Intimate Matters: A History of Sexuality in America* (New York: Harper and Row, 1988).

5   On associations with slavery, abolition, and Progressive-era histories, see: Elizabeth Bernstein, "The Sexual Politics of the 'New Abolitionism,'" *differences* 18.3 (2007): 129–51; Jo Doezema, *Sex Slaves and Discourse Masters: The Construction of Trafficking* (New York: Zed Books, 2010); Joel Forbes Quirk, "The Anti-slavery Project: Linking the Historical and the Contemporary," *Human Rights Quarterly* 28.3 (August 2006): 565–98; Gretchen Soderlund, "Running from the Rescuers: New U.S. Crusades Against Sex Trafficking and the Rhetoric of Abolition," *NWSA Journal* 17.3 (Fall 2005): 64–87.

6   For general studies of Abastenia St. Leger Eberle and her work, see: Alexis
    L. Boylan, "'The Spectacle of a Merely Charming Girl': Abastenia St. Leger
    Eberle's *Girl Skating*," Tolles, ed., *Perspectives on American Sculpture before
    1925* (New Haven, CT: Yale University Press, 2003), 116–29; Melissa
    Dabakis, *Visualizing Labor in American Sculpture: Monuments, Manliness,
    and the Work Ethic, 1880–1935* (New York: Cambridge University Press,
    1999), 127–73; Louise R. Noun, *Abastenia St. Leger Eberle Sculptor (1878–
    1942)* Exh. Cat. Des Moines Art Center, Des Moines, Iowa, 1980.

7   On *White Slave* explicitly, see: Susan P. Casteras, "Abastenia St. Leger
    Eberle's *White Slave*," *Women's Art Journal* 7 (Spring/Summer 1986):
    32–7; Christina Merriman, "New Bottles for New Wine: The Work of
    Abastenia St. Leger Eberle," *The Survey* 30 (May 3, 1913): 196–9; Charles
    Musser, "1913: A Feminist Moment in the Arts," in *The Armory Show at
    100: Modernism and Revolution*, Marilyn Kushner and Kimberly Orcutt,
    eds. (New York: New York Historical Society, 2013), 178.

8   Dabakis, *Visualizing Labor in American Sculpture*, 156–7.

9   Clifford G. Roe, "The Auctioneer of Souls," in Ernest A. Bell, ed., *War on the
    White Slave Trade: A Book Designed to Awaken the Sleeping and Protect the
    Innocent* (Chicago: The Charles C. Thompson Co., 1909), 163.

10  Merriman, "New Bottles for New Wine," 198.

11  James Mann, January 26, 1910, quoted in Grittner, *White Slavery*, 95.

12  Quoted in ibid., 70, 74.

13  Quoted in ibid., 46. On white slavery, social purity, and age of consent
    laws, see Mary E. Odem, *Delinquent Daughters: Protecting and Policing
    Adolescent Female Sexuality in the United States, 1885–1920* (Chapel
    Hill: University of North Carolina Press, 1995), chapter 1.

14  Quoted in ibid., 16.

15  Steven Mintz, *Huck's Raft: A History of American Childhood* (Cambridge,
    MA: Belknap Press, 2004), 180.

16  Jean Turner Zimmerman, MD, *Chicago's Black Traffic in White Girls*
    (1912), 10. Emphasis in original. [www.gutenberg.org/files/31615/31615-
    h/31615-h.htm]

17  Ibid., 49.

18  Grittner argues that the comparison was primarily intended to shock people,
    but it seems clear that reformers and their contemporaries were more sincere
    in their belief that white slavery was far more terrible.

19  Cynthia M. Blair, *I've Got to Make My Livin': Black Women's Sex Work
    in Turn-of-the-Century Chicago* (Chicago: University of Chicago Press,
    2010), 204–11. On African American women's Progressive-era reform,
    prostitution, and "white slavery" generally, see also: P. Gabrielle Foreman,
    "'Reading Aright': White Slavery, Black Referents, and the Strategy of
    Histotextuality in *Iola Leroy*," *Yale Journal of Criticism* 10.2 (1997): 327–
    54; Kali N. Gross, *Colored Amazons: Crime, Violence, and Black Women
    in the City of Brotherly Love, 1880–1910* (Durham, NC: Duke University
    Press, 2006), 74–6; and Deborah Gray White, *Too Heavy a Load: Black
    Women in Defense of Themselves, 1894–1994* (New York: W.W. Norton &
    Company, 1999).

20 Richard Wightman Fox, "Performing Emancipation," in Steven Mintz and John Stauffer, eds., *The Problem of Evil: Slavery, Freedom, and the Ambiguities of American Reform* (Amherst: University of Massachusetts Press, 2007), 289–311; Walter Johnson, "The Slave Trader, the White Slave, and the Politics of Racial Determination in the 1850s," *JAH* 87.1 (June 2000): 13–38; Mary Niall Mitchell, "'Rosebloom and Pure White,' Or So It Seemed," *American Quarterly* 54.3 (September 2002): 369–410; and Mary Niall Mitchell, "The Real Ida May: A Fugitive Tale in the Archives," *The Massachusetts Historical Review* 15 (2013): 54–88.

21 Henry James quoted in Joy S. Kasson, *Marble Queens and Captives: Women in 19th Century American Sculpture* (New Haven, CT: Yale University Press, 1990), 48. On *The Greek Slave* generally, see ibid., chapters 3 and 4, and Kirk Savage, *Standing Soldiers, Kneeling Slaves: Race, War, and Monument in 19th Century America* (Princeton, NJ: Princeton University Press, 1997), 28–31.

22 Kasson, *Marble Queens and Captives*, 67.

23 Savage, *Standing Soldiers, Kneeling Slaves*, 28.

24 Harriet Beecher Stowe, *Uncle Tom's Cabin; or, Life Among the Lowly* (New York: Penguin Classics, 1986, orig. 1852), 473.

25 Maurie D. McInnis argues this similarity, and notes that Powers' work was exhibited in London, where Cruikshank lived the year before he made his illustrations, in her *Slaves Waiting for Sale: Abolitionist Art and the American Slave Trade* (Chicago: University of Chicago Press, 2011), 196–7.

26 Gilroye, 127.

27 Kenneth Goings, *Mammy and Uncle Mose: Black Collectibles and American Stereotyping* (Bloomington: Indiana University Press, 1994); M. M. Manring, *Slave in a Box: The Strange Career of Aunt Jemima* (Charlottesville: University Press of Virginia, 1998); Micki McElya, *Clinging to Mammy: The Faithful Slave in Twentieth-Century America* (Cambridge, MA: Harvard University Press, 2007).

28 David W. Blight, *Race and Reunion: The Civil War in American Memory* (Cambridge, MA: Harvard University Press, 2001): esp. chapters 1 and 10; Nina Silber, *The Romance of Reunion: Northerners and the South, 1865–1900* (Chapel Hill: University of North Carolina Press, 1993), 178–85.

29 Merriman, "New Bottles for New Wine," 197.

30 Casteras, 35.

31 Jane Addams, *A New Conscience and an Ancient Evil* (New York: The Macmillan Company, 1912), 12–13.

32 Merriman, "New Bottles for New Wine," 198. This woman's experience challenges Melissa Dabakis's argument that *White Slave* assumes a specifically male gaze. It appears that Dabakis misidentifies the quoted speaker as a man.

33 Ray F. Carter, letter to the editor, *The Survey* 30 (July 12, 1913): 507–8.

34 Rudolph I. Coffee and Howard A. Kelley, letters to the editor, *The Survey* 30 (May 31, 1913): 312.

35 Albert E. Selcer, letter to the editor, *The Survey* 30 (July 12, 1913): 508.

36 Ibid.

37    L. E. Opdycke and Edith Opdycke, letter to the editor, *The Survey* 30 (May 31, 2013): 312.

38    Ibid., 311–12.

39    Estelle R. McVeckar, letter to the editor, *The Survey* 30 (June 14, 2013): 382.

40    For analysis of Beecher's "slave auctions," including the central place of light-skinned girls and women within them, see: Jason Stupp, "Slavery and the Theater of History: Ritual Performance on the Auction Block," *Theatre Journal* 63.1 (March 2011): 72–80.

41    *The Survey* 30 (May 31, 2013): 313–14.

42    Rachel Schreiber, "Before Their Makers and Their Judges: Prostitutes and White Slaves in the Political Cartoons of 'The Masses' (New York 1911–1917)," *Feminist Studies* 35.1 (Spring 2009): 161–93; Rebecca Zurier, *Art for the Masses: A Radical Magazine and Its Graphics, 1911–1917* (Philadelphia. PA: Temple University Press, 1988).

43    Taina Bien-Aime, Rachel Lloyd, Elizabeth A. Sackler, and Gloria Steinem, "Sex Trafficking and the New Abolitionists," December 27, 2008 [www .brooklynmuseum.org/eascfa/video/videos/sex-trafficking-and-the-new-abolitionists]. For a more recent example, see the 2013 portrait exhibit and organization work of New York's New Abolitionists [www .nynewabolitionists.com].

# 4

# Child's Play: Schools, Not Jails

## Erica Meiners

*Ending the School-to-Prison Pipeline*, a December 2012 congressional hearing, featured twenty-year-old Edward Ward, a volunteer member of Blocks Together, a community organization that works to support residents of the near west side of Chicago to change their community. At the hearing, Ward spoke about his experience at Orr High School. For the Black and Brown[1] students at the school, Ward testified, Orr was "like we stepped into prison," and "from the moment we stepped through the doors in the morning, we were faced with metal detectors, x-ray machines, and uniformed security." Orr security officers "spoke to us as if we were animals," and "being in detention was like being in solitary confinement." Like many non-restrictive enrollment schools in the Chicago Public School system, Orr had:

A police processing center so police could book students then and there. The officers don't get any special training to be in the school so they don't treat us like we are misbehaving; they treat us like we are committing crimes.[2]

Now an undergraduate student at a Chicago University, Ward highlighted during his testimony how his peers are treated within a prison-like institution: disrespected, harassed, threatened, profiled, and preemptively detained.

Despite being enrolled in a high school, across the United States young organizers like Edward Ward fight to be viewed as students and children/youth, not as criminals or adults. Ward's 2012 demand that his peers access the status (and benefits) of childhood triggers concepts with deep attachments to chattel slavery. Ward seeks the status of youth/ child (or at least a non-adult) hopeful this status will bring associations with innocence and some form of protection from our prison nation. Yet childhood, still not available to all, comes with integral linkages to a racialized and unequal nation: culpability, incompetence, lack of reason. Chattel slavery constructed Black people as without sentience and reason, yet also as childlike, and in need of surveillance and management. As the United States continues to struggle to view people of color, particularly African Americans, as fully human, this demand for a (Black) childhood potentially reinforces, rather than dismantles, a wider and foundational racialized carceral state.

The congressional hearing occurred after more than a decade of local and national convenings and mobilizations on the "school-to-prison pipeline" (STPP), a term coined to describe analysis and organizing aimed at interrupting the movement of youth of color from schools and neighborhoods into the criminal justice system.[3] While the public education system in the United States has historically tracked non-White communities toward school push out, non-living-wage work, participation in a permanent war economy, and/or incarceration, the development of the world's largest prison nation within the United States over the past three decades has strengthened policy, practice, and ideological linkages between schools and prisons.[4] With police enmeshed in urban high-poverty schools, punishments for students of color often translate into a punch card on the road to prison. Once young people are removed from school and marked by law enforcement agencies and school disciplinary personnel as disruptive, their relationships to learning and schools are further corroded, steering them toward school push out, non-legal employment, and potential incarceration.

This hearing also signified a growing recognition by select key political stakeholders that the criminalizing of young people, particularly in schools, could not be ignored. In the past decade, a wealth of studies on incarceration and confinement has critically historicized and analyzed how one of the world's largest democracies has produced the highest rate of imprisonment and the largest number of people confined in prisons, jails, and detention centers. Approximately 2.3 million people are incarcerated in the United States, or one in every 99.1 adults. Since the 1980s and the war on drugs, "three strikes" laws, mandatory minimum sentencing, and a plethora of other regulations and associated legal maneuvering have confined more people – disproportionately people of color and/or poor people – for longer sentences than any other period in American history. The terms *mass incarceration, prison nation, carceral state,* or *new Jim Crow* (the last popularized by Michelle Alexander's 2010 book *The*

*New Jim Crow*[5]) aim to capture the staggering number of people locked behind bars and the naturalization and the racialization of punishment and policing.[6]

Community-based groups, networks, and institutions – Chicago's Blocks Together organization, the American Civil Liberties Union, and multiple colleges and universities – have focused on organizing, convened high-profile meetings, developed institutes, and created campaigns around the intersections of education, juvenile justice, and our racialized prison nation. Frequently called Schools, Not Jails or Educate, Not Incarcerate, these organizing and research campaigns mobilize youth and communities to challenge school discipline policies and the allocation of resources toward policing and incarceration, instead of education.[7] Often youth-led, campaigns frequently center on narratives such as Ward's, which highlight how Black and Brown *male* youth are viewed as criminals, sanctioned as adults rather than children or youth, and targeted for excessive and *prison-like* school disciplinary practices that function as pathways to prison.[8]

A March 2013 rally in Detroit, led and attended by many youth of color, featured signs such as *Books Not Bars* and *End the New Jim Crow/ End the School to Prison Pipeline*.[9] In March 2014, high school students from NC HEAT, a local organization challenging the county's "school-to-prison pipeline," wore orange prison jumpsuits to a meeting of North Carolina's Wake County School Board to protest disproportionately high suspension and expulsion rates for Black students. In May 2014, after a rally at the Paderewski Elementary School, closed in 2013 as a part of a wave of fifty public school closures in Chicago, young people rallied and marched to the Cook County Juvenile Detention Center. Organized by a collective of Chicago's youth-led groups, many of the rally's speakers directly connected prisons to education, including Malcolm London from the Black Youth Project: "When you close a school and open a prison, a lot of people who don't look like me make a lot of money."[10]

Invoking prisons tethers work against the *school to prison pipeline* to wider racial justice struggles, including criminal justice reforms. Movements against the STPP also create ongoing and powerful associations with antebellum slavery. Prison is an explicitly racialized institution; as theorist Frank Wilderson writes, "whoever says 'prison' says Black."[11] Further, incarceration is, as Kanye West's 2013 song "New Slaves" calls out, linked to slavery.[12] Our current prison nation is a plank in what historian Saidiya Hartman has termed the "afterlife of slavery," including "skewed life chances, limited access to health and education, premature death, incarceration, and impoverishment."[13] While Hartman and others argue that the structures or the conditions of our current prison nation are not the same as chattel slavery, work against twenty-first-century incarceration and state punishment struggles to negotiate this "afterlife" of enslavement.

Images and representations throughout the STPP movement demonstrate how *prison and slavery-like* conditions harm children. Signs at rallies and campaign materials often feature images of Black and Brown children behind bars or razor wire, handcuffed, and being fingerprinted. Other images feature youth clothed in oversized prison-like garb and guarded by towering, uniformed adults carrying weapons. Black male youth, such as Malcolm Young and Edward Ward, narrate experiences of extreme harm to young Black (and Brown) bodies – in schools, juvenile justice systems, and adult prisons – for a range of audiences, often White, including policy makers, politicians, and the broader public. These testimonies frequently identify public institutions' inability to recognize Black and Brown bodies as those belonging to youth, students, or children. The harmed and imprisoned youth fighting to be understood as a child or a student functions as evidence of failed public institutions and of the persistence of the punishing ideological structures, including White supremacy, that legitimated slavery. Young people are pushing back on the policing of childhood, which was a key attribute of slavery itself.[14] Yet there is a profound tension in this claim to childhood. After all, in the eighteenth- and nineteenth-century United States, to be viewed as child-like, and thus without reason, was grounds for enslavement by allegedly benevolent patriarchs. Yet in our own historical moment, young people of color are desperate to be understood as a child, not as a (Black) adult, an identity seemingly tied to criminalization.[15]

Yet while harmed youth emerge within STPP campaigns, "our opponents," including prison guard unions and "law and order" politicians, invoke eerily similar images and narratives of harmed children. Campaigns to halt prison closures or to open new immigration prisons are often predicated on keeping employment opportunities available for the town's children. Austere "tough on crime" laws are rationalized for child protection. As Ruth Wilson Gilmore writes in *Golden Gulag*: "In fact, people who organize against prisons invoke the same beneficiaries ('the kids') as those who organize for prisons."[16] Jobs, protection, and a better future for our children are cited in arguments for opening new prisons and against closing existing ones. At the same time, children, both real and imagined, surface repeatedly in anti-prison messaging. The children at stake in these struggles are very different, and these parallel campaigns illustrate an old debate over who gets to lay claim to childhood itself.

The use of images and ideas surrounding the child and childhood to shape public policy is not new. Abolitionists and those seeking to uphold slavery used ideas about children – inherent goodness, innocence, and diminished capacity – to advance radically different political goals.[17] Child welfare is used to legalize *and* to challenge same-sex marriage. The sentimental figure of the child, as Lee Edelman chronicles dismally in *No Future*, "remains the perpetual horizon of every acknowledged politics, the fantasmatic beneficiary of every political intervention."[18] Yet while Edelman describes a heterosexualized White (male) child who dominates futurity, a closer examination of the use of childhood within anti-STPP organizing illuminates José Esteban Muñoz's observation: "The future is only the stuff of some kids. Racialized kids, queer kids, are not the sovereign princes of futurity."[19]

Given the past three decades of U.S. carceral expansion and the history of the child as a malleable and politically useful artifact, mobilization of child imagery across contemporary pro- and anti-prison movements is perhaps not surprising.[20] Yet the dizzying array of ideological work performed by the child motivated me to do a little field clearing. Schools and prisons, incarceration and slavery – how do these institutions and their divergent historical eras overlap to arrest life pathways and to shape resistance? What are the collateral consequences when images of the child/youth are mobilized within these struggles as harmed figures (or as revolutionary organizers)? When harmed Black and Brown youth try to claim childhood, to demand a future, does this expand or contract the prison nation? While it might be child's play to name and protest linkages between schools and prisons, less visible and yet potentially more dangerous are the punishing and capricious conceptions of innocence and consent. Embedded within and masked by the idea of the child, conceptions of innocence and consent are foundational facets of our mode of governance and the criminal justice system. While widely held to be both static and race- and gender-neutral, innocence and consent are key artifacts that reproduce inequality for all, including even those that count as children. Our investments in an innocent child, *perhaps*, naturalize jails and unfreedom, not education or liberation, for too many.

## A Prison Nation as Slavery's Afterlife

The Thirteenth Amendment legalized criminalization and imprisonment as a valid loophole to the abolition of slavery (slavery was illegal except as a punishment for crime), and Southern industries took advantage of this loophole to place needed Black laborers in conditions that approximated slavery. Angela Davis' "From the Convict Lease System to the Super Max Prison," Douglas Blackmon's *Slavery by Another Name: The Re-enslavement of Black Americans from the Civil War to World War II*, and Daniel Novak's *The Wheel of Servitude: Black Forced Labor after Slavery* outline how laws and regulations, often termed the Black Codes, sought to criminalize the everyday life of non-White people. Such measures included criminalizing those unemployed, levying special taxes against Black people for a range of everyday activities, charging those who would or could not pay those fines with vagrancy, and criminalizing movement itself, including being out after dark.[21] These Codes increased the number of Black people under formal state control, used the criminal legal system to attempt to intimidate communities into maintaining a racial caste system, and helped to produce racialized constructions of "crime" and "criminals." Once convicted under racialized unjust laws and tried by a White judicial system, the conditions of imprisonment, including forced labor, were not that dissimilar to slavery. Imprisoned labor, the "convict lease system," was used to rebuild the Southern economic base. Geoff Ward, sociologist and author of *The Black Child-Savers: Racial Democracy and Juvenile Justice* (referencing the work of historian Eric Foner), argues that the convict lease system exerted particularly cruel conditions:

> The economic principles of convict leasing reduced black convicts to a form of chattel less valued than the enslaved laborers they replaced. Brutal mistreatment, terrible working conditions, and high death rates resulted.[22]

The convict lease system made it possible to produce and maintain a low-cost labor force to support Southern mining and agricultural industries that had lost their enslaved Black workers through the abolition of slavery. The prison system ensured that Black labor was cheap and available.

Often framed as progressive, criminal justice reforms also worked to expand, and often to mask, the state's ability to regulate and police Black families and communities. The first juvenile justice court was established in 1899 in Chicago to wrest "better" treatment for a small class of people under the age of seventeen within the criminal system. These individuals would be tried in another court, deal with alternative institutions, and be entitled to more confidentiality. They would also have limited access to constitutional rights, and, at least initially, would have no right to due process or legal representation.[23] Yet far from improving or shrinking the number of people under punitive control, the juvenile justice system expanded the carceral state through the creation of new categories of crime and illegality – the truant, the delinquent, the runaway – or "status violations" typically applied only to juveniles. Predicated on the logic that wayward youth were potential citizens who required the guiding hand of reformers in order to secure the future, juvenile justice initially focused on immigrant "White" (or non-Black) youth for assimilation.[24] Ward argues that juvenile justice was a "racial project" linked to "Americanization" from inception and policed access to childhood.[25] Ward outlines that, until as late as 1940 in many Southern states, Black children were excluded from these early forms of juvenile justice. At their "best and worst," nineteenth- and twentieth-century juvenile justice systems "variously organized to perpetuate black second class citizenship and white advantage in what remained a white democracy."[26] When non-White youth began to enter in increasing numbers during the later half of the twentieth century, the juvenile justice system adjudicated which youths (overwhelmingly non-White) could count as a juvenile, and which would be transferred to adult court. As Richard Mendel's *No Place for Kids: The Case for Reducing Juvenile Incarceration* painstakingly chronicles, the conditions inside juvenile prisons continue to be gruesome.[27]

While the total number of juveniles locked up over the past thirty-five years continues to decline, today African American youth are five times more likely than White youth to be behind bars.[28] Even if not transferred to an adult court, a child restrained by the juvenile justice system does not have facilitated access to rehabilitation and to freedom. As long-time juvenile justice researcher and journalist Nell Bernstein argues in *Burning Down the House: The End of Juvenile Prison*, the number one predictor of adult incarceration is not gang participation or a missing father, but whether a person was incarcerated as a juvenile.[29] Historically, juvenile justice systems functioned to mark eligible White youths as potentially innocent, meriting differential and potentially better treatment by the judicial system.[30] Today, invoking old patterns from slavery, the criminal justice system negotiates and racializes the boundaries between childhood and adulthood. Fifteen- and sixteen-year-old Black youth, particularly boys, count as adults or are confined within punishing juvenile prisons. While historically the juvenile justice system worked to define White youth, particularly immigrants, as children, today this system works to deny Black (and Brown) youth access to childhood.

While the New Jim Crow is not chattel slavery and the political structures that enable or sustain our contemporary prison nation are not the same as those that produced and legitimated slavery, the "afterlife of slavery" includes the Thirteenth Amendment and the juvenile justice system. Ideologies of White supremacy survived (and flourished) within the twentieth- and twenty-first-century U.S. criminal justice system and its attendant conceptions of juveniles, criminals, and crime.[31] Our prison nation ensures that Black communities experience higher rates of premature death and associated forms of civil or social death: disenfranchisement, incarceration, and school expulsion. For this reason, images and references to slavery and its afterlife ricochet across popular critiques of our prison nation. Police seized protest signs proclaiming "Stop Mass Incarceration/Stop the New Jim Crow" at the August 24, 2013, fiftieth anniversary March on Washington.[32]

Given these intertwined relationships, the work to end the prison nation and close the chapter on slavery is a part of the work to build an *abolition democracy*. The use of "abolition" by contemporary anti-prison agitators and scholars is intentional. Angela Davis writes: "I choose the word 'abolitionist' deliberately. The Thirteenth Amendment, when it abolished slavery, did so except for convicts. Through the prison system, the vestiges of slavery have persisted. It thus makes sense to use a word that has this historical resonance."[33] In a nation predicated on the humiliation and exclusion of too many, W.E.B. DuBois argued that an *abolition democracy*, a system of governance and living capable of abolishing of slavery, was needed. Freedom, he noted, is not simply the absence of laws that disenfranchise and dehumanize.[34] An abolition politic is a reminder that our prison nation is not broken but is functioning precisely as designed. The invocation of abolition, as scholar and anti-prison activist Joy James writes, creates "a political present inextricably linked to the past" suggesting a contemporary "future for abolitionism, emancipation, and freedom."[35] Abolition also suggests the need to finish the tasks left undone by earlier emancipation movements. Not only was the policing of what childhood is/means a key facet of chattel slavery and therefore a site of struggle, but childhood itself continues to be one of the most sophisticated mechanisms to mask the reproduction of ideologies central to animating the "afterlife" of slavery. These contradictions are starkly visible within justice movements to end the school to prison pipeline.

## School-to-Prison Pipeline

Like Edward Ward, many young people of color in urban schools have their first interaction with policing and arrest in a public high school. Students who are queer and/or gender nonconforming, African American, Latino, First Nations, and/or with disabilities are overrepresented not only in arrests that happen in public schools but in school-based disciplinary proceedings.[36]

Grassroots and youth-centered community groups across the United States seeking to interrupt the schoolhouse-to-jailhouse track frequently center images and narratives of harmed Black and Brown youth in their argument. Youth-led projects, including Chicago's Blocks Together and national grassroots conferences such as Free Minds Free People and the Allied Media Conference, have all provided leadership, analysis, and movement building around challenging discriminatory educational policies at the local and state levels that track youth to prisons.[37] Notably, one early component of the "schools, not jails" movement was a fierce youth-led critique of the status quo of schooling that included exposing non-relevant curriculum and providing a sharp analysis of the unequal forms of schooling available to urban youth. Yet some of this analysis gets lost in more mainstream scholarship on the relationships between education and incarceration, which simply posits schooling as the antidote to carceral expansion without linking the two structures.[38]

Making the case that the young Black male body *is* being harmed and does count as a child is not a shallow or reactionary evidentiary move. To be understood as a child is to inherit a thicket of affective possibilities, particularly a status that one's harm, vulnerability, and potential or past pain will potentially ensure full and unfettered access to the category of "victim." To be harmed, a body must be sensate, capable of experiencing pain, and count as fully human. While the work of these organizations, advocates, and scholars is compelling and has raised the visibility of the racialization of school discipline policies and practices, my ongoing practice pushes me to shift gears. The concept of the school to prison pipeline has enabled, in some spheres, an understanding of the STPP as ahistorical, as a free-standing problem that can be solved by more education or better school discipline policies, thereby missing the centrality of capitalism, heteronormativity, and White supremacy in the practices of educational disqualification. While tying the educational experiences of Black and Brown male youth to our prison nation and to slavery, some anti-STPP rhetoric argues not only that different educational policies can save people, but also that children are the only ones worth saving. Displacing the focus from structural forces, such as White supremacy, to child saving, campaigns against the STPP can actually work to shore up concepts that uphold punitive regimes of innocence and guilt, and consent and coercion, that harm many.

Mainstream media's stories of outrage at the arrest or detention of young people overlook the reality that the carceral state is a designed set of interlocking systems that have descended from earlier systems of slavery and oppression. Beyond a critique that suggests that current work against the STPP is too narrowly drawn and often posits school-based reforms as solutions, campaigns that seek to dismantle the STPP also potentially reinforce and reproduce other artifacts and affects that hold the power to reinforce not only the criminalization of select young people, but the wider carceral landscape. Acknowledging this history and recognizing the unique role that the figure of the child plays in it might move liberation movements in the afterlife of slavery away from trafficking and reproducing new carceral forms, and instead move them toward freedom.

### Child Reification/Adult Demonization

STPP campaigns developed at the same time that juvenile justice reform advocates gained significant legal traction by arguing that psychology and, most important, neurology demonstrate that juveniles are different than adults and therefore must be protected and given access to rehabilitation. As the *New York Times* reported, this "explosion in scientific research on adolescent brain development" has a significant impact on the status of those younger than eighteen years of age within the criminal justice system.[39] This brain research changed how adolescents were adjudicated, translating into them facing less legal culpability for crime and more access to state protection, because they were presumed capable of development and change. In fact, the science of brain development occupies the core of the arguments behind a series of Supreme Court decisions.[40] *Roper v. Simmons*, a 2005 case that eliminated the death penalty for juveniles, *Graham v. Florida*, a 2010 case that abolished life without parole (LWOP) for juveniles convicted of non-murder crimes, and *Miller v. Alabama*, a 2012 case that identified mandatory life sentences for juveniles as unconstitutional, all featured arguments about the potential of adolescent brain development.

Lawyer and juvenile justice advocate Patricia Soung terms the trend of basing criminal reforms on neurological research as "neurolaw." Soung identifies key questions surrounding the use of this research in recent juvenile justice reform initiatives:

Interpretations of the science [are] too often laden with deficits-language, even describing youth as a form of mental deficiency. Moreover, the application of neuroscience to a juvenile and criminal justice system disproportionately populated by people of color perpetuates and naturalizes associations between race, criminality and intellect. In the end, biologizing youth and race in the same moment distracts from a fuller social understanding of how youth, race and context interact, and what measures should be taken to address youth crime and racial inequity.[41]

For Soung, the use of "neurolaw" obscures the root causes and contexts that produce youth, particularly low-income youth of color, as criminals. The shift to "biologizing" youth of color also, Soung argues, simultaneously ensures that youth are not understood as shaped through ideological contexts and histories.

As anatomy has historically provided specious evidence of the inferiority of those non-White – brain weight, hair texture, length of nose, cranial shape, genital size, and on and on – this turn to the body to legitimate diminished capacity should give us pause. Though evaluating brain research is out of the scope of this chapter, assessing the impact of the turn to neurology to defend children on a wider carceral landscape is not. Psychology, experience, and neurology legitimate delay, and science is organized as inscrutable evidence that juveniles are in need of state protection. Yet, the inverse of this research frames adults as wholly culpable. Rehabilitation, transformation, and protection are available because of the curious, delayed, temporal status of the child-juvenile, yet becomes categorically unavailable for adults. If (select) children can be rehabilitated, are adults static and therefore only eligible for incapacitation? Does rehabilitation require developmental normativity – sexual, gendered, racial? While the work to dismantle the school-to-prison pipeline clearly does not aim to demonize adults, juvenile justice reformers traffic in complex terrain. The possibility of diminished capacity for some animates a landscape that instantiates full capacity, or guilt, for many. All people are harmed by the carceral state, and I would argue that a particular focus on the child, as defined and legitimated by brain research, justifies the abandonment of adults.

## Innocence

While schools, policing, prisons, and affiliated carceral systems continually redefine who qualifies as a child, the category of the child also produces other artifacts with complex benefits and costs. While previously associated with sin and the possibility of eternal damnation, emergent eighteenth-century discourses created children as holy, angelic, and, persistently innocent, as Robin Bernstein suggests in her study of early American narratives of racialized childhood:

> By the nineteenth century, sentimental culture had woven childhood and innocence together wholly. Childhood was then understood not as innocent but as innocence itself; not as a symbol of innocence but as its embodiment. The doctrine of original sin receded, replaced by a doctrine of original innocence.[42]

Yet childhood innocence was a racialized and heterogendered project. Just as the racist term "pickaninny" was constructed to categorize and desensitize the enslaved Black child, the artifact of innocence embedded in childhood was persistently and seemingly invisibly White.[43]

Childhood participated in shaping a racialized form of innocence and provided as Bernstein argues, a "perfect alibi" for this ideological work.[44] Bernstein contended that while nineteenth-century abolitionists were successful in illustrating that African American enslaved bodies were capable of feeling pain (and were thus human), the "libel of insensateness" did not fade with the abolition of slavery, but instead "stealthily" moved into "children's culture," where innocence "provides a cover under which otherwise discredited racial ideology survives and continues, covertly, to influence culture."[45] White supremacy was not eradicated with the abolition of slavery. Bernstein argues that categories such as "children," still widely understood as a race-neutral scientific and developmental marker, functioned as the perfect container to house and reproduce deeply racialized (and heterogendered) conceptions of innocence.

While Edward Ward is justifiably aghast at the conditions in his high school and should be able to mobilize politicians and media to pay attention to racial profiling in schools, arguing that harmed Black and Brown young people should have access to the benefits and privileges of childhood neither exposes nor challenges the reproduction of this uneven category. Within contemporary campaigns against the STPP, innocence and childhood are invoked, circulated, and unexamined. Specifically, the circulation of the racialized *male child* in strategies to derail the school-to-prison pipeline, actually reproduces heterosexualized and gendered constructions of freedom, a strategy Angela Davis critiques as an early (adult) abolitionist strategy.[46] Anti-STPP campaigns also reproduce the child and the idea of innocence as neutral and *a priori* categories. Claiming freedom through access to childhood innocence does not allow us to ask why so many are considered fully culpable and therefore unfree.

While innocence is, as literary theorist James Kincaid writes, "a lot like air in your tires: there is not a lot you can do with it but lose it,"[47] within our contemporary political landscape the linkage with innocence is a potent and powerful asset. Racial disproportionality at every level of the juvenile justice system – surveillance, arrest, removal from home, conviction, sentencing – clearly shows that White youth have the clearest access to innocence.[48] Yet simply shifting select, or even all Black youth, into the "innocent" category does not allow for a critical exploration of the conception of innocence: who benefits, who does not, and why. Nor does widening the category of who might have access to childhood (and therefore possibly innocence) unpack the underlying nexus of other, more oppressive associations tied to childhood.

### Reason

Concurrent with the era of chattel slavery, children in early America also became defined by a lack of reason and their inability to consent. The construction of children with their "almost complete inability to exercise judgment" functioned, as historian Holly Brewer writes, to "elevate reason beyond other human attributes."[49] Literary scholar Anna Mae Duane, building from Brewer's analysis, suggests: "The child effectively came to represent all that should exclude a subject from citizenship."[50] While potentially benefiting from innocence, claiming childhood also sets one outside of reason and full citizenship. The construction of the child as a subject not in possession of reason opened the door to disqualify and marginalize other groups in need of control and management. While some granted the status of a child could potentially benefit from the dubious protections affiliated with this categorization, many – including women, African Americans, people with disabilities, and indigenous communities – have been, and still are, assessed as childlike.[51]

Through metaphor or policy, infantalization shapes life pathways and necessities systems of experts, surveillance, and management: social welfare policies, juvenile detention centers, social workers, and truancy officers. Assigning diminished capacity can rationalize disenfranchisement, capture, enforced sterilization, and enclosure or incarceration. Those identified as "childlike" do not merit rights or due process and can be subject to a host of violations from the state. As Brewer argues, the child, an integral and under-theorized category within legal and democratic structures, was produced in part to scaffold the development of a new regime of governance – a democratic republic – in tandem with slavery.[52] The unreasonable child, incapable of consent, shaped the life pathways of young White people but also wider colonial, patriarchal, political, and economic regimes that required the enslavement and disqualification of many.

Contemporary youth activists' demands to be seen as a child, as a body incapable of reason or self-governance, are a tricky affair. If, as campaigns against the STPP suggest, those harmed by the STPP should count as children, what new vulnerabilities are produced? As select fourteen-year-old Black and Brown youth demand to be viewed as children, rather than as thugs or dangerous adults, are they also demanding to be considered of diminished capacity, and incapable of reason? Being a non-adult renders one under parental or state control. Is one less vulnerable as a reasonless child or as a culpable, dangerous adult? The juvenile justice system, as many have argued, functions not as a *kind and just parent*,[53] but as a system that captures young people of color and confines them in prisons that significantly diminish their life chances.[54] In the past decade, increased legislation has sought to control bodies, movement, and assembly particularly for low-income urban youth of color. In conjunction with zero-tolerance school policies, these bills and laws target "baggy pants," criminalize homelessness or loitering, and establish age curfews. Identified by some jurisdictions as "ungovernable" or "incorrigible," juveniles are picked up for these status violations. Particularly impacted by status violations are youth of color and/or young women. As indicated in the 2013 report, *National Standards for the Care of Youth Charged with Status Offenses* by the Coalition for Juvenile Justice: "Girls make up 61 percent of all runaway cases, and spend twice as long in detention facilities for status offenses as boys."[55]

Not only does the demand to be seen as a child potentially place those within the STPP at greater levels of vulnerability to state intervention, but it also shores up the wider logic of reason that justifies such intervention in the first place. Our entire criminal justice system rests, possibly precariously, on fixed notions of reason, consent, and culpability. What if these are not fixed? Not bright lines? What if they are social contracts, invented in tandem with slavery, requiring excavation and renegotiation? Campaigns against the STPP that seek to liberate youth by claiming childhood thus, inadvertently and tragically reinforce an expanding carceral logic.

## Child's Play

For contemporary abolitionists, the work, beyond closing prisons, is to transform or remake other supposedly democratic institutions that have locked out too many. Recovering public safety from the racialized and punitive "law and order" paradigm requires a radical imagination. Correspondingly, abolition necessitates inventive practices to reclaim conceptions such as safety and justice and the wider frames and artifacts that serve as their condition of possibility.

While Black youth continue to be denied access to childhood, a part of the "afterlife of slavery," "the child" houses, redefines, and refines the category of innocence and simultaneously protects this concept from critical engagement. Shoring up the twinned logics of punishment and protection, the child exemplifies unfreedom, incapacity, and yet also protection, potential, and radical futurity. Dynamic and flexible, this container remains racialized and heterogendered and unavailable to many. In an expanding prison nation, all bodies matter. As fourteen-year-olds are transferred to adult court, seven- and eight-year-olds are moved into juvenile detention, men and women over the age of eighteen are consigned to indefinite prison terms, and those female, queer, and gender nonconforming are still targeted for containment and sexual surveillance, it matters, desperately, who is viewed as innocent, disposable, or incapable of consent. Access to the status of a child can potentially provide benefits: fewer school disciplinary sanctions, rehabilitation instead of retribution, and the possibility of innocence.

Even if those working against the STPP lack the ability to reframe the terms of the debate – for example, to deconstruct innocence and guilt – it is vital to recognize how these ideas are embedded and masked in many of the containers pro-prison and pro-punishment forces provide as the "neutral" players in our debates: *children*. While organizers and scholars have critically deconstructed empty tropes such as "family values," the concept of *child* has received less scrutiny. Those working against the STPP must scrutinize what flexible containers such as *the child* mask. The denaturalization of categories requires an intellectual rigor in our movement work, as well as consistent linking and reformulating of practices and analysis. This matters. Different ways of framing contemporary justice work and corresponding forms of organizing can save lives. (What if the same-sex marriage movement channeled resources and lobbying from marriage or military inclusion to universal free health care?) Deconstructing the uses of the symbolic child in contemporary carceral spheres offers windows into thinking about the most central questions in justice work today – specifically, those surrounding tensions between reform work and structural, systematic changes that have the capacity to build the work we need to abolish the "afterlife" of slavery.

## Notes

1  Throughout this chapter, I often use *Black* interchangeably with *African American*, and *Brown* to refer to *Latinos*. I use Black and Brown, as young people frequently use these terms to describe themselves in contemporary organizing against the criminalization of young people in schools that is referenced in this chapter. While the "afterlife" of slavery and colonialism are not the same, many of the youth-led mobilizations against the criminalization of young people in schools center around Latino (Brown) and African American (Black) youth.

2  Edward Ward, U.S. Congress, Senate Hearing Testimony, 2012. Available at www.dignityinschools.org/document/testimony-edward-ward-senate-committee-hearing-%E2%80%9Cending-school-prison-pipeline%E2%80%9D.

3  J. A. Browne, *Derailed: The School to Jailhouse Track* (Washington, DC: The Advancement Project, 2003); Victor Rios, *Punished: Policing the Lives of Black and Latino Boys* (New York: New York University Press, 2011); Erica Meiners, *Right to be Hostile: Schools, Prisons and the Making of Public Enemies* (New York: Routledge, 2007); The Advancement Project, *Test, Punish, and Push Out: How Zero Tolerance and High-Stakes Testing Funnel Youth into the School-to-Prison Pipeline* (Washington, DC: The Advancement Project, 2007); Garret Albert Duncan, "Urban Pedagogies and the Celling of Adolescents of Color," *Social Justice: A Journal of Crime Conflict and World Order* 27 (2000): 29–42.

4  See, for example: James Anderson, *The Education of Blacks in the South, 1860–1935* (Chapel Hill: University of North Carolina Press, 1988) on the history of Black under- and un-education; Ruth Wilson Gilmore, *Golden Gulag: Prisons, Surplus, Crisis, and Opposition in Globalizing California* (Berkeley: University of California Press, 2007) on the building of a U.S. prison nation; for numbers of people locked up, see Pew Center on the States Public Safety Performance Project, *One in 100: Behind Bars in America*, 2008, accessed February 10, 2014, www.pewcenteronthestates.org/uploadedFiles/One%20in%20100.pdf.

5  Michelle Alexander, *The New Jim Crow: Mass Incarceration in the Age of Colorblindness* (New York: The New Press, 2010).

6  The build-up of a prison nation shaped government functions that were historically perceived as either less punitive or not punitive – immigration, education, health care, welfare – creating a carceral state. See, for example, Katherine Beckett and Naomi Murakawa, "Mapping the Shadow Carceral State: Toward an Institutionally Capacious Approach to Punishment," in *Theoretical Criminology* 16.2 (2012): 221–44; Kaaryn Gustafson,

*Cheating Welfare: Public Assistance and the Criminalization of Poverty* (New York: New York University Press, 2011); Dorothy Roberts, *Shattered Bonds: The Color of Child Welfare* (New York: Basic Civitas Books, 2002); Loïc Wacquant, *Punishing the Poor: The Neoliberal Government of Social Insecurity* (Durham, NC: Duke University Press, 2009).

7  A portion of my professional and organizing work has been centrally linked to this movement.

8  While male youth of color are most frequently represented in mainstream media coverage and in organizing, research suggests a more complex ecology. Gender, race, sexuality, disability, and socioeconomic status intersect. Girls of color, students with disabilities, and/or LGBTQ students are also targeted for surveillance or removal from the home, are suspended and expelled at higher rates, and receive longer sentences/more harsh disciplinary measures. Black girls are particularly impacted, although not as well represented as those targeted in on-the-ground mobilizations. See, for example, Katherine Himmelstein and Hannah Bruckner, "Criminal Justice and School Sanctions against Non-heterosexual Youth: A National Longitudinal Study," *Pediatrics* 12.1 (2011): 48–57; Damon Hewitt, Catherine Kim, and Daniel Losen, *The School to Prison Pipeline: Structuring Legal Reform* (New York: New York University Press, 2010); Kimberle Crenshaw, *Black Girls Matter: Pushed Out, Overpoliced and Underprotected* (*African American Policy Forum*, 2015) accessed July 15 2015, www.atlanticphilanthropies.org/sites/default/files/uploads/BlackGirlsMatter_Report.pdf; Victor Rios, *Punished: Policing the Lives of Black and Latino Boys* (New York: New York University Press, 2011).

9  Gus Burns, "Youths March against Detroit Schools' Suspension Policies; Call it a 'School to Prison Pipeline,'" *mLive*, March 23, 2013, accessed February 10, 2014, www.mlive.com/news/detroit/index.ssf/2013/03/detroit_youths_protest_strict.html.

10  Kari Lyderson, "Shutting Down the (Closed) Schools to Prison Pipeline," *In These Times*, May 21, 2014, accessed June 30 2014, http://inthesetimes.com/working/entry/16733/shutting_down_the_closed_schools_to_prison_pipeline.

11  Frank Wilderson III, "The Prison Slave as Hegemony's (Silent) Scandal," *Social Justice Journal* 30.2 (2003): 18–27.

12  West's "New Slaves" from his 2013 album *Yeezus* called out the profiteering private prison agency Corrections Corporation of American and the aggressive role corporations and government have played to lock up Black people, creating new forms of Black slavery.

13  Saidiya Hartman, *Lose Your Mother* (New York: Farrar Giroux Strauss, 2007), 6.

14  Anna Mae Duane, *Suffering Childhood in Early America: Violence, Race, and the Making of the Child Victim* (Athens: University of Georgia Press, 2010).

15  See, for example, Khalil Gibran Muhammad, *The Condemnation of Blackness: Race, Crime, and the Making of Modern Urban America* (Boston, MA: Harvard University Press, 2011).

16  Gilmore, *The Golden Gulag*, 177.

17  Duane, *Suffering Childhood in Early America*.
18  Lee Edelman, *No Future: Queer Theory and the Death Drive* (Durham, NC: Duke University Press, 2004), 2–3.
19  José Esteban Muñoz, *Cruising Utopia: The Then and There of Queer Futurity* (New York: New York University Press, 2009), 95.
20  I center on the *child* because a core value of the category's awkward siblings – youth and juvenile – is their propensity to engage the category of innocence.
21  Angela Davis, "From the Convict Lease System to the Super Max Prison," in *States of Confinement: Policing, Detention and Prison*, ed. Joy James (New York: St. Martin's Press, 2000), 63–74; Douglas Blackmon, *Slavery by Another Name: The Re-enslavement of Black Americans from the Civil War to World War II* (New York: Doubleday, 2008); Daniel Novak, *The Wheel of Servitude: Black Forced Labor after Slavery* (Lexington: University Press of Kentucky, 1978).
22  Geoff Ward, *The Black Child-Savers: Racial Democracy and Juvenile Justice* (Chicago: University of Chicago Press, 2012), 68. See also Ward's reference: Eric Foner, *Reconstruction: America's Unfinished Revolution: 1863–1877* (New York: Harper, 2002).
23  See, for example, Barry Krisberg, *Redeeming our Children* (Thousand Oaks, CA: Sage Publications, 2005); Barry Feld, *Bad Kids: Race and the Transformation of the Juvenile Court* (New York: Oxford University Press, 1999).
24  Ward, *The Black Child-Savers*, 33.
25  Ibid., 33.
26  Ibid., 65, 70.
27  Richard Mendel, *No Place for Kids: The Case for Reducing Juvenile Incarceration* (Annie E. Casey Foundation, 2011) accessed May 30, 2014 www.aecf.org/m/resourcedoc/aecf-NoPlaceForKidsFullReport-2011 .pdf#page=4
28  Annie E. Casey Foundation, "Reducing Youth Incarceration in the United States," The Annie E. Casey Foundation, February 2013, 2, accessed February 23, 2014, www.aecf.org/~/media/Pubs/Initiatives/KIDS%20COUNT/R/ ReducingYouthIncarcerationSnapshot/DataSnapshotYouthIncarceration .pdf.
29  Nell Bernstein, *Burning Down the House: The End of Juvenile Prison* (New York: New Press, 2014).
30  See, for example, Ward, *The Black Child-Savers*.
31  See, for example, Muhammad, *The Condemnation of Blackness*.
32  David Zirin, "Seeing 'New Jim Crow' Placards Seized by Police & More from the March on Washington," *The Nation*, August 24, 2013, accessed February 10, 2014, www.thenation.com/blog/175890/seeing-new-jim-crow- placards-seized-police-more-march-washington#.
33  Angela Davis, "Incarcerated Women: Transformative Strategies," *Black Renaissance/Renaissance Noir* 1.1 (1996): 26.
34  W. E. B. DuBois, *Black Reconstruction in America, 1860–1880* (New York: The Free Press, 1998/1935).

35  Joy James, *The New Abolitionists: (Neo)slave Narratives and Contemporary Prison Writings* (Albany: State University of New York Press, 2005), xxxv.

36  See, for example, New York Civil Liberties Union, *New NYPD Data Shows Racial Disparities in NYC School Arrests* (ACLU, 2012), accessed February 23, 2014, www.nyclu.org/news/new-nypd-data-shows-racial-disparities-nyc-school-arrests.

37  Free Minds Free People: www.fmfp.org/ and Allied Media Conference: http://amc.alliedmedia.org/.

38  Camille Acey, "This Is an Illogical Statement: Dangerous Trends in Anti-prison Activism," *Social Justice Journal*, 27.3 (2000): 206–11.

39  Ethan Bronner, "Sentencing Ruling Reflects Rethinking on Juvenile Justice," *New York Times*, June 26, 2012, accessed February 10, 2014, www.nytimes.com/2012/06/27/us/news-analysis-ruling-reflects-rethinking-on-juvenile-justice.html?_r=2&pagewanted=all&.

40  Ibid.

41  Patricia Soung, "Social and Biological Constructions of Youth: Implications for Juvenile Justice and Racial Equity," *Northwestern Journal of Law and Social Policy* 6.2 (2011): 428–44.

42  Robin Bernstein, *Racial Innocence: Performing American Childhood from Slavery to Civil Rights* (New York: New York University Press, 2011), 4.

43  For a discussion of "pickaninny," see ibid., 35.

44  Ibid., 8.

45  Ibid., 51.

46  While not referring to male children, Angela Davis, in her introduction to the 2010 reissue of Frederick Douglass's biography, highlights the gendered complexities of narratives authored by those enslaved to advance the abolition of slavery. Heterosexuality and masculinity were central to these constructions of liberation, and slavery was often narrated as the loss of the "natural" rights attached to patriarchy and masculinity. Davis writes that "lurking within the definition of Black freedom as the reclamation of Black manhood is the obligatory suppression of Black womanhood." See Angela Davis, *Narrative of the Life of Frederick Douglas, an American Slave, Written by Himself. A New Critical Edition* (San Francisco, CA: City Lights Books, 2010), 24.

47  James Kincaid, *Erotic Innocence: The Culture of Child Molesting* (Durham, NC: Duke University Press, 1998): 53.

48  Barry Krisberg, *And Justice for Some: Differential Treatment of Youth of Color in the Justice System* (National Center on Crime and Delinquency, 2007), accessed February 6, 2014, www.nccd-crc.org/nccd/pubs/2007jan_justice_for_some.pdf.

49  Holly Brewer, *By Birth or Consent: Children, Law, and the Anglo-American Revolution in Authority* (Chapel Hill: University of North Carolina Press, 2005), 351.

50  Duane, *Suffering Childhood in Early America*, 6.

51  Ann Laura Stoler's *Race and the Education of Desire: Foucault's History of Sexuality and the Colonial Order of Things* (Durham, NC: Duke University Press, 1995) suggests that these comparisons and linkages also functioned

in reverse. Manuals from the eighteenth and nineteenth centuries that addressed childrearing, she writes, often compared children to racialized others. Children are "animal-like, lack civility, discipline, and sexual restraint; their instincts are base, they are too close to nature, they are, like racialized others, not fully human beings" (151). Adulthood meant the acquisition of reason and civility, and distinguishing oneself from "lower orders." Middle-class White children's bodies and sexualities, Stoler argues, were schooled through discourses of racialized class difference (151).

52 Brewer, *By Birth or Consent.*

53 William Ayers, *A Kind and Just Parent: Children of Juvenile Court* (Boston, MA: Beacon Press, 1998).

54 For an overview of the conditions in juvenile prisons, see Mendel, *No Place for Kids.*

55 Coalition for Juvenile Justice, *National Standards for the Care of Youth Charged with Status Offenses* (Coalition for Juvenile Justice, 2013), 39, accessed February 23, 2014, www.juvjustice.org/sites/default/files/ckfinder/files/National%20Standards%20for%20the%20Care%20of%20Youth%20Charged%20with%20Status%20Offenses%20FINAL(2).pdf.

# 5

# Born Free in the Master's House: Children and Gradual Emancipation in the Early American North

## Sarah L. H. Gronningsater

In 1796, a "Friend to the Equal Rights of Man" published an editorial in the *New York Argus* urging the state legislature to pass a bill for the gradual abolition of slavery. Like many antislavery advocates of the era, "Friend" appealed to the principles of the American Revolution as he urged legislators and the public to support the bill. "For shame," he admonished, "boast no more of liberty, but pray to the God of your unexampled blessings to stay his avenging arm for such inconsistency." But the writer also knew that it would take far more than Revolutionary ideals to convince his readers that gradual emancipation was a reasonable plan. He emphasized, therefore, that the law would free children only. "This bill proposes," he explained, *"that the children of slaves, born at some future period, shall be emancipated upon their arrival at some certain age."* A law focused on freeing children was "as little exceptionable as to be expected."[1]

During and after the Revolution, politicians and reformers in the northern states regularly discussed plans to emancipate the future-born children of slaves. Although slavery was not as deeply entrenched in this region as it was farther south, it was nonetheless a prized institution in dozens of towns and counties. In no northern state was abolition a foregone conclusion, but especially not in the states with the highest proportions of slaves – Pennsylvania, Connecticut, Rhode Island, New York, and New Jersey.[2] In the 1780s, to the displeasure of many slave masters, the legislatures of Pennsylvania, Connecticut, and Rhode Island approved statutes that granted freedom to children born to slave mothers. Although differing in details, these laws required that the children in question work as servants until adulthood. New York's lawmakers debated similar schemes four times between 1785 and 1798. In 1799, the state declared that all children born to slaves after July 4 of that year would be "born free," but obliged to serve their mothers' masters until age twenty-five (if female) or twenty-eight (if male). Were masters inclined to "abandon" these children, the local Overseers of the Poor would bind them out to another household "on the same terms and conditions that the children of paupers were subject to." In 1804, New Jersey passed the region's last gradual emancipation law, which was modeled closely on New York's. Thereafter, no American state initiated an abolition process within its borders until the Civil War.[3]

Although northern states enacted gradual emancipation during and after the Revolution, the origins of their statutes were rooted in colonial poor law and early Quaker antislavery activity. Atlantic Quakers, who began to circulate emancipation plans in the late 1600s and to experiment among themselves in the mid-1700s, drew on contemporary notions of child labor and the regulatory power of the household as they imagined abolition unfolding. In the Quaker model, children born to slave mothers would experience a freedom mediated by the patriarchal master's right to command the work and movement of his wards. The master, if no longer a "slave" master, would remain in charge; his duty was to train the child for independent adulthood – to "act the part of the father," as one Quaker explained.[4] As limited as this deferred-freedom model was, the project nonetheless proved a hard sell to slave masters outside of the Quaker fold (and indeed to some masters within the Quaker fold). Quaker abolitionists and their allies were often forced, during the Revolutionary era, to debate with masters and legislators about who would bear the costs of freedom and why.

This chapter, which focuses on New York as a case study within a larger regional story, makes two arguments about the design, politics, and effects of gradual emancipation.[5] The first is that legislators focused their laws on infant children because they knew that masters would more readily relinquish their ownership over this particular subgroup of their human property, and also because binding poor children to multi-decade terms of service was a familiar legal practice. Debates over who would bear the cost of raising the state's free-yet-bound children in their years of infancy demonstrate how children were perceived as either liabilities or precious commodities depending on how long they could be kept in service and how easily they could be marketed for sale.[6] The second argument is that because emancipation laws prioritized children, New York's black population developed legal, political, and philanthropic strategies

geared toward the safety, education, and well-being of younger generations. Children, especially older ones, attempted to affirm and defend
their quasi-free status. Black adults endeavored to protect and guide the
children in their midst. In the process, mothers and fathers discovered
limited but real ways in which they could make claims for their own freedom more readily than they could in the past. A child-centered emancipation, in short, bore specific ramifications for the staggered development
of freedom within black communities and families.

In highlighting northern gradual emancipation, this chapter joins a
growing body of scholarship on the end of slavery in the early United
States. This literature, which ably exposes the limits of the era's abolition
plans, on the whole pays little attention to how and why it was that
children were placed at the center of legislative emancipation. In other
words, gradual abolition laws tend to be described more than they are
excavated and contextualized. My aim, therefore, is both to examine the
effects that such laws had on children in servitude, as well as to contemplate why children made such attractive objects and subjects of slavery
and freedom in the first place.[7] I also seek to engage questions raised by
recent scholarship on abolition in the wider Atlantic world, perhaps most
notably in work exploring the importance of motherhood, childhood,
and gender to emancipation processes in Cuba and Brazil, whose governments in the late nineteenth century passed "free womb" laws similar in
structure to the American North's.[8] As these studies make clear, enslaved
and emancipated children across time and space created particular sets
of problems and possibilities for masters, legislators, and parents alike.
The consequences varied according to the politics, labor regimes, family
ideologies, religious values, and legal systems of each era and location. In
every setting, however, investigating the experiences of children reveals
the underlying beliefs that facilitated enslavement and also those that
facilitated freedom – with all of freedom's limitations, contradictions,
and delayed promises.[9]

Ultimately, studying children in the context of slavery and emancipation encourages nuanced thinking about normative definitions of freedom. For children in the early American North, genuine freedom hinged
as much upon the quality and nature of their dependent relationships –
and their right to be born to free parents – as it did upon the erasure of
masters' exercisable property rights. From whom does a child receive
food, education, labor orders? How free is a free child whose parents
are still in bondage? What, in addition to (or other than) autonomy, self-
possession, and the absence of necessity, are the hallmarks of freedom?

Masters and slaves, parents and children, magistrates and citizens, and politicians and reformers in the early American North had various answers to these questions. Not only their debates but also their on-the-ground struggles provide insight into the lived content of freedom for children as well as for men and women of all ages living in and emerging from slavery.[10]

Although a scattered number of philosophers, jurists, and religious dissenters expressed qualms about New World slavery in the sixteenth and seventeenth centuries, Quakers were the first self-defined community to develop a coherent antislavery movement within the imperial Atlantic sphere. Initially, Quakers' objections to slavery were limited: they worried about slaves' exclusion from Christian brotherhood, the impropriety of lifelong bondage, the violence of forced labor, and the dissolution of families. These doubts about certain aspects of slavery did not, at first, translate into organized abolitionism, but they did suggest the persistent difficulty of reconciling Quaker beliefs with slaveholding.[11]

When seventeenth-century Quakers first suggested methods for emancipation, they focused on freeing slaves after a period of bondage, but they did not single out children. In 1671, for example, George Fox – the sect's principal founder – urged Quakers in the sugar colony of Barbados to manumit slaves after a "term of years."[12] In 1682, William Penn, the first proprietor of Pennsylvania, approved a charter that stipulated, "if the *Society* [of Traders] should receive *Blacks* for *servants*, they shall make them *free* at *fourteen years* end."[13] When early Quakers mentioned children specifically, they focused on the Christian master's obligation to provide training and education for his dependents. In 1693, for instance, Quaker schismatic George Keith and his allies published a pamphlet in New York suggesting to Friends that enslaved "Children born in their House" be freed "after a reasonable time of service"; in the meantime, masters should "teach them to read, and give them a Christian Education."[14] These early Quaker calls for manumission focused on individual duty rather than community-wide emancipation. It was not until the mid-eighteenth century that a critical number of Friends began to think systematically about compelling collective emancipation within the Society.[15]

Mid-eighteenth-century Quakers who deliberated community-wide emancipation fretted in particular over the difficulties of freeing the old, the sick, and the young.[16] It was no secret, for example, that colonial masters sometimes freed elderly or diseased slaves simply because they did not want to provide for their care. Indeed, laws specifically forbade this practice, largely because officials did not want dependent ex-slaves burdening systems of poor relief. According to a similar logic, children were also problematic as subjects of emancipation – like the old and the sick, they could not readily provide for their own shelter and food, nor, in many cases, could their parents. Death, illness, estate sales, and the slave market routinely forced relatives to separate, and even in cases where parents were alive and local, creating independent ex-slave households in short order was and would be challenging; slaves did not own property (at least not legally), nor did they receive remuneration for their labor.[17] Freeing a child would solve the problem of slavery, but not necessarily the problems of sustenance and education. From this perspective, Quakers argued that it would be morally and legally appropriate to free able-bodied adults while at the same time apprenticing children until they came of age.

Apprenticing children was in itself a widespread custom, common among Quakers and the wider population. Throughout the colonies, local Overseers of the Poor, whose practices were guided by English legal traditions, routinely bound out impoverished and orphaned children. These pauper children and their parents had little say in the choice of the master or in the nature of the child's work; poverty hindered a person's right to consent to the particulars of a labor placement. In other instances, middling parents voluntarily apprenticed their young, seeking out suitable masters who agreed to train and support their sons and daughters in return for the child's labor. There was little question that parents could transfer their children to another adult in this way; until children reached the age of maturity (eighteen for a girl, twenty-one for a boy), their labor capacity legally belonged to their fathers or widowed mothers. The notion that a freed slave child would become a servant or an apprentice, therefore, did not depart radically from the broader labor practices that affected many children's lives.[18] The prevalence of child apprenticeship helps explain why mid-eighteenth-century Quakers conceived of emancipation as they did.[19]

Quakers' antislavery paternalism allowed for the emancipation of children, but de-emphasized uniting black families and relinquishing control to black parents. In 1759, for example, Quakers in Buckingham, Pennsylvania, upon learning that one of their members had bought slaves, informed the man that he would "bring up such of his negroes as are young in useful learning, endeavoring to instruct them in the principles of Christianity, and at a proper age, if they desire it, to set them free" or face excommunication.[20] That same year, Friends in Dutchess County, New York, began insisting that members who bought slaves free them after a "reasonable time."[21] In 1774, the New York Yearly Meeting, after pressure from Dutchess County Friends, decreed that members in their jurisdiction could no longer own slaves past the "Age of Eighteen, or twenty one years according to their Sex."[22] Friends were also required to assess during their meetings whether "care is taken to learn Negro Children to read and qualify them for Business."[23] It was not only the Quaker household's duty to educate black children spiritually, but also to provide training that would allow them to support themselves as adults.

At the same time that mid-Atlantic and New England Quakers were beginning to enforce emancipation within their local meetings, several committed members began a campaign to convince masters throughout the colonies to follow suit. As these abolitionist Quakers began to speak more frequently in the public sphere about the wisdom of government-mandated emancipation, they forthrightly addressed colonial masters' more worldly feelings about the uses and the expenses of enslaved children. They also acknowledged local officials' broader anxieties about the public costs of pauper care and the regulation of dependent labor.

Quaker abolitionists argued that slavery could be abolished without disrupting the social order and without penalizing masters financially. Philadelphia's Anthony Benezet, for example, disseminated plans that specifically addressed the cost of raising enslaved children and the need to supervise their path to freedom. The "Government," he wrote,

> might bring [slaves] under such Regulations, as would enable them to become profitable Members of Society.... [A]fter [they] serve so long as shall be adequate to the Money paid, or the Charge of bringing them up ... let them by Law be declared free [but remain] under the inspection of the Overseers of the Poor. Thus ... children have an opportunity of such Instruction as might be provided for them, under the Tuition of proper Instructors.[24]

Benezet thus reassured taxpayers and politicians that existing structures of poor relief could regulate ex-slaves. Children's labor would reimburse their masters for their upkeep and education. Adults' service, by contrast, would reimburse their masters for their lost market value. A slave's age, in short, was an important factor in determining the nature and the cost of his or her emancipation.

Benezet was not alone in considering the implications of freeing young versus adult slaves. In 1772, a New Jersey Quaker named David Cooper anonymously published a pamphlet anticipating debates that would soon grip the newly independent northern legislatures. He argued that the Golden Rule obliged masters to "set negroes free at the same age your own children are, without unjustly coveting their labour until they are 25 or 30 years of age, or compelling them to pay a yearly sum. They have just as good a right to their freedom at twenty-one in the eyes of unbiased justice as your own sons." A father, he continued, surely had the right to sell his daughter's labor to another master, but only "till she came to the age of a woman" at eighteen.[25] For Cooper, the distinction between masterhood and fatherhood revolved around the question of profit. The Golden Rule did not preclude a master/surrogate father from supervising or exchanging the labor of an enslaved mother's child until the child reached adulthood – but the objective was to raise and train the child, not to commodify him or her.[26]

Cooper understood, however, that many masters would be hard-pressed to decommodify children born to slave mothers, and he made a series of observations crucial to understanding the broader politics of gradual emancipation laws. He knew that northern masters found infant children to be a financial burden, but that, at the same time, these same masters greatly prized the labor and market value of older children. He took these facts into account as he pre-empted potential objections to his program. Cooper imagined a master protesting the idea that he "act the part of a father by negroes! be at the cost of raising them, schooling and what not, and when they are able to earn something set them free! ... Why at that age they'll bring me near one hundred pounds per head." Cooper replied by acknowledging that the master had men's laws on his side, but that Christ's doctrines were "diametrically opposed to the slave trade."[27] This was a morally sincere if not entirely economically convincing reply.

Like Cooper, the "Friend to the Equal Rights of Man" – the abolitionist whose 1796 plea appeared in the *Argus* – directly confronted the issue of a child's changing market value over time. Urging the New York legislature to pass a gradual emancipation bill, he wrote that "very few people would receive a negro infant as a gift – The risk, expense, and trouble of training them to a state of profitable service, overbalancing their probable future value – And even when nurtured by their mothers, the same considerations, with her loss of time, fully warrant the same conclusion." Children, "Friend" was arguing, were attractive objects of emancipation precisely because they were not, at least in their infancy, particularly coveted pieces of property. In fact, they were a drain on resources, which was why some masters might abandon them to the Overseers of the Poor.

"Friend" reminded his readers, however, that these same children, once older, provided lucrative labor. In his view, "any person would receive them for their services" after "the age of six."[28] A hardworking older child could reimburse the master for the cost of supporting and educating him or her as an infant.

In prioritizing these arguments, "Friend" revealed his grasp of the demographic nuances of slavery in New York. In the eighteenth century, slaves were between 10–15 percent of the population. By 1790, almost 40 percent of the households in the three rural counties surrounding New York City owned slaves. That said, the number of slaves in each household was generally small. The nature of New York's economy – one focused on farms and urban trades – meant that most masters desired only a few slaves at a time. In this context, infants were considered a burden. A strong, healthy "spinster" was a more reliable source of labor than a mother distracted by the care of a child or weakened from pregnancy.[29] Unattached older children, however, were attractive commodities. They worked as domestics, waiters, nurses, chimney sweeps, gardeners, grooms, dairy maids, and farmhands. Aware of these labor patterns, "Friend" thought that an abolition bill like the one before the legislature balanced "private right and convenience" with "public good" and "right."[30]

Sale notices and wanted advertisements from New York newspapers in the 1770s, 1780s, and 1790s confirm Cooper's and "Friend"'s perception of this differentiated value system for slaves of different ages. These printed notices also suggest that there was a wide public understanding of what kinds of slaves masters most desired. In 1776, for example, a master offered to exchange "A Negro wench about 27 years old, with a child about two years old" for "a handy boy." In 1780, a master stated frankly that he wanted to sell his "negro wench" and her one-year-old because he "does not like noise." Such notices continued to be published well into the 1790s, the decade when the legislature regularly debated gradual abolition bills.[31]

As some masters tried to rid themselves of mothers with young children, others placed wanted ads for the types of slaves they *did* want. Many desired older children. They were often specific about the ages they preferred. In 1775, for instance, a master "wanted to purchase a Negro boy, about twelve years of age, with a girl of sixteen or eighteen." Another asked for a "20 year old" who was "capable of waiting at Table, and doing the usual Business of a Footman, and … understands something of the Gardeners Branch." A "9 or 10"-year-old boy was sought who "must have had the Small Pox." Also needed were: "A Negro Wench" who was "twelve Years old, this Country born," "A Smart likely Negro Boy, brought up in the Country; from Twelve to Fourteen years of age," "A Negro Boy ... 17 or 19 years of age, Who has been brought up to Family or House-Work," "A Negro-Girl, between nine and twelve years of age, not exceeding the latter." Masters often specified the type of work children would provide. In 1795, for example, a master requested an "American Negro" of "about 18 to 20 ... smart, and that can do all kinds of house work, wait at table, take good care of one or two horses, & c, and occasionally drive a carriage."[32] Cooper was surely correct when he imagined a master huffing at the idea of having to free a child at eighteen or twenty-one; these were just the sort of slaves who would fetch a high price in the marketplace.

During the American Revolution, a number of non-Quaker politicians and ministers in the northern states embraced the antislavery cause. In 1773, Philadelphia Patriot Benjamin Rush published an address urging the same form of emancipation that his friend Anthony Benezet had long promoted: "Let [the young Negroes] be taught to read, and write – and afterwards be instructed in some business, whereby they may be able to maintain themselves. Let laws be made to limit the time of servitude." Rhode Island minister Samuel Hopkins's 1776 *Dialogue on Slavery* praised the Quaker example and argued that existing systems of poor relief could structure the lives of ex-slaves: "Let them be subject to the same restraints and laws with other freemen.... [B]e as ready to direct and assist those who want discretion and assistance to get a living as if they were your own children, and as willing to support the helpless, infirm and aged."[33] Non-Quakers were now considering the possibility of widespread abolition.

In 1780, Pennsylvania passed the nation's first gradual emancipation statute. The law made no provisions for freeing adult slaves – to the chagrin of some abolitionists and of course to slaves themselves – but it did address the freedom of unborn children. "An Act for the Gradual Abolition of Slavery" declared that "slavery of children, in consequence of the slavery of their mothers ... hereby is utterly taken away, extinguished and for ever abolished." The law further decreed that any child born of a slave would be "the servant" of his or her mother's master until the age of twenty-eight "in the manner and on the conditions whereon servants [are] bound by indenture" and receive "like freedom dues." Any master wishing to abandon a child could place him or her with the Overseers of the

Poor to be bound out like other pauper children. Masters would remain liable for any "Negro or Mulatto [who] shall become chargeable."[34]

Quakers like David Cooper would not have been pleased to learn that black children would serve until the age of twenty-eight; this was far past the age that white child servants or apprentices typically served. Other northern states were similarly reluctant to follow the Golden Rule to determine the length of black children's service. Connecticut's 1784 statute stated that "no Negro or Molatto Child ... shall be held in servitude, longer than until they arrive to the Age of twenty-five Years." Rhode Island explained that "children declared free" should "remain with their mothers a convenient time from and after their birth." The mothers' masters would receive funds from their local towns to "maintain and support such children," "provided, however, that the respective town councils may bind out such children as apprentices" until eighteen and twenty-one. A year later, the Rhode Island legislature repealed the clause that required towns to support freeborn children. Instead, such children would be "maintained by the owner of the mother ... to the age of twenty-one-years." All of these statutes bear evidence of the clashes between the ideological and financial interests of legislators, masters, local governments, and state governments.[35]

In 1785, with the Society of Friends' strong support, New York's legislature made its own attempt to enact gradual emancipation.[36] The Assembly approved the clause in a Senate bill declaring that children would "remain with the master or mistress of his or her mother ... in the character or capacity of a servant ... entitled to the remedies provided for indented servants" until the females reached twenty-two and the males twenty-five. The Assembly also agreed that masters would teach both sexes how to read and boys how to write, as well as provide a Bible and clothes upon release from service – stipulations that mirrored indentureship laws.[37] But the lower house also wanted to restrict black citizenship, and succeeded in inserting a disfranchisement clause.[38] The bill ultimately failed to become law, however, because the state's Council of Revision argued that New York could not deprive "children that shall be born of slaves" the right to vote "without shocking those principles of equal liberty."[39] Emancipation foundered in 1785 because the Council thought that the bill to make children free did not make them free enough. As a result, no children were freed at all.

The disputes over slavery, children, and citizenship in the New York legislature captured in microcosm a broader contemporary Anglo-American debate over hereditary status, the relationship between age and rights, and the nature of government by consent.[40] The American Patriots' emphasis on reasoned consent as the source of just political authority could cut both ways for black children. On the one hand, some elites explicitly compared slaves, women, paupers, and the insane to children in order to explain their necessary subordination within republican government; all lacked the capacity to reason. On the other hand, some theorizers claimed that black children, just like white children, could become consenting adult citizens as long as they received proper training.

In New York, the most prominent organization to promote the notion that black children could make effective citizens was the New York Manumission Society. Founded in 1785, the Society was comprised of both well-heeled Quakers and prominent politicians, including John Jay and Alexander Hamilton.[41] In its first months of operation, the Society embarked on three projects. First, members petitioned the legislature for a gradual emancipation act.[42] Second, the Society disseminated 2,000 copies of Samuel Hopkins's *Dialogue on Slavery*.[43] Third, the Society established the African Free School, an institution designed to educate black children for citizenship.[44] The school's mission echoed the logic of gradual emancipation plans in that it provided for independent white men to train black children for freedom. What made the school's mission distinct, however, was the notion that the students' freedom would be defined by access to intellectual and civic equality, not just by freedom from the poor rolls. The school thus addressed contemporary concerns about the need for responsible citizenship in the new republican nation.[45]

The Manumission Society's republican antislavery vision in fact melded nicely with older ideals of gradual emancipation. Gradual emancipation could now be fashioned as an apprenticeship for citizenship, designed for the very group of slaves who were the right age to be apprentices and also young enough, and therefore malleable enough, to be trained in good civic habits. Over the next several years, as the Society expanded the African Free School and publicized black children's intellectual capabilities, it also sent committees to Albany to lobby the state for gradual emancipation laws.[46] In 1795, these abolitionists were heartened when former Manumission Society president John Jay was elected governor.[47]

During Jay's two terms in office, the legislature debated gradual emancipation bills on three separate occasions. Among the sticking points was whether state or local taxes would be raised to pay for the costs of caring for infant children who were born to slave mothers and then "abandoned." Slave masters and their allies preferred that state rather than local taxes be used for pauper care of abandoned infants, even though

local taxes traditionally funded poor relief. Under this scheme, localities
with high rates of slaveholding would be spared higher pauper fees since
lower-slaveholding areas in the state would subsidize the cost.[48] In 1799,
the *Daily Advertiser* reported that the Assembly was in deep debate over
whether the "town or city" versus the "state" would bear "the expense
of maintaining all poor children [born to slaves]."[49] In the end, the legislature decided that the state would provide local towns with funds to
support abandoned black servants after the first year of their lives – a
departure from fiscal custom.[50]

In March 1799, the Council of Revision approved an "Act for the
gradual abolition of slavery." The statute was an amalgam of poor laws,
slave laws, and Quaker emancipation proposals. Overseers of the Poor
were put in charge of managing black children's indentureships. Local
clerks would file birth certificates for each freeborn child; any master who
neglected to file a certificate would be fined, with the proceeds funneled
to maintenance of the poor. Should a master wish to abandon a freeborn
child, the Overseers would bind the child out. Masters were required,
however, to support infants for a year before abandonment. After this
year, the Overseers would pay the newly assigned master a monthly fee
for supporting the child, following traditional rules for pauper children.[51]
The end of slavery was designed to come slowly.[52]

Indeed, it is reasonable to question whether New York's 1799 law
really freed children at all; it might be more accurate to say that gradual emancipation laws freed, at far future dates, young adults who had
been born into a form of servitude that did not look very different from
slavery. Were *children* really being freed? While it is crucial to emphasize
that the infants subject to gradual emancipation laws were not born truly
free, they were not, on paper, born slaves either. Antislavery lawmakers in
New York deliberately declared such children to be "born free" because
they intended for law-abiding masters to treat these children differently
from enslaved children. Of course, just because abolitionists and some
politicians wanted these children to inhabit a new status category did not
mean that all masters complied. However, black children and their parents seized upon the legal niceties attached to being "born free" to wrest
some rights from masters and to garner some control over their own
fates. "Born-free" children could, theoretically and sometimes in reality,
do things and ask for things that enslaved children could not. The crucial question for individual boys and girls was the degree to which their
masters would act in the ways that reformers like David Cooper wanted

masters to act, and the degree to which they or their parents could make their birth status mean better life circumstances in practice.[53]

The daily lives of children born to slaves before and after July 4, 1799, did not look materially different at first. Both slave child and servant child were born into service, tied to a master, relegated to menial labor, and vulnerable to violence and family separation. But with slowly gaining momentum, black New Yorkers began to find ways to protect and enhance the freedom of children and families. By ensuring that masters followed the law and by taking advantage of new possibilities within the state's changing social and economic environment, free and enslaved men, women, and children at times made gradual emancipation less gradual.

In the years following the 1799 act, black parents and their allies learned how vital it was to begin protecting a black child's freedom from the moment he or she was born. Although some masters duly registered children born to slaves after the 1799 law went into effect, others tried to skirt the regulations. These underhanded masters well understood that gradual emancipation laws weakened their authority and potential wealth. As the Manumission Society explained the problem, "many disputes" would arise "when these children arrive at legal age [because of] unprincipled men whose interest it will be to retain them in slavery long after their legal right so to do ceases."[54] To thwart cheating and negligent masters, the Society enlisted the help of those New Yorkers who were on the front lines: slaves and servants. Using a regular strategy, the Society designated a committee to attend "several meetings of the Coloured People on the Subject." Soon thereafter, the Society "received and reported to the City Clerk the names of Fifty children who had not previously been registered as the law directs."[55]

The 1799 act was but one of several statutes that interfered with masters' traditional property rights. The legislature also decreed that masters could no longer import or export slaves or servants for sale; if a smuggler were caught, the victim was immediately freed. Ensuring that the export and import laws were followed was particularly important for black children; masters and traders found it especially tempting to smuggle freeborn children out of the state and into jurisdictions where they could be sold as slaves for life. It was also tempting for masters to move into New York with servants or free children from nearby northern states and try to pass them off as slaves. To forestall this last problem, the legislature passed an act forbidding masters from moving into the state with their slaves (or "slaves"); visiting masters who wanted to stay for more than nine months were required to free the slaves in their possession.[56]

Black parents used all of these laws to their families' advantage. For example, in 1809, a mother reported to the lawyers of the Manumission Society "that her son James who was born since 1799" had been sold "to Matthias Ward who proposes sending him to Jersey." James's master, upon "hearing a representation of the case," agreed to release the boy from the sale.[57] In a similar example, William Bradshaw reported that his daughters were in danger of being sold as "slaves for life" by the heirs of their deceased master. With Bradshaw's information, the Society freed the girls.[58] In 1811, an enslaved mother named Mary managed to free not only her children, but herself. Mary's family had been brought to New York from New Jersey the previous May. It was now ten months later – and thus the master had broken the nine-month limit. In April, "Mary & her three children [were] free, according to the … law."[59]

It is critical to stress, however, that not every parent knew the details of state law, nor did every negative situation find remedy in the statute book. It was particularly difficult for rural black New Yorkers to access legal help, although there is evidence that slaves and servants from all over the state managed to communicate with the Manumission Society or to find similar local support, especially from Quakers. Sojourner Truth, a slave from Ulster County who became one of the nation's most famed abolitionists, recalled that she had originally learned about changes in state law by eavesdropping on her masters. She later managed to protect both her own freedom and her kidnapped son's freedom through a combination of persistent legal action, support from local white acquaintances, and assistance from the Manumission Society. Truth was a particularly remarkable woman, but her experiences of gradual emancipation were not unique. Despite the challenges, black parents like Truth shared and utilized legal knowledge in ways that sometimes changed their own and their children's lives. Success was all the more likely when an informed antislavery lawyer, abolitionist, or patron could be enlisted to assist.[60]

There is evidence that black children themselves knew that they were free, or at least that they were no longer slaves. In 1811, for example, a servant girl named Charlotte who was accused of setting her master's barn on fire insisted to the local district attorney that despite having a master, she was not a slave. After stating, "I am free" to the grand jury, Charlotte explained that she had been sold to her master, Mr. Ward, by a Mr. Duncan because she had tried to run away. The district attorney asked her "what right had Mr. Duncan to sell you to Mr. Ward if you

[were] free." Charlotte replied, "I am not sold for life. I am sold for a certain number of years only and then to be free."[61] She would serve Ward "until I was a big woman." Charlotte did not deny she had set the barn on fire. That morning, she had been beaten because "I did something naughty – I pulled up my petticoats before a little white boy which my mistress had forbidden." The district attorney asked if this beating prompted the fire. Charlotte answered, "I intended to burn it all down." Charlotte was tried for arson, found guilty, and sentenced to prison for twelve months.[62]

Charlotte's testimony cuts to the heart of what gradual emancipation meant for thousands of northern black children.[63] Her story depicts several ways in which being a black servant was little different from being a slave. But her testimony also indicates that some servant children were aware that, at least according to law, they inhabited a distinct legal category with access to certain rights. Charlotte knew that her master was not supposed to keep her forever. Similarly, other black servant children in New York knew that the state's ever-expanding list of emancipation laws required that their masters provide them with a basic education, forbade masters from treating them "cruelly" (rules governing "cruel treatment" applied to servants but not to slaves), and prohibited masters from migrating with them out of the state (another rule that applied to servants but not slaves).[64]

These knowledgeable children and their allies – parents, friends, abolitionists – did their best to spread the word that masters were required to release children early from service if they broke certain laws.[65] A girl named Phillis Jackson, for example, told the lawyers of the Manumission Society that she believed she was eligible for early release because she was born in August, 1799 and "has had no schooling." After investigating her case, the Society ensured her release and reported that Jackson was "enjoying freedom."[66] In another instance, a boy who worked for a neglectful mistress got word to the Manumission Society that he "is discontent, wants his freedom, not having had any schooling." He was also freed.[67] In some cases, concerned adults intervened on behalf of children they knew. A "colored girl" named Franciska who was "frequently cruelly beaten" by her master was aided by the household's "cook and waiter," who were both willing to testify on her behalf. Franciska was freed.[68]

As important as state laws were to the process of dismantling slavery, changes in the labor market also affected the pace and culture of emancipation. The 1799 act, in conjunction with the import and export laws, had damaged the commodity value of children, making them in effect easier to give up. Moreover, by the early 1800s, masters found it increasingly attractive to draw from a growing population of immigrants to fulfill their labor needs, especially in urban areas. (Slavery died far more slowly in the countryside.) Masters – or rather "employers" – could hire and fire such free laborers at will, paying wages rather than assuming responsibility for dependents' care within the household. This new flexibility in the labor market sometimes worked to slaves' and servants' advantage; black workers found that they had more leverage to negotiate with masters for conditional manumission and early release, or to persuade masters to sell or to give them their children. In 1815, for example, a free father in Albany named Thomas Allison bought his enslaved wife and their three freeborn children for $150, a price that in earlier market conditions would almost certainly have been higher.[69]

At times, New York State's interests, black parents' interests, and masters' interests aligned in novel ways. For example, in 1809, the state legalized slave marriage and allowed slave parents to bequeath property.[70] This statute was particularly unusual given that slaves' status had long been defined by their inability to make contracts, including the contract of marriage, and their inability to *be* and *own* property simultaneously.[71] But there were practical reasons, within the context of gradual emancipation, to permit slaves to marry and to alienate property. The 1799 law had freed children while simultaneously making them legal "bastards." Denying free children legitimacy and automatic inheritance rights increased the likelihood that they would burden state resources and fail to become independent adults.

The 1809 law also made it easier for masters to abandon servant children to their parents, rather than to the Overseers of the Poor, as long as local authorities certified that the parents were "able and willing to maintain and provide." Previously, this was difficult for masters to do, at least legally. Prior to 1809, even if a master wanted to use manumission laws to release a child servant, he would have to prove that the child was sufficiently able to care for him- or herself (which was unlikely) or to post an expensive bond. The new law allowed a master simply to release a child to his or her parents, placing the burden of responsibility on mothers and fathers. Viewed another way, the law gave black parents the right to raise their own children.

In some instances, this 1809 law assisted black families in achieving collective freedom. In 1818, for example, the mayor and recorder of Albany registered the decision of John Douw to free his slave Sarah Banker along with her two young children. The officials certified that

"Sarah Banker the mother of the children Helen Hensen and Eliza Edwards ... appeared to us and declared herself willing to support and maintain said children."[72] Mary Francis's master manumitted her along "with her female negro child of four weeks old whose services I hereto had retained." Francis "consent[ed] to take and support the said child."[73] These examples are not only revealing of the 1809 law's potential to ease restrictions on families' freedom, but also provide clues into many masters' own thinking about emancipation. Perhaps the manumissions were genuine "acts of benevolence," but they also emphasize that masters often considered freeborn infants burdens. As children became, at law, people and not property, masters found reasons not to keep black children and black families found new opportunities to stay intact.

Due to these legal, social, and economic forces, by the time the first generation of freeborn children was reaching maturity, slavery in New York was teetering. In 1817, the state struck another blow to the institution when Governor Daniel Tompkins, a former lawyer for the Manumission Society, advocated and then approved a law declaring that all slaves in New York would be emancipated on July 4, 1827. After this date, all black children would be born to free black mothers – with no mandatory terms of service attached. Children born to slave mothers in the interim, however, would remain eligible for service until they reached the age of twenty-one (rather than twenty-five or twenty-eight, as the 1799 law had stipulated).[74]

Children, the first subgroup of slaves to qualify for freedom in New York's gradual emancipation scheme, were now the last remaining cohort to owe services to a master. It was precisely their youth that kept them, well after the 1827 general abolition, in the category of personal dependents whose labor it remained ideologically consistent and easy to control. The state, both before and after 1827, granted masters considerable flexibility with respect to the labor and care of black children. Masters willing to support infants could keep them as adolescent laborers; masters who wanted to forego the costs and obligations of raising black children could easily let them go. Until 1848, it was still possible – if increasingly rare – for a black child to owe service to a master.

In practice, the abolition of slavery in New York proceeded gradually, but not nearly as gradually as eighteenth-century plans predicted. Children and their families pursued routes to early freedom. The state, for its part, proved willing to intervene in relationships between masters and servants and masters and slaves, tipping the balance of power away from masters cautiously but meaningfully. Masters themselves at times found reasons to accelerate the process, discovering incentives – whether moral or economic – to hasten emancipation.

Scholars who study the daily life of emancipation in a variety of historical settings invariably find that freedom was, in Barbara Fields's memorable phrase, "a constantly moving target."[75] Her metaphor highlights the gulf between laws on paper and events in reality, the differences between owning one's self and attaining a secure livelihood, and the vulnerability of freedom in any situation where the mere crossing of a jurisdictional border might result in re-enslavement. The experiences of black children born and raised during the era of gradual emancipation in New York remind us, as well, that freedom's contours shift over the course of a given life as age and family relationships change. What does it mean for children not only "to be born free" but to live and mature as free? Perhaps it is the ability to remain dependent, vulnerable, and costly to parents or kin who see their children's growing independence as a virtue to be nourished and encouraged over time. Freedom, the children of gradual emancipation suggest, is relational and contingent, defined not only by autonomy, but also by the capacity to reach adulthood having been nurtured safely enough in order to make, at evolving moments of maturity, one's own choices about one's labor, movement, and ties of obligation.

## Notes

For invaluable advice on improving this chapter, I thank Greg Ablavsky, Anna Mae Duane, Chris Florio, Katharine Gerbner, Jim Gigantino, Brendan Gillis, Matt Hellmann, Ruth Herndon, Tom Holt, Amy Levine, Anna Levine-Gronningsater, Max Mishler, Nic Wood, the University of Pennsylvania Law School's Legal History Writers' Bloc(k), and the anonymous reviewers.

1   "For the Argus," *New York Argus*, February 3, 1796. Italics in original. It is possible that this "Friend to the Equal Rights of Man" was a Quaker (a religious "Friend"), but the article does not say.
2   In 1780, there were 21,054 black residents in New York, 10,460 in New Jersey, 7,855 in Pennsylvania, 5,885 in Connecticut, and 2,671 in Rhode Island. The vast majority were enslaved. Slaves comprised 2.5–10 percent of the population in these states. Susan B. Carter et al., eds., *Historical Statistics of the United States, Millennial Edition* (New York: Cambridge University Press, 2006), Series Eg1–59.
3   "An Act for the Gradual Abolition of Slavery" (1780) in *Laws Enacted in the Second Sitting of the Fourth General Assembly, of the Commonwealth of Pennsylvania* (Philadelphia, 1780), 296–9; "An Act Concerning Indian,

Molatto, and Negro Servants and Slaves" (1784) in *Acts and Laws of the State of Connecticut, in America* (New London, 1784), 233–5; "An Act Authorizing the Manumission of Negroes, Mulattoes and Others, and for the Gradual Abolition of Slavery" (1784) in *Records of the State of Rhode Island and Providence Plantations in New England*, vol. 10, *1784 to 1792* (Providence, 1865), 7–8; "An Act for the Gradual Abolition of Slavery" (1799) in *Laws of the State of New-York, Passed at the Twenty-Second Session* (Albany, 1799), 721–3. "An Act for the General Abolition of Slavery" (1804) in *Acts of the Twenty-Eighth General Assembly of the State of New-Jersey ... Second Sitting* (Trenton, 1804), 251–4. James Gigantino argues that emancipation in New Jersey was particularly affected by the political and labor landscape of New York. *The Ragged Road to Abolition: Slavery and Freedom in New Jersey, 1775–1865* (Philadelphia: University of Pennsylvania Press, 2015), 11–16, 84–97. Massachusetts, Vermont, and New Hampshire abolished slavery more quickly and by other means (a state supreme court case, state constitutions). For an overview, see Arthur Zilversmit, *The First Emancipation: The Abolition of Slavery in the North* (Chicago: University of Chicago Press, 1967). Gradual emancipation was discussed in Delaware, Maryland, and Virginia during the Revolutionary era, but never implemented.

4 [David Cooper], *A Mite Cast into the Treasury: Or, Observations on Slave-Keeping* (Philadelphia, 1772), 16.

5 While staying attuned to regional patterns, I focus on New York for two reasons. First, New York was home to the largest number of slaves in the North (roughly 10 percent of the population of the state); emancipation was thus a substantial undertaking. Second, New Yorkers spent well over a decade (1785–99) debating emancipation bills, a fact that allows historians an opportunity to eavesdrop on the arguments that mattered over time to various stakeholders.

6 This first argument, in its economic dimension, builds on but also clarifies the arguments of two seminal studies. In "Philanthropy at Bargain Prices," Robert Fogel and Stanley Engerman rightly argue that the "central economic issue of emancipation [was] who should bear the costs of [masters'] compensation." Concluding that the burden mostly "shifted to the slaves," they note that "little is known about the motivation of particular groups with respect to particular legislative proposals or the ways in which economic or social class, political objectives, and ideological commitments interacted to produce one or another coalition." They do not, therefore, have a strong claim to make about why *children* were central to northern laws. Furthermore, they calculate the distribution of emancipation's costs between slaves and owners by using slave prices from Maryland, foregoing the chance to explore particular market understandings of children, child labor, and fertile women in the mid-Atlantic and New England. I do not want to overstate my claim, but it seems that many northern masters would have calculated the numbers differently; masters usually valued a young or adolescent child at the same price as a woman with an infant (or a pregnant woman). Fogel and Engerman concede, in fact, that they "may have overestimated both the value of the female childbearing capacity and the earnings attributable to that capacity."

We still need to do more work to understand how prices according to age both reflected the region's particular labor needs and shaped the development of gradual emancipation. In *The First Emancipation*, Arthur Zilversmit provides information on slave prices, emphasizes Quakers' abolitionism, and demonstrates (particularly for New Jersey) that policy makers debated the costs and benefits of child labor. My goal here is to connect the dots more explicitly – to explain why theological, ethical, economic, practical, and legal concerns converged on children at a specific antislavery moment. Fogel and Engerman, "Philanthropy at Bargain Prices: Notes on the Economics of Gradual Emancipation," *Journal of Legal Studies* 3 (June 1974), quotes on pp. 377–8, 380, 387; Zilversmit, *The First Emancipation*, chs. 2–3, 5, 7.

7   Important studies of northern emancipation include: David Gellman, *Emancipating New York: The Politics of Slavery and Freedom, 1777–1827* (Baton Rouge: Louisiana State University Press, 2006); Gigantino, *Ragged Road to Abolition*; Leslie M. Harris, *In the Shadow of Slavery: African Americans in New York City, 1626–1863* (Chicago: University of Chicago Press, 2003); Graham Russell Hodges, *Root and Branch: African Americans in New York and East Jersey, 1613–1863* (Chapel Hill: University of North Carolina Press, 1999); Joanne Pope Melish, *Disowning Slavery: Gradual Emancipation and "Race" in New England, 1780–1860* (Ithaca, NY: Cornell University Press, 1998); Gary Nash and Jean Soderlund, *Freedom by Degrees: Emancipation in Pennsylvania and Its Aftermath* (New York: Oxford University Press, 1991); Shane White, *Somewhat More Independent: The End of Slavery in New York City* (Athens: University of Georgia Press, 1991). An account that focuses on women, and through this lens addresses children's experiences more closely, is Erica Armstrong Dunbar's *A Fragile Freedom: African American Women and Emancipation in the Antebellum City* (New Haven, CT: Yale University Press, 2008). Some scholars note that newborn children made attractive objects of emancipation because policy makers believed that children had not yet been "degraded" by slavery; children could be trained to wield freedom responsibly and could become useful citizens. While this idea was indeed important in the late 1700s, especially in the context of the American Revolution, it was less essential to colonial antislavery ideology, politics, and practice. I do discuss the vital "useful citizen" argument in this chapter, but I nonetheless want to stress a longer history of gradual emancipation – a history that shows children's work and freedom discussed within other ideological and economic frameworks.

8   Camillia Cowling, who emphasizes the importance of conceptions of "motherhood" and "womanhood" in late nineteenth-century emancipation projects in Cuba and Brazil, sees "women at the front line in the struggle for legal and social change." *Conceiving Freedom: Women of Color, Gender, and the Abolition of Slavery in Havana and Rio de Janeiro* (Chapel Hill: University of North Carolina Press, 2013), 12. Although black mothers were crucial actors in the early United States North, they did not hold the same power and role in the eighteenth-century abolitionist imagination as they would in future decades. See also Martha Abreu, "Slave Mothers and Freed Children: Emancipation and Female Space in Debates on the 'Free

Womb' Law, Rio de Janeiro, 1871," *Journal of Latin American Studies* 28 (Oct. 1996): 567–80; Michelle McKinley, "Freedom at the Font: Baptismal Manumission in Seventeenth-Century Lima" (paper presented at the Berkshire Conference on the History of Women, Toronto, 2014); Rebecca Scott, "Paper Thin: Freedom and Re-enslavement in the Diaspora of the Haitian Revolution," *Law and History Review* 29 (Nov. 2011): 1061–87. Forms of gradual emancipation also occurred in Spanish America during the revolutions of the 1810s and 1820s. George Reid Andrews argues that these antislavery outcomes were the product of the critical role slaves played in the wars for independence. *Afro-Latin America, 1800–2000* (New York: Oxford University Press, 2004), ch. 2. Britain abolished slavery in the West Indies with the 1833 Act of Parliament that freed children under six while apprenticing adults. See Thomas C. Holt, *The Problem of Freedom: Race, Labor, and Politics in Jamaica and Britain, 1832–1938* (Baltimore, MD: Johns Hopkins University Press, 1992), esp. pp. 64–78, 151–63. I would also point to this volume's chapters by Audra Diptee and Sarah Winter, which highlight how the bonds of slavery and family affected children during emancipation in African and British contexts. In addition, Karen Sánchez-Eppler's historiographical discussion underscores the fact that scholars of southern U. S. slavery have worked more specifically on children than have scholars of northern U. S. slavery. A book that explores the themes I discuss here, in the context of post-Civil War southern emancipation, is Mary Niall Mitchell's *Raising Freedom's Child: Black Children and Visions of the Future After Slavery* (New York: New York University Press, 2008).

9   On applying a child-centered approach to slavery studies, see Anna Mae Duane's introduction to this volume.

10  Works that have influenced my thinking about the relationships between freedom and dependence, belonging, and obligation – troubling the "obvious" relationship between freedom and individualist independence – include: Gregory P. Downs, *Declarations of Dependence: The Long Reconstruction of Popular Politics in the South, 1861–1908* (Chapel Hill: University of North Carolina Press, 2011); James Ferguson, "Declarations of Dependence: Labour, Personhood, and Welfare in Southern Africa," *Journal of the Royal Anthropological Institute* 19 (2013): 223–42; Walter Johnson, "Clerks All! Or, Slaves with Cash," *Journal of the Early Republic* 26 (Winter 2006): 641–51; Dylan C. Penningroth, *The Claims of Kinfolk: African-American Property and Community in the Nineteenth-Century South* (Chapel Hill: University of North Carolina Press, 2003); Amy Dru Stanley, "Instead of Waiting for the Thirteenth Amendment: The War Power, Slave Marriage, and Inviolate Human Rights," *American Historical Review* 115 (June 2010): 732–65; Suzanne Miers and Igor Kopytoff, eds., *Slavery in Africa: Historical and Anthropological Perspectives* (Madison: University of Wisconsin Press, 1977), ch. 1.

11  On early modern antislavery, see Christopher L. Brown, *Moral Capital: Foundations of British Abolitionism* (Chapel Hill: University of North Carolina Press, 2006), 33–101; David Brion Davis, *The Problem of Slavery in Western Culture* (Ithaca, NY: Cornell University Press, 1966). On

Quakers, see Bryccan Carrey, *From Peace to Freedom: Quaker Rhetoric and the Birth of American Antislavery, 1658–1761* (New Haven, CT: Yale University Press, 2012). On the ways in which Quakers accommodated themselves to slavery, see Kirsten Block, "Cultivating Inner and Outer Plantations: Property, Industry, and Slavery in Early Quaker Migration to the New World," *Early American Studies* 8 (Fall 2010): 515–48; Katharine Gerbner, "The Ultimate Sin: Christianizing Slaves in Barbados in the Seventeenth Century," *Slavery and Abolition* 31 (March 2010): 57–73.

12    George Fox, "Gospel Family Order" (1676) in *The Quaker Origins of Antislavery*, ed. J. William Frost (Norwood, PA: Norwood Editions, 1980), 48–9.

13    "The Articles, Settlement, and Offices of the Free Society of Traders in Pennsylvania," *Pennsylvania Magazine of History and Biography* 5 (1881): 37–50. Italics in original. The Free Society of Traders collapsed rather quickly, far before the plan to free slaves after fourteen years could go into effect.

14    [George Keith and others], *An Exhortation & Caution to Friends Concerning Buying or Keeping of Negroes* (New York, 1693), 2–3.

15    For explanations of this timing, see: Jack Marietta, *The Reformation of American Quakerism, 1748–1783* (Philadelphia: University of Pennsylvania Press, 1984), ch. 5; Nash and Soderlund, *Freedom by Degrees*, ch. 2.

16    New York Yearly Meeting, Minutes, 1746–1800, Friends Historical Library, Swarthmore College, pp. 57–8 (1768); Westbury Monthly Meeting Manumissions, New York Yearly Meeting Records, Periodicals and Microfilm, New York Public Library; Nash and Soderlund, *Freedom by Degrees*, 89–93.

17    Vivienne Kruger has estimated that "family life under one roof" was unlikely for at least half of New York's slaves in the 1700s. "Born to Run: The Slave Family in Early New York, 1626 to 1827" (PhD dissertation, Columbia University, 1985), 147–9.

18    Poor adults (whether immigrant or native) also served multiyear terms of service, both voluntarily and involuntarily. But it was far more common in law and in practice to see children bound for multi-*decade* terms. Holly Brewer, *By Birth or Consent: Children, Law, and the Anglo-American Revolution in Authority* (Chapel Hill: University of North Carolina Press, 2005), 243–58; Farley Grubb, "Babes in Bondage? Debt Shifting by German Immigrants in Early America," *Journal of Interdisciplinary History* 37 (Summer 2006): 1–34; Ruth Wallis Herndon, *Unwelcome Americans: Living on the Margin in Early New England* (Philadelphia: University of Pennsylvania Press, 2001), ch. 1; John E. Murray and Ruth Wallis Herndon, "Markets for Children in Early America: A Political Economy of Pauper Apprenticeship," *Journal of Economic History* 62 (June 2002): 356–82. For a rich primary source, see New York City Indentures, 1718–27, 1792–1915, New-York Historical Society.

19    It is also worth noting that for Quakers – a small religious group that began without large landholdings, physical church structures, or government support – the household was a particularly important site of social and religious

reproduction. The poor-to-middling Friends who emigrated from England to the mid-Atlantic colonies in such high numbers were well-practiced in supervising the labor and education of children as a means of addressing godly and financial anxieties. Barry Levy, *Quakers and the American Family: British Settlement in the Delaware Valley* (New York: Oxford University Press, 1988), 22. See also Block, "Cultivating Inner and Outer Plantations," 520–8.

20 Thomas Woody, *Early Quaker Education in Pennsylvania* (New York, 1920), 238–9.

21 Oblong Monthly Meeting, Men's Minutes 1757–88, Records of New York Yearly Meeting of Friends, Milstein Division, New York Public Library (hereafter NYYMM). Quotation on p. 42.

22 Flushing Monthly Meeting, Women's Minutes, 1771–1806, NYYMM, December 6, 1775.

23 See, for example, Flushing Monthly Meeting, Men's Minutes 1703–84, NYYMM, for the years 1779–81, passim. Quakers throughout a yearly meeting would use the same queries.

24 Anthony Benezet, *A Short Account of that Part of Africa Inhabited by Negroes* (Philadelphia, 1762), 70–1.

25 [Cooper], *A Mite Cast into the Treasury*, 13–15.

26 For changing perceptions of the economic and sentimental value of children in the late nineteenth century, see Viviana Zelizer, *Pricing the Priceless Child: The Changing Social Value of Children* (Princeton, NJ: Princeton University Press, 1985). Levy, in *Quakers and the American Family*, argues that Friends were pioneers of modern American domestic ideology.

27 [Cooper], *A Mite Cast into the Treasury*, 17. Cooper's discussion of slavery and family recalls Sarah Winter's observation in this volume that "childhood represents a crux where the deep connections between familial relationships and the proprietary relations of slavery become visible in ways that could lead some observers to call into question slavery's ostensible legality" (see Chapter 2).

28 "For the Argus." Massachusetts minister Jeremy Belknap made a similar point about slave infants' lack of value to Virginian jurist St. George Tucker in 1795. Belknap wrote, "Negro children were reckoned an encumbrance in a family; and when weaned, were given away like puppies." *Collections of the Massachusetts Historical Society for the Year 1795* (Boston, 1835), 200.

29 *Historical Statistics*, Series Eg1–59; Kruger, "Born to Run," 147–9; White, *Somewhat More Independent*, 5, 16, 49–50. For enslaved pregnancy and childcare in the plantation South, see: Damian Alan Pargas, "From the Cradle to the Fields: Slave Childcare and Childhood in the Antebellum South," *Slavery and Abolition* 42 (Dec. 2011): 477–93.

30 "For the Argus." Although "Friend" did not make the following argument, it was sometimes suggested that freeing future-born children was a useful way to avoid violating masters' property rights. According to this logic, masters could not own someone who did not yet exist, nor claim a vested right. See "An Act to Prevent the Further Introduction of Slaves and to Limit the Term of Contracts for Servitude within this Province" (1793) in *A Collection of the Acts Passed in the Parliament of Great Britain ... Applying to the Province of*

*Upper Canada* (York, 1818), 30; Bergen County petition to the Legislature requesting repeal of the NJ Abolition Act of 1804, January 4, 1806, State Library MSS Collection, Folder 419, Box 5-3, New Jersey State Archives; Robert Pleasants to St. George Tucker, May 30, 1797, Letterbook of Robert Pleasants, Haverford College Quaker and Special Collections, 236.

31  *New-York Gazette*, March 25, 1776; *Royal Gazette*, February 26, 1780; *American Minerva*, January 23, 1797.

32  *Rivington's New York Gazetteer*, February 16, 1775; *Rivington's New York Gazetteer*, March 16, 1775; *New-York Gazette*, May 19, 1777; *New-York Packet*, December 25, 1783; *Independent Journal*, June 30, 1784; *New-York Packet*, October 7, 1784; *New-York Packet*, September 12, 1785; *American Minerva*, November 26, 1795.

33  Benjamin Rush, *An Address to the Inhabitants of the British Settlements in America, upon Slave-Keeping* (Philadelphia, 1773), 22–23. Samuel Hopkins, *The Works of Samuel Hopkins ... with a Memoir of His Life* (Boston, 1852) 2:581, 594.

34  "An Act for the Gradual Abolition of Slavery" (1780).

35  See footnote 3 for statute citations. For Rhode Island's 1785 amendment, see "An Act Repealing Part of an Act Entitled 'An Act Authorizing the Manumission of Negroes' " in *Records of the State of Rhode Island*, 132–3.

36  Edmund Prior to James Pemberton, February 26, 1784, March 3, 1784, March 10, 1784, Pemberton Family Papers, Historical Society of Pennsylvania; *Journal of the Senate of the State of New-York* (New York, 1785), 8, 15.

37  *Journal of the Senate of the State of New-York* (New York, 1785), 15, 23; *Journal of the Assembly of the State of New-York* (New York, 1785), 53, 55, 56. For laws related to child pauper apprenticeship, see "An Act Concerning Apprentices and Servants" (1788) and "An Act for the Better Settlement and Relief of the Poor" (1788) in *Laws of the State of New York ... 1785, 1786, 1787 and 1788, inclusive* (Albany, 1886) 2:620–5, 731–44; "An Act Concerning Apprentices and Servants" (1801) in *Laws of the State of New York* (Albany, 1802) 1:186–92. The Assembly also considered a bill that would have freed future-born children of slaves *and* children born since the Declaration of Independence; this plan would have freed children age eight and under. *Journal of the Assembly* (1785), 14.

38  Changes to Bill, March 2, 1785, Manuscripts and Special Collections, New York State Library.

39  Alfred Street, ed., *The Council of Revision of the State of New York* (Albany, 1859), 268. The Council of Revision was an executive-judicial body that reviewed bills before they became law. The eventual 1799 New York gradual abolition law did not place any restrictions on citizenship, office holding, or voting.

40  Brewer, *By Birth or Consent*.

41  Records of the New-York Manumission Society, 1785–1849, vol. 6, February 4, 1785, pp. 2–3, 8–10, New-York Historical Society (hereafter cited as NYMS).

42  NYMS, vol. 6, February 10, 1785, p. 17.

43  Ibid., 26–8, 35, 37.

44  For a contemporary account of the African Free School, written by one of its headmasters, see Charles C. Andrews, *The History of the New-York African Free Schools* (New York, 1830).

45  On the African Free School, see Sarah Levine-Gronningsater, "Delivering Freedom: Gradual Emancipation, Black Legal Culture, and the Origins of Sectional Crisis in New York, 1759-1870" (PhD Dissertation, University of Chicago, 2014), ch. 3; Carla L. Peterson, *Black Gotham: A Family History of African Americans in Nineteenth-Century New York City* (New Haven, CT: Yale University Press, 2012), ch. 2.

46  "The Trustees of the African School," *American Minerva*, August 22, 1794; *Herald*, August 25, 1794.

47  Jay's election was important, but so was the fact that the electorate was changing as non-slaveholding immigrants from New England moved into the state. John L. Brooke, *Columbia Rising: Civil Life on the Upper Hudson from the Revolution to the Age of Jackson* (Chapel Hill: University of North Carolina Press, 2010), ch. 6.

48  Samuel Ten Broeck to William Wilson, March 24, 1798, Wilson Papers, Clements Library, University of Michigan.

49  "Legislature of New York," *Daily Advertiser*, February 6, 1799.

50  *Journal of the Senate of the State of New-York* (Albany, 1799), 102, 107–8. On the fate of various gradual abolition bills in the state legislature in the 1780s and 1790s, see Levine-Gronningsater, "Delivering Freedom," ch. 1.

51  "An Act for the Gradual Abolition of Slavery" (1799). When masters started cheating the "abandonment" system, legislators ceased *state* funding for free-born children's care. "An Act to Repeal the Tenth Section of the Act, Entitled 'An Act Concerning Slaves and Servants'" (1804) in *Laws of the State of New York, Containing All the Acts Passed from the Revision of 1801, to ... 1804* (Albany, 1804), 479–80.

52  This emancipation program mirrors the *tutelle* system that Audra Diptee describes in this volume (see Chapter 8). Diptee notes that "free" Senegalese children were assigned "guardians" who wanted to perpetuate slavery. She also notes that some enslaved women, after marrying free men, found "the relationship was one of master and slave." Similarly, even though some American abolitionists wanted masters to "act the part of the father" to black children, masters often remained simply masters. Household relationships in both contexts maintained uneven power relationships based on age and gender despite that fact that the dependents in question were technically "free."

53  Although black servant children throughout the gradual emancipation states were born into a different status than their mothers were, the degree to which they inhabited a legal category distinct from slavery varied by state. In New York, black children gained access, on paper and sometimes in fact, to new rights and privileges. Antislavery lawmakers deliberately defined these children as laborers akin to white apprentices. Children in other states fared worse. Gigantino stresses that in New Jersey, servant children were "fundamentally different from apprentices and paupers and therefore more

closely related to slaves." *Ragged Road to Abolition*, 100. See also Melish, *Disowning Slavery*, pp. 88–95. Hodges provides a more sanguine view of emancipation in Connecticut in *David Ruggles: A Radical Black Abolitionist and the Underground Railroad in New York City* (Chapel Hill: University of North Carolina Press, 2010), ch. 1. Dunbar describes a range of experiences of child servitude in Philadelphia in *Fragile Freedom*, ch. 2.

54  NYMS, vol. 9, July 19, 1808, pp. 188–9.

55  NYMS, vol. 9, December 21, 1808, January 1, 1809, pp. 195, 201.

56  "An Addition to the Act Concerning Slaves and Servants" (1810) in *Public Laws of the State of New-York … 1810* (Albany, 1810), 32–3.

57  NYMS, vol. 10, March 3, 1809, March 21, 1809, pp. 60–1.

58  NYMS, vol. 10, March 16, 1812, April 18, 1812, pp. 167, 169.

59  NYMS, vol. 10, March 5, 1811, April 4, 1811, pp. 121–2.

60  Like Sojourner Truth, black abolitionist Austin Steward published an account of his legal activism in New York's countryside. As an adolescent, Steward discerned that his Virginian master may have broken importation laws when the household moved to northwest New York. Austin Steward, *Twenty-Two Years a Slave, and Forty Years a Freeman* (Rochester, 1857), ch. 11. On Truth, see Olive Gilbert and Sojourner Truth, *Narrative of Sojourner Truth: A Northern Slave, Emancipated from Bodily Servitude by the State of New York, in 1828* (Boston, 1850), esp. pp. 23, 44–55; Margaret Washington, *Sojourner Truth's America* (Urbana: University of Illinois Press, 2011), ch. 4. The Manumission Society's minutes indicate that slaves and servants outside of New York City contacted the Society for help; members sometimes tried to enlist local antislavery support for these supplicants.

61  Statement of Charlotte, *The People v. Charlotte, a Black Girl*, filed June 7, 1811, District Attorney Indictment Papers, Municipal Archives of the City of New York.

62  *The People v. Charlotte, a Black Girl*, June 1811, New York County Court of General Sessions, Minutes of the Sessions, Municipal Archives of the City of New York.

63  Sánchez-Eppler notes in this volume that even though the majority of American slaves in 1860 were under age twenty, historians often fail to "recognize recollections of slave childhoods as valid accounts of slavery" (see Chapter 1). The same lesson might apply to scholars of the North. Although northern emancipation laws certainly affected and freed some adults, it was children whose lives were most intensely regulated by the states' most wide-ranging abolition laws.

64  "An Act to Amend the Act, Entitled, 'An Act Concerning Slaves and Servants'" (1807) in *Laws of the State of New-York Containing all the Acts … 1809*, vol. 5 (Albany, 1809), 92–3; "An Addition to the Act Concerning Slaves and Servants" (1810); "An Act Relative to Slaves and Servants" (1817) in *Laws of the State of New-York, Passed at the Fortieth Session* (Albany, 1817), 136–44.

65  For the rules on early release, see "An Act Relative to Slaves and Servants" (1817).

66  NYMS, vol. 11, November 8, 1821, February 13, 1822, pp. 107, 110.

67 NYMS, vol. 11, January 10, 1826, October 7, 1826, pp. 149, 155.

68 NYMS, vol. 11, February 23, 1829, July 14, 1829, pp. 181, 184.

69 Manuscripts and Special Collections, New York State Library, Call #15598. For a similar example, see Call #18079. For discussion of conditional manumissions, negotiated self-purchases, and the changing labor market, see Shane White, *Somewhat More Independent*, ch. 2; Michael Groth, "Slaveholders and Manumission in Dutchess County, New York," *New York History* 78 (Jan. 1997): 33–50. For examples of slave prices, see: Zilversmit, *The First Emancipation*, appendix; Carter et al., *Historical Statistics of the United States*, Series Bb209–214.

70 "An Act to Enable Certain Persons to Take and Hold Estates within this State" (1809) in *Public Laws of the State of New-York Passed at the Thirty-Second Session of the Legislature* (Albany, 1809), 450–1.

71 On the incompatibility of marriage and slavery, see: Jacob Wheeler, *A Practical Treatise on the Law of Slavery* (New York, 1837), 199; Amy Dru Stanley, *From Bondage to Contract: Wage Labor, Marriage, and the Market in the Age of Slave Emancipation* (Cambridge: Cambridge University Press, 1998).

72 "Albany County Register of Manumitted Slaves 1800–1828" in Local Records on Microfilm (Reel #74-40-5), p. 165, New York State Archives, Albany.

73 Ibid., p. 193.

74 "An Act Relative to Slaves and Servants" (1817).

75 Barbara Jeanne Fields, *Slavery and Freedom on the Middle Ground: Maryland during the Nineteenth Century* (New Haven, CT: Yale University Press, 1985), 193.

# THE CHILD AS A PIVOT POINT BETWEEN CONSENT AND COMPLICITY

## Anna Mae Duane

Consent is inextricable from freedom. Consent, is also, by definition, incompatible with childhood. So, if children are inherently incapable of consent – as both law and custom determine in many places throughout the world – how can we determine if they are free or enslaved? Certainly, children everywhere have to do things they do not freely choose. Even the most privileged children attend school when they'd rather play outside; they have to do the dishes and clean their rooms when they would prefer to be doing just about anything else. Certainly no one would equate these chores with enslavement. But just as certainly, no one would consider it acceptable to insist that any free person over the age of eighteen be compelled to do unremunerated labor. The three chapters in this section take on the largely unquestioned assumption that people under a certain age are – and should be – incapable of consent, and urge us to lean into the difficult questions that arise when we consider the implications of that useful fiction.

In the circuitry of the law, consent is a master switch, determining who counts as child and who counts as a citizen, whether that person is innocent or culpable, and whether he or she is enslaved or free.[1] The authors in this third section argue that the law's reliance on consent renders childhood and slavery conceptually interdependent in ways that render legal remedies to post-emancipation enslavement at best ineffective, and at worst harmful to the very population they purport to help. Our authors take on some of the most visible sites of neo-abolitionist fervor – child soldiering and child prostitution – to illustrate how Western investment in children's innocence and vulnerability often supports the very forces exploiting those qualities. All three of these pieces eschew the abolitionist rhetoric of rescue to better engage the stories of actual children, often placed in difficult circumstances by economic hardship, war, or governmental policy. Their analyses push for a more realistic assessment of how people of *all* ages often have to choose between bad options. For both adults and children find themselves in circumstances that cannot be reduced to violations of individual innocents by particular bad actors, but rather emerge as the product of systemic forces that don't yield easily to humanitarian appeals.[2] In other words, relying on the rubric of consent in order to render particular acts deplorable when directed toward children denies the reality of many people struggling for survival throughout the world. As Walter Johnson has argued, to apply "the jargon of self-determination and choice" – key words in Western understandings of freedom as a personal responsibility – to historical "civil objectification and choicelessness," we can too easily obscure "a consideration of human-ness lived outside the conventions of liberal agency."[3] Indeed, as John Wall argues later in this volume, children are explicitly constructed as unqualified for this very liberal agency: "The fact is that the Enlightenment architects of human rights theory, from Locke to Rousseau and Kant, not only did not apply human rights to children, but argued explicitly that children should not have them."

Jessica Pliley's focus on white slavery allows us to see how childhood was explicitly used to define slavery in the post-emancipation period, even as that definition was deployed to obscure the memory of pre-emancipation slavery's brutal toll on men, women, and children of African descent. In order to refashion the historical reality – still in living memory for many – of the systemic enslavement and sexual exploitation of people of African descent, reformers refashioned slavery in explicit relationship to femaleness, youth, and whiteness. Pliley demonstrates how "the rhetoric of white slavery allowed slavery to be redefined, not on racial grounds, but around notions of capacity, consent, and childhood." "We can also see these traits," Pliley points out, "echoed in current twenty-first-century debates about juvenile incarceration (Meiners) or child soldiering (Rosen)." Thus, age, consent, and race are shifting parts in a perpetually moving gear works where a new justification replaces an old one that no longer functions effectively. In both the cases of the white slavery scare and the child soldiering debate, the chronological age of the individual in question – an age that has been moved up explicitly to expand the population considered enslaved – has become the sole determinant of whether that person can count as a slave.[4]

Taking a wide geographical and historical perspective, Rosen argues that child soldiering was a part of American and European history until quite recently (he finds evidence of child soldiers as late as World War II) and only became equated with slavery when Western states no longer needed to recruit soldiers under eighteen to maintain military force. Here, as in Pliley's piece on the white slavery panic, chronological age emerges as the primary rubric for determining whether a particular practice is slavery, a rubric Rosen wants us to question. For Rosen, "the entire history of the malleability of the age of consent should make us extremely cautious about using age as a proxy for consent in the definition of slavery." In cases of twenty-first-century sex work and soldiering, slavery is literally defined by childhood: certain practices are reprehensible (and thus should be rendered illegal), not in and of themselves, but because they violate a particular sense of childhood innocence. As Rosen writes, many "practices that are rejected and widely vilified in the West, including child labor, child fostering, child prostitution, child marriage, have nowadays been recast by children's rights activists and so-called New Abolitionists as forms of child enslavement." Thus our attachment to scenes of helpless innocent childhood victims and heroic adult rescuers hinders our ability to study the lives of real children, because we can't bear how young people's savvy negotiations of complex demands defy our understanding of what children are capable of, and what our relationship to them should be. Neither Pliley nor Rosen suggest that many children haven't been or aren't currently being exploited or enslaved. Nor are they implying that that some conditions aren't much better for child development than others. Rather, they remind us that a clean line between slavery and freedom, like a clean line between childhood innocence and adult complicity, blocks our view to the realities underlying the practices we find so distressing.

The first two chapters in this section chart how Western beliefs about consent render children more likely to be called slaves when they are performing acts we believe to be solely reserved for the realm of adults. Audra Diptee's chapter offers a divergent perspective, in which antislavery legislation aimed at adults renders children more likely to be enslaved in the first place. In part because colonial authorities imagined freedom as an attribute that was coded as male adulthood, and partially because African children were viewed as outside the realm of innocent vulnerability accorded to white European children, colonial officials created and facilitated situations that increased the likelihood of enslavement for both women and children. For instance, the "protection" that French colonizers offered to formerly enslaved children, especially girl children, involved replacing former slaveowners with either "guardians" or "husbands" who exploited them in precisely the same ways their previous masters had.

Diptee's chapter illuminates particularly damning side effects of the supposedly protective impulse to imagine children as incapable of consent. Their lack of legal standing rendered them wholly subject to adult decisions about their physical and sexual labor, with no say in refusing the exploitative "protection" authorities offered. Although we often imagine consent as the capacity to say yes – to commit to a contract, to take a job, or to engage in sexual acts – Diptee reminds us that consent also implies the ability to say no. In the cases she describes, children's attempts to remove their consent – to refuse the marriage or guardianship that simply perpetuated slave-like conditions under a different name – were dismissed as childish recalcitrance.

All three chapters remind us that childhood has always been a slippery concept, in which assumed categories – vulnerability, innocence, an inability to consent – simplify complex situations. By focusing only on children who, both in our fantasies of innocence and in the reality of their vulnerability, can create a sympathetic subject for rescue, we sidestep larger questions about whether particular practices are unjust in and of themselves, no matter who participates in them. In short, the reliance on a false binary between the innocent, non-consenting, passive child and the complicit criminal does important ideological work, much of it to adding to the comfort of Western would-be benefactors, and the states and corporations that benefit from cheap labor. Here as elsewhere in this volume, we argue that a failure to treat enslaved children with nuance harms both children and adults. If one needs to have the innocence of a child to qualify as a victim of either sexual or military enslavement, then those over eighteen are, by default, presumed "guilty" of consent. In truth, enslavement, past and present, often functions within systems that allow for the semblance of consent, even as all choices are highly constrained. By focusing on children's alleged inability to choose for themselves, we can write off adults caught in coercive and exploitative situations as the victims only of their own personal choices, rather than of market and military forces that compromise all people's ability to choose freely.

## Notes

1 For analyses of the flaws of this model, see Martha C. Nussbaum, *Frontiers of Justice: Disability, Nationality, Species Membership* (Cambridge, MA: Harvard University Press, 2009); and John Wall, "Human Rights

in Light of Childhood," *International Journal of Children's Rights* 16.4
(2008): 523–43.

2  For example, see an analysis of impoverished people "choosing" to sell organs
in Miran Epstein, "The Ethics of Poverty and the Poverty of Ethics: The Case
of Palestinian Prisoners in Israel Seeking to Sell Their Kidneys in Order to
Feed Their Children," *Journal of Medical Ethics* 33.8: 473–4.

3  Walter Johnson, "On Agency," *Journal of Social History* 37.1 (2003): 115.

4  See Rosen and Pliley's chapters for further explication.

# 6

## Protecting the Young and the Innocent: Age and Consent in the Enforcement of the White Slave Traffic Act

### Jessica R. Pliley

"The human chattels of these traffickers are practically slaves," declared O. Edward Janney in 1911, "for the girls and women who are lured, deceived through affection, or in some instances forced into prostitution, are held in bondage by subtle and compelling means. Whether the victim is confined behind closed doors, or is allowed to go out under close watch, or kept in submission by fear of personal violence, she is, under any of these conditions, *a slave* – one forced to do her master's bidding and obliged to give him the money she receives."[1] When the white slavery panic broke into the general American consciousness in 1907, the sensationalized stories of sexual slavery inevitably featured victims that shared the same constellation of characteristics.[2] They were young. They were white. They were innocent. From 1907 to 1914, American popular culture was dominated by stories of sexual slavery, as white slavery provided rich material for the imaginations of playwrights, filmmakers, and journalists. According to most stories, young, white girls faced an array of dangers that would leave them trapped in a brothel where they would be exploited by "human vultures who fatten on the shame of innocent young girls."[3]

The crisis of sex slaves entrapped in America's quasi-legal, very public brothels conflated racial anxieties with fears over the commercialization of sexuality to produce white slavery narratives that constructed a category of victim so innocent that all moral Americans would desire to protect her rather than consume her. Newspaper reports, magazine exposes, public investigations, and the numerous books produced on the topic emphasized the young age of American white slaves, which rendered these victims by definition as lacking any agency, and certainly having not the mental nor moral capacity to consent to sex work. Entertainment, outrage, rescue, and reform became intertwined as activists turned to Congress to put a halt to the traffic in white slaves. In 1910 Congress delivered such a law when it passed the White Slave Traffic Act, popularly known as the Mann Act, which outlawed the transport, or inducement of transport, over state lines of women and girls for the purposes of prostitution, debauchery, or "any other immoral purpose."

Much of the anti-vice legal reform agenda of the Progressive Era, to which the Mann Act contributed, centered on protecting young women's sexuality by positioning adolescent girls' consent to sexual encounters as a legal impossibility. Narratives about white slavery took this logic even further by asserting that in most cases the girls who entered sex work had never consented to their own degradation, but rather had been tricked, coerced, lured, or forced into commercial sex work, from which they could never be redeemed. Age emerged as a key axis in the Progressive-era anti-vice legal reform agenda in two interconnected ways. First, social purity activists found the rhetoric of threatened innocence aided in campaigns to pass laws to fight the sexual exploitation of children. Second, hand in hand with these campaigns were age of consent campaigns that sought to extend the length of childhood by tying notions of childhood to a fixed chronological marker of girlhood because those classified as children (below the age of consent) lacked the legal capacity to consent to sex, and also lacked the instrumental capacity to change the conditions of their lives. The white slavery discourse wove together both of these strands by simultaneously conceiving white slaves universally as young girls and asserting those girls' inability to act on their own behalf. In this way, the rhetoric of white slavery allowed slavery to be redefined, not on racial grounds, but around notions of capacity, consent, and childhood. Age, consent, and innocence were vital characteristics of post-emancipation slavery, as we see in the white slave narratives in the early twentieth century. We can also see these traits echoed in current twenty-first-century debates about juvenile incarceration (Meiners, Chapter 4, this volume) or child soldiering (Rosen, Chapter 7, this volume).

Yet, when it came to enforcement of the new federal white slavery law, the Bureau of Investigation confronted a much more challenging social milieu than reformers imagined. Faced with young women who grasped at the financial opportunities sex work offered, the Bureau had to contend with the complicated and vexing question of female consent and agency, while also trying to figure out if the law should be used to protect or police young women's sexuality. The Bureau's enforcement of this broad law quickly encountered the limits of placing young women and girls' sexuality within a slavery framework.

## White Slaves in Bondage: Myth, Melomentary, and the Power of Innocence

The tales of white slavery had their roots in the 1880 purity movement's stories of sex slavery. Though W. T. Stead's 1885 exposé of London's market in child prostitution was widely covered in the American purity press, it wasn't until Dr. Katherine Bushnell investigated rumors of forced prostitution of girls in Wisconsin and Michigan lumber camps in 1888 that a uniquely American narrative of white slavery developed.[4] Bushnell's investigation uncovered a miasma of vice where young sex workers were recruited to service the lumberjacks and kept in debt bondage to brothel owners. After interviewing 575 sex workers, she described them all interchangeably as young girls, girls, and women, though how she distinguished between these categories is exceedingly unclear.[5] Her imprecision functioned to collapse all of these sex workers into the single category of girls. The combination of youth with femaleness within the term "girl" converted these prostitutes into objects worthy of rescue.[6] She declared that these girls were a new type of slave "in that they are compelled to acquire property for others and not for themselves."[7]

By combining the constant references of the women as "young girls," Bushnell constructed a story where her sex workers were cleansed of blame due to their presumed youth, with its concomitant notion of the inability to consent. Instead she drew attention to the structures keeping them in slave-like bondage. After reading her report, social purity leader Aaron Macy Powell, who was also the editor of *The Philanthropist*, declared, "The girls and women inveigled into these dens under promise of remunerative employment or whatever other pretense ... are virtually held as slaves. The cruelties practiced [sic] to subordinate and intimidate them, are akin to the worst horrors of the old-time chattel slavery."[8]

Drawing on the language of slavery offered Powell, Bushnell, and other purity activists a way to quell arguments that blamed the existence of prostitution on women's immorality, lustfulness, and laziness. Invoking the specter of force, coercion, bondage, and, in the case of Bushnell, direct references to women in chains, transformed the unsympathetic adult whore into a blameless child sex slave.

Explicit comparisons between white slavery and African American chattel slavery were common because such comparisons functioned to highlight the inability of the enslaved to alter the exploitative conditions that structured their lives. In 1899, one writer declared: "There is a slave trade in this country, and it is not black folks this time, but little white girls – thirteen, fourteen, fifteen, sixteen, seventeen years of age – and they are snatched out of our arms, and from our Sabbath-schools and from our communion tables."[9] This writer was not satisfied with merely comparing white slavery with African American chattel slavery; rather she saw white slavery as far more outrageous because she considered the "victims" as especially innocent in terms of youth (the repetitious listing of ages). Their prior morality was emphasized by the references to the Sabbath schools and communion tables. Most activists invoked the comparison to heighten outrage over the idea of white girls trapped in enslaved conditions. William Burgess claimed that white slavery was:

far worse than negro slavery. Many a negro had an honest home, was able by the provision of his employer to establish a domestic circle and the have the same tender feeling towards his offspring as the white man had. Many an owner of black slaves conserved their purity and never thought of them for beastly purposes.... But no slave ever enters into this white slave system, no girl is ever drawn by the panderer or tricked by the enforced action of men and women into this slavery whose soul is not instantly blackened.[10]

In a world with a vivid memory of the term "slave" being equated with blackness, statements like this emphasized the very wrongness of the existence of white slaves.[11] The linking together of the category "white" with the category "slave" was almost unimaginable in a country that had always defined whiteness, at the minimum, as meaning the privilege of not being a slave – of being "free."[12] Much of the discursive power of the term "white slave" drew from its basic inversion of racial definitions. "White slaves were enslaved not because of their skin color," notes historian Gunther Peck, "but in spite of it."[13]

The metaphor of white slavery had the troubling effect of analogizing white prostitution with African American slavery. This analogy cast African American slavery as non-sexual, which it clearly wasn't,[14] and exploitative prostitution as only a white affair, a blatant dismissal of the place African American, Asian, and Latina women occupied in the sexual marketplace.[15] Further, as the quote cited earlier suggests, the analogy romanticized African American slavery, scrubbing it of its inherent brutality – sexual, familial, or physical. Coinciding as they did with the entrenchment of Jim Crow segregation and the nadir of black life in America, white slavery narratives bolstered white supremacy by remaking African American slavery into an institution that held no sexual component, and describing sexual exploitation as only outrageous when white girls were abused. Anti-white slavery activist Clifford Roe did note that women of color could be trafficked, writing in 1911, "The phrase, white slave traffic, is a misnomer, for there is a traffic in yellow and black women and girls, as well as in white girls. However, the term has become so widely and extensively used that it seems futile to ever change it." Indeed, the ubiquity of the term "white slavery" ensured that for many, the term was racially exclusive, and it was the sexual exploitation of white girls that prompted outcry.[16]

The slavery analogy was most potent when fused to ideas of youth and innocence. The late nineteenth-century purity press gladly embraced the idea that women in brothels were young girls. The *Philanthropist* blamed well-to-do men for the "cruel traffic in girlhood."[17] By speaking vaguely of girlhood, the exact boundaries of girlhood remained obscured. While the purity movement fretted about the traffic of girls, it also campaigned to raise the age of consent from its typical setting at ten or twelve years of age. The idea articulated in the age of consent campaigns was that girlhood needed to be protected from sexual exploitation, of which white slavery was an extreme manifestation, and that young women lacked the ability to properly consent to sexual encounters until they reached adulthood. In 1887, Congress passed a law raising the age of consent in DC and the territories from ten to sixteen years old. State-level campaigns had more mixed results, but by 1920, all states had raised the age of consent to either sixteen or eighteen years of age.[18] Within purity circles, the age of consent campaigns sought to carve out a wide space in adolescence for protection, essentially lengthening childhood. Similarly, the rhetorical dependence on referring to sex workers as "girls" and "young girls" within the white slavery narratives of the purity press ensured that readers would see these women as lacking the full capacity to consent, as victims of their circumstances, and youths to be protected.[19] In contrast to Karen Sánchez-Eppler's suggestion that the category of slave and child were often seen as mutually exclusive, in the white slavery narrative, the amalgamation of these categories functioned to fuse both with greater salience and importance (see Chapter 1, this volume). Tropes of endangered girlhood added a sense of urgency to anti-prostitution reforms. As Gayle S. Rubin aptly notes, "No tactic for stirring up erotic hysteria has been as reliable as the appeal to protect children."[20]

Statements painting America's prostitutes as sex slaves and then discursively converting them into child slaves through the white slavery idiom quietly circulated in the purity press until 1907, when they exploded into the mainstream media, giving birth to the white slavery narrative that dominated American popular culture from 1907 to 1914.[21] By far the most popular and far-reaching portrayals of the white slave myth that exposed the vulnerability of American girls could be found in the numerous films, plays, and pulp novels circulating the country. For example, on November 24, 1913, the film *Traffic in Souls* opened to audiences at New York's Joe Weber, and was an instant blockbuster. It is estimated that the theater turned away more than 1,000 people opening night and 30,000 New Yorkers saw the movie during its first week.[22] The movie offered an exciting story that featured two sisters, one of whom, the younger, is seduced by the unsupervised recreational opportunities of the city, where she unknowingly encounters a pimp who drugs her and sells her to a brothel, where she languishes in suffering until rescued by a policeman (hero) at the behest of her more responsible (and older) sister.

The success of *Traffic in Souls*, which was estimated to have earned $450,000 in the first month, launched a subgenre within movies known as vice films. These films capitalized on the same fears that anti-white slavery activists held – the danger urban entertainment and employment posed to young women, the anonymity of the city where cross-class and interethnic courtship could flourish, and the sexual vulnerability of young women. Often under the guise of educating audiences about social evils, such films entertained viewers with sensational representations of urban vice, and provided voyeurism that titillated audiences, most of whom, according to the *New York Times*, were teenage girls and young women.[23] Within the six months following the opening of *Traffic in Souls*, New Yorkers were treated to a near-constant stream of films with titles like *The Inside of the White Slave Traffic*, *The Exposure of the White Slave Traffic*, *The Shadows of Sin*, *Smashing the Velvet Trust*, *The House of Bondage*, *A Soul in Peril*, *The Wages of Sin*, and *The Traffic in Girls*.[24] These melodramatic white slave stories were animated by a tension between good and evil, and the white slaves were marked by their naïveté, vulnerability, and innocence, constructed in reference to girlhood rather than womanhood (a state more firmly associated with marriage and reproduction, i.e., procreative sex). There is no uncertainty within these tales, no nuance. The heroine/victim's innocence propelled the entire plot.

The richest voices within the white slavery narratives were those experts who claimed a special knowledge of the reality of white slavery.[25]

These anti-vice reformers, investigators, and journalists infused their exposés of white slavery with a melodramatic tone, yet claimed that they were merely pulling back the curtain of the brothel to reveal the true dimensions of white slavery in America. Clifford G. Roe, an assistant state's attorney in Chicago who built his reputation by prosecuting cases of white slavery, asserted that "secrecy has been the chief cause of the success of this nefarious system, for it has hidden from the young girls, who are in the greatest danger, all the methods and devices by which they may be entrapped."[26] He concluded his first exposé on white slavery, *Panders and Their White Slaves*, with the proclamation: "In the effort to cast a white light upon these arch enemies to society who lurk in the darkness, who buy and sell the souls of daughters, who gather in the miserable dollars coined from the tears of girls, I have tried to handle hard, cold facts as delicately as possible."[27] In emphasizing the "hard, cold facts" while steeping such narratives with the insipid tone of melodrama, Roe and his ilk produced what Carole Vance has termed "melomentary."

Melomentary refers to works that are presented as "documentary reports, but the bits of empirical evidence (interviews, comments of experts, facts) are organized by a highly predetermined plot line, with a limited set of characters (or subject positions), all moving towards a triumphant endpoint that is highly overdetermined."[28] Within white-slave tracts written by experts claiming insider knowledge of the business of white slavery, white slaves were always rendered as blameless in their degradation, the victims of deceit, fraud, trickery, or kidnapping. These tracts uniformly emphasized young sex workers' innocence, which was then conflated with youth and associated traits of weakness, dependency, helplessness, and an idealized naïveté.[29] Within these popularly consumed books, there was no room for female will – the desire for money or for freedom from parental control. Rather, white slaves were rendered as passive victims awaiting rescue.

The tendency to highlight the youth (and presumed innocence, dangerous ignorance, and reckless curiosity) of white slaves was shared by other anti-vice activists who quickly jumped onto the white slavery bandwagon by publishing their own exposés. All of them shared the same tendency to characterize sex workers as "young girls" or "girls," and to emphasize, somewhat paradoxically, their innocence in spite of their sexual experience. Edwin Sims, a U.S. attorney in Illinois, declared that "Literally thousands of innocent girls from the country districts are every year entrapped into a life of hopeless slavery and degradation [by] 'white slave' traders who have reduced the art of ruining young girls to a national and international system."[30] These writings frequently collapsed the innocent girl and the immoral girl into one category. Little or no distinction was made between those who entered sex work by coercion and those who entered by choice. As Wirt Hallum argued in 1912, "As for White Slavery, the girls who are forced into this or into immorality through the physical violence or intimidation of the vice promoter, are not the only ones that need our sympathy and our help. The girls who are *enticed into vice by other means* are often as much helpless victims as though they were taken into nets by force. Both classes soon become hopeless human wrecks. They are somebody's daughters and, sensational as it might sound, somebody is slowly killing them for profit."[31] These narratives treated innocent and immoral young women as the same in their victimhood, conflating the forced prostitute and voluntary prostitute into the same thing, while also transforming young women into children. The protection of the innocent young girl, somebody's daughter, encouraged the overly melodramatic, hysterical tone that saturated white slavery narratives. In addition to collapsing all young women into the category of victim (or potential victim), and eliding issues of consent by casting the victims as children, which rendered them as slaves because they could not (legally) consent or meaningfully control the conditions of their lives, while also portraying them a shockingly young, authors of white slavery tracts almost all agreed that once a girl has lost her innocence, "it all leads to the same end, the brothel and the potter's field."[32]

White slavery narratives reconstituted young women's sexual agency in fascinating ways, not so much fully denying that agency as suggesting that a young girl's decision to enter sex work, as Pamela Haag notes, "would hardly be seen as a free or meaningful, legitimate enactment of their will, given the social context in which it was made."[33] The anxieties white slavery narratives expressed were steeped in the same logics that inspired a wide range of legal reforms aimed at purifying society by policing mostly female heterosexuality. At the heart of the progressive mentality was a problematic understanding of sexuality that posited the sexual double standard as the origin of women's sexual exploitation amidst a rapidly sexualizing commercial culture. Consequently, much of the legal reform agenda centered on protecting young women's sexuality by positioning adolescent girls' consent to sexual encounters as a legal impossibility. Narratives about white slavery took this logic even further by asserting that in most cases the young women who entered sex work had been tricked, coerced, lured, or forced into commercial sex slavery, from which they could never be redeemed. Thus, white slavery was conceived as a form of slavery that was worse than African American chattel slavery because not only was the white slave's labor stolen, but her innocence and reproductive potential had also been squandered.

### The White Slave Traffic Act and the Challenges of the Subjectivities of the Young

In 1910, the U.S. Congress responded to the growing outcry about the white slavery crisis by passing the White Slave Traffic Act, popularly known as the Mann Act, which made it illegal to take a woman or child over state lines for the purposes of prostitution, debauchery, or "any other immoral purpose," with or without hire, or in other words, with or without her consent. Most congressmen who supported the law embraced the white slavery myth. Thetis W. Simms (D-TN) urged passage of the law to "take care of the girls, the women – the defenseless,"[34] and, he suggested, "we will prevent, I hope forever, the taking away by fraud or violence, from some doting mother or loving father, of some blue-eyed girl and immersing her in dens of infamy."[35] Reflecting as it did the underlying logics of the white slave narratives, the White Slave Traffic Act rendered all sex workers into sex slaves. The White Slave Traffic Act passed the House with minimal debate and went on to sail through the Senate. President William Taft signed it into law on June 25, 1910.

Almost immediately, questions arose concerning how the Department of Justice's Bureau of Investigation could enforce this law. Established in 1908 by executive order, the Bureau of Investigation formed the investigative unit of the Department of Justice (after 1935, renamed the Federal Bureau of Investigation). Bureau Chief Stanley W. Finch had to formulate the Bureau's approach to enforcement. For his part, Finch firmly believed white slavery was a very real threat to America's girls, proclaiming that the cause of prostitution was "ninety percent the fault of the man,"[36] and arguing that dissolute men seduced young girls because they could earn as much as twenty-five dollars from a brothel for bringing in a "broiler," a girl between the ages of thirteen and sixteen, and slightly less for a "chicken," a girl between sixteen and eighteen.[37] For Finch, the "white slave traffic is a species of involuntary servitude."[38]

Though the rhetoric surrounding white slavery functioned to lessen young women's agency by denying them the ability to consent, the passage of the White Slave Traffic Act forced the Bureau to confront a very different reality on the ground: while they remained open (until 1917), brothels did provide young sex workers for their pampered customers, and some young women freely entered sex work and often resisted the suggestion that they should leave prostitution. Young girls of the 1900s and 1910s might have several reasons for entering sex work.[39] One woman, born to a prostitute and raised in New Orleans' notorious Storyville vice district, recalled learning how to prepare opium for her mother's customers by the age of five. Shortly after, her virginity was auctioned off for $7.75. As a teenager, she became a waitress, occasionally turning tricks to cover living expenses. When asked about her experiences, she asserted, "I ain't ashamed of what I did, I didn't have much to do with it ... to me it seems just like anything else – like a kid whose father owns a grocery store. He helps him with the store. Well, my mother didn't sell groceries."[40] Much of the white slavery rhetoric claimed that white slaves became indelibly marked, tainted, by their sex work; they could only be white slaves and nothing else. Yet this woman's occasional prostitution did not, in her own eyes, define her. Though certainly exploited as a child by both her mother and the brothel in which she was raised, she interpreted her participation in casual prostitution as a teenager as a rational option in moments of economic need. She rejected the Progressive-era notion that she was permanently marked as "fallen" due to her experience with sex work. Still others may have chosen sex work because it provided the most secure and steady source of income, with the pay frequently far outpacing the pay for "legitimate" work. The 1911 Chicago Vice Commission reported that the average factory girl earned six dollars a week, while the average prostitute earned twenty-five dollars a week.[41]

When it came to enforcing the Mann Act, sex workers quickly took steps to protect themselves from the federal "protection" offered by arguing that they traveled of their own volition, thereby boldly asserting their own agency. When tracking the movement of prostitutes, the Bureau repeatedly had to contend with defiant young women who rejected the white slavery script. One agent in El Paso, in 1911, reported he was certain the suspected victim of trafficking, a sixteen-year-old prostitute, had been "wised up on the kind of story to tell if she is ever questioned about her past. Leona Reed [her madam] is familiar with the new law and would hardly fail to post a new girl on what to say."[42] Girls like this one protected their ability to continue to labor in sexual marketplaces by resisting any attempts to call them white slaves (note that they also protected their employers from potential prison sentences).

Other girls embraced the white slavery script and suavely used it to protect their interests and deflect any blame that might be directed at them. In March 1929, the police chief in West Frankfort, IL, arrested fifteen-year-old Eva King and twenty-two-year-old Velma Okman for solicitation and prostitution. Once at the police station, Eva divulged a tale that prompted him to call the Bureau of Investigation. Eva told the Bureau special agent that she was from a rural farming family (emphasizing her authentic, rural credulity), and that she had been living with her older sister in the town of Paducah, KY, when she met Velma Okman in February 1929. Her statement is worth quoting at length because it shows us the way she skillfully deployed the white slavery narrative to mitigate her own culpability:

She [Velma] asked me if I ever went out with fellows. I told her my sister wouldn't allow it. I asked her what she did and Velma said she was hustling for a living. I didn't know what hustling meant. Velma also told me at this time she was keeping up with a fellow. Velma said for me to come and live with her and make some money by doing what she did. I didn't know what she was doing but after I went home I thought over what Velma had told me so I decided to go and live with her and find out what she was doing.... Velma went out and brought two men back. We sat around for a while and Velma and one man went into the kitchen. The other man and I had intercourse on the bed. This was the first time I had ever had sexual relations with a man. The man I had intercourse with paid Velma two dollars, which Velma kept.[43]

Eva went on to say that a few days later, Velma took her to Jimmy Webb, who started pimping both young women, eventually taking them to Illinois after the Paducah police threatened Velma with arrest. Eva claimed that Jimmy and Velma set up all of her dates in Illinois, and "they always kept the money" earned from her sex work.[44] Given Eva's young age, and her claims of reckless ignorance and dangerous curiosity, plus the fact that she never kept the money she earned, this case struck both the chief of police and the special agent as clear-cut white slavery. Here was a young, innocent girl from a respectable background induced to practice prostitution for the profit of another – a perfect white slavery story.

Interviews with Jimmy Webb and Velma Okman painted a very different picture of Eva's behavior. Jimmy claimed that Velma had talked him into taking in Eva because she was a runaway and Velma had felt sorry for the girl. Jimmy repeatedly asserted that he never took any money for Eva's sex work and instead hinted that it was likely that she had sex without pay, for pleasure rather than profit.[45] Similarly, Velma claimed that Eva had told her that she had experience as a sex worker prior to their meeting, and that their shared experience in prostitution is what they had bonded over when they first met. Both Velma and Jimmy had a very real stake in discrediting Eva's story of violated innocence. They could face white slavery charges if the special agent trusted Eva's veracity.

What was evident to the investigating agents was that Jimmy Webb pimped his girlfriend, Velma – arranging dates, getting hotel rooms, living off of her earnings – and that he probably had done the same for Eva. Jimmy and Velma had also been the obvious instigators in the move from Kentucky to Illinois, crossing a state border, which had brought their behavior under federal jurisdiction. Based on these facts, the U.S. attorney presented the case to a grand jury, which moved to indict both Jimmy and Velma for trafficking Eva. Jimmy quickly changed his plea from not guilty to guilty. He received the maximum sentence available under the law, five years in Leavenworth, while charges against Velma were ultimately dismissed.[46] The case file is completely silent as to Eva's fate, though in all likelihood she probably was incarcerated in a juvenile justice facility in Illinois, or perhaps in Kentucky.

Eva's skillful tale of naïveté, youthful curiosity, and exploitation converted her from a hardened, street-walking prostitute to a blameless victim. Her tale echoed the basic plot points offered in movies like *Traffic in Souls*. This attempted manipulation was really only possible due to her young age. By tapping into the cultural expectations of the white slavery narrative she was able to mitigate her own guilt while casting her travel mates as the true villains. By telling the police chief this tale of exploited innocence, she probably hoped to deflect blame and get the charges against her dismissed, but she also started a process (the initiation of a Mann Act case) that she could not control. Ultimately, further investigation showed that Eva's story of innocence diverted could not be sustained, especially after her own sister told the Bureau "that she had no control over her younger sister. She understood that she had fallen into evil company and could be found at one of the sporting houses."[47] The white slavery narrative depended on the passivity of the "victim," yet Eva demonstrated a remarkable amount of agency: deciding to leave her sister's home, traveling to Illinois, reporting her alleged exploitation to the police. Further investigation revealed that she had always been willful, a characteristic that set her outside of the ideal victim, regardless of age. She seemed to behave like a fully adult woman: making independent decisions and engaging in sexual relations. Her easily demonstrated agency undercut her status as a white slave.

Sometimes parents did turn to the Bureau to stop their daughters from entering prostitution. In 1921, the mother of fifteen-year-old Josephine Merchant complained that her daughter had run away from home. She had heard a rumor the Josephine had been transported to Wyoming to practice prostitution for two men with whom she had been seen galli-vanting around Denver. The Bureau tracked Josephine down, returned her to her mother, and arrested the men who had set up an illegal brothel in Laramie. But Josephine had no interest in being described as a white slave or the Bureau's "protection." She promptly ran away again and was later discovered working in a brothel in Casper, WY.[48]

The wide range of Progressive-era anti-vice laws offered state author-ities and parents multiple ways to police young women's sexuality under the guise of protecting them. As Mary Odem's work has demonstrated, this policing tended to be very harsh, as juvenile justice institutions – reformatories, training schools, and the like – could soon be found throughout the nation for the purpose of dealing with troublesome girls.[49] Because the Bureau needed a complainant before it launched investigations, the White Slave Traffic Act provided parents with yet another weapon in their arsenal for controlling their daughters' sexual behavior. After fifteen-year-old Reba Cline Clendenon ran away from home in July 1932, her father took out a juvenile warrant for her deten-tion. Frank Clendenon suspected that Reba had run away with twenty-six-year-old Edwin Fowler, a man with a reputation as a shiftless drunk. When Reba returned home in August, her father committed her to the State Industrial School for Girls at Tullahoma, TN, for three years on charges of being incorrigible and associating with immoral people. "He stated that his daughter had never been in any trouble before, and he and his wife felt it best and safer to place her where she could be pro-tected."[50] But her father was not satisfied with taking only this step; he wanted Fowler punished.

The aspect of the case that made the greatest impression on the inves-tigating agent was Reba's youth, which he imagined to be greater than it was. "She has the appearance of being much younger than fifteen years, and, in fact, is nothing more than a child."[51] When the agent interviewed her, he carefully coached her testimony to affirm that in engaging in sex with Fowler, she had been "overpersuaded [*sic*]."[52] The investigating agent, the Alabama U.S. attorney, and Reba's father banded together to get Edwin Fowler arrested and tried on Mann Act charges. After two years of legal wrangling, the case finally moved forward in northern Alabama, though at this point Reba Clendenon was no longer the fifteen-year-old ingénue. The entire case hinged on Reba's youth and innocence, but after she had lived in a state home and, by virtue of her merely getting older (she had aged out), the case lost some of its logic and Fowler was found not guilty.

After the Supreme Court empowered a wide reading of the White Slave Traffic Act's "any other immoral purpose" clause in 1917, the Bureau used the law to police young women's sexuality more broadly, a trend that both reflected and fortified similar developments occurring within state-level and local law enforcement and disciplinary institutions. Of the 47,500 cases investigated between 1921 and 1936, most featured elements that had no connection to prostitution, but were rather cases of seduction, runaway daughters, bigamy, adultery, and sexual assault.[53] This shift in investigative priority reflected a shift in Bureau priorities as the Bureau positioned itself as a defender of traditional morality in the post–World War I period. But it also reflected the demands of citizens who launched the complaints that initiated a majority of investigations. During the same period, from 1917 to 1936, the term "white slavery" had largely disappeared from popular discourse as it had been thoroughly discredited by leading media critics.[54] Due to the requirement of having to have a private individual, really an affronted party, launch an investigation, the most exploited sex workers – separated from their families, working in clandestine sites, and dominated by pimps – rarely received any legitimate protection the Mann Act might offer.

The emergence of the white slave narratives during the Progressive Era reflected a host of anxieties about young women's entry into the workforce, their exploration of urban environments, and a new sexual culture. Prostitution had thrived in urban environments like New York City and Chicago during the nineteenth century, prompting only sporadic and ineffectual protest.[55] The anti-white slavery narratives, in contrast, offered anti-vice activists a potent re-conceptualization of the sex worker from a hardened, immoral dollymop to a tragic child slave robbed of her innocence. On the basis of this new victim, much legal reform was achieved. Not only did Congress pass the White Slave Traffic Act, but forty-five states also passed state-level anti-trafficking laws.[56] These laws joined a number of anti-vice laws – tin plate laws, injunction and abatement laws, venereal disease reporting laws – most of which were intended to protect America's youth. This legal revolution culminated in the closing of public brothels in 1917, marking the end of the brothel era in the United States.

Clearly the white slave narrative accomplished much, but with ambivalent results. The narrative worked for a number of reasons. It articulated white slaves as victims who had been innocent, and who, with the loss of their innocence, became utterly tragic. As anthropologist Heather Montgomery notes, "Innocence is a quality projected onto, and expected of, children by adults."[57] It is their innocence that motivates protection. But as Erika Meiners notes in chapter four of this volume, "innocence embedded in childhood was persistently, and seemingly invisibly White," and thus tales of white slavery constructed a racial border around the category of redeemable victim. White slavery narratives functioned to turn adult sex workers into child sex slaves and in doing so attempted to reclaim an idea of innocence, blameless-ness, and redeemability. The entire logic hinged on the idea that young women had ended up in the brothel due not only to their own mistakes, but solely due to the predation of others. Sympathy was key. Thus, sex workers became children, and then they were converted into slaves – individuals who, by definition, lack the ability to change the circumstances of their lives. Lacking as they did any recognizable agency – something children and slaves are denied – the white slavery narrative left no room for the agency, choice, or will of sex workers.[58]

Collapsing women and children into a single category had political implications within the context where women routinely took to streets to march for their rights to be extricated from the typical citizenship category of dependents they had long occupied; a category they shared with children and disabled persons (as well as servants and slaves in earlier periods).[59] On one hand, women agitated and demanded rights while also suggesting that one of the reasons that the sexual marketplace had thrived was because of women's lack of political participation. On the other hand, the white slave narrative asserted that women and girls were in the same class – a class vulnerable to sexual exploitation. Young sex workers confound all of these classifications by rejecting their status as victims and nothing more, using the Mann Act strategically, or, most commonly, behaving in ways or having characteristics that cast them far outside the circle of the "protected" or "redeemable." These contradictions of gender ideals, sexual anxieties, and young women's own subjectivities demonstrated a world in flux as public discussions of sexuality became more prominent. More important, the historical example of the white slave narratives and the enforcement of the laws they inspired cautions us against building law enforcement regimes on flimsy ideas of innocence that require an erasure of agency.

## Notes

1  O. Edward Janney, *The White Slave Traffic in America* (New York: National Vigilance Committee, 1911), 15.

2  Jeffrey Weeks, *Sex, Politics and Society: The Regulation of Sexuality since 1800* (New York: Longman, 1981), 14–15; Frederick K. Grittner, *White Slavery: Myth, Ideology and American Law* (New York: Garland Press, 1990), 61–6; Gayle S. Rubin, "Thinking Sex: Notes for a Radical Theory of the Politics of Sexuality," in *Social Perspective in Lesbian and Gay Studies: A Reader*, ed. Peter M. Nardi and Beth E. Schneider (London: Routledge, 1998), 100–33.

3  Edwin E. Sims quoted in Janney, *The White Slave Traffic*, 34.

4  W. T. Stead, "The Maiden Tribute to Modern Babylon" (July 6–10, 1885) in *Josephine Butler and the Prostitution Campaigns: Diseases of the Body Politic*, Volume IV, ed. Jane Jordan (London: Routledge, 2003), 115–234; Judith Walkowitz has offered the most trenchant analysis of Stead's exposé in *City of Dreadful Delight: Narratives of Sexual Danger in Late-Victorian London* (Chicago: University of Chicago Press, 1992), 82.

5  Kate C. Bushnell, "Working in Northern Wisconsin," *W.C.T.U. State Work* (Madison, WI) 3.7 (Nov. 1, 1888): 1–8.

6  During the long nineteenth century, children and women occupied the same category of legal "dependents" with other groups like servants, slaves, and disabled persons. See Barbara Young Welke, *Law and the Borders of Belonging in the Long Nineteenth Century United States* (New York: Cambridge, 2010).

7  Kate C. Bushnell, "The Wisconsin Lumber Dens," *The Philanthropist* 3.12 (Dec. 1988): 3.

8  "Wisconsin's Shame," *The Philanthropist* (Dec. 1888): 1.

9  Charlton Edholm, *Traffic in Girls and Work of Rescue Mission* (Chicago: Charlton Edholm, 1899), 15–14.

10 William Burgess, *White Slavery and Its Remedies* (n.p., n.d. [probably 1911]), 2. Obviously, Burgess's claims contained multiple fallacies and should be interpreted as an artifact of the Lost Cause. See Steven Deyle, *Carry Me Back: The Domestic Slave Trade in American Life* (New York: Oxford University Press, 2005); Eugene D. Genovese, *Roll, Jordan, Roll: The World the Slave Made* (New York: Pantheon, 1974); Ariela J. Gross, *Double Character: Slavery and Mastery in the Antebellum Southern Courtroom* (Princeton, NJ: Princeton University Press, 2000); Walter Johnson, *Soul by Soul: Life inside the Antebellum Slave Market* (Cambridge, MA: Harvard University Press, 1999); Wilma King, *Stolen Childhood: Slave Youth in Nineteenth-Century America* (Bloomington: Indiana University Press, 1995); Peter Kolchin, *American Slavery, 1619–1877* (New York: Hill and Wang, 1993); Dylan C. Penningroth, *The Claims of Kinfolk: African American Property and Community in the Nineteenth-Century South* (Chapel Hill: University of North Carolina, 2003); Michael Tadman, *Speculators and Slaves: Masters, Traders, and Slaves in the Old South* (Madison: University of Wisconsin Press, 1996); and Deborah Gray White, *Ar'nt I a Woman? Female Slaves in the Plantation South* (New York: W.W. Norton, 2000).

11   Grittner, *White Slavery*, 130–1.

12   E. J. Hobsbawm, *The Age of Empire, 1875–1914* (New York: Pantheon Books, 1987), 64; Welke, *Law and the Borders of* Belonging, 30.

13   Gunther Peck, "Feminizing White Slavery in the United States: Marcus Braun and the Transnational Traffic in White Bodies, 1890–1910," in *Workers across the Americas: The Transnational Turn in Labor History*, ed. Leon Fink (New York: Oxford University Press, 2011), 221–44, 224.

14   Sharon Block, *Rape and Sexual Power in Early America* (Chapel Hill: University of North Carolina Press, 2006); Stephanie M. H. Camp, *Closer to Freedom: Enslaved Women and Everyday Resistance in the Plantation South* (Chapel Hill, University of North Carolina, 2004); Jacqueline Jones, *Labor of Love, Labor of Sorrow: Black Women, Work, and Family, from Slavery to the Present* (New York: Vintage Books, 1985); Jennifer Morgan, *Laboring Women: Reproduction and Gender in New World Slavery* (Philadelphia: University of Pennsylvania Press, 2004); and White, *Ar'nt I a Woman*.

15   Cynthia Blair, *I've Got to Make My Livin': Black Women's Sex Work in Turn-of-the-Century Chicago* (Chicago: University of Chicago Press, 2010); Kevin J. Mumford, *Interzones: Black/White Sex Districts in Chicago and New York in the Early Twentieth Century* (New York: Columbia University Press, 1997); Lucie Cheng Hirata, "Free, Indentured, Enslaved: Chinese Prostitutes in Nineteenth-Century America," *Signs* 5.1 (Autumn 1979): 3–29; Benson Tong, *Unsubmissive Women: Chinese Prostitutes in Nineteenth-Century San Francisco* (Norman: University of Oklahoma Press, 1994); Kazuhiro Oharazeki, "Listening to the Voices of 'Other' Women in Japanese North America: Japanese Prostitutes and Barmaids in the American West, 1887–1920," *Journal of American Ethnic History* 32.4 (Summer 2013): 5–40; Grace Peña Delgado, "Border Control and Sexual Policing: White Slavery and Prostitution along the US-Mexico Borderlands, 1903–1910," *Western Historical Quarterly* 43.2 (2012): 157–78.

16   Roe, *Horrors of the White Slave Trade*, 97. Brian Donovan argues that the white slave narratives played a key role in drawing racial boundaries during the Progressive Era in *White Slave Crusades: Race, Gender, and Anti-vice Activism, 1887–1917* (Chicago: University of Illinois Press, 2006).

17   "The Trade in Girls," *The Philanthropist* (August 1887): 1.

18   David J. Pivar, *Purity Crusade: Sexual Morality and Social Control, 1868–1900* (Westport, CT: Greenwood Press, 1973), 140–4; Mary Odem, *Delinquent Daughters: Protecting and Policing Adolescent Female Sexuality in the United States* (Chapel Hill: University of North Carolina Press, 1995), 8–27, especially 14–15.

19   This narrative ploy also functioned to bolster the rhetoric of the anti-child labor movement that saw children industrial workers as child slaves. For example, in 1888, Nell Nelson (aka Helen Cusach Carvalho) published a series of articles called the "City Slave Girls" in the pro-labor *Chicago Times*. The series was later republished as a book under the title

*The White Slave Girls of Chicago*. Nelson focused on the exploitation of young women in Chicago's garment industries, not prostitution. Yet the overlapping rhetoric of the anti-child labor campaign and the anti-prostitution campaign served to benefit both. Nell Nelson, *The White Slave Girls of Chicago* (Chicago: Barkley Publishing Co., 1888). See also Katheryn Kish Sklar, *Florence Kelley & the Nation's Work: The Rise of Women's Political Culture, 1830–1900* (New Haven, CT: Yale University Press, 1995), 211.

20  Rubin, "Thinking Sex," 102.

21  Janet Eileen Mickish, "Legal Control of Socio-sexual Relationships: Creation of The Mann White Slave Traffic Act of 1910," PhD diss. (Carbondale: Southern Illinois University, 1980), 114–18, 127–31.

22  Kevin Brownlow, *Behind the Mask of Innocence: Sex, Violence, Crime: Films of Social Conscience in the Silent Era* (New York: Alfred A. Knopf, 1990), 77–8. For more on *Traffic in Souls*, see Christopher Diffee, "Sex and the City: The White Slaver Scare and Social Governance in the Progressive Era," *American Quarterly* 57.2 (2005): 411–37.

23  Brownlow, *Behind the Mask of Innocence*, 78.

24  Shelley Stamp, *Movie-Struck Girls: Women and Motion Picture Culture after the Nickelodeon* (Princeton, NJ: Princeton University Press, 2000), 40–101, quotation on 46.

25  Reformers wrote scores of book that were peddled through magazines, reform groups, and door-to-door book salesmen, bearing titles such as *My Little Sister, Horrors of the White Slave Traffic, War on the White Slave Trade, The White Slave Traffic in America, Fighting the Traffic in Young Girls, Panders and Their White Slaves, Crimes of the White Slavers, House of Bondage, The Black Traffic in White Slaves*, and so on. Ernest Bell's *Traffic in Girls* sold more than 400,000 copies. Pamphlets and social purity magazines like *The Philanthropist*, which saw a 50 percent increase in circulations from 1908 to 1909, supplemented these publications. Amy R. Lagler, "'For God's Sake Do Something': White-Slavery Narratives and Moral Panic in Turn-of-the-Century American Cities" (PhD diss., Michigan State University, 2000), 128–31.

26  Clifford G. Roe, *Panders and Their White Slaves* (New York: Fleming H. Revell Co., 1910), 7.

27  Ibid., 222.

28  Carole S. Vance, "Innocence and Experience: Melodramatic Narratives of Sex Trafficking and Their Consequences for Law and Policy," *History of the Present* 2 (Fall 2012): 200–18, 204–5.

29  Heather Montgomery, *Modern Babylon: Prostituting Children in Thailand* (New York: Berghahn Books, 2001), 136, 139.

30  Edwin Sims, "The White Slave Trade of Today," in *Fighting the Traffic in Young Girls or War on the White Slave Trade*, ed. Ernest A. Bell (Chicago: G. S. Ball, 1910), 47–60, 48.

31  Wirt W. Hallam, "The Reduction of Vice in Certain Western Cities through Law-Enforcement," *Social Diseases: Report of the Progress of the Movement*

*for Their Prevention* (published by the Society of Sanitary and Moral Prophylaxis) 3.2 (April 1912): 27–48, 31. Italics in original.

32  Clifford Roe, *The Great War on White Slavery* (Chicago: Clifford Roe and B. S. Steadwell, 1911), 107.

33  Pamela Haag, *Consent: Sexual Rights and the Transformation of American Liberalism* (Ithaca, NY: Cornell University Press, 1999), 67.

34  U.S. House, *Congressional Record* 45 (Jan. 19, 1910), 811.

35  Ibid.

36  Illinois General Assembly, *Report of the Illinois Senate Vice Committee* (Chicago: Allied Printing, 1916), 355.

37  Ibid., 354; "50,000 Make 'Easy Living' in White Slave Traffic," *Fort Wayne Journal-Gazette*, Sept. 15, 1912, 33.

38  "United States in New War on White Slavery," *Fort Wayne Journal-Gazette*, Apr. 27, 1913, 43; Stanley W. Finch, "The White Slave Traffic," Senate Doc. 62nd Congress, 3rd Session, Document No. 982 (Washington, DC: Government Printing Office, 1912), 7.

39  In her work with child sex workers in Thailand in the 1990s, Heather Montgomery found that the children she interviewed appreciated how the money they earned from prostitution help support their families and demonstrated their filial duty. Heather Montgomery, "Children, Prostitution, and Identity: A Case Study from a Tourism Resort in Thailand," in *Global Sex Workers: Rights, Resistance, and Redefinition*, ed. Kamala Kempadoo and Jo Doezema (New York: Routledge, 1998), 139–50, 148–9.

40  Quoted in Ruth Rosen, *The Lost Sisterhood: Prostitution in America, 1900–1918* (Baltimore, MD: Johns Hopkins University Press, 1982), 101.

41  Jane Addams, *A New Conscience of an Ancient Evil* (New York: Arno Press, [1912] 1922), 58.

42  Report, Special Agent L. E. Ross, Dec. 17, 1911, "U.S. vs. Leona Reed – White Slave Case," 3095-3, Roll 140, RG 65, Federal Bureau of Investigation, Investigative Case Files of the Bureau, 1908–22, M1085, National Archives, College Park, MD [hereafter cited as BOI Microfilm Records].

43  Report, G. R. Baer, Mar 22, 1929, 31-26252-1, Reel 105A, FBI White Slave Microfilm Files, Record Group 65, Records of the Federal Bureau of Investigation – FBI Headquarters Case Files, Classification 31, National Archives, College Park, MD [hereafter cited as FBI White Slave Microfilm Files].

44  Ibid.

45  Ibid.

46  The federal government was quite squeamish about sending women to federal prison under the Mann Act. There was only one facility to house them (in Lansing, KA) and in the law's early years, judges showed a marked tendency to fine women, rather than imprison them. Nonetheless, because women frequently occupied mid-level positions in the vice world (running brothels and moving talent), the Mann Act did contribute a larger number of women imprisoned in federal facilities than had ever been seen before. Marlene D. Beckman, "The White Slave Traffic Act: Historical Impact of a Federal Crime Policy on Women," in *Criminal Justice Politics and Women: The Aftermath*

*of Legally Mandated Change*, ed. Claudine Scheber and Clarice Feinman (New York: Haworth Press, 1985), 85–101.

47 Report, A. D. Metegan, Apr. 15, 1929, 31-26252-2, Reel 105A, FBI White Slave Microfilm Files.

48 Report, Fred I. Keepers, Nov. 23, 1921, Denver, CO, 31-434-3, Box 18, FBI White Slave Files.

49 Robert M. Mennel, *Thorns and Thistles: Juvenile Delinquency in the United States, 1825–1940* (Hanover, NH: University Press of New England, 1973); Odem, *Delinquent Daughters*; Tamara Myers, *Caught: Montreal's Modern Girls and the Law, 1869–1945* (Toronto: University of Toronto Press, 2007); William S. Bush, *Who Gets a Childhood? Race and Juvenile Justice in Twentieth Century Texas* (Athens: University of Georgia Press, 2010); Miroslava Chávez-García, *States of Delinquency: Race and Science in the Making of California's Juvenile Justice System* (Berkeley: University of California Press, 2012).

50 Report, J. M. Towler, Aug. 27, 1932, Birmingham, AL, 31-36188-1, page 2, Box 73, Record Group 65, Records of the Federal Bureau of Investigation – Bureau Headquarter Case Files, Classification 31, National Archives, College Park, MD.

51 Ibid., 4.

52 Ibid., 2–3.

53 J. Edgar Hoover quoted in "White Slave Traffic Gains: Hoover Asks Public Aid in Drive to Wipe Out Violations," *Boston Evening Recorder*, Aug. 17, 1936. For more on the general enforcement of the Mann Act, see Jessica R. Pliley, *Policing Sexuality: The Mann Act and the Making of the FBI* (Cambridge, MA: Harvard University Press, 2014).

54 The debate about the prevalence of white slavery culminated in a dismissal of the issue by the outbreak of World War I. By the 1920s, the term was seen as old-fashioned and even in the interwar anti-trafficking movement, the term was eschewed in favor of the phrase: "traffic in women and children." See Jessica R. Pliley, "Claims to Protection: The Rise and Fall of Feminist Abolitionism in the League of Nations' Committee on the Traffic in Women and Children, 1919–1937," *Journal of Women's History* (Winter 2010): 90–113. For an overview of the critics of white slave, see Mark Thomas Connelly, *The Response to Prostitution in the Progressive Era* (Chapel Hill: University of North Carolina Press, 1980), 127–33.

55 Robert E. Riegel, "Changing American Attitudes Toward Prostitution (1800–1920)," *Journal of the History of Ideas*, 29.3 (Jul.–Sep. 1968): 437–52; Anne M. Butler, *Daughters of Joy, Sisters of Misery: Prostitutes in the American West, 1865–1890* (Urbana: University of Illinois Press, 1985); Barbara Meil Hobson, *Uneasy Virtue: The Politics of Prostitution and the American Reform Tradition* (New York: Basic Books, 1987); Timothy Gilfoyle, *City of Eros: Prostitution, and the Commercialization of Sex, 1790–1920* (New York: Norton: 1994); Sharon E. Wood, *The Freedom of the Streets: Work, Citizenship, and Sexuality in a Gilded Age City* (Durham: University of North Carolina Press, 2005).

56  Joseph Mayer, *The Regulation of Commercialized Vice: An Analysis of the Transition from Segregation to Repression in the United States* (New York: The Klebold Press, 1922), 31.

57  Montgomery, *Modern Babylon*, 145.

58  Of course, young people and slaves have always resisted the idea that they lacked agency and the power to testify. See Ariela Julie Gross, *What Blood Won't Tell: A History of Race on Trial in America* (Cambridge, MA: Harvard University Press, 2009), and Ariela Julie Gross, "Beyond Black and White: Cultural Approaches to Race and Slavery," *Columbia Law Review* (2001): 640–90.

59  Welke, *Law and the Borders of Belonging*.

# 7

# Slavery and the Recruitment of Child Soldiers

## David M. Rosen

During the last few decades of the twentieth century, international law and international humanitarian and human rights organizations focused significant attention on the issue of child soldiers. Since 1998, the recruitment and use of child soldiers under the age of fifteen has been widely regarded as a war crime under international law, resulting in the conviction and imprisonment of a number of child recruiters. Beyond this, a variety of human rights and children's rights treaties have sought to widen the ban against child recruitment to include all persons under age eighteen, although such treaties do not involve criminal liability for recruitment. All these efforts are grounded in the Convention on the Rights of the Child, which sets a universal definition of childhood as beginning at birth and ending at age eighteen.[1] Parallel to these developments, there has been a marked conflation of the idea of child recruitment with the crime of enslavement. Most strikingly, the International Labour Organization's (ILO) Convention on the Worst Forms of Child Labor declared the forced or compulsory recruitment of child soldiers under age eighteen a "form of slavery" or a practice "similar to slavery."[2]

Since the 1999 ILO Convention, the rhetoric has sharpened and there has been increasing use by both the media and human rights organizations of the idea of "military slavery."[3] Indeed, President Obama, in a recent speech highlighting his administration's efforts to curb human trafficking, declared child soldiers to be slaves.[4] This chapter examines the relationship between child recruitment and enslavement. It argues that recruitment and enslavement are and should be treated as conceptually and empirically distinct phenomena. While it is certainly possible for child soldiers to be enslaved, I argue that child recruitment per se is not a form of human bondage.

Central to this discussion is the historical and cross-cultural fluidity of the experience of childhood and the concept of the child. The world is composed of "childhoods," and no single childhood serves as a fixed star or empirically determined universal frame of reference for others. As Heather Montgomery has pointed out, the idea that childhood begins at birth and ends at age eighteen is a bureaucratic fiction.[5] Neither the chronological boundaries between childhood and adulthood nor the range of actions, rights, and duties deemed compatible or incompatible with any single culturally and socially constructed understanding of childhood are absolutely congruent with other such understandings. If so, then the central question turns on the degree to which our understandings of the recruitment of child soldiers and of slavery itself should be built on a bureaucratic fiction.

No doubt the ILO's concerns about child soldiers arose in the context of highly cited instances of child abduction and enslavement by armed groups in a number of recent insurgencies, especially in Africa. These include the now notorious cases of child abduction by the Revolutionary United Front (RUF) during the Sierra Leone Civil War (1991–2001) and the Lord's Resistance Army (LRA) in Uganda. Since 1999, key leaders of the RUF have been convicted by the Special Court for Sierra Leone of the war crime of the recruitment of child soldiers, as well as of the crime against humanity of enslavement, a crime that encompasses forcible training for military purposes. In 2005, the International Criminal Court issued warrants of arrest for Joseph Kony and other military leaders of the LRA on the separate charges of child recruitment and enslavement. These two cases seem to show an empirical connection between at least some forms of child recruitment and enslavement. There is little doubt that at least some child soldiers in recent conflicts have been treated as slaves.

But the question the ILO treaty raises is far more complex; namely, whether the conscription of any person under age eighteen either by government armed forces or by non-state armed groups is per se a form of slavery. It is to this broader issue that this article is addressed. The entire discussion of child soldiers itself is an unfortunate example of how changing social policies define research categories. It is crucial to note that the concept of the "child soldier" was not created by historians or social scientists as a guide to empirical research and analysis, but rather emerged in the late twentieth century as a legal and moral concept fashioned by humanitarian and human rights organizations, law enforcement, criminal law codes, and political leaders interested in creating a new universal definition of child. These efforts were guided by the idea that children were to be understood as essentially innocent and vulnerable and in need of protection.

The concept of the child soldier as an abused and exploited victim of war has become so deeply embedded in a Western discourse of deviancy that it is virtually impossible to treat it as a socially constructed codification. Clearly, conflating the idea of the child soldier with the condition of slavery serves as a metaphorical strategy for exaggerating deviancy, rather than a way of accounting for the experiences of real children and youth during wartime. As both Jessica Pliley and Micki McElya make plain in their contributions to this volume (Chapters 6 and 3, respectively), this rhetorical strategy has also been associated with other social panics implicating children and childhood – such as the nineteenth-century white slavery scare – where activists invoked both chattel slavery and abolition to dramatize and mark perceived forms of injustice. As a result, research on nearly any issue that touches on the exploitation of children opens up a conceptual, legal, and moral minefield. Many practices that are rejected and widely vilified in the West, including child labor, child fostering, child prostitution, and child marriage, have nowadays been recast by children's rights activists and so-called New Abolitionists as forms of child enslavement. The problem facing historians, anthropologists, and others seeking to understand the complexity of childhood, including problems of exploitation and suffering, is how to address these issues without abandoning independent inquiry.

### Child Soldiers: The Western Historical Experience

The widespread presence of child soldiers in the Western military challenges the views of modern advocacy. Youngsters below age eighteen were widely present in the militias and armies that fought the American Revolution. In January 1776, on the eve of the Revolution, Massachusetts required that the militia be constituted from "all able bodied male persons therein from sixteen years old to fifty."[6] Colonial legislation focused on persons to be conscripted into to military service by government was ambiguous or indifferent to the age of volunteers: it seems to have followed a general understanding that exists to this day in many armed forces and groups, namely that the age of conscription (forced recruitment) is almost always set higher than that of voluntary enlistment.

Colonial militias also played a vital role in the emerging youth culture in early America. This culture, organized in opposition to dominant Puritan values, took shape around militia training days, which afforded young people the opportunity to meet. These training days, to the alarm of many, allowed youngsters to gather, smoke, carouse, and swagger.[7] Between 30 percent and 40 percent of adolescent males participated in war between 1740 and 1781.[8] American Revolutionary leaders themselves were much younger than loyalist leaders and local militias were often organized at college campuses that were themselves cauldrons of revolutionary thinking.[9] Teenagers played a major role in resistance to British rule. Between 1765 and 1760, there were at least 150 anti-British riots in the American colonies and the rioting mobs were filled with teenage apprentices and youthful laborers.[10] Not surprising, these teenagers filled the ranks of the revolutionary army, which in itself was composed largely of men and boys drawn from the poor, the young, the marginal, and the unfree.[11] With half the American population under age sixteen, it was not surprising that the Continental Army was filled with boys of every age.[12]

The presence of youngsters is also evidenced in narratives of the time. Most famous is that of Joseph Plumb Martin, who joined the Connecticut state forces in June 1775 when he was fifteen. In his autobiography, Martin describes his urge to enlist and how he frequented the "rendezvous" where many of his "young associates" would join up. Of his decision to enlist, he said, "I had obtained my heart's desire."[13] When, on June 14, 1775, the Continental Congress resolved to raise the first companies of the Continental Army, it made no mention of age. It called for the voluntary recruitment of officers and men ranging from captains to privates, riflemen, trumpeters, and drummers. On July 18, 1775, the Continental Congress resolved "that it be recommended to the inhabitants of all the united English Colonies in North America that all able bodied effective men, between sixteen and fifty years of age in each colony, immediately form themselves into regular companies of Militia."[14]

Demographic data also provide evidence of the youthfulness of the revolutionaries. Existing records of the many regiments camped at Valley Forge with Washington during the winter of 1777–8 show many youngsters in regiments from all over the country. In the 1st–8th Connecticut regiments, 179 out of 655 soldiers, or 27.3 percent, were between twelve and seventeen. In the nine companies of the NY 2nd Regiment, 52 out of 188 soldiers, or 27.6 percent, were between twelve and seventeen. In Rhode Island's 1st and 2nd Regiments, 35 of 109, or 32 percent, were between thirteen and seventeen. Of the 922 soldiers of the Pennsylvania Line of the Continental Army between 1775 and 1783, 113, or 12 percent, were between ten and seventeen. The age range of soldiers serving in the Revolutionary war was far greater than those of modern armies. In the Pennsylvania Line, there were four youngsters aged ten and one man aged seventy-three. Of course, the vast majority of young soldiers across the militias and regiments of the revolutionary forces were ages fifteen, sixteen, and seventeen. Many of the youngest were fifers and drummers, but many were also ordinary private soldiers. Of course the age ranges may differ by regional and other circumstances, but there is no escaping the fact that the armies of the revolution were filled with youngsters from twelve to seventeen.[15] All the data support the conclusion that youngsters were a regular and unremarkable part of the armed forces of the American Revolution.

## The American Civil War

The U.S. Civil War tells a similar story. Although the official age of conscription was set at age twenty, this did not affect the river of underage volunteers. The Enrollment Act of 1863 introduced conscription for men between ages twenty and forty-five on the Union side. But the Enrollment Act did not create a system of universal conscription. Unlike the national systems of conscription that would later be established both in Great Britain and the United States during World War I, the real purpose of the Enrollment Act was to coerce or stimulate voluntary enlistment, but not to replace it.[16] At war's end it was clear that thousands upon thousands of underage boys had made their way into the armed forces of the United States. The crisis of war, the power of patriotic sentiment, the desire of youth for adventure, the inherent corruptions in recruitment based on a bounty system, and other factors made certain that a steady stream of young boys filled the ranks of the Union Army.

The recruitment of boys into Civil War armies was not without controversy. By the beginnings of the nineteenth century, new ideas about childhood were gradually taking root in the West. These ideas involved the widening conviction that the family is a sacred unit and children, purer and more innocent than adults, were to be treated as treasured objects deserving exceptional care.[17] As this new view of childhood became more entrenched, many areas of social life, the courts, legislators and society as a whole began to have greater concern for the interests of children and to articulate their own ideas about children's interests and needs. In Britain,

America, and other places in the West, the cultural and social distinctions between childhood and adulthood hardened, and childhood gradually came to be regarded as a separate and distinct stage of life characterized by innocence, vulnerability, and the need for protection. Great deference was paid to the psychological autonomy of the child, but though the family's authority per se waned vis-à-vis the child, the practical autonomy of the child also lessened considerably. Childhood autonomy may have been celebrated both philosophically and conceptually, but the psychologically autonomous child was placed within a gilded cage.

But none of this happened overnight. Real changes took place more rapidly among the middle class than among the working class and poor, but these new sensibilities did spread quickly into law, which was increasingly fashioned around middle-class sensibilities in both America and Britain.[18] So rapidly did this evolve into the hegemonic view of childhood that the lives of real children were nearly rendered invisible. In a similar way, Karen Sánchez-Eppler argues in this volume (see Chapter 1) that concepts of childhood innocence pushed some historians to argue that childhood was incompatible with slavery. In fact, much the same can be said about children in the military. The growing assumption in the West that children should be protected dependents and that military service was incompatible with childhood has often blinded us to the reality of their lives under arms in Western society. However important these ideas were to become in the twentieth century, they were not as firmly rooted in society at the time of the Civil War, and, at this period of national crisis, they were set aside as a peacetime luxury.

Is it possible to determine how many youngsters served in the military during the American Civil War? It is generally accepted that about 2.1 million soldiers and sailors served in the Union forces during the Civil War and that about 882,000 soldiers and sailors served in the Confederate forces.[19] During the war, Benjamin Gould of the U.S. Sanitary Commission undertook a statistical analysis of the ages of soldiers in the Union Army as of 1864. He examined the recorded ages in military rosters of 1,049,457 soldiers. It showed that 1.2 percent of the soldiers were under eighteen years of age.[20] But Gould's figures were believed to be unreliable because of the large numbers of volunteers who misrepresented their age. In 1905, George Kilmer reviewed Gould's data and pointed out a number of statistical anomalies that led him to assert that at least 100,000 boys who were listed as age eighteen were often not even sixteen or seventeen. This did not include the thousands officially listed as sixteen or seventeen or younger.[21] In 1911, Charles King asserted that the Civil War was fought by a "grand army of boys." He claimed that 800,000 soldiers were below age seventeen, 200,000 were under sixteen, and another 100,000 were no more than fifteen.[22] King did not explain how he obtained these figures. King, however, had a long and distinguished career in the U.S. military. He was a West Point graduate who participated in the Civil War and retired from active service in 1879. He continued on in military service through the Spanish-American War and World War I. Thus, while we have no way of fully judging the accuracy of his claims, it is fair to say that he probably had a good understanding of the general age, makeup, and composition of military units. If his figures are taken at face value, more than half the Union Army of 2.1 million would have been below age eighteen, a figure that seems somewhat exaggerated.

More accurate recent evidence points to a very large number of children, even if not quite the numbers King suggested. In 2006, Pizzaro, Silver, and Prause examined the full medical records of recruits from 303 randomly selected companies of the Union Army. The data were drawn from the descriptive roll books in the U.S. National Archives, resulting in a sample of 35,730 individuals. Of this larger sample, 15,027 recruits who lived until at least 1890 were selected for the analysis of their medical histories. Of these 15,027, however, 3,013, or 20 percent, were recruited into the Union ranks between ages nine and seventeen.[23] Assuming the random sample is representative of all recruits across the armed forces, then approximately 420,000 of the 2.1 million soldiers in the Union forces were between ages nine and seventeen. While this number is less than half of what King suggested, they are very significant numbers. The number of youngsters in the Union forces alone would have been greater than the numbers of child soldiers said to exist in the world today. While we do not have comparable data for the armies of the Confederacy, it is not unreasonable to assume that the figures would be proportionately similar. There is no reason to believe that the Confederacy was more lax in this respect, despite the charges made by General Grant that the Confederacy in particular had robbed both the cradle and the grave to sustain its forces.[24] Accordingly, even if it is impossible to pin down exact numbers, the presence of underage recruits throughout the army was a well-known and accepted fact of life throughout the Civil War.

A larger question is why are these numbers important? What they tell us is that in our not-too-distant past, the United States was a prime recruiter of youngsters into the armed forces. This contrasts with the view of many contemporary critics of the recruitment of child soldiers, who argue that the use of child soldiers is an aberrant phenomenon of the modern world. Accompanying this view is the undocumented but commonplace assertion that the recruitment of persons less than eighteen years of age in Western armies was a rarity in the past.[25] Wittingly or unwittingly, the historical amnesia of these critics only serves to make contemporary recruitment appear even more appalling and deviant. Understanding the recruitment of child soldiers in its historical context makes plain the ordinariness of child recruitment both historically and cross-culturally, making clear that the issue of child recruitment is far more complex than contemporary critics allow in their zeal to rid the world of child soldiers.

### The Great Transformation: World War I

World War I was pivotal in the history of child recruitment in both England and the United States. In both countries, the introduction of national conscription had a profound impact on the recruitment of child soldiers. First, it brought a virtual halt to the systematic enlistment of underage soldiers. Although enterprising youngsters with the will to enroll could always figure out a means of disguising their true ages to evade enlistment regulations, national conscription eliminated institutional incentives to enroll the young. With the end of the volunteer army, the mass mobilization of the entire male population could take place and the entire logic of recruitment changed with mass conscription. With virtually the entire adult male population subject to conscription, no incentives to recruitment were required. More important were the bureaucratic challenges of placing and training soldiers and weeding out the unfit. There simply was no need to recruit the young.

But there was no conscription at the beginning of World War I (1914–18). In both Great Britain and the United States, there was widespread unease at the creation of this new national project. In fact, at the outbreak of the war in August 1914, the British Army remained the same army of volunteers who had served the country quite well during the many colonial wars it had fought in the nineteenth century. In 1914, the army consisted of approximately 400,000 soldiers, made up of the regular army and part-time and reserve forces. Army regulations governing recruitment provided that volunteers had to be at least eighteen years of age and that only those over age nineteen could be sent overseas to fight.

At the beginning of the war, the army was flooded with recruits as Great Britain became engulfed by a wave of patriotic and anti-German sentiment. But the patriotic outburst for what many believed would be a short war was not long-lived. The summertime recruits did not march home victorious for Christmas, and by 1915, talk of conscription was in the air, and Britain instituted a national registration system requiring all males between fifteen and sixty-five to register. By 1916, Britain's volunteer army was abandoned as Parliament introduced national conscription.

But during the first two years of the war, volunteerism was the norm and the army was filled with boy soldiers as boys from all over the country sought to enlist in violation of army regulations. In the great rush to enlist, scant attention was paid to any serious method of determining age. The army, hungry for soldiers, was a reluctant enforcer of its own regulations. George Croppard, who in 1914 enlisted at age sixteen in the Royal West Surrey Regiment, described himself as an "ordinary boy of elementary education and slender prospects" who was "drawn [as if] by a magnet" to the recruiting office. When he told the recruiting sergeant his true age, the sergeant said, "Clear off, son. Come back tomorrow and see if you're nineteen, eh." He was back the very next day to accept the king's shilling as a new recruit.[26] Victor Silvester, the famous British dancer and orchestra leader, enlisted in November 1914 at the headquarters of the London Scottish Regiment at the Buckingham Palace gate. He was fourteen years and nine months old. When asked his age, he said eighteen and nine months. He was examined by the medical officer, determined fit, and quickly sworn in. He returned home to break the news to his parents.[27]

During the course of the war, some 8.7 million individuals served and 956,703 died from wounds, injury, or disease. By conservative estimates (perhaps underestimates) some 250,000 soldiers were underage and about 55 percent of these were killed or wounded during the war.[28] Thus in World War I Great Britain alone recruited as many child soldiers as are estimated to exist in the world today. Underage enlistment was at its highest in the beginning of the war with between 10–15 percent underage.[29] Young people could enlist without providing any documentation of age, so that boys ages fourteen to eighteen joined the steady stream into the ranks and formed a substantial portion of the overseas fighting forces.[30] Ultimately, the national registration system and conscription substantially reduced the flow of under-eighteen-year-olds into the army, but the majority of those who enlisted underage remained in the service.

## Conscription and the End of Boy Soldiers

The British volunteer army that entered World War I in August 1914 was modeled on the army that had long been used to police the empire and suppress anticolonial revolts in the nineteenth century. The force of regular enlisted men was led by a socially elite officer corps who were secure in the belief that the war would be short and victorious and that the volunteer army would more than meet Britain's needs. As in the American Civil War, the public and the new recruits were promised a short war, an easy victory, and personal glory. The troops, it was widely proclaimed, would be "home before Christmas." More than a million men and boys volunteered to serve during the first months of the war.

War fever gripped nearly every segment of society, drawing volunteers from all social classes. The children of the wealthy and well-educated joined skilled laborers, craftsmen, and workers from every industry in the mass but unregulated volunteerism of the early days of the war. As the war dragged, however, and casualties reached grotesque numbers of killed and wounded, voluntary enlistments began to plummet. It was clear that mass warfare required a remedy for the chaotic boom-and-bust character of voluntary recruitment. It demanded a more efficient bureaucratic system of organizing men and allocating labor between the shop floor and the trenches. Long before the war, supporters of mandatory national service had advocated national conscription, but it was the inability of the volunteer army to meet the combined needs of both full-scale national mobilization and efficient wartime production that moved Great Britain to embrace it. As a prelude to conscription, in July 1915, Parliament passed the National Registration Act that required the registration of all persons between the ages of fifteen and sixty-five who were not members of the armed forces. This wartime census provided detailed age and manpower statistics, and allowed the military to distinguish between persons to be called up for military service and those who would remain employed "in the national interest" in areas such as agriculture, coal mining, munitions, and shipbuilding and repair. In January 1916, Parliament passed the Military Service Act, making all men from ages eighteen to forty-one subject to conscription, creating a system of national service for the first time in British history.[31] With virtually the entire adult male population of Great Britain registered, classified, and subject to conscription, there was no need to recruit boy soldiers. No doubt some boy soldiers continued to evade regulations and enlist, but the incentives for the recruitment of the young rapidly disappeared. The enormous numbers of dead and wounded on the front lines meant that there would always be significant resistance to the draft, but overall, the combination of voluntary recruitment and conscription led to the enlistment of 5 million soldiers by the end of the war in November 1918.[32]

The issue of boy soldiers provided added moral weight for the arguments in favor of national service, but it was hardly the decisive factor. Advocates of conscription asserted that the recruitment of underage boys had a pernicious effect on the army. In particular, they argued that the sight of wounded boys evoked both compassion and mothering among the adult troops, which interfered with their duties. They also argued that the killing and wounding of boys gave ammunition to views of pacifists and other so-called peace at any price advocates and thereby undermined the war effort. In addition, they claimed that the open lying and deceit involved in the recruitment of underage boys undermined the faith of the British people in the army and other institutions. On the other side of the argument, however, many of those who opposed conscription also saw the recruitment of youngsters as an evil. Some argued that compulsory military service constituted a new form of tyranny against a freeborn people and reflected a growing militarism in the state. In this light, the recruitment of underage boys was another sign that democracy had succumbed to militarism. The War Office rejected all attempts at modifying recruitment policies. It spurned the idea that enlistees be required to provide birth certificates, on the grounds of administrative efficiency and the overwork and confusion in governmental offices required to produce these records. It rebuffed the view that young recruits be accepted provisionally until actual birth certificates were obtained.[33] It was national service alone that served as the death knell for the recruitment of boy soldiers. Those boys recruited before conscription were rarely released from service, but the flow of youngsters into the military came to a sudden and decisive end.

The American experience with recruitment in World War I was quite different from that of the British. The United States entered the war April 6, 1917, almost three years after the war began, and was involved in the war until the end on November 11, 1918, a period of about seventeen months. While President Wilson originally hoped to create a volunteer army, this idea was quickly abandoned and Congress passed the Selective Service Act of 1917. Between 1917 and the end of the war, the United States drafted nearly 2.8 million men. The total number raised was about 4.1 million, including voluntary enlistments and those who were part of the prewar military.[34] The vast majority of American troops were conscripts and the new selective service system created a nation system of registration in which all U.S. male citizens or persons who had declared their intention to become citizens between age twenty-one and thirty-five were required to register for the draft. The age for conscription was set at twenty-one. The age for voluntary enlistment was set at eighteen, and by 1918, the Selective Service Act itself was amended to require registration of eighteen-year-olds. Selective Service was a national system that mobilized millions of soldiers for war. In contrast to the Civil War era, volunteerism was no longer at the heart of national conscription and military recruiters were no longer in search of volunteers to meet the demand of war. Selective Service did not completely eliminate underage soldiers. Some youngsters continued to lie their way into military service, but conscription allowed for the mass mobilization of society with little need to dip into younger age cohorts for recruits. Turning a blind eye was no longer necessary.

In contrast to Great Britain, the organization of conscription in America was overtly hostile to volunteerism from the very beginning. Military recruitment embraced Taylorism and scientific management. Voluntary recruitment, it was argued, disturbed the "scientific administration of the task" and "impaired the efficiency" of the entire selective service enterprise. In this view, voluntary enlistment failed to distinguish between those persons whose labor might be indispensable for industrial production from those who were deemed "industrially worthless." Volunteerism in the age of mass warfare and mass mobilization was inefficient in distributing manpower between military and industrial needs. By the end of the war on November 11, 1918, more than 2.8 million men had been conscripted. Voluntary enlistment was discontinued in the army on December 15, 1917, and slowly came to an end in the other armed services by the end of the war.[35] The American view was that each registrant must await his time and perform his military obligations only in an orderly process.

The number of persons mobilized in the British Empire during World War I was 8,904,467; of these 908,371 died from battle death, disease, and accidents, 2,090,212 were wounded, and 191,652 went missing or were taken prisoner. Total casualties were 3,190,235 persons. In the United States, 4,355,000 were mobilized, 116,516 died from battle deaths and other causes, 204,002 were wounded, and 4,500 went missing or were taken prisoner. Total casualties were 323,018 persons. It is an ironic note that in the West the recruitment of child soldiers came to an end with the advent of mass war and the implementation of the bureaucratic and highly organized mobilization of the populace for war. Whatever the changing sentiments about children and war may have been, and however heartfelt the idea that childhood was incompatible with war, it was the bureaucratic management of recruitment that brought an end to the recruitment of child soldiers in the United States and Great Britain.

### Child Soldiers and the Partisan Armies of World War II

In Britain and the United States, the systematic recruitment of child soldiers came to an end with World War I. But the end of that war in 1918 did not bring about an era of peace. Though touted by U.S. President Woodrow Wilson as "the war to end all wars," World War I was only a prelude to countless horrific conflicts that spread across the globe in the twentieth century. The Second World War began only twenty-one years later, with the Nazi invasion of Poland on September 1, 1939. By the time World War II began, the landscape for child recruitment had changed dramatically, for with the notable exception of Nazi Germany, the Western European powers no longer systematically recruited children. This did not mean, however, that no child soldiers were involved in the conflict. Child soldiers were certainly involved in the conflicts in Spain during the rise of fascism and the Spanish Civil War (1936–9), which have come to be widely understood as a "dress rehearsal" for the Second World War. Child soldiers were a constant presence in Spain during these years, although numbers are uncertain. Julian Laplaza Perez, who was fifteen when he joined the Nationalist Army in Spain, noted that boys his age came from all over Spain to fight.[36] George Orwell fought on the Republican side and was wounded in the conflict. In his war memoire *Homage to Catalonia*, he described the presence of child soldiers as young as age eleven in the Republican ranks, although he generally thought that there were few soldiers below age fifteen on the front lines. Orwell also thought that younger soldiers did not make very good fighters. In his view, they needed too much sleep and the youngest of them were so undisciplined as to constitute a "public menace."[37] Anna Starinov, who was sent to Spain by the Soviet Union to organize Republican guerillas behind the lines of Franco's rebel forces, had to contend with the presence of children in the Republican forces, and found them more of a nuisance than an asset.[38] The presence of children in fighting forces was undergoing an important shift; instead of being part of regular armed forces, children were finding their way into the partisan groups that were attempting to resist the Nazi conquest and occupation of Europe. These groups were made up largely of civilians, although they often included former soldiers who had taken up arms after the regular armies of their countries had been defeated and had surrendered.

These trends in recruitment, namely nation-states' general abandonment of using younger soldiers, have continued to hold. Most nations no longer systematically recruit children. There are some notable, sometimes notorious exceptions. During the Iran–Iraq War, it was widely reported that Iran recruited some 95,000 children above age twelve and some as young as age nine to be used as human waves to clear areas of land mines. The official age of recruitment in Iran is nineteen, but government-allied paramilitary groups, and even foreign Iranian allies such as Hezbollah, systematically recruit volunteers with little concern about age.[39] It has also been reported that child soldiers as young as fourteen were used to violently suppress antigovernment political demonstrations in Iran in 2011.[40] Indeed, it may well be the case that some nations have shifted recruitment of children to paramilitaries in order to maintain the fiction that their armed forces have a higher age of recruitment. Other nations that continue to recruit child soldiers in violation of international law include Afghanistan, the Democratic Republic of the Congo, Chad, Myanmar (Burma), Somalia, Sudan, South Sudan, Syria, and Yemen. In some instances, such as Somalia and South Sudan, the governments have now entered into agreements with the United Nations to end the recruitment of child soldiers. In South Sudan, former child soldiers, once members of the so-called Red Army, have now transformed themselves into a movement for social change in the country with an eye toward providing future political leadership.[41]

Outside of these nations, the problem of child soldiers is largely one of recruitment by non-state armed groups such as rebel forces, revolutionaries, guerrillas, insurgents, terrorist groups, paramilitaries, global terrorist networks, regional tribal, ethnic, and religious militants, and local defense organizations, which unlike national armed forces, depend more on the use of youngsters as combatants. This shift is evident in a quick review of the UN list of the most persistent users and recruiter of child soldiers.[42] What should be clear from this list is the diversity of groups recruiting child soldiers. They range from those whose stated goals are to overthrow dictatorships and create democratic societies to those who intend to create regimes of terror. Rather than simply imagining a world of evildoers who abuse and enslave children with impunity (although clearly there are some of these here), there is a need to recognize the reality that many are simply people who reject or are indifferent to new and sometimes alien concepts of childhood, people for whom Western ideas of childhood simply do not jibe with their own understanding of the world. This does not mean that the world is a museum in which old ideas of childhood must be preserved in a diorama. But it tells us that the entire child soldier project, with its goal of universally separating children from military service, is not only a matter of finding and jailing a few bad apples, but also an extraordinarily complex and ambitious project of directed social change.

### The War Crime of Child Recruitment

The recruitment of child soldiers under age fifteen is now considered a war crime under international criminal law. In addition to the defendants tried and convicted for child recruitment before the Special Court for Sierra Leone, another child recruiter, Thomas Lubanga Dyilo, a Congolese militia leader, was tried, convicted, and sentenced by the International Criminal Court (ICC). The recruitment of under-fifteen-year-olds stands as absolute prohibition. International criminal law makes no distinction between children who volunteer, children who are conscripted, or children who are abducted. Recruitment in any form is prohibited as a war crime and violations subject recruiters to individual criminal liability. In the eyes of the law, children under age fifteen are not legally entitled to consent.

Beyond this, a number of human rights and children rights treaties have expanded the definition of the child soldier, raising to eighteen the age below which recruitment should be prohibited. These treaties, though not part of the system of international criminal law, may influence legal interpretations. They are designed to affect the recruiting practices of both state and non-state actors. Treaty compliance is voluntary and enforced through international peer pressure informally designated as "name and shame." There are no formal penalties for violators. The primary purpose of these treaties is to establish new international behavioral norms. The target age of eighteen is in keeping with the definition of childhood found in the 1989 Convention on the Rights of the Child, which defines a child as any person below age eighteen. But rights treaties are not normatively consistent. For example, the 2000 Optional Protocol to the Convention on the Rights of the Child on the Involvement of Children in Armed Conflict prohibits non-state armed groups from recruiting persons under the age of eighteen, but allows far more flexibility to the recruiting practices of states. The latter are only prohibited from conscripting under eighteen-year-olds, but are still permitted to engage in the voluntary recruitment of those above the age of fifteen. Thus the issue of exactly who falls into the category of a child soldier remains complicated, with international criminal law focused on persons under fifteen while a variety of human rights and children's rights treaties and their civil society advocates actively promote eighteen as the normative age of recruitment.

## Military Slaves

The effort to end recruitment did not originally focus on linking the recruitment of child soldiers with slavery. The primary goal was to establish the recruitment of child soldiers as a war crime. Child soldiers are frequently described as slave-like commodities. They are said to be "used," "manipulated," or "cheap and disposable."[43] The latter term likens them to cheap modern goods and products – disposable cameras, razors, plastic cups, or wristbands – easily consumed and discarded. At times, child soldiers have been depicted as "harvested" by various armed factions, a kind of post-apocalyptic metaphor that casts them as expendable feed or fodder. Children are frequently called "cannon fodder." Historically, of course, critics of war have often used the term "cannon fodder" to describe raw, untrained recruits, both young and old, who were deemed expendable and cynically thrown into the face of enemy fire with little regard for the loss of life. But contemporary critics of the recruitment of child soldiers have adopted this term as especially applicable to all children who are recruited into armed conflict, deeming them "the cannon fodder of choice."[44] Child soldiers are routinely said to be "programmed" in both advocacy literature and media accounts. They are "programmed to kill," "programmed to lie about their age," "programmed to feel little revulsion for their actions and to think of war and only war."[45] Filmmaker Sharmeen Obaid Chinoy described Taliban child soldiers as looking like "they're in a trance; they rock back and forth; it's as if they're reciting things that they have been programmed to recite."[46] The idea of the child soldier as programmed has become sufficiently engrained in public consciousness that Australian ethicist Robert Sparrow likens child soldiers to "autonomous robots," which he foresees as the weapons systems of the future – the next generation of smart weapons.[47]

The idea of slave armies of children challenges traditional notions of slavery. The dominant view of historians has generally been that that slavery and military service were largely incompatible. In antiquity, captured soldiers and civilians were often reduced to slavery, and war itself was sometimes specifically started for the specific purpose of obtaining slaves.

Moreover, since captured soldiers (and civilians) were routinely slain, those allowed to live in a state of slavery were said to have little cause to complain. So while it was routine for captured soldiers to be reduced to slaves, it was far rarer for slaves to be armed as combatants. The boundaries between slavery and freedom are often sharply drawn, even more so where, as in the antebellum South, slavery was highly racialized. The dominant examples of mass slavery during in modern warfare provides even further evidence of the brutality of slavery and the unbridgeable gaps between slavery and freedom. During World War II, tens of thousands of soldiers captured by Germany and the Soviet Union went to their deaths in slave labor camps.[48] Civilians, especially those defined by Nazi racial ideology as subhuman, suffered much the same fate. Jews in Germany and in German conquered territories were targeted for death, but were often used as slave labor in concentration camps before being murdered. In addition, Nazi Germany industrial production was tied to the Nazi slave labor regime and renowned German corporations such as Krupp, AEG, Telefunken, and Siemens made systematic use of thousands of Jewish slaves transported to German production sites from concentration camps.[49] The possibility of slave masters arming slaves under these circumstances seems simply beyond all credibility. As a result of the experience of World War II, slavery came to be treated in international law as both a war crime and a crime against humanity.

But recent historical evidence has provided a basis for some modification of traditional views about the arming of slaves. Instead, it now appears that there have been a variety of documented instances in which slaves were, in fact, armed either by their masters or by ruling governments. In keeping with traditional views, it also appears that in most of these cases, the arming of slaves was, in fact, coupled with explicit or implicit promises of personal freedom, even if the individual manumission of slave soldiers did not otherwise serve as a harbinger of the end of the institution of slavery.[50] In colonial America, both English colonists in South Carolina and Spanish colonists in Florida conscripted slaves in militias in time of war.[51] During the American Revolution, large numbers of slaves did enlist in both the Patriot and Tory militias and armies.[52] Former slaves flocked to the Union Army during the American Civil War, where military service served as a symbol of newfound freedom. As the Confederate cause collapsed at the end of the Civil War, plans to arm slaves in defense of the Confederacy were widely discussed and debated, but with the widespread recognition that arming slaves would inevitably lead to the end of slavery.[53]

The more radical departures from the traditional model involves the military use of slaves in Africa and in the Muslim world. John Thornton argues that "the regularity with which slaves were armed in Africa suggests that fighting was as much the part of the work routine of slaves as any other labor."[54] One factor that makes the African data difficult to assess is the many multiple relationships of patrimonial dependency that so envelope the African social landscape, rendering historians and anthropologists reluctant to characterize all these relations of dependency as slavery. But some were clearly recognized as such, making plain that the military use of slaves was widespread across the continent. The use of militarized slaves solved a variety of practical political problems, as rulers could use dependent slaves to enhance their power, with few local checks and balances. Frequently, military slavery in Africa involved the conscription of young boys. Military slavery in the Muslim world (which included parts of Africa) also appears to have been very widespread, and in numerous instances appears to have involved the use of young boys to be trained in the military. In many instances, such slaves were clearly distinguished from ordinary slaves by the power and prestige they held despite their slave status.[55]

In both the African and Muslim contexts, the use of military slaves gave rise to numerous complications. Most important, the arming of slaves always remained very problematic, as armed slaves tended to form independent centers of power, often achieving and exercising *de facto* political control despite their ascribed servile status. All this suggests that where slavery exists in a world generally organized in and through multiple relationships of patrimonial dependency, the *de facto* distinctions between freedom and slavery may sometimes blur. In such contexts, the arming of slaves may not seem as anomalous as it does in the Western context.

Beyond this, despite the jural status of slavery, there is scant evidence that military slaves as a class could easily be simultaneously armed and brutally exploited. Whatever the particular circumstances, historical experience suggests that the idea of the creation of a well-armed but at the same time exploited servile class of persons seems somewhat improbable. But can such a class of persons be created from children? If we are to take the claims of a wide variety of human rights and children rights advocates concerned with the problem of child soldiers seriously, we are being asked to accept that hundreds of thousands of children across the globe – or at least a significant portion of such children said to be associated with armed conflict – are being enslaved in precisely this manner.

Further complicating this picture is the fact that the vast majority of the "children" classified as child soldiers are actually armed adolescents and teenagers, who might be more accurately described as youth.[56] Children's rights advocates, relying on the definition of childhood set down in the Convention on the Rights of the Child, define a child as any person under age eighteen.

## Slavery in International Criminal Law

The 1926 Slavery Convention defines slavery as "the status or condition of a person over whom any or all of the powers attaching to the right of ownership are exercised."[57] In international criminal law, slavery is a crime against humanity. This definition clearly incorporates chattel slavery as in the African slave trade, but also applies to the exercise of ownership powers in the course of trafficking in persons, in particular women and children. Criminal liability depends on the exercise of all of the powers attaching to the right of ownership over one or more persons, such as by purchasing, selling, lending, or bartering such a person or persons, or by imposing on them a similar deprivation of liberty. Under some circumstances, forced labor, reducing a person to a servile status, and trafficking in persons, in particular women and children, can also be understood as enslavement to the extent that these involve the exercise of powers of ownership.[58] Slavery can also take the form of sexual slavery, which is both a crime against humanity and a war crime. Since legal slavery no longer exists, all criminal cases of enslavement turn on an individual factual determination of the circumstances to whether a person is enslaved.[59] There may very well be instances in which the situation of some child soldiers would fall under this category.

## Slavery in International Labor Treaties and Human Rights

Under some circumstances, international criminal law may also criminalize forced labor, but only when it involves a deprivation of liberty that rises to the level of slavery.[60]

While criminal law requires investigation, international labor agreements have provided an opportunity for classifying all forms of child recruitment as slavery. The idea that the conscription of child soldiers is a form of slavery per se has emerged out of the conventions of the International Labor Organization. The International Labor Convention (No. 29) concerning forced or compulsory labor defines forced labor as "all work or service which is exacted from any person under the menace of any penalty and for which the said person has not offered himself voluntarily."[61] Forced labor is usually understood to differ from slavery in that it does not necessarily involve exercising the powers of ownership. Moreover, and by way of emphasizing the contrast between forced labor and slavery, the ILO restrictions do not constitute an absolute ban on all forms of involuntary labor. Indeed the Convention specifically exempts any work or service exacted in virtue of compulsory military service laws for work of a purely military character. Also exempt are work or services exacted in emergency situations, including warfare and other circumstance that endanger the existence or well-being of a population.[62]

The ILO exemption of military service is consistent with the tradition of law in this area. Historically, nations have refused to treat compulsory military conscription for adults as a form of slavery or involuntary servitude. Service in the military is usually conceived of as a duty of citizenship, not as a form of ownership. In fact, the very idea that slaves might have legal rights and duties was usually deemed inconsistent with the ownership logic of slavery. Accordingly, the Thirteenth Amendment to the U.S. Constitution, which banned slavery and involuntary servitude in the United States did not contemplate banning conscription. The U.S. Supreme Court in *Butler v. Perry*, 240 U.S. 328 (1916) also explicitly ruled that conscription was neither slavery nor involuntary servitude.

The exemptions for involuntary labor in the ILO Convention on Forced Labor, however, are restricted to adult able-bodied males of the apparent age of not less than eighteen and not more than forty-five years. While this restricted the use of children in forced labor, it did not necessarily mean that such violations constituted enslavement. But the ILO's Convention on the Worst Forms of Child Labor fills this gap by explicitly equating the conscription of persons under eighteen years of age as slavery.

Labor rights have traditionally not been treated as human rights. But in 1998, in the Declaration on Fundamental Principles and Rights at Work, the ILO endorsed certain labor rights, including the elimination of forced or compulsory labor, the abolition of child labor, as fundamental human rights.[63] It is important to note, however, that unlike International Criminal law, which focuses on individual criminal culpability, human rights law – although its concerns are the rights of individuals – focuses on influencing the behavior of states, and imposes no criminal liability. It is very important to be cautious here, because it is by no means universally accepted that labor rights are in fact human rights.

If compulsory recruitment of anyone below age eighteen is a form of slavery, it is certainly an odd form of slavery at best, and one that has not yet found its way into international criminal law. Traditionally, abolitionists regarded slavery as a violation of natural law. In legal terms, slavery was *mala in se*, something absolutely evil in and of itself and not merely something prohibited as a mere matter of social policy.[64] In chattel slavery, age and gender played no role: slavery was an evil for men, women, and children alike. In contrast, if age eighteen were the legal dividing line between slavery and freedom, two identically positioned persons, each conscripted into the military, each with identical rights and duties in the military, but one seventeen years of age and one eighteen years of age, find themselves radically separated by law – the former a slave and the latter a patriot fulfilling his or her duty to society. The boundaries between slavery and freedom would become essentially calendric. Likewise, two seventeen-year-olds, one conscripted and the other a volunteer, would likewise find themselves equally divided by extremes, the one a slave and the other not. The distinctions between slavery and freedom would be derived from social policy unlinked to the actual experience of child soldiering. It is very clear what the ILO and a host of human rights and children rights organization are attempting to accomplish, namely to drive a wedge between children and the military. But given the comparative and historical variation of the experience of under-eighteen-year-olds under arms, including all these experiences under the universal rubric of slavery appears to make little legal or empirical sense.

Much of the argument supporting an age-based definition of slavery turns on the age of consent. Under international criminal law, children under age fifteen are presumed not to be able to consent to recruitment.[65] Accordingly, they are deemed forcibly conscripted even where they have clearly volunteered. But the law currently remains unsettled for fifteen-to-eighteen-year-olds. Complicating this argument is that historically the age of consent has been a moving target. British common law did not draw a single hard line about age. Instead, it contained the legacy of earlier thinking in which the boundaries between childhood and adulthood were not clearly distinct, coupled with a recognition that children move gradually toward full maturity. Accordingly, common law recognized different levels of rights and responsibilities by both age and gender. A male could take the oath of allegiance at age twelve (presumably required for any person enlisting in the armed services); at age fourteen, he could consent to marry, choose a guardian, and attain the age of legal discretion or make a will; at age seventeen, he could be an executor of an estate; and at twenty-one, he would reach "full age." A female could be betrothed at age seven, at age twelve, she could consent or disagree to a marriage or bequeath her personal estate; at fourteen she was regarded as having reached the age of legal discretion, and she reached "full age" at twenty-one. The common law recognized the arbitrariness of the idea of "full age," acknowledging, for example, that in other countries such as France the absolute right to marry did not occur until age thirty.[66] We might today disagree with the details of the common-law schema, but the legal recognition of a gradual unfolding of rights, duties, and responsibilities makes far more sense than the growing tendency in contemporary international law to draw a single bright-line distinction between childhood and adulthood at age eighteen. Erica Meiners, in her contribution to this volume (see Chapter 4), notes the punishing and capricious elements that underlie the concepts of childhood innocence and consent. Similarly, the entire history of the malleability of the age of consent should make us extremely cautious about using age as a proxy for consent in the definition of slavery.

There clearly are situations in which the forced recruitment of child soldiers results in persons under age eighteen being placed in conditions that may fairly be characterized as forced labor and perhaps slavery. Note, however, that usually these are situations in which adult conscripts are treated in much the same manner. The cruelty with which some of the most notorious armed groups such as the Lord Resistance Army in Uganda treat their conscripts is not necessarily a matter of age. Children's rights advocates are correct in wanting to protect children from all forms of cruelty. The central question is whether using the issue of child conscription as a general proxy for slavery, regardless of the actual situation in which children find themselves, makes empirical, legal, or moral sense. Virtually all rules of laws that substitute proxies for evidence are over-inclusive and satisfy the cultural and political logic of the moment in their desire for efficiency.[67] The ILO is not a legislative body, and its agreements are not laws, but forms of norm entrepreneurship – the creation of new norms. This raises the question as to whether the term *slavery*, as applied to child soldiers, is used primarily to amplify distaste for a social practice that many in the international community find morally abhorrent. In essence, the use of child conscription as a proxy for slavery creates a form of "constructive slavery," in which a phenomenon whose features and circumstances lack the essential characteristics of servitude become treated as slavery solely as a function of law or policy.

## Child Soldiers as Slaves

Arguing that labeling all child soldiers slaves is a form of normative over-kill does not mean that there are no instances in which child soldiers may in fact be slaves. During the civil war in Sierra Leone (1991), the recruitment of child soldiers was widespread. Three main armed forces and groups were involved in the struggle. The main rebel force was the Revolutionary United Front (RUF); the main government army was the Sierra Leone Army (SLA) and the Civilian Defense Forces (CDF), a coalition of ethnic militias that fought against the RUF. Following a military coup in Sierra Leone, the RUF joined forces with the Armed Forced Revolutionary Council and its armed forces (AFRC). What is clear is that the experience of children in these groups was radically different.

### Revolutionary United Front

The RUF has been the subject of considerable study and analysis. It was widely known for its abduction of children and its widespread campaign of terror against the civilian population of Sierra Leone. A significant study of RUF recruitment was undertaken by Myriam Denov, who examined seventy-six children (thirty-six boys and forty girls), all of whom reported being abducted by the Revolutionary United Front.[68] The children were four to thirteen years old at the time they were taken into the RUF, and remained with the rebel forces from periods ranging from a few months to eight years. Using the collected narratives of the children, Denov developed a model of forced recruitment into the RUF. She describes an especially cruel threefold rite de passage by which children were 1) separated from their former lives and incorporated and accultur-ated into the RUF's culture of violence; 2) learned to adapt to, participate in, and sometimes resist the intensely brutal and cruel world of the RUF fighters; and 3) finally left the RUF at war's end, transformed by their experiences and only uneasily reintroduced to the daunting challenges of postwar Sierra Leone.

Within this framework, children were abducted, separated, and isolated from their families and communities into RUF-controlled enclaves. Children generally reported a period of training and ideological orientation similar to that found in most armed forces and groups. This included weapons and physical training, along with instruction in the care and use of small arms and the careful management of ammunition. Children were also schooled in a wide variety of battlefield tactics and killing techniques. There was also a major ideological component that required recruits to attend meetings, and listen to speeches and motivational lectures on the philosophy of the RUF and its social and political goals and sing war songs.

What set the RUF apart from other armed groups in Sierra Leone was the degree to which it was infused by an extreme culture of violence, designed to break down resistance, ensure obedience, and celebrate and routinize cruelty and terror. The RUF, Denov states, was "indiscriminate in its brutality."[69] It engaged in wholesale murder and terror throughout Sierra Leone and visited daily cruelties upon its own recruits, whether they were men or women, boys or girls. The abuse of child soldiers took place within the larger context of abuse visited upon all members of the RUF by its chain of command. But there seems to be little doubt this was slavery and that these children, like all slaves, had, as David Brion Davis observed, "no legitimate independent being except as instruments of their masters' will."[70]

A major strength of Denov's study is that her findings stress the limited agency of children, even under extreme circumstances over which they have little control. Denov points to the strength of peer relationships among recruits and the degree to which children and youth mentored one another, took on key leadership positions within the RUF, actively recruited other children into the ranks of the RUF, and forged strong bonds of friendship. The data also point to the fluidity of roles both boys and girls took up in the RUF. Without minimizing the treatment and suffering of many of these children and youth, it is clear that their identities and experiences cannot be reduced to the simple categories of "victims" and "sex slaves" that are so prominent in many accounts of child soldiers. Equally important is the way children, both boys and girls, were able to resist, sometimes violently, the abusive behavior of others. Both boys and girls were frequently able to challenge or evade the culture of violence within the RUF so as to preserve their own senses of personal identity and morality.

But demonstrating the existence of agency among the children of the RUF does not negate a condition of slavery. Indeed, the agency of slaves was widespread in the American chattel slave system. The agency of slaves did not necessarily challenge the system of slavery but often worked to ensure its continuity.[71] Whatever agency RUF child soldiers seem to have had, they never, given the culture of terror that enveloped them, could convert this into explicit resistance. Many of these children, especially girls, were truly slaves in any conceivable sense of the word. As Denov puts it, "among powerful patriarchal structures, girls became mere 'property' of males, with their bodies being used as resources to be exploited, and even as gifts and rewards."

## Civilian Defense Forces

At the same time that children were being forcibly recruited into the RUF, children were also joining the Sierra Leone Civilian Defense Forces. The CDF was a loose amalgam of independent ethnic militias and self-defense groups that emerged to defend a largely unarmed and defenseless civilian population from the rapacious and violent rebels of the Revolutionary United Front and the predatory military forces of the Sierra Leone state. The best-known militias groups and their ethnic affiliations in Sierra Leone were the Kamajors (Mende), the Donsos (Kono), the Kapras (Temne), and the Tamboro (Koranko). These ethnic militias played a major role in defeating the RUF but also had distinctly different local and national agendas that divided them from one another. The Mende based Kamajors were the dominant militia group and the CDF leadership was largely drawn from the Mende. Kamajor militias were widely described as being rooted in a long-standing practice of traditional hunters who serve as guardians and protectors of villages and communities, but in fact they were a modern force that made use of the trappings of tradition. There is little doubt that the CDF, which began as a force committed to defending civilians, came to also target and victimize them. The young fighters of the CDF became marginalized bottom feeders who turned to depredation. The violence of all soldiers, children, and adults became a trade and an identity, and was one of the few ways youth could actually participate in the economy. But whatever their failings, the CDF forces were far less ruthless than the enemies against whom they fought.

But at the end of the war, the Special Court for Sierra Leone was jointly created by the government of Sierra Leone and the United Nations. Its mandate was to try those who bear the greatest responsibility for serious violations of international humanitarian law and Sierra Leonean law during the civil war. Several of the key leaders of the RUF and the CDF stood in the dock before the Special Court for Sierra Leone, charged with (and later convicted of) orchestrating and carrying out numerous war crimes against civilians, including the recruitment of child soldiers.

In its examination of the conscription of child soldiers, the Special Court made clear that the use of actual force was central to the conviction of the RUF and AFRC leaders. The evidence showed that they forcibly abducted children of a wide variety of ages and that the abduction of children was only part of a broader pattern of atrocities.[72] As the Trial Chamber in the AFRC case stated, "the only method described in the evidence is abduction.[73] "In the court's opinion, in the RUF cases, abduction and conscription were virtually synonymous.[74] The RUF and

AFRC leadership were also charged and convicted of enslavement and sexual slavery. The trial chamber made clear that the children abducted and conscripted by the RUF were also slaves and that the crime against humanity of enslavement encompassed the forcible training for military purposes, including the forcible training of children.[75]

In contrast, before the Special Court for Sierra Leone, kamajor violence was portrayed as a result of a movement gone wrong. The kamajors were described as an erstwhile but authentic self-defense movement that had somehow lost its traditional moorings in village, community, and chiefdom life and, as a result, also lost its moral compass.[76] But despite this unhappy turn of events for the CDF, it remains clear that the recruitment of youth by the CDF was radically different from that of the RUF. Both the RUF and CDF leadership were charged with war crimes and crimes against humanity, including the conscription or enlistment of child soldiers under age fifteen. But only the RUF leadership was charged with and convicted of enslavement, sexual slavery, rape, and other forms of sexual violence. It was the RUF that stood out for its widespread and systematic murder, extermination, and terrorization of the civilian population.

Around the world, millions of people are involved in wars, rebellions, insurgencies, and civil conflicts. It is widely asserted that 250,000–300,000 soldiers below the age of eighteen are involved in contemporary armed conflicts, but in reality there are no reliable statistics to support these numbers. The figure of 300,000 was put forth by advocacy groups promoting a ban on child recruitment as a way of dramatizing the issue, but it is very likely that the actual numbers are significantly lower.[77] Whatever the actual number, over the past several decades, many hundreds of thousands of children have experienced and continue to experience war as soldiers. To understand the issue of child soldiers, there is a pressing need to penetrate both the fog of war and the fog of advocacy. Reducing the involvement of children and youth in all these conflicts to an issue of slavery obscures rather than clarifies the role of children in both historical and contemporary conflicts.

## Notes

1   Convention on the Rights of the Child, 1577 U.N.T.S. 3 (November 20, 1989), Article 1.
2   Convention Concerning the Prohibition and Immediate Action for the Elimination of the Worst Forms of Child Labour, ILO Convention No. 182, adopted by the ILO General Conference, Geneva, June 17, 1999, Articles 1, 3(a).

3    "Warlords Keep Huge Army of Child Soldiers in Slavery," *Dawn*, July 7, 2012. www.dawn.com/news/733530/warlords-keep-in-huge-army-of-child-soldiers-in-slavery; "Terror Organization PKK and Their Slaves: Child Soldiers in the PKK," *Cartel 1923*, April 16, 2012, www.liveleak.com/view?i=ce5_1334599659.

4    Barak Obama, Remarks at the eighth annual Clinton Global Initiative Meeting, September 25, 2012. Accessed March 5, 2014. www.c-span.org/video/?308392-2/president-obama-remarks-clinton-global-initiative.

5    Heather Montgomery, *An Introduction to Childhood: Anthropological Perspectives on Children's Lives* (Chichester UK: Wiley-Blackwell, 2008), 114.

6    An Act for Forming and Regulating the Militia in the Colony of Massachusetts Bay, January 22, 1776, *Acts and Resolutions, Public and Private, of the Province of Massachusetts Bay, Volume 5* (Boston, MA: Wright and Potter, 1886), 445.

7    Steven Mintz, *Huck's Raft: A History of American Childhood* (Cambridge, MA: Harvard University Press, 2004), 29.

8    Ibid., 51. Also see Harold E Selesky, *War and Society in Colonial America* (New Haven, CT: Yale University Press, 1990).

9    Mintz, *Huck's Raft*, 69.

10    Ibid. at 62.

11    Ibid. at 63.

12    Ibid. at 62.

13    Joseph Plumb Martin, *Memoire of a Revolutionary Soldier: The Narrative of Joseph Plumb Martin* (Halowell, ME: Glazier, Masters & Co., 1830; reprint, Mineola, NY: Dover, 2006), 12.

14    *Journals of the Continental Congress*, 1774–89, Volume 2 (Washington, DC: Library of Congress 1904–37), 187–8. Available at http://memory.loc.gov/ammem/amlaw/lwjclink.html.

15    Harold Selesky, "A Demographic Survey of the Continental Army that Wintered at Valley Forge, Pennsylvania, 1777–1778" (Washington, DC: Nation Park Service, 1987). Available at www.nps.gov/vafo/historyculture/demographic-survey.htm (See particularly Selesky's unpaginated age tables in text).

16    James M. McPherson, *Ordeal by Fire: The Civil War and Reconstruction* (New York: Alfred A. Knopf, 1982), 356.

17    Janet Dolgin, "Transforming Childhood: Apprenticeship in American Law," *New England Law Review* 31 (1997): 1113–91, 1114.

18    Lawrence Friedman, *The History of American Law, 3rd Edition* (New York: Touchstone, 2005), 70.

19    James McPherson, *Battle Cry of Freedom: The Civil War Era* (Oxford: Oxford University Press, 2003), 306 n. 4.

20    Benjamin Gould, *Investigations in the Military and Anthropological Statistics of American Soldiers* (New York: Hurd and Houghton, 1869), 35.

21    George L. Kilmer, "Boys in the Union Army," *The Century* 70 (1905): 269–75.

22    Charles King, "Boys of the War Days," in Francis Trevelyan Miller, ed., *A Photographic History of the Civil War*, Volume 8 (Springfield, MA: Patriot Press, 1911), 190.

23 Judith Pizzaro, Roxanne Cohen Silver, and JoAnn Prause, "Physical and Mental Health Costs of Traumatic War Experiences among Civil War Veterans," *Archives of General Psychiatry* 63.2 (2006): 193–200. Available at www.ncbi.nlm.nih.gov/pmc/articles/PMC1586122. Age at first enlistment was obtained from military records, and ranged from nine to seventy-one years. This variable was categorized into five age groups of approximately equal size to highlight the effect of younger ages: 9 to 17 years (n = 3013), 18 to 20 years (n = 3694), 21 to 25 years (n = 3435), 26 to 30 years (n = 2225), and 31 years and older (n = 2660).

24 Bell Irvin Wiley, *The Common Soldier in the Civil War: Book II The Life of Johnny Reb* (New York: Grosset and Dunlop, 1943), 331.

25 See, for example, Peter W. Singer, *Children at War* (New York: Pantheon, 2006), 15.

26 George Croppard, *With a Machine Gun to Cambrai* (London: Her Majesty's Stationary Office, 1969), 1.

27 Victor Silvester, *Dancing Is My Life* (London: Heinemann, 1958), 16.

28 Richard van Emden, *Boy Soldiers of the Great War* (London: Headline, 2005), 317–18, 321.

29 Ibid., 319.

30 Ibid., 321.

31 An Act to Make Provision with Respect to Military Service in Connection with the Recent War, 1916 (5 & 6 Geo. C. 104) UK Parliamentary Archives, HL/PO/PU/1/1916/5&6G5c104.

32 The official number is 4,970,902. *Statistics of the Military Effort of the British Empire during the Great War* (London: His Majesty's Stationary Office, 1922), 364.

33 Letter from George C. Curnock to Sir Arthur Markham, November 2, 1915. Papers, Correspondence, and Press Cuttings Relating to the Life and Careers of Arthur Basil Markham, MP Markham 22/Code PA3143, Archival Material of British Library of Political and Economic Science, London School of Economics. Markham 22/Code PA3143.

34 Richard Rinaldi, *The United States Army in World War I – Order of Battle* (Takoma Park, MD: Tiger Lily Publications, 2005), 5.

35 *Second Report of the Provost Marshal General to the Secretary of War on the Operations of the Selective Service System to December 20, 1918* (Washington, DC: Government Printing Office, 1919), 6.

36 "Nationalist Veteran," *Spanish Civil War University of Texas Austin*. Accessed December 12, 2013. http://journalism.utexas.edu/coursework/spanish-civil-war/nationalist-veteran.

37 George Orwell, *Homage to Catalonia* (New York: Harcourt, 1969), 26.

38 A. K. Starinov, *Behind Fascist Lines: A Firsthand Account of Guerilla Warfare during the Spanish Revolution* (New York: Ballentine Books, 2001), 33.

39 Child Soldiers International, *Child Soldiers Global Report 2001 – Iran*, 2001. Accessed June 20, 2013, www.refworld.org/docid/498805f02d.html.

40 Robert Tait, "Iran 'Using Child Soldiers' to Suppress Tehran Protests," *The Guardian*, March 13, 2011. www.guardian.co.uk/world/2011/mar/13/iran-child-soldiers-tehran-protests.

41  Andrew Green, "South Sudan's Red Army Comes of Age," *The Guardian*, March 27, 2013. www.guardian.co.uk/global-development/2013/mar/27/south-sudan-red-army-comes-age.

42  "Children and Armed Conflict: Report of the Secretary General," *General Assembly-Security Council* A/64/742–S/2010/181. April 13, 2010. Accessed February 6, 2014. http://daccess-dds-ny.un.org/doc/UNDOC/GEN/N10/311/28/PDF/N1031128.pdf?OpenElement.

43  "Children Affected by Armed Conflict/ Child Soldiers," *Youth Advocacy Program International*, April 1, 2014. http://yapi.org/youth-wellbeing/children-affected-by-armed-conflict-child-soldiers.

44  Tom Masland, "Voices of the Children: We Killed and Beat People," *Newsweek*, May 13, 2002. www.newsweek.com/2002/05/12/voices-of-the-children-quot-we-beat-and-killed.html.

45  Alcinda Honwana. *Okusiakala ondalo yokalye: Let Us Light a New Fire: Local Knowledge in the Post-war Healing and Reintegration of War-Affected Children in Angola.* 1998. www.forcedmigration.org/psychosocial/inventory/pwg001/pwg001.pdf.

46  Kalsoom Lakhani, "Pakistan's Child Soldiers," *Foreign Policy*, March 29, 2010. http://afpak.foreignpolicy.com/posts/2010/03/29/pakistans_child_soldiers.

47  Robert Sparrow, "Killer Robots," *Journal of Applied Philosophy* 24 (2007): 62–77.

48  Arnold Krammer, *Prisoners of War: A Reference Handbook* (Westport, CT: Greenwood Publishing Company, 2008), 33–6.

49  Benjamin B. Ferencz, *Less than Slaves: Jewish Forced Labor and the Quest for Compensation* (Bloomington: Indiana University Press, 2002), xxvi.

50  David Brion Davis, "Introduction," in Christopher Leslie Brown and Philip D. Morgan, eds., *Arming Slaves: From Classical Times to the Modern Age* (New Haven, CT: Yale University Press, 2006), 6–8.

51  Ira Berlin, *Many Thousands Gone: The First Two Centuries of Slavery in North America* (Cambridge, MA: Belknap Press, 2000), 66.

52  Phillip Foner, *Blacks in the American Revolution* (Westport, CT: Greenwood Press, 1976).

53  Bruce Levine, *Confederate Emancipation: Southern Plans to Free and Arm Slaves during the Civil War* (Oxford: Oxford University Press, 2006), 2.

54  John Thornton, "Armed Slaves and Political Authority in Africa in the Era of the Slave Trade, 1450–1800," in Christopher Leslie Brown and Philip D. Morgan, eds., *Arming Slaves: From Classical to the Modern Times* (New Haven, CT: Yale University Press, 2006), 79.

55  Daniel Pipes, *Slave Soldiers and Islam: The Genesis of a Military System* (New Haven, CT: Yale University Press, 1981), 5–23.

56  Mark Drummond, *Reimagining Child Soldiers in International Law and Policy* (Oxford: Oxford University Press, 2012), 50. See generally David M. Rosen, *Armies of the Young: Child Soldiers in War and Terrorism* (New Brunswick, NJ: Rutgers University Press, 2012).

57  "Convention to Suppress the Slave Trade and Slavery," *League of Nations*, September 25, 1926, 60 LNTS 253, Registered No. 1414. Accessed February 28, 2014. www.refworld.org/docid/3ae6b36fb.html.

58 "Rome Statute of the International Criminal Court (last amended 2010)," July 17, 1998. Article 7 (1) and 7(2)(c). Accessed February 28, 2014. www .refworld.org/docid/3ae6b3a84.html; "Elements of Crimes," *International Criminal Court*. Art. 7 (1) (c) and footnote 11. Accessed February 28, 2014. www1.umn.edu/humanrts/instree/iccelementsofcrimes.html.

59 Finally other acts not enumerated in criminal statute can sometimes be considered crimes against humanity and may involve enslavement. For example, the Special Court for Sierra Leone determined that "forced marriage," defined as "forced conjugal association with another person resulting in great suffering, or serious physical or mental injury on the part of the victim," was a crime against humanity, but did not equate it with slavery, despite some obvious similarities.

60 *Elements of Crimes*. 2011. The Hague: International Criminal Court. Art. 7 (1) (c) and footnote 11. Available at www1.umn.edu/humanrts/instree/ iccelementsofcrimes.html.

61 "Convention Concerning Forced or Compulsory Labour (No 29), 1930," International Labour Organization. www.ilo.org/dyn/normlex/en/f?p= NORMLEXPUB:12100:0::NO:12100:P12100_ILO_CODE:C029.

62 John Ryle, "Forced Labor," Crime of War Project, 2011. Accessed March 1, 2014. www.crimesofwar.org/a-z-guide/forced-labor.

63 "Declaration on Fundamental Principles and Rights at Work," *International Labour Organization*, 1998. Accessed March 2, 2014. www.ilo.org/public/ english/standards/relm/ilc/ilc86/com-dtxt.htm

64 See, for example, Massachusetts Anti-Slavery Society, *Fourteenth Annual Report* (Boston, MA: Scarlet and Laing, 1846), 65–6.

65 See *Prosecutor v. Dyilo*, Doc. No. ICC-01/04-01/06.

66 William Blackstone, *Commentaries of the Laws of England*, vol. 1 (Philadelphia: Robert Bell, 1771), 463.

67 The use of proxies is a common legislative tool almost always used to solve social problems in an over-inclusive manner. In American jurisprudence, gender has frequently been used a proxy for parental unfitness. Examples include the cases *Tanley v. Illinois* 405 U.S. 645 (1972) where gender served as a proxy for unfitness so that children of unwed fathers were deemed wards of the state, while those of unwed mothers were not. Another instance is *Orr. v. Orr* 1440 U.S. 268, (1979) in which the U.S. Supreme Court ruled unconstitutional Alabama alimony statutes that provided that husbands, but not wives, be required to pay alimony upon divorce. In this case, Alabama argued, among other things, that gender was a proxy for need and that no actual evidence or inquiry into the actual circumstances of a husband or wife was required. In contrast, California statutory rape law used age and gender as a proxy for harm when it held males, but not females, criminally liable for having sexual intercourse with an individual under eighteen years of age See *Michael M. v. Superior Court*, 450 US 464 (1981). Statutory rape laws, and all forms of legislative proxies, end up expressing multiple and historically contingent policy initiatives of powerful political groups and public officials. See Carolyn E. Cocca, *Jailbait: The Politics of Statutory Rape Laws in the United States* (Albany: State University of New York Press, 2004). The

American war on drugs was essentially a proxy war on violent crime with nonviolent drug offenders often sentenced more harshly than those who committed violent crimes. In American criminal law, drug possession above a specified quantity served as a proxy for distribution, resulting in long prison sentences for persons unconnected or marginally connected to the drug trade. It is much simpler to prove possession than to actually prosecute for distribution, but once possession serves as a proxy for distribution, conviction becomes cheap, efficient, and unjust. See William Stuntz, *The Collapse of American Criminal Justice* (Cambridge, MA: Harvard University Press, 2011), 267–8.

68  Myriam Denov, *Child Soldiers: Sierra Leone's Revolutionary Front* (Cambridge: Cambridge University Press, 2004), 96–120.

69  Ibid., 123.

70  David Brion Davis, *Inhuman Bondage: The Rise and Fall of Slavery in the New World* (New York: Oxford University Press, 2006), 31.

71  For an extended critical discussion of agency in the context of chattel slavery, see Walter Johnson, "On Agency," *Journal of Social History* 37.1 (2003): 113–24.

72  Steven Rapp, "The Compact Model in International Criminal Justice, the Special Court for Sierra Leone," *Drake Law Review* 57 (2008): 11–49.

73  "Prosecutor v. Brima." *Special Court for Sierra Leone.* Case No. SCSL 04-16-T, Trial Court Judgment, June 20, 2007, ¶ 275.

74  "Prosecutor v. Sesay," *Special Court for Sierra Leone.* Case No. SCSL 04-15-T, 9, Trial Court Judgment, March 2, 2009, ¶¶ 1699–1701.

75  Ibid., ¶¶1488, 1694, 1695, and 2156.

76  Danny Hoffman, *The War Machines: Young Men and Violence in Sierra Leone and Liberia* (Durham, NC: Duke University Press, 2011).

77  G. Scott and S. Reich, "Think Again: Child Soldiers: What Human Rights Activists Never Tell You About Young Killers," *Foreign Policy*, May 22, 2009. www.foreignpolicy.com/articles/2009/05/21/think_again_child_soldiers.

# 8

# Notions of African Childhood in Abolitionist Discourses: Colonial and Postcolonial Humanitarianism in the Fight Against Child Slavery

Audra A. Diptee

Stories of child slavery in present day Africa are so pervasive that few would be shocked by the horrific circumstances under which captive children are made to live. Nor would many be surprised, given the high level of public awareness about the transatlantic slave trade, to learn that child slavery in Africa has a very long history. During the slave trade, children were often the "major targets" of slavers, and there was a continuing slave trade "consisting mostly of children" long after Europeans imposed prohibitions on the export of enslaved African people to the Americas.[1] In many areas, children were particularly vulnerable to being illegally enslaved as they were "more easily kidnapped, controlled and acculturated."[2] According to historian Martin Klein, in western Sudan during the early 1880s, there were sometimes slave caravans comprised of only children. By the early twentieth century, when the French made more deliberate efforts to end the slave trade in Africa, those being enslaved were "almost exclusively children." In Klein's words, they were "easier to hide" and "easier to intimidate into silence."[3]

Explanatory narratives aimed at addressing the root causes of African child slavery tend to fall into two camps: Slavery is either seen as a "survival of the past" or, in sharp contrast, as a function of present-day globalization forces.[4] To date, historians have been increasingly trying to make links between their research and the contemporary problem of child slavery. The tendency, however, has been to restrict their analysis and contribution to providing historical context.[5] If the matter of child slavery – be it past or present – is to be properly understood, it is important to contextualize, and ultimately historicize, the ways in which the concepts of childhood and slavery have been defined. Michael Barnett has argued that humanitarian efforts to "stop suffering and confer dignity" should not be seen as transhistorical. These efforts are informed by "contemporary notions of humanity and victimhood."[6] In other words, the nature of abolitionist efforts to end child slavery depended on how slavery was understood and who was considered enslaved. They were also informed by fluid notions of childhood. As David Rosen's article on child soldiers and Jessica Pliley's article on prostitution – both in this collection – have made clear, the use of the term *child slavery* by humanitarian and human rights activists – in both contemporary and historical contexts – needs to come under greater analytical rigor. Their studies raise questions about the ways in which notions of innocence are embedded in conceptions of childhood and the ways in which the "universal rubric of slavery" obscures the variety of historical and contemporary contexts in which children have been used and exploited.

Understanding children's experience under slavery is relevant for another reason. From the perspective of life course theory, it is important to contemplate the totality of a person's life and the ways in which the circumstances of a particular historical moment affect later outcomes. It gives priority to the understanding that an individual's past shapes that individual's future. Put another way, the story of children and the story of adults are, in fact, part of the same story. The story of the enslaved child is the first part of the story of the enslaved adult. In other words, without proper consideration of childhood under slavery, the adult's story is incomplete, and the narrative lacks depth. Understanding experiences during childhood can shed light on "decisions, opportunities, and conditions that affect later outcomes."[7] Hence, the history of slavery as it relates to children brings us closer to understanding the totality of the human experience under slavery. Of course, not all children make it into adulthood. There can be little question that child slaves, in particular, would have above average mortality rates as they are more likely to face physical abuse, be poorly fed, and receive little, if any, medical attention. Yet the history of these children can also provide valuable insights. By contextualizing their experiences within its appropriate sociohistorical context scholars, activists, and policy makers can better determine those factors that have differentially shaped the experiences of exploited children.[8]

As many of the chapters in this collection have demonstrated, activist discourses addressing childhood are often racialized, gendered, and embedded with notions of innocence.[9] Less clear, however, are the ways in which these Western conceptions of childhood interact with the concept of childhood as it is constructed elsewhere. In other words, childhood is not an unproblematic term, as it is often conceptualized differently, embedded with different assumptions, and given different meanings in varying contexts.[10] As in the case of West Africa, for example, during the precolonial and colonial period, societies did not traditionally use age to define social status. Instead, the focus was on "generations." Youth was defined "by unique historical circumstances and narratives that set their generation apart." Hence ideas of youth were in a state of greater "negotiation, flux and invention." It was understood to be a phase in the life cycle "enshrined by a continuous cycle of public rituals."[11] Colonial interventions, which were often articulated in humanitarian terms, however, would serve to disrupt these notions and introduced new definitions of youth that were informed by notions of age, gender, race, and also shaped by changing ideas of maturity.[12]

This study explores abolitionist discourse generated during the colonial period in West Africa and its relationship with the narratives constructed by present-day humanitarians working to end child slavery in the contemporary period. Relying primarily on colonial sources for French West Africa, it demonstrates that parameters of childhood and slavery, as defined by colonial officials, were far removed from many of the other studies in this collection. For better or for worse, there is no denying that antislavery was the ideological framework Europeans used to justify the colonization of Africa. Yet notions of childhood innocence and children's need for protection, though part and parcel of the abolitionist discourse of the day, gave way to practical realities and other colonial priorities. There was a sharp difference between the antislavery ideals embedded in colonial law and the actual practices taking place on the ground as actively enforcing idealized notions about childhood and freedom proved untenable. Although there were very real efforts to end child slavery, quite often compromises were made, policies were not aligned with actual practices, and humanitarian efforts were competing with other colonial interests that sometimes trumped efforts to liberate captive children. This required stripping African children of the supposed innocence and protection that was generally associated with childhood in other contexts.

Furthermore, the colonial project brought a racialized dimension to childhood in Africa, and this was manifested in the humanitarian discourses of the early twentieth century. It was understood that at the core of the "mission civilisatrice," there was a battle over *African childhoods*.[13] The very concept of childhood, then, was unstable. It was continually being defined and redefined depending on the particularity of circumstances and according to the desires of the various stakeholders. Unsurprisingly, there were colonial efforts to remake African childhoods in a way that supported and justified the priorities of the colonial project. Because efforts to eliminate child slavery were often in conflict with other colonial objectives, the idealism that grounded the concept of freedom was mediated in its application by the practical realities of circumstances. This resulted in the parameters of freedom being defined according to age and gender and African youth making their own efforts to claim their freedom and to define the terms of their childhood. Finally, this chapter suggests that the complicated, morally compromised efforts to end slavery in colonial Africa are often given short shrift in present day humanitarian discourses. In effect, this oversight serves to obscure analyses of the practice and policies geared toward ending child slavery.

## Saving the Children from their Africanness

Ironically, although European efforts to abolish the transatlantic slave trade in the nineteenth century ended the forced transport of Africans off the continent, it actually led to an expansion in slave systems *in Africa* and so to an increase in the number of enslaved children.[14] From the African point of view, the European blockade against the export of Africans across the Atlantic would have a significant impact on the political economy of the continent. When and how change occurred varied across Africa, but the nineteenth century was, without question, a period of transition.[15] For much of West Africa, the shrinking of the Atlantic slave trade led to an expansion of economic activities (often referred to as "legitimate commerce") in the agricultural sector in order to meet the growing regional and international demands. In addition, and this is perhaps one of the greatest ironies in the history of the Atlantic slave trade, European prohibitions against the trade may have ended the forced migration of Africans to the Americas, but it only served to increase the use of enslaved labor within much of Africa in order to meet the needs of this expanding agricultural sector.[16] With the decline in demand for captives in the Americas, there was an oversupply of slaves in Africa and a corresponding fall in slave prices on the continent. In other words, slave labor became more affordable and an increasing number of the enslaved were made to labor in the expanding peanut sector (Senegal) as well as the palm oil and palm kernel sector in Dahomey (present-day Bénin) and Cameroon. In the savanna states, the enslaved were made to labor as porters, and in the production of grains and textiles.[17] In the French Sudan, officials estimated that two-thirds of the population was enslaved. Patrick Manning estimates that for all of French West and Central Africa there were approximately 10 million people living as slaves.[18] Women and children accounted for the majority of these captives.

Unlike other studies in this collection, such as those by Erica Meiners and Micki McElya, which have emphasized the ways in which discourses on childhood were grounded in notions of innocence, this chapter focuses on how enslaved African children rarely benefited from this kind of thinking. Instead, as a result of racialized notions of childhood in the nineteenth-century African context, it was believed that African children needed to be Christianized and civilized and their labor channeled into sectors that would facilitate European commerce. Notions of childhood innocence were often at odds with their "Africanness." Abolitionist discourses in Africa were intimately linked to discourses about progress. It was understood that progress in Africa would be attained through the imposition of "Christianity, commerce, and civilization." These three elements, it was believed, could "penetrate to the root of evil" in Africa.[19] Unsurprisingly, colonial officials had an outlook that clearly privileged the emancipation of men. In 1904, in a report addressing slavery in French West Africa, the Commandant at Bobo-Dioulasso (in modern-day Burkina Faso) noted that the trade in men was over and that *only* women and children were being sold as slaves.[20] The Commandant's comment hints at the ways in which age and gender informed discussions about slavery and freedom in French West Africa.

Although abolitionist ideals were commonly espoused, in reality, both colonial officials and missionaries found themselves addressing the liberation of child slaves in some morally ambiguous – if not outright hypocritical – ways. In part, this was because, although antislavery was the justification Europeans used to colonize Africa, actively enforcing any such position was proven unrealistic and at times undesirable. This necessarily meant abandoning idealistic notions about liberating African children. In fact, any interest in ending slavery in Africa was subordinate – very subordinate – to other colonial priorities.[21] For this reason, colonial administrations only gave *indirect* support to end slavery. In the case of the French, not unlike the British, there was ambivalence about stopping slavery in West Africa. In 1848, when slaves in St. Louis and Gorée (Senegal) were freed, traders from outside the colony refused to trade. Thus, there was an immediate need to *reduce* the efficacy of the laws. This might mean, for example, colonial officials returning the slaves of their allies instead of freeing them as stipulated under the law. To further address the "problem" of freeing slaves, the French even disannexed some of their territories, turning them from colonies into protectorates. As emancipation laws applied only to the colonies, colonial administrators were spared the inconvenience of antagonizing slaveholders who lived in these areas.[22] Similarly, in the Gold Coast, in 1874, the British made slave trading illegal, but did no such thing for slavery. Instead, slavery "was declared to have no legal status."[23] The distinction was a powerful one and the goal was to have slavery gradually die out as the two chief means of producing and reproducing the slave population were dealt with in colonial law: slave trading was no longer permitted; and children born after a certain date would be considered free.[24]

It might be tempting to assume that French colonial administrators at least held on to their ideals when it came to enslaved children, but this was not the case. Child slavery continued to thrive.[25] In fact, when the French colonial state finally abolished the legal category of slave in 1903, it meant only that slave owners could no longer expect help from the state if they sought to get a slave returned. It would not be until 1905 that the French would actually outlaw the capture and sale of slaves.[26] Although this made the process of enslavement illegal, and also guaranteed that all children would be born free, the situation was not necessarily something to be celebrated. To get their liberty those people who were already living as slaves, the majority of whom were women and children, had two choices: they could petition for their liberty before the courts; or, they could purchase their freedom. If neither of these options were possible, they would retain their slave status throughout their lives.[27] Put another way, from the perspective of the law, *slave trading* would suffer an abrupt legal death and the institution of *slavery* would die a "slow death."[28] Ironically, what these early twentieth-century abolition laws created was a new era of human trafficking, and it was children who were particularly vulnerable. Despite the implementation of these twentieth-century abolitionist laws, various means and methods were used to separate children from their mothers. This might include "custody disputes, pawning, and various forms of fosterage." All of these would result in children living under slavery or slave-like conditions.[29]

In other words, this particular brand of colonial humanitarianism operated in a conflicted manner and so reinforces Michael Barnett's assertion that humanitarian efforts have the capacity to both advance *and undermine* moral progress and to emancipate and *dominate*.[30] Thus, although one of the objectives of the colonial project was to end slavery, it simultaneously served to facilitate systems of slavery. While the French hoped to emancipate enslaved children, they also intended to control the terms of their freedom. For example, the French use of "liberty villages" highlights the ways in which the principle of freedom was, in practice, subordinated to the French colonial agenda.[31] During the 1880s, approximately 180 liberty villages were established in the West African savanna. As the name suggests, these villages were set up as a place of residence for recently liberated slaves.[32] In reality, however, these "liberty" villages were a way to control freed slaves in order to meet labor needs. Children (and women) made up a significant percentage of the population of these villages.[33] In short, colonial efforts at economic development in French West Africa demanded African labor "for porterage, building infrastructure, and for producing food" for administrative and urban centers.[34] Not only were Africans required to perform this labor as a means of paying taxes to the French colonial state, but they were also required to pay a "head tax" for children that varied depending on location. The tax could be applied to children of various ages: in some places there was a head tax on children as young as eight; in other places the head tax could be for children aged ten or sixteen.[35] Furthermore, as Martin Klein has demonstrated, colonial conquest contributed to the growth of the slave trade. Not only were French soldiers permitted to keep a small number of slaves, but African auxiliaries to the colonial army were often permitted war booty that included enslaved children.[36]

Ultimately, the battle against child slavery was constrained by a larger battle – one over the very idea of African childhood and how it should operate in the colonial context. The chapters of Micki McElya and Jessica Pliley, both in this collection, emphasize the ways in which conceptions of childhood innocence have been linked to whiteness in the early twentieth-century United States. During the same period in the French West African colonial context, however, African childhood was rarely seen as embedded with innocence, and the need to protect these children was articulated primarily when it served the colonial agenda.[37] Colonial officials believed that the future of France (and no doubt other European powers) in Africa meant finding ways to control the next generation of Africans. This explains why Henri Canard, the governor of Senegal (1881–2), could lament that the young "captives libérés" continued to live in a state that closely resembled slavery while, in the very same letter, he also contemplated ways to make these children good laborers and "bons Français."[38] In other words, liberating enslaved children did not merely mean liberating them from African control. It also meant preparing them to serve French colonial interests. In many ways, then, emancipating African children was about wrestling control from adult Africans and finding ways to insert children, when possible, within the sphere of French control. Unfortunately for the French, limited resources made this ideal difficult to achieve to an extensive degree. They had a far greater concern. In the absence of the military might necessary to exercise complete control over what they understood as their territories, the French needed to contemplate ways to appease African elites, merchants, and traders.

One of their offerings to these groups was continued access to the labor of African children, which meant they often turned a blind eye to the ways in which children continued to be exploited. Enslaved children would indeed be "liberated" in those areas where the French could enforce it, but they did little to ameliorate children's actual circumstances, which were often severely exploitative. The French concern with the *de jure* status of children and not their *de facto* reality means that, for many children, their freedom would have been unrecognizable. Needless to say, colonial officials articulated their desire to control African children and their labor in terms that were self-congratulatory and heroic. In the case of Canard, he wrote that these children were "so generously granted their liberty" and, with specific reference to St. Louis, he remarked that children "continually beg for protection," though unfortunately, from Canard's point of view, they remained strangers to French mores and generally resistant to French civilization.[39] As Bernard Moitt has argued, however, the French colonial state played a "duplicitous role" when it took on the task of legally protecting children. The laws were often unenforced and the concerns of merchants and traders who relied on enslaved child labor were often privileged over any rights to freedom.[40]

Thus, children continued to suffer under domestic slave systems in French West Africa.[41] In October 1880, for example, two men were apprehended at Pont Faidherbe, St. Louis (Sénégal) for trying to sell "a young child." There is no indication of the child's age, but there is evidence to suggest it was an infant, as it was small enough to be carried in the arms of one of the men while he was on a camel. It is noteworthy that this occurred a full thirty-three years after slavery had been abolished in the colony. In fact, these men had been instructed by Mohammed Moktar, the man who claimed ownership over the child, to make the sale in Gandiol (a region further south) – no doubt because it fell outside those boundaries affected by the abolitionist laws the French imposed. To avoid making the trek, however, the two men instead decided to take their chances selling the infant in Guet n'Dar, St. Louis. For reasons that remain unclear, they were unable to sell the child, and it was in their attempt to leave St. Louis and go to Gandiol as originally instructed that they were apprehended.[42] At times, if children were old enough and brave enough, they tried to secure their liberty on their own. Take the case of the young boy named Moussa Crassalé who was being held captive in St. Louis by Madior Gueye. In February 1882, this ten-year old took it upon himself to run away and to go directly to the Commissaire de police. By his account, he had been purchased in Médine (near Kayes in present-day Mali) and brought to St. Louis (Sénégal) by Madior Gueye. Not surprising, Madior Gueye contested this version of events. Instead, he maintained that he was merely keeping the young boy in his house at the request of his owner – even though he was aware that legally there could be no slaves in St. Louis.[43] Unfortunately, the records do not give any indication of what happened to either of these two children. There is a high likelihood, however, that they were both kept in St. Louis and, assuming they survived, grew up legally free but lived in slave-like conditions because of the *tutelle* system.

The *tutelle* system was a highly problematic system of guardianship for minors (anyone under eighteen years old) that the French introduced in Sénégal in 1857.[44] The liberation of enslaved children presented a particular set of challenges for the French. Children needed to be tended to, taken care of, and supervised by adults. Thus, the French were in a situation that required them to place recently liberated children with responsible adults. Put another way, the end of slavery necessitated the development of institutions that would address the "problem" of children's freedom. Unfortunately for the children involved, the *tutelle* system of guardianship was far from perfect. According to Moitt, the majority of children were entrusted to traders and merchants – both African and European – who had formerly claimed ownership over enslaved children. In other words, legally these children were assigned guardians; in reality they were put into the hands of individuals who had a vested interest in keeping child slavery as a thriving institution. Others were left with Catholic missions and correctional institutions until they turned eighteen years old.[45] Thus, the use of the *tutelle* system ensured that although the French had strong ideals about "la droite d'être libre," in practice liberty was circumscribed by age.[46]

Although protecting young people was certainly part of the colonial discourse, in reality, the chief concern was about control. Youth often took an active role in trying to shape the terms of their childhood, and their efforts were often at odds with colonial objectives.[47] Furthermore, under certain circumstances and when convenient to the colonial cause, decisions were made that moved African youth into the realm of adulthood.[48] In other words, French colonial notions of childhood and youth were by no means stable and fixed. Enslaved young girls, for example, were often "given" as wives to *tirailleurs* (infantry men). Traditionally, girls could be married off quite young in West Africa. However, under the French-imposed *tutelle* system, anyone under eighteen was considered in need of a guardian. In forcibly marrying these girls, the French could claim to have liberated them from slavery, but would also be requiring them to participate in a ritual that effectively ended their childhood. In the words of one military officer, "some captives are given to our [African] *tirailleurs* in order to make them their wives. The marriage renders them free."[49] Yet, as Martin Klein makes clear, a female captive did *not* "gain rights when she became a wife."[50] These "marriages" gave men rights that far surpassed what might be traditionally expected from a husband. From the African point of view, female slaves married under such circumstances maintained their slave status. In the words of one colonial official, African soldiers who had been "given" wives continued "to see their wives as slaves."[51] In fact, it was not uncommon for men to sell their "liberated wives."[52] Thus although colonial officials were seeking the liberty of these enslaved girls, the terms of their liberty and their ability to consent was clearly circumscribed by their sex.[53] As Erica Meiners has put it in her chapter in this volume, the notions of "innocence and consent" embedded in racialized notions of childhood are two elements that "reproduce inequality." While African children were rarely assumed to embody childhood innocence, the *mission civilitrice* certainly assumed that their "Africanness" was testimony to diminished capacity and so they were denied any rights to consent.[54] In other words, African youth were not denied the right to consent because they embodied innocence, they were denied it because they were African.

This was certainly the case of "three young girls" who had been "distributed" to the African infantry fighting in support of the French.[55] The girls were from the village N'Dande (in modern-day Sénégal) and were captured in 1887, during a war that was mounted by the marabout Mamadou Dramé to resist French colonization. Upon their capture, they were "given" to a sous-lieutenant named Samba Maram. After an attempted escape, however, they were stopped near Kayes (modern-day Mali) and returned to "their master."[56] Gouveneur Jules Genouville's response to the situation leaves little doubt about French colonial ambivalence about slavery. In short, Genouville made clear that as far as individuals captured in the interior were concerned, particularly near the newly captured region Cayor, there needed to be much tact and care. He hoped to avoid intervening in the matter as political tensions would ultimately result in a desire to "detach and separate" from France. Genouville further added that if the French were to take one captive under their protection, it would not be long before they were overwhelmed with captives seeking their freedom. More important, however, this action would give a justification for recrimination and would be "the source of political difficulties and never-ending conflicts" with Africans who relied on slave labor.[57]

Given all that was at stake, as articulated by the governeur, it should come as no surprise that he later reported, in a letter to the Ministre de la Marine et des Colonies, that the situation was exaggerated and the three young girls, who were named Kadidia, Aminata, and Coumba Sidibé, were in "normal condition." By his account, they were not captives but were being kept by the wife of sous-lieutenant Samba Maram as they awaited the return of their husbands. According to the governeur, they seemed perfectly content.[58] In the reports it was claimed that one of the young girls, named Kadidia, was married to the *tirailleur* De M'diaye (coincidentally the brother of Samba Maran). She supposedly received a "bride price" of 220 francs that was given to her (former) master, who was also a member of the military.[59] How French officials were able to make an ideological distinction between the selling of a captive young girl (to which they were opposed in principle) and what can only be seen as the forced marriage of a young, captive female, whose bride price was passed from her "husband" to her former master, is unclear. And yet, they clearly did – with little hesitation and repeatedly. Both of the other girls, Aminata and Coumba Sidibé, were "married" with a sizeable "bride price" transferred to their former owners.[60]

Furthermore, as we have seen in several other studies in this collection, when notions of innocence are bestowed on the young, there is also the assumption that these perceived innocents cannot be held responsible for their actions. In the French colonial imagination, however, precisely because African youth bore no qualities of innocence, they could *not* be absolved of responsibility for anything they did. In those circumstances when they chose to act independently, these youth were labeled as rebellious and troublesome.[61] Thus, as might be imagined, when enslaved girls who had supposedly been liberated through arranged "marriages" resisted their transfer from slave owner to purported husband, colonial officials generally perceived them unsympathetically.

The French concern with "reconciling humanitarian considerations with political necessities" required them to construct a narrative that not only masked the moral ambiguities of forcibly marrying enslaved girls, but that also placed responsibility with the girls.[62] Even the attempt at escape by the three girls discussed earlier was trivialized into a youthful indiscretion. The report, which is deserving of much skepticism, concluded that, upon investigation, it was clear that the oldest and most "adventurous" of the girls (Coumba Sidibé) had encouraged her friends to return to their homeland, but they were stopped at a neighboring village. There was no acknowledgment that the girls might have been trying to escape a forced marriage, or resist what they might have understood not as a marriage, but as enslavement. It also noted that after the girls had been apprehended, they made quite clear they were "satisfied with their fate" and that they "had *never* been victims of bad treatment." In response to the initial concerns about the girls' liberty, it was suggested that these observations were made by someone with little awareness of the "ways of the region" and that the authorities were greatly concerned with ensuring the liberty of those who lived in communities that still had slavery as the foundation of their social order.[63]

In colonial French West Africa, abolitionist discourses that advocated for the liberation of enslaved children were severely compromised by racialized notions of childhood and morally ambiguous ideas about what constituted freedom for African children. From the French colonial perspective, African children not only lacked innocence, but they needed to be saved from their "Africanness." These children, not unlike adults, were victims of an infantilizing discourse about Africans. The primary concern, then, was not about protecting African children, but about controlling them so that they served French colonial interests. Paired with notions of childhood innocence is the assumption that children do not bear responsibility for their actions.[64] Because African youth were racially infantilized, however, they were also demonized if their behavior did not suit French colonials. Yet, as the foregoing examples illustrate, despite the challenges, children often attempted to claim their own freedom. This might be through the law or by means of escape. In so doing, these children were being proactive in shaping the "cultural politics of childhood."[65] For colonial officials and slaveholding Africans, this created a problem. These youth were rejecting the imposed institutions that gave others rights over them or the right to determine the circumstances under which they should live.

## Historical Consciousness and Humanitarian Discourse

The complicated and morally compromised practices that were part of the abolitionist effort during the colonial period are rarely given a full analysis in present-day humanitarian narratives addressing child slavery. As Benjamin Lawrance has shown, however, in the early twentieth century, humanitarian discourses on childhood became increasingly racialized so that the narratives of African and European children "began to part ways." Whiteness became an organizing category in child rescue. Increased legislative support for children in Europe and North America was not matched in the colonies. As a result, discourses involving African children and childhood became increasingly racialized and gendered. They were seen as rebellious, delinquent, and the cause of much anxiety.[66] In line with these rescue discourses, in 1931, Save the Children International Union organized a conference on "The African Child" which was held in Geneva. The conference was attended primarily by European humanitarians who hoped to take European notions of childhood to Africa.[67] Their objectives were grounded in a globalized vision of childhood that they hoped would have universalizing tendencies, but that often came into conflict with the various local productions of childhood that existed in Africa.[68]

In many ways, the racialized and gendered constructions of childhood from yesteryear continue to be embedded in contemporary humanitarian and human rights discourses. Today we are guided by the 1989 UN Convention on the Rights of the Child (UNCRC).[69] The UNCRC and its precursors are the manifestation of globalized laws related to children. They reflect attempts to create an "international vision of childhood."[70] That said, while the globalization of laws might have the *tendency* to universalize perspectives on childhood, a tension remains between this international vision and the local conceptions of childhood that have been shaped in various social, political, and economic contexts across the globe. This explains why in 1990 the Organization of African Unity (now the African Union) felt compelled to develop the African Charter for the Rights and Welfare of the Child (ACRWC) which aimed to better address childhood in the African context. The Organization of African Unity (OAU), comprised of African heads of state and government, thought it prudent to develop a charter that better reflected the concerns stemming from "socio-cultural and economic realities of the African experience."[71]

Ironically, although enslaved African children have long been fighting to shape the terms of their childhood, present-day notions of human rights have been formulated in a fashion that denies children full citizenship. Human rights "are extended to children only secondarily" as the notion of rights are modeled in a fashion that assumes individuals are "independent and autonomous." In the introduction to this collection, Anna Mae Duane has cautioned that the binaries of "child versus citizen" and "victim versus agent" are problematic paradigms and are inadequate for understanding the "undertheorized assumptions about childhood" as they relate to power and dependence. Instead, it is suggested that children should be seen as "part of a continuum of human need" and not as a "wholly different class of person." This argument is reinforced by John Wall, who contends that children need to be understood not merely as "vulnerable people in need of protection but also as full social beings with agency and dignity."[72] In the twenty-five years since the Convention on the Rights of the Child, small progress has been made in this area. The most notable change is the Third Optional Protocol of the UNCRC which was implemented in 2014. Prior to this, there was no way to ensure that countries that ratified the convention actually enforced the laws of this international agreement. The Third Optional Protocol, however, puts children at the center of the process. For the first time, in the history of the UNCRC, individual children, groups of children, or advocates for specific children can file a complaint with the United Nations when there is a perceived violation of their rights. Unfortunately, the protocol is, as the name suggests, optional – which means countries that have ratified the UNCRC have no obligation to adopt it.[73]

In addition to concerns about the need for international laws to push past the notion that enslaved children are more than just vulnerable beings in need of protection, conceptions of child slavery *in Africa*, in particular, are also deserving of critique. Several studies have shown the ways in which decontextualized notions about Africa and images of African children exist, not only in popular culture, but in rescue discourses generated by nongovernmental organizations and humanitarian and human rights organizations, as well as sites of policy formation.[74] Put another way, these discourses are grounded in historical narratives comprised of "selective remembrances" used to justify decisions in the present. In efforts to resolve the problem of child slavery in Africa – more than most other parts of the world – history is quite often seen as "the problem." Present-day child slavery in Africa is often presented as an extension of the continent's long history of slavery. It is used to explain counterproductive traditions, such as child slavery, as well as the imagined collective inertia that is believed to prevent putting an end to this practice. Thus, those African societies in which child slavery continues to be pervasive are seen as having a need to be saved from their history and traditions.[75] Furthermore, these rescue discourses assume that the application of initiatives and policies will enable the societal change and transformation necessary and will put these societies on the road to modernity and progress.[76]

As it currently stands, historical references continue to be made with brevity. Take, for example, an excerpt from the "historical background" section in an article on contemporary child slavery. Authored by affiliates of the International Labour Organization (ILO), it historicizes efforts to end slavery as follows:

Perhaps because slavery was such a widespread phenomenon and a particularly serious violation of human rights, it also became one of the first causes of international action to abolish it. Even though the trade continued for many decennia after 1807, the 1807 UK legislation proved to be the beginning of the end of the western slave trade. In 1815, the first international document against slavery was adopted, the Declaration Relative to the Universal Abolition of the Slave Trade being adopted by the six countries participating in the Vienna Congress. Many international agreements to abolish the slave trade followed in the ensuing century, none of them fully effective (Weisbrodt and Anti-Slavery International, 2002). In 1926, the member States of the League of Nations adopted the Slavery Convention, which for the first time defined slavery internationally, and set globally binding rules to abolish it.[77]

An abbreviated and sanitized narrative, such as this, is not without its problems. First, it offers an uncomplicated rendering of abolitionist efforts that puts distance between these humanitarian initiatives and their colonial pasts. As Uma Kothari puts it, there is a "political imperative to avoid tarnishing humanitarian efforts and to keep them intellectually far removed from the colonial exploitation of an earlier period."[78] Unfortunately, divorcing humanitarian efforts aimed at ending contemporary child slavery from the messiness of their history, brings a level of obscurity to analyses and masks "historical continuities and divergences in the theory, practice and policies" being implemented.[79] Second, it minimizes, if not ignores, the ways in which humanitarian efforts can be implicated in *helping to sustain* systems of slavery – including, of course, child slavery. Embedded in abolitionist discourses – past and present – are very particular notions about time and progress. More specifically, the assumption that "linear changes take place in linear time" grounds much of what is being said.[80] As with the excerpt just cited, rarely do humanitarian narratives of the present day foreground the ways in which, during the period of colonial humanitarianism, compromises were quite often made, policies were not aligned with actual practices, and humanitarian efforts were competing with other interests that sometimes trumped efforts to liberate enslaved African children.

## Conclusion

Through its reflection on French colonial attitudes toward the liberation of enslaved African children, this chapter has described how colonial practices were contradictory and how their policies were largely ineffective.[81] In fact, as Richard Roberts has argued, not until the Commission on Slavery (1926) by the League of Nations were there "periods of heightened administrative engagement" by the French. Despite this, however, there were a number of factors that undermined the efficacy of colonial policy. This included not only the implementation of contradictory policies, but also the existence of policies that conflicted with practices at the local level. Furthermore, the colonial officials did not have the means to effectively implement policy beyond those places in which they had a strong foothold.[82]

Nonetheless, colonialists understood that their future in Africa meant finding ways to control the next generation of Africans. They faced a particular predicament: The French, and other European powers more generally, simultaneously wanted to put policies in place that would end slavery – an institution comprised primarily of children – while also wanting control over African labor. Thus the battle over African childhood was not a battle over the liberty of children, but instead how to wrestle control from Africans and ensure that children could be put to service in a way that benefited colonial ambitions. Limited colonial resources, however, meant that French colonial officials had to make heavy compromises and turned a blind eye to the circumstances of exploited children. As for the children themselves – they also made efforts to influence and define the terms of their childhood. Quite simply, the problem of child slavery was a case of imperial ideas confronting colonial realities in the African context. Unfortunately, for the children, colonial efforts to end slavery were far from satisfactory, as the various stakeholders each contested the ways in which African childhoods should be shaped.

The messy and complicated unfolding of abolitionist efforts in Africa rarely make it into contemporary humanitarian discourses focusing on child slavery. The tendency has been to draw on historical narratives that emphasize very particular notions of time and progress. Although practitioners are increasingly developing an awareness of the ways in which a better engagement with history might help with humanitarian initiatives, it remains to be seen if, how, and to what extent the application of history will be incorporated into their work.[83] As Micki McElya points out in her study on American girlhood and race in this volume (see Chapter 3), the advocacy, activism, and policy of today are often grounded in "webs of memory, representation, and titillation" that require more intense examination. There are very real costs to ignoring history, how historical memory informs policy formation, and how the historical consciousness of communities respond to the imposition of these policies. Certainly, good intentions are not good enough. The cost for failing to do this, of course, is that millions of vulnerable children continue to live in slavery today. In the words of Linda Polman, humanitarian efforts can no longer be exempt from criticism as "too much has gone wrong."[84]

## Notes

1   Paul E. Lovejoy and Jan S. Hogendorn, *Slow Death for Slavery: The Course of Abolition in Northern Nigeria, 1897–1936*, African Studies Series (Cambridge: Cambridge University Press, 1993), xvi.

2   Suzanne Miers and Richard Roberts, eds., *The End of Slavery in Africa* (Madison: University of Wisconsin Press, 1988), 40.

3   Martin A. Klein, "Children and Slavery in the Western Sudan," in *Child Slaves in the Modern World*, eds. Gwyn Campbell, Suzanne Miers, and Joseph C. Miller (Athens: Ohio University Press, 2011), 129.

4   For an example of a work that unproblematically links child slavery of the past with that of the present, see Kwabena Adu-Boahen, "Post-emancipation Slave Commerce: Increasing Child Trafficking and Women's Agency in Late Nineteenth-Century Ghana," *Lagos Historical Review* 9 (2009): 119. For a theory on the impact of globalization on slavery, see Kevin Bales, "Testing a Theory of Modern Slavery," 2014(2006), www.freetheslaves.net/Document.Doc?id=14.

5   See Benjamin N. Lawrance and Richard Roberts, eds., *Trafficking in Slavery's Wake: Law and the Experience of Women and Children in Africa* (Athens: Ohio University Press, 2012). On the issue of slavery more generally, see Suzanne Miers, *Slavery in the Twentieth Century: The Evolution of a Global Problem* (Walnut Creek, CA: Altamira Publishers, 2003); Joel Quirk, *The Anti-slavery Project: From the Slave Trade to Human Trafficking* (Philadelphia: University of Pennsylvania Press, 2011).

6   Michael Barnett, *Empire of Humanity: A History of Humanitarianism* (New York: Cornell University Press, 2011), 11.

7   Barbara A. Mitchell, "Life Course Theory," in *International Encyclopedia of Marriage and Family*, ed. J. J. Ponzetti (New York: MacMillan Reference, 2003), 1051–5.

8   Mitchell makes this argument about the utility of life course analyses gener-
    ally and not with respect to slavery in particular. Ibid.

9   See, for example, the chapters by Micki McElya, Erica Meiners, Jessica Pliley,
    and Kelli Johnson in this volume.

10  Allison James and Adrian L. James, *Constructing Childhood: Theory, Policy
    and Social Practice* (New York: Palgrave MacMillan 2004), 7–8.

11  Richard Waller, "Rebellious Youth in Colonial Africa," *Journal of African
    History* 47(2006): 78. See also Burton and Hélène Charton-Bigot, eds.,
    *Generations Past: Youth in East African History* (Athens: Ohio University
    Press 2010).

12  Waller, "Rebellious Youth in Colonial Africa," 78–81.

13  As I have argued elsewhere, there needs to be great care when generaliz-
    ing about the historical experiences of African children as there were mul-
    tiple notions of childhood in colonial Africa. For that reason, the author
    opts to make reference to African childhoods (plural) instead of a single
    African childhood. Audra Diptee and Martin A. Klein, "African Childhoods
    and the Colonial Project," *Journal of Family History* 35.3 (2010): 3–6. For
    a discussion on contestations over childhood in Zimbabwe, see Beverly
    Grier, *Invisible Hands: Child Labor and the State in Colonial Zimbabwe*
    (Portsmouth, NH: Heinemann, 2006), 8.

14  Paul Lovejoy estimates that 3.95 million captives kept in Africa were chil-
    dren. The estimate for all captives held in domestic slavery is 9.21 million.
    See table 3.9 in Paul Lovejoy, *Transformations in Slavery: A History of
    Slavery in Africa*, 2nd ed. (Cambridge: Cambridge University Press, 2000),
    66. Richard Allen, "Children and the European Slave Trading in the Indian
    Ocean during the Eighteenth and Early Nineteenth Centuries," in *Children in
    Slavery through the Ages*, eds. Gwyn Campbell, Suzanne Miers, and Joseph
    C. Miller (Athens: Ohio University Press, 2009), 36–8. For recent works on
    African slavery in the Indian Ocean, see Edward A. Alpers, Gwyn Campbell,
    and Michael Salman, *Resisting Bondage in Indian Ocean Africa and Asia*
    (New York: Routledge, 2006); Gwyn Campbell, "The East African Slave
    Trade, 1861–1895: The 'Southern' Complex," *The International Journal of
    African Historical Studies* 22.1 (1989); Shihan de S. Jayasuriya and Richard
    Pankhurst, *The African Diaspora in the Indian Ocean* (Trenton, NJ: Africa
    World Press, 2001). See also Fred Morton, "Small Change: Children in
    the Nineteenth-Century East African Slave Trade," in *Children in Slavery
    through the Ages*, eds. Gwyn Campbell, Suzanne Miers, and Joseph C. Miller
    (Athens: Ohio University Press, 2009), 56.

15  Historians have debated whether Africa went through, to use the words of
    historian A. G. Hopkins, a "crisis of adaptation" with the end of the slave
    trade. The literature on this topic is extensive, but for some of the more
    recent works, see various articles in Robin Law, ed. *From Slave Trade to
    "Legitimate" Commerce: The Commercial Transition in Nineteenth-Century
    West Africa* (Cambridge: Cambridge University Press, 1995).

16  Adu-Boahen, "Post-emancipation Slave Commerce," 122; Benjamin N.
    Lawrance and Richard Roberts, "Contextualizing Trafficking in Women and

Children in Africa," in *Trafficking in Slavery's Wake: Law and the Experience of Women and Children in Africa*, eds. Benjamin N. Lawrance and Richard Roberts (Athens: Ohio University Press, 2012), 9.

17  Patrick Manning, *Francophone Sub-Saharan Africa, 1880–1995*, 2nd ed. (Cambridge: Cambridge University Press, 1998), 27.

18  Ibid., 26.

19  Barnett, *Empire of Humanity*, 65–7.

20  Klein, "Children and Slavery in the Western Sudan," 127.

21  See, for example, the quote from a letter written by the Ministre de la Marine et des Colonies (Paris) to Governeur Henri Canard (Senegal), May 2, 1882. "We desire the end of slavery amongst the indigenous population ... but we wait for this result from the influence of our civilizing mission, and not from measures that are alienating and contribute to a serious prejudice against our commerce." SEN/XIV, Box 15. Located in the Archives Nationales d'outre Mer (ANOM), Aix-en-Provence, France.

22  Miers and Roberts, *The End of Slavery in Africa*, 14. For a comprehensive study of slavery in French West Africa, see Martin A. Klein, *Slavery and Colonial Rule in French West Africa*, African Studies Series (Cambridge; New York: Cambridge University Press, 1998).

23  Miers and Roberts, *The End of Slavery in Africa*, 10–15.

24  Ibid., 12–13.

25  See Bernard Moitt, "Slavery and Guardianship in Postemancipation Senegal," in *Child Slaves in the Modern World*, eds. Gwyn Campbell, Suzanne Miers, and Joseph C. Miller (Athens Ohio University Press, 2011); Martin A. Klein, "Children and Slavery in the Western Sudan," ibid.; Trevor Getz, "British Magistrates and Unfree Children in Early Colonial Gold Coast, 1874–1899," ibid.

26  Miers and Roberts, *The End of Slavery in Africa*, 14.

27  Manning, *Francophone Sub-Saharan Africa, 1880–1995*, 29.

28  See Lovejoy and Hogendorn, *Slow Death for Slavery*.

29  Richard Roberts, "The End of Slavery, 'Crises' over Trafficking, and the Colonial State in the French Soudan," in *Trafficking in Slavery's Wake: Law and the Experience of Women and Children in Africa*, eds. Benjamin N. Lawrance and Richard Roberts (Athens: Ohio University Press, 2012), 69.

30  Barnett, *Empire of Humanity*, 11–12.

31  Of course the official rhetoric spoke in more humanitarian terms. "Our liberty villages ... the initiative of Lieutenant Colonel Galieni, Commandant Supérieur du Soudan Français, demonstrate one of the excellent ways we employ all the means that we have at all times to free captives." No. 860, Chef de Bataillon Commandant Supérieur au Commandant Supérieur des troupes. August 29, 1887, Kayes. SEN/XIV, Box 15 (ANOM).

32  The majority of these villages were set up by the military, though some were also established by missionaries. Manning, *Francophone Sub-Saharan Africa, 1880–1995*, 28.

33  Klein, *Slavery and Colonial Rule in French West Africa*, 81–91. See also the appendices for data on the liberty villages.

34  Miers and Roberts, *The End of Slavery in Africa*, 19–20. See also Timothy Weiskel, *French Colonial Rule and the Baule Peoples: Resistance and Collaboration, 1889–1911* (Oxford: Oxford University Press, 1980).

35 Lisa McNee, "The Languages of Childhood: The Discursive Construction of Childhood and Colonial Policy in French West Africa," *African Studies Quarterly* 7.4 (2004): 24.

36 "The inhabitants from recently occupied villages have been, either by decision or by tolerance, distributed as captives (slaves) to the infantry employed in our operations." Senateur Isaac to Ministre Etienne, June 20, 1887, St. Louis, Sénégal. SEN/XIV, Box 15. Located in the Archives Nationales d'outre Mer (ANOM), Aix-en-Provence, France. See also chapter 4 in Klein, *Slavery and Colonial Rule in French West Africa.*

37 Lisa McNee contends that colonial officials resisted measures that would genuinely protect African children. For example, they argued that it was impossible to use age as a criterion (given the absence of birth certificates and other records) and were opposed to establishing a minimum working age, among other things. See McNee, "The Languages of Childhood," 28.

38 "Au sujet des jeunes captifs libérés," Governeur Henri Canard to the Ministre de la Marine et des Colonies, May 23, 1882, St. Louis, Sénégal. SEN/XIV, Box 15. Located in the Archives Nationales d'outre Mer (ANOM), Aix-en-Provence, France.

39 "Au sujet des jeunes captifs libérés," Governeur Henri Canard to the Ministre de la Marine et des Colonies, May 23, 1882, St. Louis, Sénégal. SEN/XIV, Box 15 (ANOM).

40 Moitt, "Slavery and Guardianship in Postemancipation Senegal," 141–7.

41 The archival documents that make reference to child slavery offer only the faintest impression of children's experiences. Children did not produce records that offered an account of their enslavement, and so the records available are imperfect at best. That said, there are no shortage of documents that give a clear indication of the ways in which children were being sold.

42 "Etat indicatif des faits de ventes, achat ou recel de captifs qui ont en lieu à St. Louis du mois d'octobre au 23 mars 1882 et qui ont été déférés aux Tribunaux." March 27, 1882, SEN/XIV, Box 15 (ANOM).

43 "Etat indicatif des faits de ventes, achat ou recel de captifs qui ont en lieu à St. Louis du mois d'octobre au 23 mars 1882 et qui ont été déférés aux Tribunaux." March 27, 1882, SEN/XIV, Box 15 (ANOM).

44 Moitt, "Slavery and Guardianship in Postemancipation Senegal," 145.

45 Ibid., 141.

46 No. 860, Chef de Bataillon Commandant Supérieur au Commandant Supérieur des troupes. August 29, 1887, Kayes. SEN/XIV, Box 15 (ANOM).

47 Sociologists Allison James and Adrian James argue the "cultural politics of childhood" is also shaped by children. See James and James, *Constructing Childhood,* 7–8.

48 This parallels the argument that Erica Meiners makes in her chapter (see Chapter 4 in this volume), in which she maintains that "black and brown male youth" were assigned adulthood in the U.S. criminal system.

49 No. 860, Chef de Bataillon Commandant Supérieur au Commandant Supérieur des troupes. August 29, 1887, Kayes. SEN/XIV, Box 15 (ANOM).

50 Klein, *Slavery and Colonial Rule in French West Africa,* 95.

51 See, for example, the comment: "It is difficult to modify their ways and some of [the soldiers] continue to see their wives as slaves [captured during

war]." No. 1504, Governeur du Sénégal to the Ministre de la Marine et des Colonies, September 21, 1887, St. Louis, Sénégal. SEN/XIV, Box 15. For a study that discusses the ways in which the institutions of marriage and guardianship were used to disguise slavery, see Marie Rodet, "'Under the Guise of Guardianship and Marriage': Mobilizing Juvenile and Female Labor in the Aftermath of Slavery in Kayes," in *Trafficking in Slavery's Wake: Law and the Experience of Women and Children in Africa*, eds. Benjamin N. Lawrance and Richard L. Roberts (Athens: Ohio University Press, 2012), 86–100.

52  See, for example, the case of the indigenous soldier, Amady Samba, who sold his "wife." No. 1504, Governeur du Sénégal (Jules Genouville) to the Ministre de la Marine et des Colonies, September 21, 1887, St. Louis, Sénégal. SEN/XIV, Box 15 (ANOM).

53  It was believed that these marriages could serve the colonial government favorably by making the African *tirailleurs* more settled and by reducing the enslavement of women and girls. In fact, it did neither. It was slavery by another name. Letter written by Chef du Service Judiciare, No. 31, undated (but authored some time before July 19, 1887), St. Louis, Sénégal. SEN/XIV, Box 15.

54  For a discussion on the infantilization of Africans, see McNee, "The Languages of Childhood," 28.

55  Martin Klein discusses this case, but refers to the captives as "three young women." In the documents, however, they are consistently referred to as "trois jeunes filles," which translates as "three young girls." See Klein, *Slavery and Colonial Rule in French West Africa*, 95.

56  Letter written by Chef du Service Judiciare, No. 31, undated (but authored some time before July 19, 1887), St. Louis, Sénégal. SEN/XIV, Box 15.

57  Letter written by Chef du Service Judiciare, No. 31, undated (but authored some time before July 19, 1887), St. Louis, Sénégal. SEN/XIV, Box 15. Interesting, Senateur Alexandre Isaac, who was a "man of color" from the French Caribbean colony Guadeloupe, made a case for the girls' liberty. Senateur Isaac au Ministre Etienne, June 20, 1887. Located in the Archives Nationales d'outre Mer (ANOM), Aix-en-Provence, France.

58  No. 1510, Gouverneur du Sénégal to the Ministre de la Marine et des Colonies, September 21, 1887.

59  Chef de Bataillon Commandant Supérieur au Commandant Supérieur des troupes. August 29, 1887, Kayes. SEN/XIV, Box 15 (ANOM).

60  Chef de Bataillon Commandant Supérieur au Commandant Supérieur des troupes. August 29, 1887, Kayes. SEN/XIV, Box 15 (ANOM).

61  See Waller, "Rebellious Youth in Colonial Africa," 77–92.

62  Not everyone was prepared to say the girls were legitimately married. See for example, the letter written by Chef du Service Judiciare, No. 31, undated (but authored some time before July 19, 1887), St. Louis, Sénégal. SEN/XIV, Box 15.

63  Chef de Bataillon Commandant Supérieur au Commandant Supérieur des troupes. August 29, 1887, Kayes. SEN/XIV, Box 15 (ANOM).

64  The chapters by Jessica Pliley and David Rosen in this collection also make this argument (see Chapters 6 and 7, respectively).

65  The "cultural politics of childhood," as defined by James and James, suggests that notions of childhood are both constructed and contested. Childhood should be understood as something that is "interpreted, understood and socially institutionalized." How this is done varies between cultures and generations, and in the very way it engages with the daily lives of children. See the introduction of James and James, *Constructing Childhood*.

66  Benjamin N. Lawrance, "Documenting Child Slavery with Personal Testimony: The Origins of Antitrafficking NGOs and Contemporary Neo-abolitionism," in *Trafficking in Slavery's Wake: Law and the Experience of Women and Children in Africa*, eds. Benjamin N. Lawrance and Richard Roberts (Athens: Ohio University Press, 2012), 167–8. See also Waller, "Rebellious Youth in Colonial Africa."

67  For a fuller discussion of the 1931 conference on "The African Child" which was held in Geneva, see Dominique Marshall, "Children's Rights in Imperial Political Cultures: Missionary and Humanitarian Contributions to the Conference on the African Child of 1931," *International Journal of Children's Rights* 12 (2004): 275.

68  For a study that explores African conceptions of childhood, see Alma Gottlieb, "Babies as Ancestors, Babies as Spirits: The Culture of Infancy in West Africa," *Expedition* 46.3: 14–21. See also her fuller study, *The Afterlife Is Where We Come From: The Culture of Infancy in West Africa* (Chicago: University of Chicago Press, 2004).

69  Although the UNCRC was the most influential, note that a number of child-focused declarations preceded it in the twentieth century. This includes the 1924 Geneva Declaration of the Rights of the Child, the UN declaration in 1959, and several Hague conventions in the 1980s and 1990s. James and James, *Constructing Childhood*, 81.

70  Jo Boyden, "Childhood and the Policy Makers: A Comparative Perspective on the Globalization of Childhood," in *Constructing and Reconstructing Childhood: Contemporary Issues in the Sociological Study of Childhood*, eds. Allison James and Alan Prout (London: Routledge, 1997), 190–229.

71  'Dejo Olowu, "Protecting Children's Rights in Africa: A Critique of the African Charter on the Rights and Welfare of the Child," *The International Journal of African Historical Studies* 10(2002): 127–36. See also Danwood Mzikenge Chirwa, "The Merits and Demerits of the African Charter on the Rights and Welfare of the Child," *International Journal of Children's Rights* 10 (2002): 157–77. As of 2014, the African Charter on the Rights and Welfare of the Child was ratified by only forty-seven of the fifty-four member states of the African Union. See "The African Charter on the Rights and Welfare of the Child: 25 Years in 2015," *African Press Organisation*, January 24, 2014.

72  Citations are from the chapters written by John Wall and Anna Mae Duane (see Chapters 11 and introduction, respectively, in this volume).

73  Audra Diptee, "The UN Convention on the Rights of the Child 25 Years Later: Sara Austin Reflects on the Journey," *Atlantic Studies* 11.4 (2014): 555–64.

74  See, for example, Jo Ellen Fair, "War, Famine, and Poverty: Race in the Construction of Africa's Media Image," *Journal of Communication*

*Inquiry* 17.2 (1993): 5–22; Graham Harrison, "The Africanization of Poverty: A Retrospective on 'Make Poverty History,'" *African Affairs* 109.436 (2010): 391–408; Sam Gregory, "Kony 2012 through a Prism of Video Advocacy Practices and Trends," *Journal of Human Rights Practice* 4.3 (2012): 1–6.

75 The authors make these assertion with specific reference to development policy, but it can be extended to child slavery–focused humanitarian initiatives (which are quite often related to development concerns). Michael Woolcock, Simon Szreter, and Vijayendra Rao, "How and Why History Matters for Development Policy," in *History, Historians, and Development Policy: A Necessary Dialogue*, eds. C. A. Bayly et al. (Manchester: Manchester University Press, 2011), 26–7.

76 Uma Kothari, "History, Time and Temporality in Development Discourse," in *History, Historians and Development Policy*, eds. C. A. Bayly et al. (Manchester: Manchester University Press, 2011), 65–70; Ravi Kanbur, "Why Might History Matter for Development Policy?," in *History, Historians, and Development Policy: A Necessary Dialogue*, eds. C. A. Bayly et al.(Manchester: Manchester University Press, 2011), 117–21.

77 Hans van de Glind and Joost Kooijmans, "Modern-Day Child Slavery," *Children & Society* 22 (2008): 150–1.

78 Kothari, "History, Time and Temporality in Development Discourse," 66.

79 Ibid., 65–6; Barnett, *Empire of Humanity*, 61.

80 Kothari, "History, Time and Temporality in Development Discourse," 67.

81 Joel Quirk makes a distinction between "legal abolition" and "effective emancipation." As he puts it, if slavery is renounced but "extreme forms of exploitation persist under other headings," abolition efforts should not be seen as effective. For Quirk, effective emancipation is a fluid concept that represents "evolving, political and ethical expectations" that may include prevention, restitution, and rehabilitation, among other things. Quirk, *The Anti-slavery Project*, 7.

82 In the case of French West Africa, for example, such places would be Gorée and St. Louis.

83 For an example of an humanitarian organization engaging with history, see Eleanor Davey, "Humanitarian History in a Complex World" (Humanitarian Policy Group, Overseas Development Institute, 2014); Eleonor Davey, John Borton, and Matthew Foley, "A History of the Humanitarian System: Western Origins and Foundations"(Humanitarian Policy Group, Overseas Development Institute, June 2013).

84 Linda Polman, *The Crisis Caravan: What's Wrong with Humanitarian Aid?* (New York: Picador, 2010), 172.

# CHILDREN'S VOICES, CHILDREN'S FREEDOM

## Anna Mae Duane

The previous three sections have looked at how adult conceptions of children – as members of a family shaped by property relations, as innocent victims of adult crimes, and as individuals unable to consent – have provided frameworks that allow acts of coercion, exploitation, and even enslavement to persist in the face of legal prohibition. Every chapter, in its own way, has suggested that adult conceptions of children occlude our understanding of how oppressive systems have migrated from pre- to post-emancipation forms of enslavement. This section, in many ways, responds to the questions raised in earlier chapters about how we might better listen to enslaved children, past and present. Our authors offer this response by asking children to relate their experiences and rights claims in their own voices. The first chapter in this section, by Kelli Lyon Johnson, and the second, coauthored by scholar-activists Jonathan Blagbrough and Gary Craig, both feature the testimony of children who identify as former slaves. This section's third chapter, by philosopher John Wall, urges us to shift the paradigms that structure current human rights protocols to create new frameworks that would respect children's ability to make choices and take political action.

Kelli Lyon Johnson's analysis of the testimony of formerly enslaved children illuminates how savvy these children are about navigating adult expectations. Even as they insist on being heard in the public sphere, they cannily engage the narratives that will allow a listening adult to recognize them as children. Thus these child narrators often claim a right to the very sort of innocent idealized childhood that many of our authors have critiqued, simply because it allows them to create common imaginative ground with the audience they seek. To take just one example, Johnson describes how "Kavita" alludes to childhood innocence, even as she describes her own oppression: "Kavita's understanding of what childhood should be like allows her to connect to an audience that shares her belief and, thus, to highlight the vulnerability children experience merely by being children and to refute any perceived complicity in her exploitation." Taking her cue from the words of the child-narrators she cites, Johnson insists – as do all the authors in this section – that we come to terms with the complex dynamics that render children both victims *and* agents.

The second chapter in this section also features children's testimony to draw an accurate picture of child domestic workers. In the first chapter in this volume, Karen Sánchez-Eppler asks how we might better listen to children who were enslaved in the nineteenth century. In this chapter in our final section, Craig and Blagbrough provide strategies for how we might engage the words of children enslaved in the twenty-first century, by asking them to both define their experiences of enslavement and, perhaps most important of all, to articulate their vision of what freedom could mean.

Child domestic workers, as Craig and Blagbrough report, constitute a large – but largely underreported--population of children subjected to coerced, exploitative, unremunerated labor. However, because these children are ensconced in private homes, with families, "helping out" with domestic chores, their experiences replicate an intense version of what many imagine the proper place for children, and thus often fails to excite the outrage – or the action – that child soldiering or sex work generates. Yet the twenty-first-century children who speak in these interviews confirm what our first section on pre-emancipation child slaves suggests: a private family home can be just as exploitative as a factory floor, a brothel, or a cocoa plantation. While coerced sexual work is often singled out as a uniquely horrifying form of child exploitation, the child domestic workers reveal that repeated sexual assaults are often a part of the domestic "work" that they are expected to endure.[1]

But if the family proves no bastion against the exploitation of children, other options are equally problematic. Intense state oversight of individual homes hardly seems an appropriate solution. Given the dangers of institutional reformers – described in the chapters by Erica Meiners, Jessica Pliley, and Micki McElya – simply handing over control of the family to either state or outside agencies would be unlikely to improve the situation of many children. As John Wall, the author of the third chapter in this section reminds us, even if somehow state oversight of the private family were either feasible or desirable, globalization continues to weaken individual state power to police abuses or address rights violations. Wall explains, "while international treaties and national and local laws have done much to keep child slavery in check, they face the fact that global markets and technologies can find unique ways to exploit child labor and circumvent children's rights instruments. In addition, globalization bends local cultural constructions of child labor toward global marketplace demands." The pull of global capital, with its relentless demand for cheap labor, supersedes the legal power of local laws, and certainly of international treaties, about which individual states may well feel ambivalent. Thus, Wall goes on to argue, "the exploitation of child labor is the product of a vicious cycle in which it most benefits precisely those globally wealthy few who have the greatest power and resources to combat it." One response to this vicious circle, Wall suggests, is to disrupt the assumptions that render children incapable of political response, and largely subject to the wishes of adults.

We end this volume where we began, by suggesting that children's unique role in the family and in our legal and cultural structures have allowed for structures of coercion, control, and even ownership to persist beyond the legal abolition of slavery. Scholars skeptical of transhistorical work might suggest that comparing past and present forms of unfree labor collapses the distinction between widely different times, places, and practices in order to create a falsely coherent narrative. But, we believe, and we hope these chapters demonstrate, placing past and present iterations of trafficking, unfree labor, and enslavement in conversation complicates our understanding both of current practices and of those that unfolded before slavery was made illegal. As John Wall reminds us, "slavery in the nineteenth century was not eradicated by opposing violence and victimization alone. It required in addition positively embracing slaves' human dignity and agency." Until we embrace children's dignity and agency – as well as their vulnerability – we cannot begin to fully imagine their freedom.

### Notes

1   For a particularly harrowing account of the abuses visited upon Haitian child domestic workers, see Jean Robert Cadet's *My Stone of Hope: From Haitian Slave Child to Abolitionist* (Athens: University of Texas Press, 2011).

## 9

# "If I got a chance to talk to the world … ": Voice, Agency, and Claiming Rights in Narratives of Contemporary Child Slavery

## Kelli Lyon Johnson

Studying child slavery highlights problematic assumptions about children as victims, about consent in the enslavement of both children and adults, and about the role of children in antislavery work and communities of action. Indeed, the chapters in this volume demonstrate the ways in which the socially constructed child can become embedded in and obscured by discourses of slavery, especially contemporary slavery, in ways that render children in slavery invisible, as Anna Mae Duane argues. "[I]t's not surprising that scholars often avoid the problem of integrating child slavery into larger slavery studies," Duane writes in the introduction to this volume, because "thinking about children as a fundamental element within slavery forces us to confront questions about power and dependence, about authority and force that structure how we think about rights, about power, about citizenship, and about human development." Either, she argues, historians, analysts, and activists "don't 'see' child slaves, or don't include them in their analyses because children's needs and vulnerabilities complicate the already difficult work of creating viable definitions." I suggest that historians, analysts, and activists also fail to "hear" children in slavery and that by inviting, listening to, and heeding children's voices – the stories of their own enslavement and what their experiences *mean* – we may begin to live up to the aspiration of children's rights.

Children's voices in human rights struggles remain peripheral at best. Their relative silence stems at least in part from a persistent belief in children as essentially rightless: children have been traditionally understood as not fully human in the sense of being refused access to a full range of civil, social, cultural, and economic rights. In the Enlightenment philosophy that has so influenced the Global North, Gwyn Campbell and his colleagues write, "children, alongside females and nonwhite males, were considered irrational and 'animal-like' and thus debarred from civic rights and responsibilities."[1] The result, Duane determines, was the construction both of a "passive, victimized, silent, and sheltered" child, which produced "the state of childhood [as] antithetical to full humanity – the child, like the barbarous nation, may have the potential for future rational autonomy, but both must undergo rigorous training to overcome their current state of incompleteness."[2]

In the field of contemporary slavery studies, and in human rights discourses generally, *voice* is frequently deployed as a metaphor for agency. In fact, *voice* and *agency* are so closely related they are often used interchangeably, predicated on the assumption that someone able to *exert* voice must have adequate *agency* to do so. Voice is taken as an article of faith among human rights advocates and practitioners in the struggle for children's rights, enshrined in both the Universal Declaration of Human Rights (UDHR) and the 1989 Convention on the Rights of the Child (CRC). For Joseph Slaughter, human rights themselves are contingent on voice: "[h]uman rights violations target the voice, and therefore, the voice should be the focus of human rights instruments." Ultimately, he writes, "[t]he right to narration is not merely the right to tell one's story, it is the right to control representation." Sarada Balagopalan suggests that one of the three major domains of inquiry in children's rights "is concerned with giving children a 'voice,' an active capacity to speak and narrate their lives."[3] Article 12 of the CRC explicitly mandates the inclusion of children's voices: "States Parties shall assure to the child who is capable of forming his or her own views the right to express those views freely in all matters affecting the child, the views of the child being given due weight in accordance with the age and maturity of the child." There remains, however, a dearth of children's voices in research about and representations of contemporary slavery and in antislavery campaigns despite its widely recognized role in the defining and claiming of human rights.

Children's voices remain marginalized or suppressed in much antislavery work in part because of a pervasive practice of using *images* of children to represent child slavery. The figure of "the child slave" has been mobilized in the moral lingua franca of human rights as a symbol of vulnerability, victimization, exploitation, and exclusion. This use of the image of "the child slave" resonates with the "conceptual slippage" revealed by Allison James and Adrian James in which "the child" is used as "one part standing in for the whole, in this case the social collectivity

that is '*children*.' " The result of the use of the singular ultimately collec-
tivizes and regulates "what is held culturally to constitute a 'normal,' or
even 'ideal' childhood."[4] In the same way, "the child slave," especially as
image, distills all enslaved children's experiences into one. The appeal of
"the child slave" for antislavery advocates rests on the *a priori* innocence
of the socially constructed child. Laura Suski's work on images of children in humanitarian appeals reveals that the image of "the child" plays
a narrative role that "does not fundamentally require a voice and, as
many development campaigns have discovered, is often better commu-
nicated visually, through tears or vacant looks." Instead, the images are
understood "as equivalent to voices in their ability to convey the denial
of innocence, freedom, and play that children experience in suffering."[5]
In this context, "the child slave" constitutes an ideal, innocent subject to
be saved, rehabilitated, and returned to that idealized and romanticized
state of grace – childhood.

Ascribing dependence and lack of competence to children also serves
to silence children's voices and inhibit children's rights claims. The antithesis of slavery (and goal of antislavery) – freedom – is generally not available to children because of their legal and social status as dependents. As
a result, children risk being defined out of slavery by virtue of their age
(on which their legal and social status is often predicated). Moreover,
children are constructed as lacking competence, so even when they are
"counted" among enslaved people, their competence to render meaningful (through narrative) their own experiences may be dismissed and, thus,
excluded by antislavery activists and researchers. Karen Sánchez-Eppler
confronts the same doubts and dismissals in her analysis of the Work
Projects Administration (WPA) narratives collected in the 1930s in the
U.S. South in this volume (see Chapter 1). While some historians' resistance to the use of the WPA slave narratives has been overcome, Sánchez-
Eppler asserts, "[T]he now ridiculed racist insistence that slaves cannot
offer reliable testimony resonates against the still prevalent assumption
that children cannot." This assumption about children's competence to
narrate their own experiences then robs enslaved children of their "right
to narration."

"If I got a chance to talk to the world," Ravi tells Peggy Callahan of
Free the Slaves, "I would relate my life story. I would tell them that I was
working on the loom. I would tell them about my rescue. I would talk
to them about how I came to this wonderful place and how I was given
the opportunity to study, to learn. I would tell them about my life experiences."[6] Ravi realizes that it is not only his experiences, but also *telling*

his experiences that has relevance in the fight to end slavery. Ravi, like many narrators enslaved as children, sees his story and his voice as the mechanisms through which to claim rights *as* and *for* children. Through this claiming of voice and rights, children who tell their stories of enslavement also complicate our beliefs about children and childhood, about agency and consent, and about victimization and empowerment on their own terms.

### "At this age, when other children play and enjoy": Children, Childhood, and Vulnerability

One important means by which narrators enslaved as children complicate beliefs about children and childhood slavery lies in their identification of themselves as children. The most common allusion to children or childhood is a specific reference to their age, as in Adelina's story, which she begins this way: "I am fifteen years old, and I became a sex worker when I was thirteen."[7] As with Adelina's story, references to age at the time of enslavement frequently appear in the first line or lines of their narratives, asserting their identities as children and framing the following narrative as the narrative of a child. Significant numbers of narrators invoke children and childhood explicitly by using the word *child* itself or referring to themselves as "small," "young," or "little." William says, "You're a little kid, you're thinking, Grandmother will come along and yell at them and get you out."[8] Shanawaz contrasts his experience in carpet loom slavery to other children's experiences, saying, "I never dreamt of such a poor condition at this age when other children play and enjoy."[9] Recalling a time when she was enslaved in domestic work, Kavita asserts, "People who do such things must understand that we are children. We are so innocent, so vulnerable. They must understand they must not do this to anyone, anywhere. What I would like to say to the world is when it comes to children, they're small, they're innocent, they're vulnerable. They just like playing, laughing, having fun, and very often they are unable to comprehend the repercussions of what the elders are doing to them."[10]

Kavita's assertion about children highlights another problematic convergence in childhood studies and slavery studies: vulnerability. Because of perceived innocence and lack of competence, the socially constructed child is often portrayed and perceived as vulnerable, and scholars of childhood have sought to clarify the concept by analyzing actual children's lived experiences and by deconstructing developmental approaches to children and childhood that imagine all children in all places at all ages as the same. In slavery studies, vulnerability (to enslavement) appeals to scholars seeking to identify root causes of slavery by moving beyond explanations at the individual level that emphasize blame and individual responsibility. In "Child Trafficking: A Modern Form of Slavery," Hans van de Glind seeks to bring these two approaches together when he argues that "the general public often misunderstands the circumstances that lead to trafficking. Poverty is undoubtedly an important factor explaining why some children are trafficked, yet poverty alone cannot explain why some countries have more child trafficking than others." Instead, he contends, "[G]overnments, NGOS and other agents fighting child trafficking should be familiar with the concept of vulnerability, that is, moving beyond the idea that poverty is at the root of all trafficking, and understanding that there is a range of risk factors affecting the level of vulnerability of each child: at individual child, family, community, institutional and workplace levels, and in source communities and at destinations."[11] So we cannot reject Kavita's assertion of children's innocence and vulnerability out of hand in an effort to emphasize agency. Her narrative points to a tension in studying child slavery that centers on vulnerability. On one hand, we need to recognize and validate Kavita's description of her *own experience* and what she sees as root causes, or at least risk factors, in childhood enslavement. Indeed, as Jenny Kitzinger argues, "it is childhood as an institution that makes children 'vulnerable.'"[12] In other words, for many children, childhood as an identity category and social status creates vulnerability, not children themselves. On the other hand, reading vulnerability and innocence into all children's slave narratives (as a cause of enslavement) further renders children invisible in antislavery work by focusing attention too narrowly on weakness and risk. Kavita's story allows us not only to see this tension, but also to recognize the consequences of children's lack of rights: in a context in which children can both access and claim rights, their vulnerability dissipates or even disappears.

The words some children use to describe their experiences and identities – *child, small, little, vulnerable* – could be read as representations of disempowerment, but these narrators – Adelina, William, Shanawaz, and Kavita – invoke these ideas as a means of *interrogating* vulnerability to dispel another identity commonly ascribed to children – victim. Arising here, then, are questions not only of agency, but also of whether enslaved people should be considered victims at all. Francesca Polletta points out the problematic assumption that "representing oneself as a victim, as passive, pitiable, and generic, cannot but diminish one's sense of agency." This assumption "underestimate[s] both the advantages and dangers of telling stories of victimization. To claim oneself as a victim is not necessarily to trade agency for passivity."[13] Child narrators assert their full right to be free from slavery despite denials of those rights in cultures around the world that see children as appropriately placed in domestic slavery and forced labor, particularly girls and children in poverty. Kavita's understanding of what childhood should be like allows her to connect to an audience that shares her belief and, thus, to highlight the vulnerability children experience merely by being children and to refute any perceived complicity in her exploitation. I argue that, rather than representing themselves as powerless victims, people who tell their stories of child enslavement claim their rights as children and seek mechanisms for building communities of children across space and time. I do not read these assertions of their identity as children as signs of their passivity or victimization; rather, narrators refer to constructions of childhood to speak back to common discourses of blame associated with contemporary slavery. As a result, their agency is not diminished but rather enhanced.

## "It is no fault of my own at all": Agency, Consent, and Innocence

Focusing on children's assertions of their vulnerability illuminates issues of agency, one of the most important and difficult problems in contemporary slavery studies. For the study of slavery and for the study of children, agency presents a particular problem: both children and enslaved people are constructed and then essentially defined as lacking agency. With the recognition of the constructedness of "the child" as passive, victimized, and silent has come an opposing response to affirm children's agency and power. As part of a widespread critique of the universalist, developmental, and/or imperialist definition of "the child," some scholars have asserted that, as human beings, children are – and should be understood as – powerful agents in their own lives. Neil Stammers argues that these two approaches – the "old" (children as powerless) and "new" (children as powerful) – remain "couched in binary terms where, from the 'old' perspective, children are structurally positioned as victims (or potential victims) with no agency, while, from the 'new' perspective, children are seen as subjects/agents potentially in control of their own destiny with apparently little facing them by way of structural constraint." He suggests, instead, "recognising that children can be both victims and social actors with agency," experiencing "complex and ambivalent encounters with power."[14] James and James argue that conjuring children's agency "is not to say, however, that children are necessarily powerful political actors who can take a major part in shaping their own histories," but rather "to draw attention to their capacity to act and to recognise that these actions have consequences, consequences that are unintended as well as intended."[15]

Contemporary slavery studies must similarly contend with the alternating and sometimes simultaneous power and powerlessness of enslaved people. The stories told by people enslaved as children embody this tension both in narrating a horrific human rights abuse and, at the same time, in asserting a sense of empowerment through its telling. As John Wall argues in this volume, "[H]uman rights might be better applied to the phenomenon of child slavery if children themselves are understood not only as vulnerable people in need of protection but also as full social beings with agency and dignity." Instead, he concludes, children "need to be understood as fully public members of the human rights sphere in all their victimhood and agency at once." Recognizing the ways that children have often been understood as not fully human, narrators enslaved as children engage these debates by identifying themselves not only as children, but as children possessing the right to freedom from slavery. In their stories, they clearly demonstrate their understanding of enslavement as a violation of their rights as children.

To account for disjunctions in assertions of children's agency and their actual empowerment, Natascha Klocker uses the idea of "thick" and "thin" agency. "'Thin' agency," she writes, "refers to decisions and everyday actions that are carried out within highly restrictive contexts, characterized by few viable alternatives. 'Thick' agency is having the latitude to act within a broad range of options." Agency, then, can be thickened or thinned throughout a person's life. In this way, "[S]tructures, contexts, and relationships can act as 'thinners' or 'thickeners' of individual agency, by constraining or expanding their range of viable choices." This conceptualization of agency "convey[s] a sense of the 'layering' or 'eroding' effects of the multiplicity of factors that affect young people's agency," such as, in her study, "age, gender, 'tribe,' and poverty," all of which "thinned" Tanzanian girls' agency.[16]

Narrators enslaved as children thus recognize the ways in which their status and identity as children can thin their agency, both before and during their enslavement. In *Daddy's Little Earner*, Maria Landon portrays her status as a child as disempowering and, in fact, the very reason for her commercial sexual exploitation by her own father: "One of the rights he insisted on was to do as he pleased with his children, and part of that meant beating us whenever the urge took him. We were as much his property as Pussy the Corgi or his well-shone boots."[17] For Maria, her status in her family thinned her agency, and this kind of childhood- and family-status vulnerability weaves throughout dozens of narratives as formerly enslaved children describe violence and abuse in the home as a greater threat than life on the streets.

Another means through which narrators enslaved as children assert their agency is by shaping their narratives – at least in part – in response to perceived audience beliefs about them, judgments that find enslaved people complicit in or to blame for their own exploitation. Through their descriptions of their status, many narrators, like Maria and Kavita, also seek to balance judgments about their complicity, responsibility, and blame. They recognize the potential for audience assumptions about refusing, fleeing, or escaping, assumptions that emerge out of the dominant ideology in the Global North about independence, a belief in individual choice, and the presumption of individual empowerment – ideas not typically associated with children. Their responses to those assumptions and judgments demonstrate their recognition of the factors that can or have thinned their agency prior to and during enslavement. At issue here is consent: Consent is particularly problematic in contemporary slavery research and activism. First, consent assumes agency, enough personal power to agree to participate. Second, consent assumes rights – a subject with access to a full array of human rights from which one is positioned to consent. Third, consent subsumes blame, as adults who consent to any type of work (including prostitution) but end up being enslaved are often portrayed in dominant discourses as responsible for their own enslavement.

Sex trafficking serves as a rhetorical and political flashpoint focusing on consent in the context of prostitution. This debate engages many of the same issues that Jessica Pliley describes in her chapter in this volume on white slavery in the Progressive-era, when age-of-consent campaigns coincided with white slavery campaigns to portray girls as children who "lacked the legal capacity to consent to sex, and also lacked the instrumental capacity to change the conditions of their lives" (see Chapter 6, this volume). Today, many activists and scholars contend that women can and sometimes do choose to enter into prostitution, asserting women's agency in their consent. Opponents argue that no woman can consent to prostitution, and, thus, that all women in prostitution have been trafficked or enslaved.[18] Because of the frequently binary terms of this debate, "the child" enslaved in prostitution has emerged as a particularly compelling figure in media stories because she is defined by law as unable to consent and thus avoids this fractious and sometimes vicious debate and the blame or disempowerment that result.

Children enslaved as soldiers also provide an opportunity to look at questions of children, consent, and agency that weave throughout contemporary slavery studies and other human rights discourses. The experiences of child soldiers fall along a continuum of consent, from enthusiastic enlistment to outright abduction with many falling somewhere between these two extremes. The question of whether children can voluntarily join armed forces centers on age, which is then conflated with assumed developmental abilities (or dis/abilities) and thus renders children unable – because of their developmental deficiencies and lack of competence – to consent. The question for child soldiers is: At what age are children capable of consenting to fight in wars?

Rachel Brett and Irma Specht's study of child soldiers sheds some light on the question of consent. In *Young Soldiers: Why They Choose to Fight* (2004), they engage the controversy over the idea of "voluntary participation" in armed conflict. They present and analyze interviews with fifty-three "boys and girls" from nine countries on four continents (including Afghanistan, Columbia, the Democratic Republic of Congo, Ireland, and Sri Lanka), exploring the contexts, the world views, the triggers, and the risk factors that surround children's decisions to fight. They hope "that giving these young people the chance to speak out and bringing their diverse voices together will invite a more honest look at the common reasons for young people joining armed forces or groups," which, in turn, "assist local, national, regional, and international actors to respond better to them" (1–2). They found that "it tends to be assumed that those who join want to fight," which is true in some cases but not in others (105). "What the research shows," they conclude, "is that frequently the distinction between voluntary and compulsory or forced recruitment is not clear-cut."[19]

Like Brett and Specht, I look to the narrators themselves to shed the most light on the child soldier debate about consent as they describe how they came to be soldiers and how they may have been prevented from escaping. Fifty-eight percent of former child soldiers in this study report being taken by force. Manju is very straightforward about her time as a child soldier in Sri Lanka: "Today I am here. Why? Not because I wanted to join; it is no fault of my own at all. I was forcefully taken away into the movement."[20] She wants to make very clear that she did not join the movement and that she did not consent to enslavement. Clementine emphasizes her identity in the face of her abduction, saying, "When the rebels came, I was small, they forced me to go with them."[21] More than three dozen more narrators describe a similar experience, being captured, tied up, and, often, beaten. That such a large proportion of these published narratives include abduction is important because abduction maintains their subject position as "'pure' victims" and thus more attractive for human rights or humanitarian appeals. For appeals involving children, their victimization rests on the popular belief that they are always already innocent *by virtue of being children*.

Equating childhood with innocence, however, is not a simple formula. Barbara Harlow, for example, points to a common claim about child soldiers – that children "make the best soldiers because they have no fear. They obey orders without question. They are uninhibited by moral concerns." The problem, she argues, is that "at the heart of these justifications is a sense that children are not inherently innocent. Nothing in their nature need be overcome or corrupted to turn them into fighters for whatever cause."[22] Child soldiers, then, highlight problematic assumptions about childhood and innocence. Moreover, a second, related problem is that while this preference for "pure" – that is, abducted – child victims reinforces their innocence, it also has the potential to deprive them of agency. Many child soldiers do, in fact, join armed forces and thus refute their characterization as helpless, abducted victims. Among the narratives in this study, twenty-five percent of former child soldiers report "voluntarily" joining an armed group. As Brett and Specht point out, however, this volunteerism occurs on a continuum.

While abductions follow similar patterns, volunteering often looks distinct from one narrator to another. Dieudonné describes being motivated by patriotism: "I joined the *maquis* [*mayi-mayi*] in 1998, when I was 10. Because I wanted to serve my country."[23] Several child soldier narrators "joined" after witnessing the death or, more often, the execution of family members, pointing them toward the opposing force out of a desire for revenge or the offending force out of fear. In Chad, Souleiman recalls, "[S]ome of our family were killed by the Zahhawa, and I wanted to take revenge on behalf of my family. I had talked about this with my friends, and we all decided to leave the village and join the rebellion. Five of us left, all close neighbours and brothers. One was younger than me. We did not talk about it with our parents; we made the decision on our own."[24] Souleiman asserts his own personal power in designing and executing a plan for revenge, embarking on the first step: joining the armed rebels. In Liberia, Comfort explains to Agnes Kamara-Umunna, "[T]hey killed my father in front of me. I could not stand it. That's how I came to join. I became a warrior."[25] Not only does Comfort declare her (albeit informal) enlistment in an armed group, but she also invokes a role typically reserved for male adults: warrior. These narrators see the potential for the thickening of their personal agency – to fight, to avenge, or even to survive – by joining armed groups, their status as children notwithstanding.

### "I have a duty to those who are still slaves": Narrative, Empowerment, Rights

Perhaps the most important vision of their agency begins with narrators' assertions of empowerment through narrative. Through their stories, child narrators seek to incite the listener or reader to take some action against slavery as they envision a transformation of their words – their voices – into political, cultural, and/or social change that will (help to) eliminate slavery everywhere for everyone. Mende Nazer says about her own story, "For me the reason for talking out is to help make another slave free – not just a slave from Sudan, but anywhere in the world. By talking out, people will be aware and more able to help people become free."[26] Nujood's sense of empowerment comes from her story. In her memoir, *I Am Nujood, Age 10 and Divorced*, she writes, "I was proud to learn that my story had helped [other girls] find the means to defend themselves, and I feel responsible in a small way for their decision to rebel against their husbands."[27] Such an effort suggests that they see their slave narratives as having power outside their own experiences. Many narrators see helping others as the most important thing they can do themselves in the fight against slavery, and a variety of narrators demonstrate a belief in the "thickening" of their agency through voice, evident in their expressed desire to help others and to speak for them. This tactic is common in advocacy work by activists and scholars, but in their narratives, some adults who were enslaved as children claim this act as their own – their responsibility, their duty, and, for some, their mission. Francis says, "As a former slave, I have a duty to those who are still slaves," so "I speak on behalf of the 27 million who do not have a voice."[28] So while their agency may be thinned by their status as children, child slavery narrators see their agency as "thickened" through narration, a belief they share with authors of historical slave narratives. Francis and scores of others recount their stories to help others, believing their narratives to be vehicles that thicken others' agency as well.

Narrators who tell the story of their enslavement claim rights through assertions of their status as children and, at the same time, assert their own agency by insisting on their stories – their voices – as a means of helping other children escape from or avoid slavery. Telling their stories of enslavement does not occur without personal cost as narrators must relive painful experiences. Enslaved as a child in a brothel in Cambodia, Chantha tells her story as she suffers the end stages of AIDS: "My life has had no significance, no value," she says. "I hope that by sharing my story, my life will finally have meaning and can help prevent others from the deep sadness of my life."[29] Chantha's hope rests in her ability and willingness to recount the painful events of her enslavement in order to help others. In *Child Soldier*, China Keitetsi reveals a similar hope, writing, "This is my final humiliation to speak of myself, about shameful abuse and inferiority, because that's the only way I can save my friends."[30] Theresa describes the cost to the narrator and the benefit to a community of survivors: "Telling the story makes me relive it. Brings the buried memories to the surface. Voluntarily. Making me vulnerable once again. But this is a vital component in moving from a victim to a survivor. When I use my painful experience to help others, when I enter into worthy relationships and learn to trust another person, I move from survivor to victorious."[31] At the same time, despite pain or humiliation, Theresa and a number of other narrators enslaved as children seek to comfort and educate others who have been enslaved or are at risk of being enslaved. With her memoir, Theresa says, "I want to educate society on the horrors of trafficking, and give hope and healing to those that have suffered unbearable things."[32] Jill's sense of purpose is multiple: "I write this story so that maybe someone who hears it will somehow be able to avoid the pain that was forced on me, and for others to know that things like I experienced really do happen – and they can happen to anyone's daughter, sister, girlfriend, niece, or wife."[33] She is recapturing the agency denied her during her enslavement, using narrative as empowerment.

While stories are often associated with the evocation of empathy to create affective connections, a variety of narrators also suggest that their agency can be further thickened through communities of action, enacted through narratives that create connections across space and time. First, some narrators envision their own actions as a mechanism of change, particularly at the local level. Many narrators enslaved as children envision a profession in which they help other people, a kind of other-directed (rather than self-focused) agency. Kavita says, "I want to grow up and I want to study to become a nurse. I want to become a nurse so I can help other people and look after them in their hour of need."[34] They sometimes see their futures in helping professions, goals shaped by their experiences in slavery. Freed from debt bondage, Battis hopes to "open a tailoring shop and stitch clothes for my villagers. They will give me money and I will definitely not come into bondage again. I will set up an example for my friends and children of the village and prevent them from getting into the trap of bondage."[35] Sandeep's enslavement at the loom also shapes his future plans: "I wish that in the future I will become a policeman and break the knees and elbows of these slaveholders, and not allow any children to go along with them even if he gives scores of money."[36] After his enslavement at a carpet loom, Rambho says, "I want to go to my village and be a guard there, and I think I'll be able to study and earn money. And I won't let anybody go to the looms even by mistake. I'll tell them, 'They hit you and they beat you.' I would not let them go there, ever. If the children make any mistakes they beat them up. I won't let them go there."[37] Formerly enslaved at a carpet loom, Rama has specific instructions for the Indian government. "I want to tell the government that these kids exist," he says. "It's time for you to take these children out of the loom. And it's not so difficult. All you need to do is surround the factory on all sides, come in and take the children. That's all you have to do."[38] After his escape from the loom, Ashok points to what he sees as the root causes of his enslavement. "The world is too cruel for those who don't have money and education, hence I ask you to please support us and stop child labor."[39] Anand also seeks to advocate for others, requiring the use of his own voice and his own experiences. He tells Siddharth Kara, "I want to be a lawyer so I can protect the rights of children. Children must be protected from bad people."[40] Anand does not represent children as victims, but as subjects with rights that must be recognized and protected. Communities of action must be predicated on those rights.

Second, those who are adults when they tell the story of their enslavement as children are more likely to see *voice itself* as a means of empowerment and action. Emmanuel Jal concludes his memoir by declaring, "I'm still a soldier, fighting with my pen and paper, for peace till the day I cease."[41] For Emmanuel, for the narrators in this study, and for those who have not yet told their stories, they find hope in the transformation of trauma into empowerment by raising their voices. Their desire to help others who have been enslaved – or who might be vulnerable to enslavement – frequently hinges on their story. Frequently disempowered by

poverty, gender, ethnicity, caste, or other element of their identity or experience that thins their agency (and, sometimes, led to their enslavement),
a number of narrators see their stories – specifically, in these cases, their
voices – as a means of thickening their agency. Theresa wants "parents
to see how easily this could happen to an average kid from the suburbs."
She then addresses her readers directly: "My desire is that you share this
with other parents. May this book provide hope that a survivor can heal
and turn something horrific into a catalyst for good."[42] For her, action
and voice are closely related; the primary action she seeks is the dissem-
ination of her voice.

Voice, however, is not a panacea. William initially appears ambivalent
about the power of voice, about the significance or value of telling his
story. Speaking of slavery in Sudan, William refuses an oversimplified
equation of voice and change: "Today, 'human rights' is about talking.
It's not about action anymore. When you think that the United Nations
is speaking up today – a UN resolution, section this, number that – what
does that mean? Will it help me in the village?" He argues, "When we
talk about slavery and don't talk action, it feels like, why should I say
my words?" But he appears to conclude, ultimately, that telling his story
constitutes some sort of action: "You have to speak to people, to let them
know."[43] Most narrators, however, celebrate voice and its power in telling their stories, believing in its role in asserting agency, claiming rights,
creating community, and, finally, fighting slavery. Abuk is less ambivalent
about her story and its role in ending slavery in Sudan. Near the beginning of her narrative, she says, "My hope, the reason why I speak out
whenever I can, is that those people will do more than just listen, that
they will raise their voice along with me," and she returns to the idea after
having recounted her own experiences, asserting that "though I am far
away from it all, I know my voice has power." And that power, for her, is
tangible, not metaphorical: "I will speak out about what is happening to
the people in my country until the raids and the violence and the slavery
have stopped."[44]

Narrators who tell their stories of child enslavement ultimately show
us both that voice can create connections with the potential to construct
community and that voice remains the most promising mechanism for
claiming rights, especially for children for whom rights have not been
reliably or regularly imagined. When we listen to the voices of children
in slavery, we gain a more complex and complicated understanding of
contemporary slavery in general as children's stories shift the debate
about consent away from a focus on innocence or morality to a more

comprehensive understanding of the constellation of factors that create vulnerability because of their status as children. Children's stories also shift the debate about agency away from dichotomous oppositions of empowerment against vulnerability and of innocence against agency toward a more nuanced interpretation of the ways that agency can be thickened and thinned according to identity, family situation, and societal status, for example.

In the end, these shifts hinge on a move away from the "child slave" or even the "child victim" to a framework of children's rights, which they themselves claim in their assertions of their identity as children, their understanding of what constitutes childhood, and the role they can and do play in contemporary antislavery work. A framework of rights allows for recognizing the vulnerabilities of children as a result of their identities, statuses, and roles without the oversimplification of victimization, disempowerment, and rightlessness. In their insistence on the significance of their stories and on the power of their voices, narrators enslaved as children remind us that agency in contemporary slavery takes a variety of forms. These narrators as children and adults describe their enslavement as children often at great personal cost because they believe in the power that emanates not only from telling it but from others hearing it. In this way, the power of the teller and the power of the audience come together to create the kind of community of action that many of these narrators envision. But until we listen to the voices of people enslaved as children, we cannot together constitute a community of action in which formerly or currently enslaved people work together with scholars, activists, advocates, and community leaders to end contemporary slavery.

## Notes

1   Gwyn Campbell, Suzanne Miers, and Joseph C. Miller, *Children in Slavery through the Ages* (Athens: Ohio University Press, 2009), 3.
2   Anna Mae Duane, *Suffering Childhood in Early America: Violence, Race, and the Making of the Child Victim* (Athens: University of Georgia Press, 2010), 6.
3   Sarada Balagopalan, "The Politics of Failure: Street Children and the Circulation of Rights Discourses in Kolkata (Calcutta), India," in *Reconceptualizing Children's Rights in International Development: Living Rights, Social Justice, Translation* (Cambridge: Cambridge University Press, 2013), 135.
4   Allison James and Adrian L. James, *Constructing Childhood: Theory, Policy and Social Practice* (New York: Palgrave Macmillan, 2004), 15.

5 Laura Suski, "Child Suffering and the Humanitarian Appeal," in *Humanitarianism and Suffering: The Mobilization of Empathy* , ed. Richard Ashby Wilson and Richard D. Brown (Cambridge: Cambridge University Press, 2008), 207, 208.

6 Ravi, "Ravi," in *To Plead Our Own Cause: Personal Stories by Today's Slaves*, ed. Kevin Bales and Zoe Trodd (Ithaca, NY: Cornell University Press, 2008), 77. With the exception of book-length published memoirs, I use only first names for narrators, which is how most of them appear in publications. After the first mention of memoir authors, I continue to use their first names for continuity. About the narratives in this study: I analyzed 166 published contemporary slave narratives by people enslaved as children, thirty-nine of whom can be identified as children at the time of narration. Sixteen of these narratives are book-length memoirs.

7 Adelina, "Adelina," in ibid., 52.

8 William, "William," in ibid., 248.

9 Shanawaz, "Shanawaz," in ibid., 78.

10 Kavita, "Kavita," in ibid., 139.

11 Hans van de Glind, "Child Trafficking: A Modern Form of Slavery," in *Child Slavery Now: A Contemporary Reader* (New York: Policy Press, 2010), 106, 112–13.

12 Jenny Kitzinger, "Who Are You Kidding? Children, Power, and the Struggle against Sexual Abuse," in *Constructing and Reconstructing Childhood: Contemporary Issues in the Sociological Study of Children* (New York: Routledge, 2003), 177.

13 Francesca Polletta, *It Was Like a Fever: Storytelling in Protest and Politics* (Chicago: University of Chicago Press, 2006), 111.

14 Neil Stammers, "Children's Rights and Social Movements: Reflections from a Cognate Field," in *Reconceptualizing Children's Rights in International Development: Living Rights, Social Justice, Translation* (Cambridge: Cambridge University Press, 2013), 286.

15 James and James, *Constructing Childhood*, 24.

16 Natascha Klocker, "An Example of 'Thin' Agency: Child Domestic Workers in Tanzania" in *Global Perspectives on Rural Childhood and Youth: Young Rural Lives* (New York: Taylor and Francis, 2010), 85.

17 Maria Landon, *Daddy's Little Earner* (New York: Harper, 2008), 15.

18 See, for example, Jo Doezema's *Sex Slaves and Discourse Masters: The Construction of Trafficking* (London: Zed, 2010) for an excellent overview of the debate.

19 Rachel Brett and Irma Specht, *Young Soldiers: Why They Choose to Fight* (Geneva: International Labour Organization, 2010), 1–2, 105, 112.

20 Manju, "Manju," in *To Plead Our Own Cause*, 198.

21 Clementine, *How to Fight, How to Kill: Child Soldiers in Liberia* (New York: Human Rights Watch, 2004), 32.

22 Barbara Harlow "Child and/or Soldier?: From Resistance Movements to Human Rights Regiments," *CR: The New Centennial Review*, 2010, 301.

23 Dieudonné, *Democratic Republic of Congo: Children at War, Creating Hope for the Future* (London: Amnesty International, 2006), 30.

24 Souleiman, *A Compromised Future: Children Recruited by Armed Forces and Groups in Eastern Chad* (London: Amnesty International, 2011), 17.

25 Agnes Kamara-Umunna, *And Still Peace Did Not Come: A Memoir of Reconciliation* (New York: Hyperion, 2011), 230.

26 Mende Nazer, *Slave: My True Story* (New York: Public Affairs, 2004), 227.

27 Nujood Ali, *I Am Nujood, Age 10 and Divorced* (New York: Broadway, 2010), 164.

28 Francis Bok, *Escape from Slavery: The True Story of My Ten Years in Captivity and My Journey to Freedom in America* (New York: St. Martins, 2004), 276.

29 Chantha, "Chantha," in *To Plead Our Own Cause*, 207.

30 China Keitetsi, *Child Soldier* (Abingdon, UK: Souvenir Press, 2011), 272.

31 Theresa L. Flores, *The Slave across the Street* (Garden City, ID: Ampelon Publishing, 2010), 139.

32 Ibid., 147.

33 Jill, "Jill," in *To Plead Our Own Cause*, 180.

34 Kavita, "Kavita," in ibid., 140.

35 Battis, "Battis," in ibid., 80.

36 Sandeep, "Sandeep," in ibid., 81.

37 Rambho, "Rambho," in ibid., 72.

38 Rama, "Rama," in ibid., 74.

39 Ashok, "Ashok," in ibid., 79.

40 Siddharth Kara, *Bonded Labor: Tackling the System of Slavery in South Asia* (New York: Columbia University Press, 2012), 234.

41 Emmanuel Jal, *War Child: A Child Soldier's Story* (New York: St. Martins, 2010), 256.

42 Flores, *The Slave across the Street*, 14.

43 William "William," in *To Plead Our Own Cause*, 250.

44 Abuk in Rahila Gupta, *Enslaved: The New British Slavery* (London: Granta, 2008), 41, 59–60.

# 10

# "When I play with the master's children, I must always let them win": Child Domestic Labor

## Jonathan Blagbrough and Gary Craig

Child slavery has been a highly significant, deeply troubling aspect of modern slavery, continuing as such despite the introduction of legislation and policy in most countries outlawing the physical, sexual, emotional, and financial exploitation of children (those under eighteen years old).[1] There is an extensive literature on slavery, dominated by the European, North American, and African accounts of the transatlantic slave trade, but most focuses on the experiences of adults (some of it written latterly by slaves themselves). There is very little available on children's experiences, particularly presenting children's voices. As Campbell, Miers, and Miller comment, "Children in slavery (is) a subject that has only recently become the subject of academic research.[2] Scholarly attention has up to now centered primarily on adult male slaves ... [and t]hroughout the history of slavery, children were in a minority." As they also note, most children "did not keep diaries or other records of their lives and treatment."

Our contribution to this volume focuses on child domestic workers (CDWs) – a group of uniquely vulnerable and exploited children, many living and working in circumstances covered by the 1956 UN Supplementary Convention on the Abolition of Slavery, the Slave Trade, and Institutions and Practices Similar to Slavery. Much of the historical literature that does exist on child slaves sees their voices, if engaged at all, mediated through the agency of adults. By presenting accounts here based on the powerful voices of children themselves, we provide insights into children in domestic work situations, locating this practice in our understanding of child slavery: children as victims, after all, have the greatest right to speak truth to power and, as we show, can have agency to change their positions. Hearing children's voices also helps to distinguish between unremittingly exploitative and slavery-like situations and those where positive outcomes can be identified.

More than 17 million children worldwide, mostly girls, are estimated to be in paid or unpaid domestic work in households other than their own, many located in the world's poorest countries.[3] Of these children, more than two-thirds are considered to be in unacceptable conditions, either being below the country's legal minimum working age, or working in hazardous conditions or circumstances legitimately described as slavery. Despite the prevalence of the practice, the growing numbers, its importance as a source of employment, and its significance to local and national economies, domestic work remains a uniquely gendered, hidden, and burdensome form of work; children involved are particularly vulnerable to exploitation and abuse.

## Child Slavery: Hidden from History

As noted, the literature on historical slavery and the slave trade is now extensive; the scholarship on the latter offers very detailed accounts of a trade that was commercially driven, and thus recorded in minute detail to establish its economic viability. The purchase and use of slaves was a relatively straightforward economic proposition, particularly where slaves created further slaves by having children. The creation of slave children was a relatively cheap matter and their use as slaves similarly inexpensive; consequently there are few extant records accounting (literally) for their use. Campbell and colleagues' *Children in Slavery throughout the Ages*, while indeed addressing "children in slavery," also illustrates the difficulties scholars have in grappling with the issue: much of the content is indirect material, the voices of children generally reaching us only through those of significant others.

One shouldn't dismiss the difficulties in obtaining accounts of children's lives (a problem not limited to the domain of slavery), particularly of accessing accounts shaped substantially by children themselves.[4] It is only in the past half century that campaigns to establish children's rights and give them an autonomous voice have acquired significance. Where children's voices are heard in Campbell and colleagues' collection (even if they are the voices of adults reminiscing about their childhoods), they do provide powerful testimony to the appalling treatment of human beings as commodities, a treatment remaining as an indelible blot on the landscape of human rights today. While a very limited picture of child slavery emerges, it lays bare the huge task now facing scholars in this arena.

We can hope that Campbell and colleagues' book and the present one, with their extensive references and detailed accounts (see, e.g., Johnson, Chapter 9, this volume, on the issue of voice), provide starting points for this enterprise. We now focus on the historical and contemporary phenomenon of CDWs.

### Understanding Child Domestic Work in the Context of Slavery

It is widely understood that poverty invariably underlies a child's vulnerability to domestic work. The large majority of CDWs come from poor families and, particularly in societies lacking social protection safety nets, are sent to work to supplement family income or lessen financial strain at home.[5] However, other structural factors such as gender and ethnic discrimination, social exclusion, lack of educational opportunities, migration, displacement, and the impacts of conflict and disease are also important drivers.[6]

At the same time, other complex and fundamental "push" factors, such as the desire for a child to escape from domestic violence, flee a forced marriage, or parents' wishes to send their girls into "safe," suitable situations ahead of married life, are also at play.[7] A recent study of the psychosocial impact of domestic work on children found that the level of cultural and social acceptability of child domestic work in a society influences the age at which children enter the sector and how they are subsequently treated – with children in societies where the practice is widely accepted found to be starting work at a younger age and subject to greater exploitation than elsewhere.[8]

Children are also "pulled" into domestic work as a result of economic uncertainty (together with the widespread belief that the move offers better living conditions) and by siblings and friends already working in households. Increasing participation of women in the labor force has meant a considerable demand for domestic help, with many employers opting for younger workers because they are cheaper and considered more acquiescent.[9] In some countries, significant numbers of older children report that they themselves decide to leave home and seek work, to be able to continue in education.[10]

Many of the factors pushing and pulling children into domestic work are common to other forms of child labor, so what makes CDWs particularly vulnerable to slavery? Central to concerns about their situation is the ambiguity of the children's relationship to the employing households, and the perception that their work is not really employment.

The paternalistic thinking often accompanying this relationship – that domestic workers (especially children) are "like one of the family" – helps conceal its exploitative nature. These paternalistic notions reflect vestiges of the master-servant nexus "wherein domestic work is a 'status' which attaches to the person performing the work," consequently serving to define the worker, limiting her/his future options.[11] This thinking is amplified for children in domestic work, due to the employer's control over the child and the child's dependency on the employing family for her/his basic needs, creating a slave-like status.

Widespread acceptance of domestic work as appropriate for girls in particular serves to heighten their ambiguous relationship with their employing families. So too does the relative informality of such arrangements, which support the parental pretense that their children are being cared for within a family environment, while giving credence to employer beliefs that they are supporting a child in need. In some societies, the idea that the CDW's employer is a benefactor has been legitimized by describing this relationship as "adoption" by strangers or "fostering" by extended family members – practices continuing in parts of Asia and Latin America, as well as across much of sub-Saharan Africa including, often, in branches of extended families resident in industrialized countries. Characterizing child domestic work situations as "adoption" or "fostering" implies caring kinship relations and community support for raising children, rather than exploitation.[12]

### When Child Domestic Work Becomes Slavery

Experts have been particularly concerned about children in domestic work in various guises for the past 100 years. In 1925, the League of Nations' Temporary Slavery Commission condemned the transfer of children for domestic service under the pretext of adoption as slave dealing.[13] The Commission's Findings underpinned the League of Nations' 1926 Slavery Convention, which considered slavery to encompass "any or all of the powers of ownership" (Article 1(1)) and called for the "abolition of slavery in all its forms" (Article 2(b)). This international standard broadened the definition of slavery beyond that of chattel slavery, encompassing practices similar in nature and effect – subsequently taken to include forced labor, servitude, and trafficking.

The development of the 1956 UN Supplementary Convention on the Abolition of Slavery, the Slave Trade, and Institutions and Practices Similar to Slavery further defined "child servitude" as, *inter alia, "any institution or practice whereby a child or young person under the age of 18 years is delivered by either or both his natural parents or by his guardian to another person, whether for reward or not, with a view to the exploitation of the child or young person or of his labor"* (Article 1(d)).

This is particularly relevant to the situation of many CDWs: it addresses children living away from home to work, whether or not they are paid. Indeed, discussions during the drafting of the Supplementary Convention strongly indicate that specific practices involving children were intended to be prohibited. These practices included versions of the Chinese *Mui Tsai* (literally meaning "Little Sister") system, involving the "handing over" of young children (mainly girls) by parents/guardians to be used by their new family as domestic servants under the guise of adoption – a practice aptly describing how many children today become CDWs.[14] The issue of the boundary between childhood and child slavery, and changes in perceptions of that boundary over time is of course central to this anthology, addressed in other chapters in this book (see for example, Anna Mae Duane's introduction, and, Audra Diptee, Chapter 8,).

In a current example, in the West African states of Togo and Benin, where the vast majority of CDWs "live in," a distinction has been found between those who decided to live with their employers and those "placed" to work for extended family members by their parents, a long-standing cultural practice known in Togo as *placement (confiage* in Benin). While children in both instances reported similar difficulties, it was found that the cultural dictates of *placement* meant that children felt particularly compelled to stay, whatever the circumstances. This results in CDWs continuing to suffer in abusive households.[15]

Many thousands of CDWs in South Asia and elsewhere are considered to be in debt bondage (in these cases, when children enter domestic service in exchange for money for a third party, or to repay an outstanding debt).[16] For example, families in agricultural bonded labor in Pakistan and Nepal have often been required to send a daughter to the landlord's family to be a domestic worker. Cases are widespread of parents pledging children into individual bondage as domestic workers in exchange for money to survive or for exceptional expenses.[17]

For many years, the ILO's Committee of Experts on the Application of the Conventions and Recommendations (CEACR) has presented various manifestations of child domestic work as forced labor, and more recently as a worst form of child labor. This includes children obliged to work long hours without pay and who experience restricted freedom of movement, children sold into domestic service by their parents, those trafficked for the purpose of domestic labor, and children in various traditional systems of domestic servitude (ILO 2012a: para. 469). In 2011, the CEACR observed that "the Committee has been commenting for many years on the situation of hundreds of thousands of restavek children who are often exploited under conditions that qualify as forced labor. It noted that ... many of these children, some of them only 4 or 5 years old, are the victims of exploitation ... work long hours without pay, face all kinds of discrimination and bullying, receive poor lodging and food and are often subjected to physical, psychological and sexual abuse."[18]

More recently, child domestic work has also been identified as a trafficking issue.[19] In many cases, intermediaries broker the deals between parents and employers for children's services, and transport the children to their employing families. Some intermediaries deceive or coerce the child or her parents, who often receive false promises about the working conditions, opportunities for education, and what life for the child will be like. The way in which significant numbers of children enter domestic service can thus legitimately be described as trafficking.[20]

## Evolving Legal Frameworks

The fundamental rights of the child are set out in the United Nations' international framework document, the 1989 Convention on the Rights of the Child (UNCRC), which is almost universally ratified (barring the United States). Analyzing child domestic work in this way reveals that more than twenty Articles of the UNCRC are potentially or actually infringed; from Article 2 on the right to non-discrimination to Article 37 on the right to protection from cruel or degrading treatment, and deprivation of liberty. Despite the more than twenty-five-year existence of the UNCRC and the inroads made to realize children's rights through the efforts of international and local groups, a considerable gap remains between international recognition of these rights and their local reality. The concept of child rights, let alone of a CDW having rights of his/her own that might be violated, remains unknown to most parents and employers.[21]

From a labor perspective, the ILO has been concerned with children as domestic workers for decades. A resolution concerning the conditions of employment of domestic workers was adopted in 1948, with a further resolution in 1965 calling for normative action in this area.[22] However, it was ILO's landmark convention on the Minimum Age for Admission to Employment, 1973 (hereafter C.138) that highlighted child domestic work (and other exploitative practices) as forms of child labor. At the same time, the ILO has noted that while "a majority of countries have adopted legislation to prohibit or place severe restrictions on the employment and work of children ... child labor [of which child domestic work is a subset] continues to exist on a massive scale, sometimes in appalling conditions."[23] The acknowledgment that legislation, particularly age-based prohibition, is something of a blunt (and often ineffective) instrument in curbing such a complex and varied social phenomenon set in motion efforts to prioritize forms of child labor universally agreed to be intolerable. Through the resulting Worst Forms of Child Labor Convention, 1999 (C.182) the ILO broadened its legislative approach from an age-oriented response alone toward a nuanced conception of several key features of child domestic work (discussed later), which transform it into a "worst form" of child labor.[24]

The past twenty years in particular have seen the ILO's International Programme on the Elimination of Child Labor (ILO-IPEC) and many international and local NGOs become involved in efforts to change perceptions of child domestic work (see Wall, Chapter 11, this volume, for a further discussion of child-centered legal frameworks). More generally, by talking to children themselves, understanding among the child rights fraternity has also been shifting beyond consideration of CDWs (and other child workers) simply as passive victims of exploitation and abuse and toward recognition of them as individuals with agency, able to change their own lives and those of others. The sector-specific approach taken by the ILO's Domestic Workers Convention, 2011 (C.189), testifies to a further shift in international policy thinking. These standards are based on the conviction that domestic workers are like other workers, entitled to respect of their rights and dignity.[25] The new standards require states to protect young children from domestic work, while ensuring that adolescents entitled to work can do so without impinging on their education.

Significantly, C.189's provisions broadly reflect the views and experiences of child domestic workers themselves, in part as a result of NGO efforts in several countries to consult with hundreds of CDWs and to bring their demands to the attention of ILO delegates involved in the C.189 drafting process.[26] As a result, C.189's provisions are an important acknowledgment of the particular situation of young domestic workers who are over the minimum age for admission to employment, but who are not yet eighteen, and who require special protection and attention in order to continue their education. It is prompting ILO constituents and others to think carefully before either excluding CDWs from the scope of child labor legislation (as many countries did under exceptions to C.138), or "blanket-banning" all child domestic work by labeling it as "hazardous," as has taken place in many countries under the auspices of C.182.

While the adoption of new standards on domestic work may not have an obvious immediate impact on the situation of the many children in domestic service, signs of its use are emerging in stimulating international and local debate about challenges domestic workers face. The standards also increase pressure on governments to protect domestic workers of all ages by bringing them into public view rather than remaining, as has historically been the case, hidden from sight. As a result of listening to the views of CDWs in the standard-setting arena and on the ground, comprehension of the practice is rapidly advancing from absolutist prohibitionist approaches toward more a nuanced consideration that certain children's circumstances, while creating vulnerability to exploitation and abuse, needn't always be harmful.

## Hearing the Voices of Child Domestic Workers

As noted, child domestic work has traditionally been conceptualized as a labor and, sometimes, as a slavery issue.[27] In recent years, efforts to seek the views of children themselves have helped to broaden and deepen our understanding of their situation. We now better understand the drivers and triggers that push children from their homes, the forces that pull them into domestic work and that keep them there. These efforts have also proffered a more rounded conception of their lives, motivations, and perceptions – not just as workers, but as children, as girls, as migrants, and as individuals with some agency over their own lives – which can be harnessed to improve their circumstances.

Despite the varied manifestations of child domestic work, there are important similarities in the circumstances and experiences of CDWs – particularly lack of control over their lives, exploitative working conditions, exclusion from appropriate welfare provision, and isolation – that resonate with the concerns of slavery experts, and that ultimately blight their future life chances. The direct voices of CDWs cited here, collected from consultations, group discussions, and individual interviews over several years, present grounded insights into the real lives and perspectives behind policy and theory.

## Discrimination and Isolation

*"Once, I had tea with my employers. They told me to go in the corner and drink."* (Kavitha, India)[28]

CDWs often report that the discrimination and isolation experienced in the employer's household is the most difficult part of their burden. A study in Bangladesh found that it was "neither the verbal or physical punishments, nor the possible lack of material goods or even food, that upset [CDWs] the most; it was the discrimination, exclusion, disrespect, ingratitude, and other assaults on their emotional needs that truly hurt them."[29] Even if their relationship with household members is good, these relationships are not on equal terms. A typical example of discrimination is that the employer's children go to school, while the CDW cannot. CDWs often have to eat separately, having leftovers or food of inferior quality, and sleep in the kitchen or on the floor of their employers' children's rooms.[30]

*"Some days I stayed without food. I was not allowed to share the table with the family or to touch anything. I used to eat in the kitchen."* (Adele, Tanzania)
*"My treatment is so so. I have to make sure I am in my place.... In their eyes I am a domestic worker serving them."* (Louisa, Peru)

Denying CDWs their rights – including to education and play – is considered particularly hurtful when they often live side by side with those who do enjoy such rights. Many studies note the distress of CDWs who take their employers' children to school or for play, but are not allowed to join in.[31] This inferior treatment not only has negative consequences for CDWs, but also for other children in the employers' household, who grow up with a sense of innate superiority over others. (Ibid.)

*"The children, they insult me, you see. They call out my mother's name, every day. It's their way of telling me off if I don't do things right, if their bed is not made properly. They are very arrogant and quite big. Once they wanted to hit me because I had not done their things."* (Ruby, Peru)

In Bangladesh, an eight-year-old girl summed up the inequity governing her relationship with her employer's children: *"When I play with the master's children, I must always let them win."*[32]

## An Impediment to Education

*"I was going to study this year, but my employer said it wasn't possible; they couldn't leave the children alone. Both he and his wife go out to work."* (Luis, Peru)

It is ironic that while children in countries with universal primary and secondary education systems often bemoan attending school, those who are denied access to education are fully aware of its potential in improving future prospects and generally rank its importance above all other measures to support them. Some consider that becoming a domestic worker is a way of continuing their studies.³³ In reality, their situation is often a serious obstacle to studying, with school attendance rates particularly low among girls in domestic service.³⁴ This may simply be because employers do not allow them to go to school or training, or go back on an initial promise to do so.³⁵

*"I work as a domestic but used to attend school. Before going to school, I had to take a big pot full of cooked rice to the roadside. One day, the pot fell down and the rice was spoiled. My employer was angry and decided not to pay my school fees. So I dropped out of school but continued working for her for a long time."* (Nadine, Togo)

Even when CDWs are given the opportunity, long working hours and requirements of their job often make it impossible to take up education. In Peru, for example, some children persevere with night schools, but report that they have little time for homework and are frequently tired, which makes it difficult to progress.³⁶ Frequently, the requirements of school, in addition to the burden of domestic work duties, results in late and irregular attendance and in being unable to concentrate.³⁷

## Vulnerability to Violence and Abuse

*"My employer forced me to undress. She hit my body with a bottle, chair, or anything she got hold of."* (Izzy, Philippines)

CDWs regularly report that their isolated situation and ambiguous role in their employer's household makes them particularly vulnerable to physical, verbal, and sexual abuse. If violence occurs, the child's dependency on the employer for basic needs, her sense of duty to her parents to make the situation manageable, or her fear of the consequences of speaking up make her far less likely to report it.³⁸ Regular violence or its threat routinely leads to a loss of self-esteem: a self-perpetuating cycle of abuse can develop, which results in abused CDWs feeling unable to challenge the situation.³⁹

*"My employer also beats me when he beats his wife. But their daughter asks me to be patient when her parents get mad at me."* (Liza, Philippines)
  *"They treated me differently. The lady [employer] was very rough, but the boss [her husband] was nice to me, but I thought, 'He is nice for a reason'; that's what I thought. 'He is interested in me.' Because he would say, 'Here you are; 10 soles*

*for you,' and I would take it and say thank you of course – I was just a child. And then in the end he took advantage of me, just touching me, nothing else, he did not try to rape me."* (Isabel, Peru)

Sexual violence toward CDWs, due to the child's vulnerability and isolation, is common. In Haiti, restavek girls are sometimes called *la pou sa*, a Creole term meaning "there for that." They are accepted sexual outlets for men or boys of the household.[40] A West Bengal study indicated that a third of CDWs had their private parts touched by members of their employing family. Twenty percent had been forced to have sexual intercourse.[41] In El Salvador, an ILO-IPEC study showed that more than 15 percent of CDWs who had changed their employers had done so because of sexual harassment or abuse.[42]

*"The eldest child* [of the employer] *impregnated me and they chased me away."* (Denise, Tanzania)

### A Hazard to Health

CDWs regularly perform many tasks, such as carrying heavy loads (including water, laundry, fuel, and other children), handling toxic household chemicals, gardening, farming and working with knives, hot pans and irons. Children confirm this can be exhausting and dangerous, particularly for younger children and those fatigued by long working hours and lack of sleep.[43]

*"I wake up at six in the morning. I prepare breakfast for the couple and their children, then wash the dishes. I sweep, mop, wash clothes, feed the dogs, and finish cleaning the rest of the house. When the children come back from school I get them something to eat."* (Antony, Peru)

In Indonesia, the ILO reported that CDWs typically perform the same amount of work as adult workers, a level that is inappropriate to their physical capacity and stamina. The study commented that the long hours of work and little time for rest, recreation, or socializing impacted these children's mental, physical, social, and intellectual development.[44] In Guinea and Morocco, Human Rights Watch (HRW) documented young girls working between twelve and eighteen hours a day, seven days a week.[45] An IPEC survey of Vietnamese CDWs found that 36 percent had been sick or injured during their service, with a higher percentage among the younger workers (from nine to fourteen). Common ailments included coughs, respiratory problems, headaches, back pain, and wounds.[46]

*"I wake up at 5 am, prepare the children and escort them to school. Returning home I do the housework. Later, I pick the children up from school. Usually I sleep at 9 pm."* (Sarah, Tanzania)

Recently, concern about the health impacts of child domestic work has shifted to include aspects of their psychosocial well-being. Reporting on the situation of CDWs in El Salvador, Guatemala, Indonesia, Morocco, and Togo, HRW found that, almost without exception, interviewees suffered some form of psychological abuse. It concluded that "employer abuse, combined with isolation at the workplace, excessive work demands, and financial pressures may contribute to intense anxiety and depression."[47]

*"My punishment was not being able to see my family; they knew my family was my weak point."* (Adrian, Peru)

In Brazil, a cross-sectional survey of 3,139 children, including young workers, found that those in domestic work were particularly at risk of developing behavioral problems.[48] Another large study, in Ethiopia, established that CDWs aged eight to fifteen suffered more psychosocial disorders (such as phobia and separation anxiety) than other working and non-working children. Researchers concluded these issues were caused by CDWs' excessive working hours; lack of personal freedom; and physical, verbal, and emotional abuse.[49]

## Moving for Work

*"They don't allow me to speak with my mummy on the phone. They always say it is a wrong number."* (Meena, India)

Most CDWs move long distances, often hundreds of miles, away from their families and into employers' households, exacerbating their vulnerability. This mostly rural–urban (sometimes cross-border) movement is part of a wider pattern in many settings – a trend set to continue because of economic imperatives, conflict, state failure, natural disasters, and environmental and resource pressures.[50] Children moving for domestic work are doing so for many reasons. Some may make the decision to migrate, while others are displaced, and yet others are trafficked. Children forced to migrate alone are by far the most vulnerable group of migrant children; within it, CDWs constitute a particularly important section.[51]

(When was the last time you saw your parents?) *"Not since I came here three years ago. They live very far and I can't go on my own, and they haven't got the money to come here."* (Are you in touch with them?) *"Sometimes when they go to the village they call me ... just sometimes"* (Eddy, Peru)

CDWs living far from their families often find the resulting lack of contact difficult to bear. Some reported that their employers make matters worse by deliberately isolating them from their families, limiting opportunities for contact. In Tanzania, a third of CDWs stated they were not allowed to have visitors or visit parents or relatives. The numbers were higher amongst CDWs working in the capital, Dar es Salaam, who reported being more isolated in terms of social networks than those working closer to home.[52]

*"I started to work at 12 years old. Since then, I never saw my family. Homesickness is my greatest enemy. My mother only saw me when my employer finally told her where I was working.... I wanted to tell my parents how difficult my life was, but there was no chance."* (Elsie, Philippines)

A 2011 study of child migrants in labor conducted by ILO-IPEC and Child Helpline International in Kenya, Nepal, and Peru found that migrant working children (many of whom were CDWs) appeared to be worse off than local working children in various ways: they had to work longer hours, were paid less, denied food more, had greater exposure to hazards, were more prone to violence, and were more often unable to leave employers' households.[53]

## What Do Child Domestic Workers Need from Us?

*"We have a strong voice and the ability to speak out. But, if we do not speak out, who will hear us? We need to speak for the rights of every domestic worker. We have the right to tell others what is happening to many of us."* (Angela, Philippines)

CDWs are not only in a position to articulate their situation, but are often very clear about what assistance they need to improve their circumstances. They speak widely about which interventions have the most positive impact for them; broadly, children praise those interventions seeking to: (1) maintain or re-establish contact between the child and her/his close relatives; (2) intervene directly with their employers in a non-confrontational way; (3) support the establishment and strengthening of groups of CDWs to represent and help themselves; (4) encourage CDWs to return to education by, for example, making schooling more child-friendly, and particularly more girl-friendly.

(Do you have a day off?) *"Yes, thanks to my own effort."* (Didn't you have one before?) *"No, I used to live in, you see. When I lived in, I helped him on Sundays, so I worked every day, then my friends said, 'You are nobody's slave; you don't have to explain what you do when you are not working. Isn't that true? You have to speak up.' So now, I don't go in on Sundays; I am studying IT on Sundays and I never go in to work now. The lady was a bit annoyed; she said, 'Since you have decided all by yourself to take a holiday you don't eat on Sundays.' So I can't really talk yet. I still feel quite low. I still don't have ... {the courage.}*(Carlos, Peru)

A recent study exploring the effects of domestic employment on children's well-being reflects CDWs' identification of the determining factors appearing to have protective or negative effects on their well-being: (1) education contributes to well-being; conversely, CDWs who don't attend school have worse psychosocial outcomes (particularly low self-esteem) than those who do (see Meiners, Chapter 4, this volume); (2) the availability of support networks, including those provided by NGOs and employers alongside their own family and friends, can make a significant difference to the way working and living conditions impact CDWs' psychosocial health; (3) children with poor psychosocial outcomes are also more likely to suffer from poor physical health; (4) the nature of the tasks performed impacts CDWs' well-being.[54] Children's peers have also proven a critical source of mutual support.

(Do you know other child domestic workers?) *"Yes, and I help them, offering them my friendship, advice, encouraging them. They also helped me with their friendship and affection, which for me is more important than material things. We need friendships."* (Juan, Peru)

Under the banner "Stand With Us!" more than 400 current and former CDWs from Africa, Asia, and Central and South America were consulted during 2010/11 about the ILO's (then) proposed standards on domestic work and how children could best be protected from exploitation and abuse. These children expressed clear views about key provisions of the draft standards, in particular the right to education, the need for special protection for CDWs, and the monitoring of their living and working conditions – many of these views were subsequently reflected in C.189 and its accompanying recommendation. Four of the key concerns were that:

(1) No one should be a CDW below the national legal minimum working age. Young domestic workers above this age (usually fourteen or fifteen years) can work, but their employment should be subject to special protection.

*"Going to school makes it possible to find a good job; our employers have a job because they went to school."* (Salomé, Togo)

(2) Written employment agreements are the best way of ending exploitation and getting young domestic workers back into education.
*"There should be agreement between employers and CDWs with regard to wages, holidays and sending us to school."* (Elsa, India)

(3) CDWs need urgent protection from physical, sexual, and emotional abuse. Local leaders and law enforcers should look out for and assist young domestic workers in abusive situations.
*"There should be a clause in all contracts that obliges employers to respect adolescents and prohibit physical, sexual and emotional abuses against us."* (Marta, Costa Rica)

(4) Young domestic workers should be locally registered and given opportunities to organize.[55] This underlines our earlier point about the ineffectiveness of existing laws and protocols. It also helps to clarify the boundaries between slavery or slavery-like situations, and what might be deemed acceptable work for children and young people.
*"We should be given the chance to meet friends outside our workplaces. Without outside contact, we can never know from whom to seek help."* (Ali, Philippines)

## Conclusion

Understanding of CDWs has grown considerably in the past twenty years. With this understanding has come recognition of the complexities surrounding their varied situations and yet often similar experiences, along with greater clarity about how best to conceptualize these children and support and protect them. Perhaps the greatest advance in our knowledge has come from listening to the children themselves – not only in relation to their working lives, but their experience and ideas of how they can best be assisted and, crucially, how to help themselves and support each other (see Sánchez-Eppler, Chapter 1, this volume, for further discussion of how children's voices can be accessed). More broadly, the voices of CDWs are precipitating a profound review of the way we as adults and activists perceive them and their situation: we need to see them not only as passive victims of exploitation but also as actors capable of changing their circumstances, if assisted to do so. Significantly, recent policy shifts, codified through international standard-setting, provide us with important opportunities to help these children improve their lives – making clear that while some CDWs are rightly considered to be living in intolerable slavery, many others want to work, and are legally entitled to do so. Those children who want to work can be helped to improve their working conditions. These new developments afford activists opportunities to take more nuanced and effective measures for children's protection and to help identify the line between work undertaken in slave-like conditions, and what might be socially acceptable work, a line often difficult to define in a contemporary context. What is most important perhaps is the insight (hardly new) that listening to the voices of children themselves is the most important route to understanding their needs and wishes and to realizing how far we, as a society, are from meeting them.

## Notes

1　G. Craig (ed.) *Child Slavery Now* (Bristol: Policy Press, 2009).
2　G. Campbell, S. Miers, and J. C. Miller (eds.) *Children in Slavery through the Ages* (Cincinnati: Ohio University Press, 2009).
3　ILO, *Child Domestic Work: Global Estimates 2012* (factsheet) (Geneva: ILO, 2013).
4　G. Craig, "Children's Participation through Community Development: Assessing the Lessons from International Experience," in eds. C. Hallet and A. Prout, *Hearing the Voices of Children* (London: Routledge, 2002).
5　ILO, *Ending Child Labor in Domestic Work and Protecting Young Workers from Abusive Working Conditions* (Geneva: ILO, 2013).
6　ILO, *Helping Hands or Shackled Lives? Understanding Child Domestic Labor and Responses to It* (Geneva: ILO, 2004).
7　M. Black (2011), looking at the link between forced marriage and child domestic work, suggests there is evidence that the prospect of forced early marriage pushes some children (especially girls) to run away to the street, where they are vulnerable to exploitation and abuse, including in domestic work. Communication with Blagbrough, 2010.
8　Anti-Slavery International. *Small Grants, Big Change: Influencing Policy and Practice for Child Domestic Workers* (London: Anti-Slavery International, 2013).
9　ILO, *Children in Hazardous Work: What We Know, What We Need to Do* (Geneva: ILO, 2011).
10　J. Blagbrough, *They Respect Their Animals More: Voices of Child Domestic Workers* (London: Anti-Slavery International/WISE, 2008).
11　ILO, *Decent Work for Domestic Workers*, Report IV(1), International Labor Conference, 99th Session (Geneva: ILO, 2010: para. 45).
12　M. Dottridge and O. Feneyrol, *Action to Strengthen Indigenous Child Protection Mechanisms in West Africa to Prevent Migrant Children from Being Subjected to Abuse* (Lausanne: Terre des Hommes Foundation, 2007).
13　For further information see S. Miers, *Slavery in the Twentieth Century: The Evolution of a Global Problem* (Walnut Creek, CA: AltaMira Press, 2003).

14 Draft preliminary report of the Ad Hoc Committee of Experts on Slavery of the United Nations, 1951.

15 Anti-Slavery International, *Small Grants, Big Change.*

16 Debt bondage is defined in the United Nations' 1956 *Supplementary Convention on the Abolition of Slavery, the Slave Trade, and Institutions and Practices Similar to Slavery* as: "the status or condition arising from a pledge by a debtor of his personal services or of those of a person under his control as security for a debt, if the value of those services as reasonably assessed is not applied towards the liquidation of the debt or the length and nature of those services are not respectively limited and defined" (Article 1(a)).

17 H. Gazdar and A. Khan, "A Rapid Assessment of Bonded Labor in Domestic Labor and Begging," in *Rapid Assessment Studies of Bonded Labor in Different Sectors in Pakistan* (Karachi: Bonded Labor Research Forum, 2004).

18 *Haiti* – CEACR, observation, 2011.

19 The *Protocol to Prevent, Suppress and Punish Trafficking in Persons, Especially Women and Children* (supplementing the UN Convention against Transnational Organized Crime, 2000). In this Protocol, child trafficking is "The action of recruitment, transportation, transfer, harbouring, or receipt [of a child] for the purposes of exploitation, which includes exploiting the prostitution of others, sexual exploitation, forced labor, slavery or similar practices, and the removal of organs." Bear in mind too that children legally cannot consent to their own exploitation.

20 See, for example, *Central African Republic* – CEACR; 2010; *Chad* – CEACR, 2010; *Lesotho* – CEACR, observation, 2011; and *Mali* – CEACR, observation, 2010.

21 M. Black, *What Are the Best Ways to Develop Effective Strategies and Approaches to Reach and Support Child Domestic Workers?* (London: Comic Relief, 2011); ILO, *Helping Hands or Shackled Lives?* 29–32.

22 ILO: *Record of Proceedings*, International Labor Conference (ILC), 31st Session, 1948, Appendix XVIII: Resolutions adopted by the Conference: 545–6; ILO: *Official Bulletin* (Geneva), July 1965, Supplement I: 20–1.

23 From: www.ilo.org/ipec/facts/ILOconventionschildlabor (accessed September 23, 2013).

24 For example in paragraph 3(e) of Recommendation 190, which accompanies the Worst Forms of Child Labor Convention (C.182), 1999: in determining hazardous work situations, consideration should be given to "work under particularly difficult conditions such as work for long hours or during the night or work where the child is unreasonably confined to the premises of the employer."

25 ILO, *Effective Protection for Domestic Workers: A Guide to Designing Labor Laws* (Geneva: ILO, 2012).

26 For more information on these efforts and CDW demands, see "What Do Child Domestic Workers Need from Us?: later in this chapter.

27 This section draws on a number of consultations, focus group discussions, and interviews undertaken with CDWs by Blagbrough and others in both urban and rural contexts from countries in Africa, Asia, and Latin America

since 2004. The results of these can be found in a number of publications, including Blagbrough (2008) and *Stand with Us: Consultations with Current and Former Child Domestic Workers in 2010 and 2011 Regarding Proposed ILO Standards on Domestic Work* – available from www.childrenunite.org .uk.

28  All child domestic workers' names have been changed to protect individual identities.

29  N. Baum, "Girl Domestic Labor in Dhaka: Betrayal of Trust," in *Working Boys and Girls at Risk: Child Labor in Urban Bangladesh*, ed. G. K. Lieten (Dhaka: The University Press Ltd., 2011).

30  UNICEF-ICDC, *Child Domestic Work*. Innocenti Digest No. 5 (Florence: UNICEF International Child Development Centre, 1999). This has echoes of the segregation of nineteenth-century slaves.

31  ILO, *Helping Hands or Shackled Lives?*

32  T. Blanchet, *Lost Innocence, Stolen Childhoods* (Dhaka: University Press Limited/Save the Children, 1996).

33  ILO, *Helping Hands or Shackled Lives?* 34–5.

34  *Child Labor and Educational Disadvantage – Breaking the Link, Building Opportunity* A Review by Gordon Brown, UN Special Envoy for Global Education (New York: UN, 2012:9).

35  ILO, *Give Girls a Chance: Tackling Child Labor, a Key to the Future* (Geneva: ILO, 2009).

36  Blagbrough, *They Respect Their Animals More.*

37  ILO, *Helping Hands or Shackled Lives?* 34–5.

38  J. Blagbrough, "Child Domestic Labor: A Global Concern," in Craig, *Child Slavery Now*, 81–99.

39  P. S. Pinheiro, "Violence against Children in Places of Work," in *Report of the Independent Expert for the United Nations Study on Violence against Children* (A/61/299) (New York: United Nations, 2006: 242)

40  National Coalition for Haitian Rights (NCHR), *Restavèk No More: Eliminating Child Slavery in Haiti* (New York: NCHR, 2002).

41  Save the Children, *Abuse among Child Domestic Workers: A Research Study in West Bengal* (West Bengal: Save the Children UK, 2006).

42  O. Godoy, *El Salvador. Trabajo infantil doméstico: Una evaluación rápida* (Geneva: ILO-IPEC, 2002).

43  ILO, *Children in hazardous work: What we know, what we need to do* (Geneva: ILO, 2011: 28–9). For a full list of hazards affecting child domestic workers see ILO, *Hazardous Child Domestic Work: A briefing sheet.* (Geneva: ILO, 2007)

44  ILO, *Flowers on the Rock: Phenomenon of Child Domestic Workers in Indonesia* (ILO: Jakarta, 2004).

45  See e.g., Human Rights Watch, *Bottom of the Ladder: Exploitation and Abuse of Girl Domestic Workers in Guinea* (New York: Human Rights Watch, 2007); Human Rights Watch *Lonely Servitude: Child Domestic Labor in Morocco* (New York: Human Rights Watch, 2012).

46  ILO, *Survey Report: Child Domestic Workers in Ho Chi Minh City* (Hanoi: ILO, 2006).

47 Human Right Watch, "Swept Under the Rug: Abuses against Domestic Workers around the World," *Human Rights Watch* 18.7 (c): July 2006.

48 L. A. Benvegnú et al., "Work and Behavioural Problems in Children and Adolescents," *International Journal of Epidemiology* 34.6 (2005): 1417–24.

49 A. Alem et al. "Child Labor and Childhood Behavioural and Mental Health Problems in Ethiopia," in *Ethiopian Journal of Health Development*, 20.2 (2006): 119–26.

50 D. Reale, *Away from Home: Protecting and Supporting Children on the Move* (London: Save the Children UK, 2008).

51 ILO-IPEC, *Joining Forces against Child Labor: Inter-agency Report for The Hague Global Child Labor Conference of 2010* (Geneva: ILO-IPEC, 2010: para. 20).

52 Blagbrough, *They Respect Their Animals More.*

53 ILO and Child Helpline International, *Child Migrants in Child Labor: An Invisible Group in Need of Attention* (Geneva: ILO, 2012).

54 Anti-Slavery International. *Home Truths: Wellbeing and Vulnerabilities of Child Domestic Workers* (London: Anti-Slavery International, 2013).

55 Anti-Slavery International (www.antislavery.org) and Children Unite (www.childrenunite.org.uk), 2010 and 2011. For more information about the consultation process and the recommendations, see www.standwithus-youngdomesticworkers.blogspot.co.uk; also Children Unite, *Policy Briefing: Child Domestic Work and the 2013 World Day Against Child Labor* (London: Children Unite, 2013).

# The Global Human Rights of Modern Child Slaves

## John Wall

Despite being illegal in every country in the world, and despite almost a century of international antislavery conventions, child slavery persists. It is even, by some estimates, on the rise. The nature of the enslavement of young people under eighteen has changed due to globalization, which has eased conditions under which children and youth may be sold or trafficked and corporations and individuals may act with impunity. The International Labour Organization (ILO) currently estimates that there are approximately 5.5 million minors working under conditions of slavery, including 3,780,000 for household or private sector labor, 960,000 for sexual exploitation, and 709,000 enslaved by states.[1] Others have put the figure of overall child slavery at more than 27 million, depending on how slavery is defined.[2] Free the Slaves estimates that around 60,000 slaves currently work in the United States, at least a quarter of them children.[3] The Anti-Slavery Society claims that at least half of all slaves around the world today are minors, and that, while it has leveled off in recent years, child slavery has risen significantly over the past few decades.[4]

Not only is it difficult to know exact statistics on child slavery, but globalization has complicated how to define slavery itself. Article 1 of the League of Nations' landmark 1926 Slavery Convention defines slavery in traditional nineteenth-century terms of ownership: "the status or condition of a person over whom any or all of the powers attaching to the right of ownership are exercised." However, the ILO now uses the broader language of "worst forms of child labour" and "practices similar to slavery" in order to include activities in which ownership is not technically exercised, such as "the sale and trafficking of children, debt bondage and serfdom and forced or compulsory labour, including forced or compulsory recruitment of children for use in armed conflict."[5] The United Nations (UN) has further asserted, through its 1989 Convention on the Rights of the Child (CRC) and its subsequent Optional Protocols concerning prostitution, pornography, and armed conflict, that some forms of child labor are "forced" or "exploitative" for minors simply by virtue of the persons in question being minors. A child slave is thus generally defined today as anyone under eighteen who is forced into or unable to exit from labor under violent or exploitative conditions. Mike Dotteridge summarizes the view as follows: "In today's world, *de facto* power and control rather than de jure ownership is the basis for assessing whether a particular child should be described as a child slave."[6] Or as Free the Slaves defines it, slavery today means "being forced to work without pay, under the threat of violence, and being unable to walk away."[7]

The question addressed in this chapter is how to think about modern child slavery from the perspective of human rights. It is on one level obvious that child slavery violates basic human rights, especially rights to protection from exploitation and abuse. But at a deeper level, the realities of modern child slavery demand a more comprehensive human rights approach, one that attends not only to protection rights, but also to rights to provision of basic economic and educational necessities and rights to participation in society. Put differently, child slavery today is a problem arising out of humanity's vast and complex global interdependency, an interdependency in which children are not just passive victims, but also agents with public dignity.[8] Taking what I have called a "childist" approach,[9] this chapter suggests that child slavery demands a comprehensively reshaped vision of human rights, one in which the experiences of profoundly marginalized persons such as child slaves instigate a renewed imagination of what it means to hold human rights in today's global order.

## What Is Modern Child Slavery?

Child slavery has existed throughout all of known human history, but its particular lived experience has varied across time, societies, and cultures. Even the definition of a child has changed, though here I follow the CRC in using the term to refer to anyone below the age of eighteen. Child slavery today is a contested category and has many different manifestations. An illustration of a few of its more prominent expressions will help us begin to see why modern child slavery is a complex phenomenon calling for new kinds of global response.

Possibly the most widely practiced form of child slavery today is domestic servitude in non-familial households (see Blagbrough and Craig, Chapter 10, this volume). Such children often work twelve to sixteen hours a day cooking, cleaning, caring for other children, gardening, and/or helping with a family farm or business. Most of these child slaves are girls, and they are most predominant across Africa and South Asia. Thousands are also trafficked annually for household labor to Europe and the United States.[10] While many children work in others' households, their labor is considered slave-like by the ILO if it is "hazardous and likely to harm the health, safety or morals of children," including keeping children out of school.[11] Children become domestic slaves for various reasons such as family poverty, debt bondage (paying off a parental loan), loss of parents to AIDS, an abusive home that causes them to flee, or the belief that the new position will lead to future educational or employment benefits.[12] Because they are isolated within homes, such children are particularly vulnerable to abuse. A child domestic in the Philippines reports, for example, that "they hurt me, spank me, throw things at me, use hurtful words."[13] Often children are locked in the home, prevented from contacting parents, provided no days off, and paid nothing or only enough to cover debts to traffickers.[14]

Another venue for child slavery is larger-scale industrial and agricultural work. Many children in these positions are abducted or trafficked; others are trapped by poverty or debt bondage. Here are three examples. Eight-year-old Mohammed Sharif was abducted from his village in Nepal and sold for 1,500 Nepali rupees (about USD $20) to an embroidery factory owner in Mumbai, India. Here he works sixteen- to eighteen-hour days, receives only minimal food, is severely beaten and is never permitted to leave the factory. He reports: "If I fall asleep, they pour salt and chili powder in my eyes."[15] Tipu is a fourteen-year-old boy working for a fishery in Bangladesh. He had run away from an abusive stepfather only to be deceived by a slave recruiter and sold for around 500–800 taka ($10–16) to the local mafia. He works imprisoned with other boys on a slave island for sixteen to eighteen hours a day, often all night, sorting, cleaning, and drying fish, while receiving no compensation besides small meals and a sleeping mat on the fishery floor. The fishery owners threaten the children with violence if they try to escape, and local police and officials are paid off to look the other way.[16] Raikan is a fourteen-year-old girl working off her family's debt to a tobacco farmer in Kazakhstan. She works in the "killing fields" harvesting tobacco with dozens of other children aged ten to seventeen, where she is exposed to acute nicotine poisoning through her fingers, handles unregulated pesticides and fertilizers, performs long hours of physically debilitating labor, and uses dangerous tools. She is also prevented from enrolling in school.[17]

Another significant form of child slavery is sex work, including prostitution, stripping, and pornography. Such work takes place worldwide, and the illegal sex industry is the third largest criminal enterprise behind trade in drugs and arms.[18] It is the most common form of child slavery in the United States, involving up to 300,000 U.S.-born minors and 17,000 internationally trafficked minors, an estimated 90 percent girls.[19] In India, estimates range from 35,000 to 500,000 children, again chiefly girls, who currently perform sex work.[20] Many children are forced into sex work or tricked by promises of other kinds of work, and many are held captive by violence, threats of violence, drug addiction, or debt bondage. Some take on sex work to support their families or from long-standing cultural practice.[21] As a study of child prostitutes in Cape Town suggests, "while many children forced into prostitution exercise no control over abhorrent working conditions, and in this sense may be described as child slaves, there are numerous examples of children who deliberately engage in prostitution, or from within the institution adopt forms of agency, in order to achieve what they regard as a beneficial outcome" such as economic security or income for their family.[22]

Other forms of child slavery today are numerous. The UN and ILO consider the approximately 300,000 child soldiers around the world, 70 percent of who are boys, child slaves by virtue of child soldiering's illegality and the frequent lack of pay and use of violence for recruitment and retention.[23] The ILO also considers child trafficking itself a form of child slavery, given that the at least 1.2 million trafficked children at any given point in time worldwide are generally purchased, held captive, threatened, and prevented from escaping.[24] Some children are involved in organized crime such as the sale and traffic of illegal drugs, begging on the street, and burglary.[25] In addition, some would consider child slavery to include practices such as underage marriage, child rental for work, and bonded serfdom to a landowner.

## Modern Child Slave Rights

There is now broad international consensus on prohibiting child slavery and slave-like labor. Shortly after the 1926 Slavery Convention, the ILO adopted its broader 1930 Forced Labour Convention No. 29, now ratified by 174 states, which (with a few exceptions such as military recruitment) bans all "forced labour," which is defined as "all work or service that is exacted from any person under the menace of any penalty and for which the said person has not offered himself voluntarily."[26] Subsequently, the United Nations' foundational document, the 1948 Universal Declaration of Human Rights, states in Article 4 that, "No one shall be held in slavery or servitude; slavery and the slave trade shall be prohibited in all their forms." And Article 8 of the United Nations' 1966 International Covenant on Civil and Political Rights (ICCPR), ratified by 167 states, legally binds signatory countries to ban not only slavery, but also "servitude" and "forced or compulsory labour."[27]

Children and youth are not mentioned specifically in connection with slavery or labor in the documents just mentioned, though neither are they excluded. The League of Nations prohibited the general "exploitation" of children in its 1924 Geneva Declaration of the Rights of the Child. But not until the United Nations' nonbinding 1959 Declaration on the Rights of the Child was the labor exploitation of children singled out for attention. Article 9 prohibits "employment before an appropriate minimum age" and "any occupation or employment which would prejudice [a child's] health or education, or interfere with his physical, mental or moral development." The United Nations' legally binding 1989 CRC states in Article 32.1: "Parties recognize the right of the child to be protected from economic exploitation and from performing any work that is likely to be hazardous or to interfere with the child's education, or to be harmful to the child's health or physical, mental, spiritual, moral or social development." The CRC further prohibits the use of children in prostitution or pornography (Article 34), children's sale or trafficking (Article 35), and the recruitment of children under fifteen into armed conflict (Article 38). The United Nations subsequently expands on these articles in the CRC in its Optional Protocol on the Sale of Children, Child Prostitution and Child Pornography (2000) and its Optional Protocol on the Involvement of Children in Armed Conflict (2000), which raises the prohibition age from fifteen to eighteen.

Meanwhile, the ILO has developed two binding conventions targeted specifically to child labor. Its 1973 Minimum Age Convention No. 138, ratified by 154 states, requires parties to "pursue a national policy designed to ensure the effective abolition of child labour and to raise progressively the minimum age for admission to employment or work to a level consistent with the fullest physical and mental development of young persons." It further defines the minimum age of work "likely to jeopardise the health, safety or morals of young persons" as no younger than eighteen. These developments culminated in the ILO's 1999 Worst Forms of Child Labor Convention No. 182, ratified by 172 states and currently the most definitive and comprehensive international instrument addressing child slavery and slavery-like practices. It calls on states to eliminate and prohibit "the worst forms of child labour" for all persons under age eighteen, including not only the ownership of children for labor, but also sale and trafficking, debt bondage, serfdom, forced or compulsory labor, compulsory recruitment into armed conflict, prostitution, pornography, drug trafficking, or any work likely to harm children's health, safety, or morals.

Of course, it is one thing to ratify international agreements on child slavery and slave-like practices and quite another to implement them. It is also one thing to create national and local laws to prohibit child slavery and another to make them effective. Almost every nation in the world bans the worst forms of child labor and requires education up to a certain age. Yet child slavery remains widespread. In addition, many nongovernmental organizations are working to eradicate child slavery and forced labor, with again a diversity of results. Just a few of these organizations, besides agencies within the United Nations and the ILO, are Anti-Slavery International, Free the Slaves, Amnesty International, the African Network for Prevention and Protection against Child Abuse and Neglect, Refugees International, Plan International, and Human Rights Watch.

### The Problem of Globalization

The question remains as to why child slavery persists – and has even grown – despite global efforts to abolish it. Part of the difficulty, I now wish to suggest, lies in the new realities of hyper-globalization. While international treaties and national and local laws have done much to keep child slavery in check, they face the fact that global markets and technologies can find unique ways to exploit child labor and circumvent instruments of children's rights. In addition, globalization bends local cultural constructions of child labor toward global marketplace demands.

Globalization is a complex economic, technological, political, and cultural phenomenon over whose meaning and merits there is much debate. An influential definition of globalization is that it refers to "the widening, deepening and speeding up of worldwide interconnectedness in all aspects of contemporary social life, from the cultural to the criminal, the financial to the spiritual."[28] Globalization is not "a disconnected phenomenon floating above the local and national," but rather "the myriad forms of connectivity and flows linking the local (and national) to the global"; in other words, "a thickening 'global-local nexus.' "[29] Put differently, globalization means that "more people and places have become more interdependent and have organized new connections in more intricate ways."[30]

Those who view globalization as generally good for groups like the poor and children argue that it creates increasingly free markets and opportunities that expand worldwide economic development. A coffee farmer in Brazil can now track global commodity prices on his cell phone and sell his goods to the highest bidder across the planet. Economist Thomas L. Friedman famously claims that today "the world is flat," meaning that the hyper-globalization of markets, the Internet, outsourcing, and almost every other dimension of trade now opens up the same economic opportunities to anyone with the skills and imagination to take advantage of them.[31] Jagdish Bhagwati cites India's economic rise as evidence that global capitalism is "a system that can paradoxically destroy privilege and open up economic opportunity to the many."[32] This neoliberal perspective is put into practice not only by global corporations, whose profits can exceed entire countries' GDPs, but also by the International Monetary Fund, the World Bank, and the World Trade Organization, institutions originating in the Bretton Woods Conference of 1944 and often credited with sustaining decades of worldwide economic development.

Bhagwati has argued in particular that global markets have reduced, rather than increased, child labor. This is because, in his view, globalization generally translates into greater prosperity and increased opportunities for credit, thus reducing the incentive on parents to put their children to work and increasing their incentive to send children to school.[33] For example, in the 1990s when Vietnam reduced export quotas on its primary staple, rice, prices of rice rose 29 percent to global prices, resulting in rising incomes for many farmers and corresponding declines in labor by their children.[34] Bhagwati does acknowledge a caveat, however, that increased prosperity due to globalization does not reduce trafficking in poor children across borders or discourage black market trade such as child prostitution.[35]

There are problems with these arguments, especially when it comes to child slavery. First, they assume that the new global markets can be regulated in the same way as national and local markets. In reality, traditional labor protections are currently enforceable only by states, which can find themselves overwhelmed by the power and finances of international corporations. Our coffee farmer in Brazil has to compete with coffee farmers worldwide who each have to sell as low as possible to global companies like Starbucks who can influence state governments and take their business elsewhere. This kind of criticism is most famously made by the World Social Forum, an international network of activists, NGOs, and human rights groups:

The alternatives proposed at the World Social Forum stand in opposition to a process of globalization commanded by the large multinational corporations and by the governments and international institutions at the service of those corporations' interests, with the complicity of national governments. They are designed to ensure that globalization in solidarity will prevail as a new stage in world history. This will respect universal human rights.[36]

The claim here is that global markets will not regulate themselves democratically, but need to be balanced by international standards of human solidarity and rights. Political theorist Rosi Braidotti argues even more radically that "globalization means the commercialization of planet Earth in all its forms, through a series of inter-related modes of appropriation ... [including] the hyper-capitalist accumulation of wealth [and] the turning of the ecosystem into a planetary apparatus of production."[37] A powerful and largely unrelated global marketplace faces few obstacles from traditional state law and many incentives to exploit individuals such as poor children for their labor.

In addition, globalization has created a tremendous economic divide: great wealth and power for the few alongside entrenched poverty and instability for the many. According to Manfred Steger, the idea that globalization is an unalloyed good "is without question the dominant ideology of our time. Since the 1990s it has been codified and disseminated worldwide by global power elites [who] saturate the public discourse with idealist images of a consumerist, free-market world."[38] In reality, the world is experiencing a new robber baron era not unlike the late nineteenth century, when children found themselves enslaved in factories and farms. That era was ended through a series of national laws prohibiting labor exploitation and supporting children's education and health care. In the new global economy, however, international institutions can condemn exploitative labor practices, but they possess little power or capacity to enforce them.

Finally, child slavery in particular appears to be not simply a byproduct of global markets, but something implicitly contained within them. As Nicola Phillips argues, exploitative and other forms of unfree child labor, for example in the garment industry in India, do not arise from children's "exclusion from development processes," as neoliberals claim, but rather are phenomena "that those development processes produce and reproduce themselves."[39] Multinational corporations have the power to monopolize price and supply conditions by means of "large-scale outsourcing and ... harnessing of an informality-mobility nexus."[40] In addition, they can manipulate national governments so as to keep themselves "beyond the effective reach of private and public regulation."[41] The result is that global markets run more efficiently the more they can exploit the low costs of child labor and the more they can prevent effective child labor regulation.

Globalization may, therefore, lift some boats, but it currently does little to reduce, and in fact significantly encourages, child labor exploitation. And while it can be argued that many children who engage in prostitution, dangerous farming, or long hours of factory labor do so on their own volition to avoid destitution, the reason they face destitution in the first place is in large part because they are unprotected from global market forces. States can and should legislate against child labor exploitation and ratify antislavery treaties. But to a significant extent, they too are increasingly overwhelmed by powerful global market headwinds. In the end, the exploitation of child labor is the product of a vicious cycle which most benefits precisely those globally wealthy few who possess the power and resources to combat it.

## Rethinking Human Rights

Compounding this problem of today's hyper-globalization is a deeper historical problem of denying human rights to children. The fact is that the Enlightenment architects of human rights theory, from Locke to Rousseau and Kant, not only did not apply human rights to children, but argued explicitly that children should not have them.[42] This view has, of course, been refuted by increased acceptance of children's rights since the end of the nineteenth century, starting, in fact, with the fight against children's labor exploitation in factories, and expanding through national laws and international mechanisms such as the CRC into a wide range of children's rights to protections against violence and abuse, provisions of security and care, and participation in social freedoms. Paradoxically, however, the underlying concept of "human rights" still tends to assume a model of the human as an independent and autonomous adult, so that "human rights" are extended to children only secondarily and hence often only partially or contentiously.

Human rights might better be applied to the phenomenon of child slavery if children themselves are understood not only as vulnerable people in need of protection, but also as full social beings with agency and dignity. When it is assumed that human rights belong only to socially autonomous individuals, then child slaves appear as exactly the opposite: dependent victims violently removed from their proper private sphere. In this case, it becomes difficult to imagine child slaves as subjects who are due full human rights. Human slavery in the nineteenth century was not eradicated by opposing violence and victimization alone. It also required positively embracing slaves' human dignity and agency. Part of this embrace involved rejecting the notion that slaves were "private" property and accepting their status as public citizens. Such an approach must now be extended to the modern slavery of children. Child slaves need to be thought about as more than merely private individuals victimized by public realities. They need to be understood as fully public members of the human rights sphere in all their victimhood and agency at once.

Scholars of children's rights have recognized this problem of applying human rights effectively to children and have developed new, postmodern ways of understanding "human rights" accordingly. Barbara Bennett Woodhouse, for example, argues that human rights can include children fully only if they are understood less as protections of individual autonomy and more as means for interdependent inclusion.[43] The reality is that persons of any age, young and old, are both agents in the world and dependent on each other, social relations, and public structures. Mehmoona Moosa-Mitha argues similarly that children show that human rights should be grounded, not in Enlightenment ideals of universal rationality, but in deconstructive efforts on the part of societies to recognize human lived experience in all its differences and diversity.[44] Children may not generally enjoy as much hegemonic power as adults, but they are just as deserving of social power structures that respond to their particular lives.

My own childist view, in accordance with these postmodern ideas, is that human rights should be rethought as social responsibilities to lived experiences of human diversity. The division between "rights" and "responsibilities" was formulated in the Enlightenment to distinguish between the "public sphere" of rational autonomy and the "private sphere" of emotional dependency. This division needs to be broken down so that rights and responsibilities are understood as two sides of the same coin. Human rights, in this view, are society's responsibilities to include all people in their actual social diversity. Rights are how societies expand their moral imaginations to respond to their members' different experiences. As I have put it elsewhere, "Human rights are social responsibilities to the human diversity of otherness.... The underlying purpose of human rights is painfully but joyfully to expand the circumference of a society's unfathomable humanity."[45]

From this postmodern childist perspective on human rights, child slavery can be seen as more than just a problem of the protection of the vulnerable, however much that is the case in part. Child slavery is more fundamentally a problem of societies' failures to respond to the experiences of a systematically excluded group. Children in exploitative labor are not simply anomalies in the global marketplace, but products of a global economic order that denies the full humanity of its youngest and poorest members. An effective response will require a different kind of global economic human rights structure that includes children precisely in their differences as children. This does not mean that impoverished children should be treated as if they had the same economic agency as well-off adults. It means, on the contrary, that the global market dynamics that currently respond only to the interests of wealthy adults should be made to respond also to the real lived experiences of poor children.

### Responding to Child Slavery

What would a more expansive human rights perspective suggest about confronting child slavery in practice? While global neoliberalism may seem too powerful a force to challenge effectively, the reality is that marginalized groups have always faced hegemonic powers and frequently overcome them. As Arjun Appadurai has argued, the world today is witnessing a variety of international human rights movements in which globalization "from above" as imposed vertically by the wealthy North is being counteracted by a diversity of grassroots globalizations arising among local communities "from below."[46] As Appadurai puts it, "the global spread of the discourse of human rights has provided a huge boost to local democratic formations," and "what these horizontal movements produce is a series of *stronger* community-based partners for institutional agencies charged with realizing inclusive democracy and poverty reduction."[47] Since globalization is a living global-local nexus of heightened interdependent connectedness, local cultures have the opportunity to join together worldwide to resist the machinery of market utilitarianism. This suggests that child slavery will be systemically reduced if the global human rights community moves beyond its current focus on humanitarian protection alone, important though this remains, to include horizontally shared, locally grounded, grassroots empowerment. Globalization is not only problematic for poor children, but is also a potential means for organizing across local contexts and developing alternative market practices of non-exploitative solidarity.

Concretely speaking, it certainly remains of immediate importance to work for child slaves' rights to protection against exploitation, violence, and abuse. The CRC and its Optional Protocols are right to focus, as noted earlier, on "the right of the child to be protected from economic exploitation." Likewise, the ILO's Convention No. 182 necessarily calls for the immediate elimination and prohibition of "the worst forms of child labour." In fairness to these Conventions, they do connect child slaves' protection rights to other kinds of rights not to be denied, such as the rights to education, health care, and development. However, the CRC and ILO Convention No. 182 only make these connections to other kinds of rights in limited ways, by pointing out how child labor exploitation can also damage children's education and health. They do not ascribe rights such as to education and health care as vital to overcoming exploitation.

What is needed, in part, is for children's antislavery protection rights to be connected more comprehensively to children's rights to provision and participation. The right to protection against exploitative labor is difficult to realize when rights to a free education and public health and welfare are absent. Eric V. Edmonds and Nina Pavcnik argue that "If a more rapid reduction in the general incidence of child labor is a policy goal, improving educational systems and providing financial incentives to poor families to send children to school may be more useful solutions to the child labor problem than punitive measures designed to prevent children from earning income."[48] For example, the tobacco worker Raikan might be less likely to find herself working under dangerous and exploitative conditions in Kazakhstan if she had a real and robust right to a free education in her home community; or if in Kazakhstan she were provided specific rights to a minimum level of health care. The major cause of child slavery, after all, is family poverty. Simply protecting children from slavery without providing resources against poverty is unlikely to prove effective in the face of global economic forces. To cite another example from earlier in this chapter, the Bangladeshi fishery worker Tipu would

less likely have run away from home if the state possessed stronger measures to support children's rights to economic stability. Some children
choose factory work, agriculture, or prostitution because they have no
other economic alternatives.

Child slaves' rights to public participation are perhaps the easiest rights
to ignore or neglect. It can seem paradoxical to speak of participation by
those denied basic freedoms, but in fact, throughout history, slavery has
been stamped out only when slaves' rights to participation in society have
been fully recognized. There are two ways to think about child slaves'
participation rights. From one perspective, these rights might very well
involve the freedom to participate in exploitative labor itself. While "slavery" has traditionally been defined in opposition to "freedom," many child
slaves are in fact laboring to one degree or another voluntarily. Sometimes
this participation is only for lack of any viable alternative. At other times,
the situation is more complicated. For example, a study of young religious
girl sex workers, or *Devadasis*, in Kanataka, India, shows that "they do
not reveal themselves to be the frightened, brainwashed victims of parental or systemic violence depicted in most accounts of child prostitution.
Instead, they present themselves as girls who may not always like what
they do or what is demanded of them, but do so out of a sense of filial
duty, economic need, and because doing *dhandha* [sex work] is incorporated into their models of female maturity."[49] Here we find a mixed picture where slave-like labor brings a certain amount of social and cultural
benefit that the child herself chooses. In a similar way, as David M. Rosen
describes in Chapter 7 in this volume, many child soldiers freely choose to
fight. What is on one level exploitative labor may be on another level the
best choice a child can make from among various alternatives. However
much children should have rights against labor exploitation, these must
always be balanced against children's rights to make labor choices.

From another perspective, children working in slave-like conditions
need to be provided broader kinds of participation rights to social, cultural, and political freedoms. The CRC legally binds states to guaran-
teeing children several participation rights such as "the right to express
[his or her] views freely in all matters affecting the child" (Article 12),
"freedom of expression" (Article 13), "freedom of thought, conscience
and religion" (Articles 14), and "freedom of association and ... peaceful
assembly" (Article 15). When it comes to child labor, slavery-like conditions can be protected against in part through, for example, the ability of children to organize labor unions to improve working conditions;
the right to choose to leave one's place of employment; and the right to

a voice in local, national, and international labor policy. On postmodern grounds, slavery is not simply the opposite of freedom, but, rather, the opposite of responsiveness to differences of experience. As Mootha-Mitha has put it, "What counts for injustice, harm or oppression would be based on children's experiences of exclusion, both in ways that centre their voice and also in ways that are not prescribed solely within normative views of harm."[50] Just as for adults, then, children's labor exploitation will be overcome, not through protection rights alone, but through a broader human rights approach that also empowers children to make themselves heard and understood. What underlies the range of needed protection, provision, and participation rights is the more fundamental right to society's responsiveness to one's lived experiences of difference.

These considerations of children's multifaceted needs for agency and protection add a more comprehensively global perspective to the child labor rights the CRC and ILO call for. State and local governments, as we have seen, can do much but are also limited in the influence they can exercise over global markets. NGOs, likewise, while often working internationally, have limited powers when it comes to children's rights' actual enforcement. But a broader human rights approach could unite international organizations, NGOs, national and local governments, communities, and child laborers themselves around a global framework for grassroots anti-child-slavery activism. Such a movement should not narrowly conceive of child slaves as innocent victims. Nor should it assume that children are necessarily economic agents in exactly the same ways as adults. Rather, an effective global antislavery movement would work from the grassroots to unite a wide diversity of local participants around child slaves' human rights to equal social inclusion.

## Conclusion

Modern child slavery is one of the greatest tests of the ideals and practices of human rights. One would have to be a diehard ideologue of neoliberalism not to be troubled the presence of millions of children working long hours without pay in households and factories, spending their days picking fruit instead of going to school, and being trafficked into pornography and prostitution. The global marketplace alone will not correct these injustices. At the same time, such activities will not be ended by a narrowly conceived humanitarianism focused simply on saving child victims. Not only are local and national governments limited in what they can achieve on the global stage, but it is ultimately counterproductive not to recognize child slaves' rights to agency and dignity. Finally, modern child slavery cannot simply be opposed by demanding children's freedom, as slavery's very causes are rooted in problematically adult-centered and neoliberal conceptions of freedom as such. It demands a broader view of the human as socially and globally interdependent.

As I have argued, child slavery calls for a comprehensive human rights response based on children's full humanity, a response that recognizes children as equal participants in the global human rights community in all their difference and diversity of lived experience. We will know that the world is not simply headed for increasing global rapaciousness and inequality if its most glaringly unjust practices such as child slavery can inspire even more powerful global-local grassroots movements advancing responsiveness to the dignity of all.

## Notes

1 International Labour Organization (ILO), International Programme on the Elimination of Child Labour (IPEC), *Marking Progress against Child Labour: Global Estimates and Trends 2000–2012* (Geneva: International Labour Organization, 2013), 21–2.

2 K. Bales, *Abolishing Slavery* (Berkeley: University of California Press, 2007).

3 Free the Slaves, "Trafficking and Slavery Fact Sheet" (accessed January 6, 2014 at www.freetheslaves.net/document.doc?id=34).

4 Anti-Slavery Society, "Does Slavery Still Exist?" (accessed January 6, 2014 at www.anti-slaverysociety.org/slavery.htm).

5 International Labour Organization (ILO), "Worst Forms of Child Labour Convention 1999 (No. 182)" (accessed January 11, 2014 at www .ilo.org/dyn/normlex/en/f?p=NORMLEXPUB:12100:0::NO::P12100_ILO_ CODE:C182).

6 Mike Dotteridge, "Contemporary Child Slavery," in Gwyn Campbell, Suzanne Miers, and Joseph C. Miller, eds., *Child Slaves in the Modern World* (Athens: Ohio University Press, 2011), 254–67, 258.

7 Free the Slaves, "Trafficking and Slavery Fact Sheet."

8 Barbara Bennett Woodhouse, *Hidden in Plain Sight: The Tragedy of Children's Rights from Ben Franklin to Lionel Tate* (Princeton, NJ: Princeton University Press, 2008).

9 John Wall, *Ethics in Light of Childhood* (Washington, DC: Georgetown University Press, 2010).

10 Bridgett Carr, "Examining the Reality of Foreign National Child Victims of Human Trafficking in the United States," *Journal of Law and Policy* 37 (2011): 183–204, 185; Philip Whalen and Malika Id'Salah, "Girls as Domestic Slaves in Contemporary France," in Gwyn Campbell, Suzanne Miers, and Joseph C. Miller, eds., *Child Slaves in the Modern World* (Athens: Ohio University Press, 2011), 208–20, 212.

11 International Labour Organization (ILO), "Helping Hands or Shackled Lives? Understanding Child Domestic Labour and Responses to It," 2004 (accessed January 9, 2014 at www.ilo.org/wcmsp5/groups/public/–ed_norm/–ipec/documents/publication/kd00098.pdf), 5.

12 Jonathan Blagbrough, "This Is Nothing but Slavery: Child Domestic Labor in the Modern Context," in Joseph C. Miller, Suzanne Miers, and Gwyn Campbell, eds., *Child Slaves in the Modern World* (Athens: Ohio University Press, 2011), 193–207, 195.

13 Ibid., 200.

14 Cecilia Flores Oebanda, "Child Slavery in South and South East Asia," in Gary Craig, ed., *Child Slavery Now: A Contemporary Reader* (Portland, OR: Policy Press, 2010), 285–95, 292.

15 Dotteridge, "Contemporary Child Slavery," 261.

16 Kari B. Jensen, "Child Slavery and the Fish Processing Industry in Bangladesh," *Focus on Geography* 56.2 (2013): 54–65, 55–61.

17 Patrick Thorman, "Child and Forced Labor in Tobacco's Killing Fields of Kazakhstan," *Regent Journal of International Law*, 9 (2013): 213–45, 213–14.

18 April Rieger, "Missing the Mark: Why the Trafficking Victims Protection Act Fails to Protect Sex Trafficking Victims in the United States," *Harvard Journal of Law and Gender*, 30 (2007): 231–56, 231–2.

19 Ark of Hope for Children, "Child Trafficking Statistics," 2014 (accessed January 9, 2014 at www.arkofhopeforchildren.org/issues/child-trafficking-statistics#.Us8Nbfssx_c); Cheryl Nelson Butler, "Sex Slavery in the Lone Star State: Does the Texas Human Trafficking Legislation of 2011 Protect Minors?" *Akron Law Review*, 45 (2012): 843–82, 844.

20 Emily K. Harlan, "It Happens in the Dark: Examining Current Obstacles to Identifying and Rehabilitating Child Sex Trafficking Victims in India and the United States," *University of Colorado Law Review*, 83 (2012): 1113–47, 1124–5.

21 Treena Rae Orchard, "Girl, Woman, Lover, Mother: Towards a New Understanding of Child Prostitution among Young Devadasis in Rural Karnatiaka, India," *Social Science and Medicine*, 64 (2007): 2379–90.

22 Zosa de Sas Kropiwnicki, "Strategic Agents: Adolescent Prostitutes in Cape Town, South Africa," in Gwyn Campbell, Suzanne Miers, and Joseph C. Miller, eds., *Child Slaves in the Modern World* (Athens: Ohio University Press, 2011), 221–37, 232–3.

23 Sarah Maguire, "Children, Slavery, and Soldiering," in Gwyn Campbell, Suzanne Miers, and Joseph C. Miller, eds., *Child Slaves in the Modern World* (Athens: Ohio University Press, 2011), 238–53.

24 Hans van de Glind, "Child Trafficking: A Modern Form of Slavery," in Gary Craig, ed., *Child Slavery Now: A Contemporary Reader* (Portland, OR: Policy Press, 2010), 99–116.

25 Serdar M. Degirmencioglu, Hakan Acar, and Yüksel Baykara Acar, "Extreme Forms of Child Labour in Turkey," in Gary Craig, ed., *Child Slavery Now: A Contemporary Reader* (Portland, OR: Policy Press, 2011), 215–26.

26  International Labour Organization (ILO), Forced Labour Convention No. 29 (1930), (accessed January 6, 2014 at www.ilo.org/dyn/normlex/en/f?p=NORMLEXPUB:12100:0::NO::P12100_ILO_CODE:C029).

27  United Nations, International Covenant on Civil and Political Rights (1966) (accessed January 6, 2014 at www.ohchr.org/en/professionalinterest/pages/ccpr.aspx).

28  David Held, Anthony McGrew, David Goldblatt, and Jonathan Perraton, *Global Transformations: Politics, Economics and Culture* (Palo Alto, CA: Stanford University Press, 1999), 2.

29  Manfred Steger, *Globalization: A Very Short Introduction* (New York: Oxford University Press, 2013), 6 and 1, respectively.

30  Frank J. Lechner and John Boli, "Introduction," in Frank J. Lechner and John Boli, eds., *The Globalization Reader*, fourth edition (Malden, MA: Wiley-Blackwell, 2012), 1.

31  Thomas L. Friedman, *The World Is Flat: A Brief History of the Twenty-First Century* (New York: Farrar, Straus and Giroux, 2005).

32  Jagdish Bhagwati, *In Defense of Globalization* (New York: Oxford University Press, 2007), 15.

33  Ibid., 69–71.

34  Ibid., 71.

35  Ibid., 72.

36  World Social Forum, "Charter of Principles" (2002) (accessed January 14, 2014 at www.forumsocialmundial.org.br/main.php?id_menu=4&cd_language=2), Principle 4.

37  Rosi Braidotti, *The Posthuman* (Malden, MA: Polity Press, 2013), 7.

38  Steger, *Globalization*, 106.

39  Nicola Phillips, "Unfree Labor and Adverse Incorporation in the Global Economy: Comparative Perspectives in Brazil and India," *Economy and Society* 42.2(2013): 171–96, 175 and 182.

40  Ibid., 185.

41  Ibid.

42  John Wall, "Human Rights in Light of Childhood," *International Journal of Children's Rights* 16.4(2008): 523–43.

43  Woodhouse, *Hidden in Plain Sight*, 309.

44  Mehmoona Moosa-Mitha, "A Difference-Centred Alternative to Theorization of Children's Citizenship Rights," *Citizenship Studies* 9.4(2005): 369–88.

45  Wall, *Ethics in Light of Childhood*, 138.

46  Arjun Appadurai, *The Future as Cultural Fact: Essays on the Global Condition* (New York: Verso, 2013), 198.

47  Ibid., 156 and 176.

48  Eric V. Edmonds and Nina Pavcnik, "Child Labor in the Global Economy," *Journal of Economic Perspectives*, 19.1 (2005): 199–220, 200.

49  Orchard, "Girl, Woman, Lover, Mother," 2388.

50  Moosa-Mitha, "A Difference-Centred Alternative to Theorization of Children's Citizenship Rights," 385.

# Index